A BOORISH AFFAIR
THE WEST'S TREATMENT
OF RUSSIA

MARY P. KIRWAN

About the Author

Mary Kirwan has a degree in German and Irish (Gaelic) from Trinity College Dublin and advanced degrees in business and information technology. She is a barrister in Ireland and qualified to practice law in Ontario, Canada and New South Wales, Australia.

She lived in Toronto, Canada for many years where she worked as a commercial litigation lawyer. She also spent a period as a senior prosecutor at the Canadian Federal Department of Justice, using wiretap evidence to convict drug dealers and to seize and confiscate the proceeds of crime.

She has a keen interest in data security and extensive experience working at a senior level in the sector. She wrote a column on the subject for the (Canadian) Globe and Mail newspaper for several years. She was regularly quoted in the international media and gave interviews for radio and TV.

She is a Fellow of the American Bar Association (ABA), a member of the Steering Committee of the ABA (Section of International Law) Russia/Eurasia Committee, and a long-standing contributor to ABA activities. She lives in Dublin, Ireland.

'Whenever you find yourself on the side of the majority, it is time to pause and reflect'

Mark Twain

For

The Bionic Woman who thinks ill of no-one

CONTENTS

Part IV: More like us than not

Acknowledgements

I want to thank long-suffering family and friends who indulged my passion for all things Russian. Special thanks are due to David, Eileen and Damian in Madrid for the cover and design work. Two people in Moscow must be credited for inspiring me to put pen to paper: They know who they are. All errors made and opinions expressed are mine alone.

Prologue

I wrote this book for fear no-one else would.

Most authors are encouraged by family and friends to put pen to paper. I had the opposite experience. I was strongly advised not to. Friends in the media told me that it is now fashionable amongst the UK press to attack Russia, and particularly the Russia state. They said that certain UK writers have virtually made a career out of it.

By contrast, defending Russia was simply not done. I was warned that if I chose to do so, I would be deemed eccentric at best, and most likely portrayed as a Russian state apologist and generally made to look ridiculous.

These dire predictions did not bode well for my project.

Enthusiasm on the Russians side was even less effusive. I was told over and over again that prejudice against Russia is so ingrained in the West that I'd simply be wasting my time. There is a widespread view that the Western press is largely comprised of bigots with tunnel vision.

Based on my own analysis conducted over several years, the UK media, in particular, has cast the Russian state in the role of diabolical villain in a West End play that seems destined to run forever. The Russian people are collateral damage in this damaging war of words.

The same old stereotypes and caricatures are wheeled out time and time again about a country of over 143 million people. Western popular culture, including movies, books, and TV shows all stoke the fire with their tired portrayals of Russians as Mafiosi, terrorists, mad scientists, tacky, wild-men billionaires, strippers and prostitutes.

Many Westerners have never met a Russian so their only image of them comes from these highly dubious sources.

That being said, what was I to do about it?

I pondered the notion that I should 'Go find something else to write about'- or, as one Russian wryly observed- 'Take up yoga, pilates, or grow herbs.' I didn't want to grow herbs.

What did all the well-meaning advice amount to at the end of the day? Wasn't Russia regularly criticized for not having a free press? Yet I was being told to avoid making waves for fear of our free press. No, that wouldn't do.

In any event, silence wasn't an option. The project wasn't an impulse-it was a full blown obsession. I was also well used to being told what I couldn't do, and doing it anyway. The Irish may smile a lot, but we are also as stubborn as mules.

I came by my obdurate streak honestly. It was a trait honed in childhood, and would, I hoped, stand me in good stead as I wrote a book most everyone considered a waste of time.

We were beaten up as kids in Dublin in an all girls' school. If we didn't add our sums up fast enough, we were whacked with rulers heaped together for maximum effect. If we didn't decline our verbs properly, or fast enough, we were beaten with rulers, or slapped about the face or behind our knees, a painful spot. You could be pretty sure you'd be beaten no matter what you did. Braver, smarter kids tried on occasion to stand up for the weaker kids, and were beaten for their troubles.

It could have been worse, as we now know. At least we weren't sexually abused. It all left a mark, however. As long as I can remember, I had to fight my corner. That was Catholic Ireland in the good old days, or, as one Irish Times columnist recently described it- that was 'Crap Ireland.' None of us would willingly return to Crap Ireland days, despite our current financial woes.

The constant pummelling impacted all the kids differently. Some acquired a stutter they kept for years. I made faces and had a loud 'horse cough.' The teachers would stand me in a corner and humiliate me, laughing at my face-making and nervous cough and encouraging the other kids to slag (tease) me.

To survive in this rather brutal world, I realized that I'd have to toughen up-and fast. The penny dropped that the only defence a small person had against the bullies and the bigger, mean people was words.

I could use words to defend myself and others less able to do so. Words could also wound. It sure beat taking up Kung Fu- popular at the time, as the country was engulfed in Bruce Lee mania. Gaining respect through physical violence seemed potentially risky. What if the bully was better at Kung Fu than me? No, words would have to suffice.

Language is respected in Ireland and a smart mouth is a very valuable commodity. Over the years, I also learnt that the pen is indeed, on occasion, if not mightier, at least as mighty as the sword.

Propagandists throughout the ages have learnt that lesson well- using powerful words, phrases and images to bend our fickle minds to their will, to make us think an idea planted was indeed our own; to compel us to kill and maim innocent people with whom we had no quarrel. In 1924, in his book 'Mein Kampf' (My Struggle), Adolf Hitler wrote that propaganda is 'a truly terrible weapon in the hands of an expert.' The Nazis were experts.

Growing up in Ireland when I did, if you survived childhood, you had other challenges to overcome where erudition was not an asset, but guile helped. For instance, you engaged in sexual activity at your peril.

Besides the threat of permanent establishment in Hell (if you had sex outside marriage), if you wanted the birth control pill, you had to run the gauntlet of surveillance cameras and extreme security to attend a secret clinic that was in constant threat from various religious bigots and assorted lunatics wielding large crosses, held tightly across their breast like Jesus on Calvary.

It was a primitive society, ruled by the Catholic Church and the governing Fianna Fail party with a rod of iron: Crony capitalism at its best, with an Irish twist.

Ironically, my Russian friends, many of whom grew up during communism, had a far less eventful, even freer childhood, and they were never man-handled in school.

By sheer co-incidence, I gained an early insight into the impact that expressing an affinity with my Russian brethren would have on those around me. Around the age of 13, I announced with fanfare (having briefly read Karl Marx's Communist Manifesto) that I was now a communist.

The reaction was deeply gratifying, and exceeded my wildest expectations. I was warned in the most severe terms that communists were the spawn of the devil. I basked in the glory, but my experimentation with communism was short-lived. It was too much pressure, as I was not entirely sure what communists 'did.' I also knew no communists, so it was lonely too.

I read Russian literature at the local library-my sanctuary. I loved Dostoyevsky and Solzhenitsyn and the art of Chagall and Kandinsky. I was scarcely aware that they were all Russian. I'd never met a Russian. I'd met few people who weren't Irish- the gene pool was very narrow at that time. The odd Chinese and Italian person working the local 'chippers'- that was it.

My vision of Russians was vaguely romantic, however. I was struck by the fact that they were tough. Any man who could face a firing squad, get a reprieve, recover from the shock, and finish a best seller as the bailiffs came to remove his desk (for non-payment of debts) clearly came from solid stock.

In general, besides my admiration for Dostoyevsky, I imagined fine-boned, earnest young men and women huddled in Soviet kitchens that looked like a set from a 50's Elvis movie, passionately debating the finer points of cubism and existentialist thought.

In between, they'd move a chess piece on a board with devastating precision. Physics and maths books would be scattered about (light reading) and beautiful children practiced ballet steps in the foreground. In my imaginings, it seemed a far cry from life in Crap Ireland, although to be fair, we managed to have a great deal of fun by being resourceful: A small forested area became Sherwood Forest and we were Robin Hood and his ever Merry Men.

Girls were scarce in our circle, so I was guaranteed the role of a very enthusiastic Maid Marian. I was a dab hand with my home made bow and arrow, although I once hit a local kid in the eye and had to purchase his silence by handing over my entire collection of Dandy comic books- a devastating blow at the time.

If I wasn't out playing outlaw, I was glued to a book.

My reading material was generally pretty eclectic, but one day at the library, I found a book about the Eichmann trials- the Nazi responsible for devising the diabolical scheme to exterminate the Jews. It marked the beginning of an obsession that endures to this day, and that has played a large role in me writing this book.

It was a devastating read. By far the worst thing I had ever read, or even imagined. I could not believe it was real- that it had actually happened. It had excerpts from the testimony of Holocaust survivors about incidents so indescribably evil, I could not get the grotesque images out of my mind.

Around the same time, a local man, who considered himself a neo-Nazi drew swastikas on books in the library about the Nazi era and wrote vile slogans on the pages. He also put Nazi stickers in phone booths throughout my village.

I got on my bicycle and took all the stickers down, and waged a tit-for-tat war with him. Eventually, a friend and I started a chapter of the UK based Anti-Nazi League- an organisation trying to stamp out violence against 'punk rockers' by skinhead types who beat up anyone dark skinned or who simply wasn't a skinhead.

Meanwhile, I continued to read everything I could put my hands on about the Holocaust. I was determined to get to the bottom of it.

I studied German in school and eventually caused everyone more grief by insisting I wanted to go to the dark side by attending the Protestant university, Trinity College Dublin. By way of context, growing up we were told that if we ran around the Protestant church three times, we'd see the devil. I never quite got up the nerve to finish the third lap. However, if Trinity was good enough for Oscar Wilde, it was good enough for me. I was prepared to take my chances amongst the Protestants.

The very small number of kids at my (Catholic) school who wanted to apply to Trinity had to sit an entrance exam. We had to study alone, while those applying to University College Dublin-the Catholic establishment that all good little Catholic girls should aspire to attend, received copious grinds and help from teachers. We were, in effect, little pariahs. I scrapped through.

I majored in German and Irish (Gaelic) Studies. Before long, I took to the study of words and their impact by immersing myself in an examination of propaganda techniques in the First and Second World Wars. I wrote my thesis on anti-semitism in nineteenth century Germany. I was interested in the impact of that period on subsequent events leading up to the Holocaust.

Sadly, I learnt that the history of anti-semitism is truly ancient, with roots back in the annals of time. The foremost expert on the subject was Leon Poliakov[1] (1910-1997) - a Russian scholar, born in St Petersburg, who spent much of his life in France. He studied law in Paris, started a short-lived newspaper for German immigrants, and attended the Nuremburg trials. He seems to have led a very full, rich life. I'd dearly love to have met him.

He did not lack wit. When he was asked why he devoted his life to such a morose subject as the history of anti-Semitism, he apparently responded (in a manner reminiscent of comedian Larry David) that he 'wanted to find out why certain people have it in for me.'

In any event, with Poliakov's help, despite never having set eyes (to my knowledge) on an actual Jewish person, I concluded that Jewish history was even more miserable than Irish, or even Russian history, which clearly took some doing.

I discovered that the Jews were stereotyped in Germany for centuries. It was a slow and insidious process, and found expression in popular pamphlets, science, anthropology and literature, as well as in the mainstream press. It also featured in popular culture, folklore, and fairy tales.

It sowed a seed that took root in devastating fashion in the Third Reich, as much of the German population was long accustomed, even inured to the pernicious characterization of the Jewish people living in their midst.

Many Germans and Jews lived side by side in Nazi Germany before the latter's extermination: They knew each other. The Jews did not live in a far away land, an unknown entity. Yet history unfolded as it did, despite proximity, despite the fact that the oppressors had personal knowledge of their victims. Such is the power of stereotyping, prejudice, and rampant scapegoating.

Why does any of this matter?

It matters to me because I worry about the level of hostility that is directed towards Russia in the West. It gives me the creeps, lacks empathy for a courageous people, and frequently smacks of jingoism and superiority.

Even worse, the hostility, by and large, comes from those who should know better, e.g. Western 'influencers'- the (mainly blue-chip) media (not, predominantly the tabloids), politicians, movie makers, writers and doyennes of popular culture, many of whom are Jewish, and certainly know the impact of stereotyping that evolves into prejudice and suspicion.

Like Russians, my people, the Irish, have a troubled past. We murdered each other for decades, a two hour drive from where I sit. Blood ran down our streets and pregnant women were blown to smithereens by men who still have not been held to account (the Omagh bombing in 1998).

The scars are a long way from healing, but we have made a good start. No-one except the insane wants to go back in time. We should have empathy to spare for Russia-a neighbour still at a very vulnerable stage of renewal and re-invention. I, for one, wish the Russians peace and prosperity after decades, centuries of deprivation.

Throughout its fractious history, Russia has lurched from one crisis to the next. Its people need time to catch their breath, to feel secure. They crave stability, normalcy, things many of us have long taken for granted- they are weary of change. Revolution holds no allure for them.

Russia is far too important to be perpetually treated like the pimply kid always put in the corner by the Western teacher.

It is the biggest country in the world and possesses a wealth of riches that we need if humanity is to endure. Their seat at the table must be assured and they will not be treated as equals until the stereotypes are dispelled, and the will of the Russian people respected.

We must work together to emerge from the current financial crisis. It is not just a crisis of confidence in capital markets- it is far deeper than that. It is a global crisis that threatens to kill a far more precious commodity that underpins our society, a crisis of hope, hope and belief that we can build a better world, if not for our generation, for our children and grandchildren. We are all in it together.

We will not succeed with cartoonish stereotyping of our neighbours, or in pushing our way of life on them.

Despite the rather depressing prognosis from many quarters for my project, I refused to accept it. I believe that the world is full of fair minded people. If they think that Russians are all Mafia and President Putin, Idi Amin, it is because that is all they read in Western newspapers, and see and hear on Western television. It is not, in my mind, because they have some deep-seated hostility towards Russians or Russia. Rather, I believe the contrary is the case.

I was rather painfully aware of the difficulty of doing justice to such an important topic. In the end, I concluded that saying something, however insufficient, was better than doing nothing at all, or waiting for that elusive, perfect expression of an idea that might never come.

In this respect, I must ask for the readers' indulgence, and assure you of my good intentions.

Part One: Russia in the media

Chapter One

Our Tuppence Worth

No rational purpose can surely be served by consistently pinning the Russians into a corner. Taken to extremes, a sense that you can never do anything right can lead to a persecution complex.

I will examine some of the many inconsistencies in the treatment of Russia relative to other nations throughout this book-not with the goal of denigrating the people in such places, often hostage to government policy, but simply to point out the disparity and inequality in treatment, and manifest double standards.

Russia does not have a monopoly on either mendacity or morality. Neither does the West. Yet, the intemperate language used by the Western media about Russia is often highly provocative- reminiscent of wartime propaganda, rhetoric calculated to 'stir up the natives' and keep the home fires burning.

Except that the West is currently not at war with anyone, leaving motley terrorists aside and the occasional foray into Libya and other oil rich nations to ostensibly bring 'freedom' home.

We are certainly no longer at war with Russia. The Cold War is over. However, reading the UK press in particular, you'd be forgiven for imaging that hostilities are still very much alive in Britain, and on occasion in the US. In many respects, the Cold War seems to have given way to an even colder peace.

The more I read over the past several years, the more remarkable it seemed. I asked myself over and over: Why are certain members of the Western press trying to start a fight?

Don't we have enough problems without the resumption of hostilities with a friendly nation- a country that is not actually drowning in debt- that might conceivably be a shelter in a very violent storm for Western businesses mired in recession?

Can we in good conscience throw the first stone at a country barely out of communist shackles? Why do we cosy up to clearly totalitarian states and countries with abysmal human rights records- but remain fiercely critical of Russia?

American and UK politicians and activists take glee in pointing out shortcomings in Russia society, with expressions of outrage and provocative statements about retaliation. Yet they turn a blind eye to poverty, gross and deepening inequality at home, as well as grave problems with our own legal system and rampant miscarriages of justice. It is a kind of selective, even wilful blindness.

Yet we have had centuries of democracy and so called 'rule of law' to get our houses in order- and we have failed to do so, as the current financial crisis amply attests. Sauce for the goose is clearly not sauce for the gander, at least so long as Russia is the gander. The Western media, with the UK leading the charge, is, however, like a ferret after a Russian rabbit- once they get hold of it, they just won't let go.

I believe we must show empathy- not crass, empty-headed condescension towards Russia and its elected officials. Instead of offering cool-headed, well reasoned advice and counsel that does not revolve around the patronising, narrow-minded conceit that what works in Wyoming or Liverpool will work in Vladivostok, we hector the Russians, vilify their politicians and lecture them like small children in need of adult guidance.

The UK media frequently treats them like a bad smell in the rarefied atmosphere of a British country club. We really need to get over ourselves.

Russians are a cultured, formidable, talented people- a far cry from the barbarians the Western media and popular culture portray with marked indifference to the truth.

Russian women have long enjoyed equal status before the law, and the Russian state does not use the death penalty. By contrast, in Saudi Arabia, women are not permitted to drive or vote and violence against them is endemic and rarely prosecuted. Saudi women can't enter most professions.[2]

Yet by contrast with Russia, Saudi Arabia gets kid glove treatment from the Western media and politicians.

Russian young people live in a country with phenomenal natural resources, and huge upside potential. As a betting man might say, 'They have everything to play for.'

Russia has the lowest state debt among the G8, G20 and even the BRIC (Brazil, Russia, India and China) nations. On May 1, 2012, it stood at 9.2% of GDP. Its foreign debt is a miniscule 2.5%. Remarkably, it is one of only three G20 countries that has a balanced budget. In 2011, inflation in Russia was 6.1%, although it has since crept up to 6.8%. Four years ago, however, inflation was more than 13%.

Little or no economic growth is expected in much of the crisis-ridden Western world in the foreseeable future. Yet according to 2011 data, Russia's GDP grew by 4.3 per cent. This was the highest rate of growth among major European economies and one of the highest among the major economies of the world – only China and India were ahead.

Going forward, growth of 4% is predicted, 5% at a stretch, but still phenomenal by Western standards.

In 2011, the unemployment rate in Russia declined by 1 percent year to 6.6 percent, and according to President Vladimir Putin ('Putin'), it currently stands around 5.4%[3]. By contrast, unemployment in Germany, Europe's Bright Light, is circa 6.8%.

The Russian Central Bank's foreign currency reserves are the third largest in the world, over $512 billion as of June 8, 2012. Russia has lots of firepower available to it to jump start the economy and plenty of rainy day money to weather the inevitable storms on the horizon. The Reserve Fund has more than $60 billion in it, and the National Welfare Fund, used to support the pension system, has another $85.5 billion in its coffers.

These are statistics most Western leaders can only dream about. Yet if our media is to be believed, it is the Russians who have all the problems. Who are they kidding?

In much of southern Europe, youth unemployment stands at over 50%. The plight of Europe's young people is extremely serious, with a real risk that an entire generation will grow up and live substantial periods of their adult lives without work, with unpredictable consequences.

The debt burden now carried by Westerners is astounding. In the US, it is $35,576.72 per person (public debt as a % of GDP is 72.2); Britons carry a debt load of $34,408.27 per person (89.4% of GDP), and in Ireland, we face a colossal debt of $54,403.98 per person (112.4 % of GDP).

Even the Germans have a hefty debt load of $34,227.61 per person (82.5% of GDP).

In marked contrast, public debt per person in Russia is positively miniscule: $1,117.13 per person (8.2% of GDP), according to the Economist's rather terrifying *Global Debt Clock.*[4] The Chinese have a debt load of $960.43 per person (15.7% of GDP).

In his article on corporate governance in Russia, '*Corporate Governance in Russia-Reality & Myth,*'Alexander Branis, Chief Investment Advisor at Prosperity Capital Management in Moscow, points out a number of salient points that get very little air time in the Western media.

He wrote that although Russia defaulted on its sovereign debt in 1998, a mere 15 years ago, it has repaid this debt almost entirely since then. In a remarkable turn-about, it has even become a net creditor on the global stage.

The Russian state has also built up the world's third largest foreign currency reserves during this period and maintained a significant current account surplus for fourteen years straight, despite its much-maligned reliance on fluctuating commodity prices.

Progress has also been made in diversifying the economy: Oil and gas, which made up about 40% of GDP in 2003, accounted for 17% of GDP in 2011, about the same as Norway. Branis also emphasizes that the services sector in Russia, almost non-existent when communism fell, now has a GDP-share three-times that of the energy sector.

As Branis points out, Russia is now the second-largest consumer market in Europe and likely to overtake Germany in a couple of years as Europe's largest retail market. There are many Soviet-era companies that have not restructured or modernized-that present huge opportunities for savvy investors, in a world where few similar opportunities exist.

The facts suggest that Russians have much to be grateful for. I firmly believe (unless we make it otherwise with reckless talk) that Russia has a great future. Arguably, our best days in the West are now behind us.

Yet, they play second fiddle to us. We do not give proper recognition to the contribution that they make to the advancement of society. Their bitter experience in Afghanistan was ignored by US leaders, convinced they knew something the Russians didn't, or more likely, they simply discounted the possibility that the Cold War enemy might have highly pertinent input.

Instead, we sent in troops that don't speak the local language or comprehend local culture to bomb people who hate us, in a vain and misguided attempt to proselytize an American way of life.

What has the whole wretched affair achieved, other than guaranteeing civil war in our wake? Not to mention all the beautiful young men determined to do their duty- blown to smithereens, or sent home maimed.

If we are to evolve as a species, we need to do a great deal more talking, and far less scapegoating and killing. Yet, we seem absolutely resolute in our determination not to learn from past mistakes.

We risk a backlash against the innocent Russian people, by stigmatizing them with our ugly, insensitive, meaningless words and phrases-and by making accusations against them that ignore our own stark shortcomings and aggressive tendencies.

Leading up to the recent Duma and Presidential elections in Russia, Putin was the victim of an extraordinarily personalised campaign of vilification that on occasion verged on hate-speech. If he has developed a persecution complex, we must bear a measure of the blame for our lack of restraint and the indecorous, immoderate language used towards him.

Putin has a degree in law and an advanced degree in economics. He speaks several languages, including German. He is immensely proud of his country and its heritage in a way that cynical Westerners find hard to fathom. His legacy of quantifiable achievements for his country is rarely acknowledged in the West, as we face the stark realization that our own politicians have not exactly covered themselves in glory over the past decade.

A recent review in the Sunday Telegraph by Oliver Bullough (4 March, 2012) of a book about Putin by Masha

Gessen-'*The Man Without A Face: The Unlikely Rise Of Vladimir Putin*' (the title says it all) concluded that Gessen's diatribe probably 'just means Russia is a chaotic, crazy country where anything can happen- whether Putin wants it too or not.'

I call this the 'basket case' premise. I will discuss it at length.

Gessen's book appears to be based on an article she wrote a few years back in *Vanity Fair*. I recall it took my breath away. It was a grotesque polemic; quite repellent, brim-full of the most damaging, torrid allegations imaginable. I was dumbfounded at the time. I had no opinion of Putin one way or the other, but the piece was an affront to common decency.

I wrote to the magazine to express my disquiet that they would publish an unabashed exercise in character assassination based on unsubstantiated speculation and amateur psycho-babble. I did not receive a response.

Gessen's book is more of the same, yet it has inexplicably received glowing reviews in the West.

The tired, myopic depiction of Putin as a latter day Genghis Khan that is so in vogue in the West, is well wide of the mark based on the most cursory examination of the facts. This does not make him a saint, but I am personally acquainted with few persons who fit that designation. The one-dimensional, cartoon character persona stitched up for him in the West is more suited to characters in myth and legend than in the pages of respected Western newspapers.

Nevertheless, a huge amount of Western media bile is expended on boorish personal attacks on Putin.

I am old-fashioned. As a head of state, with an impressive record in office that gets scant recognition behind the lurid headlines, he deserves a modicum of respect. The fact he is a public figure does not grant the press an open-season licence to engage in polemics dressed up as analysis and fair comment.

I subscribe to the notion that civility and good manners are under-rated, and currently in very short supply. Society itself is debased and coarsened by diatribes, mean-spirited, highly-personal attacks on individuals unable or unlikely to defend themselves. It is all the worse if such attacks are made by respected journalists occupying a position of influence.

The hostility towards Putin, from people I suspect have never met him, is, I believe, quite unprecedented: A kind of Wild-West 'lynch-him-sky-high' mentality seems, inexplicably, to have taken hold of many ostensibly rational Western journalists at blue-chip publications.

The vast majority of the allegations made against him that I have reviewed are based on little more than conjecture and rumour. Regardless, the focus on him is hugely disproportionate to that given to numerous other world leaders-very few of whom are without fault or not amenable to criticism under a variety of headings.

It is most concerning to me that there is no discernible decency gauge when it comes to denigrating Russians, and Putin in particular, no bridge too far. How have we arrived at a place where we think we have earned the right to treat Russians, including their elected representatives, as if 'anything goes'?

I have observed the same phenomenon when wealthy and successful Russian businessmen are interviewed by Western media outlets- cordiality often goes out the window and a kind of cavalier, casual rudeness takes its place.

Ironically, many of the harshest criticisms made against Russia could be made with equal, indeed more forceful conviction against a host of other countries. Russia is, however, never given an inch, but far less benign powers are routinely given a mile.

The Western media is, for instance, cowed by Islam and its more extremist elements. A softly, softly approach is used, lest we cause the slightest offence. No such accommodation is granted the Russians.

The veritable avalanche of negative media coverage about Russian affairs impacts ordinary Russians who are a blank to most Westerners-blanks the Western media, Hollywood and popular culture most obligingly fill in.

From reading Western media coverage of Russia, you'd be forgiven for imaging that the sun never shines, that the people never laugh for joy or cry for sorrow, and that ferocious crime gangs roam the streets of Moscow like medieval brigands.

What nonsense it all is. It is also a stunning disservice to this proud nation of 143 million people who have travelled a long and tortuous road from Gulag to modernity.

Yet, despite all the coverage, what do we really know about Russians and how they go about their daily lives?

Do most Westerners know that Russians love flowers, chocolate, cats, yoga and their kids? Or that Russian men are chivalrous, and fond of British heavy metal music- and that Russians generally have a sense of the profound that we lack?

On one of my first trips to Moscow, I went grocery shopping with a Russian friend. I was amazed to find out that Moscow has supermarkets like ours, packed with a wide variety of goods. I studied everything-like an anthropologist in the wild. The supermarket aisles were much the same as ours, the car park looked as packed as my local- even the cars were the same brands: Not a beat up Lada in sight.

The shame was mine, for being so ignorant. For imaging, I don't know what. I just didn't expect everything to seem so familiar- or for the people's lives, their daily struggle to get by to strike such a chord.

The revelation from that trip was that Russians are far more like us than not, in terms of our basic, shared humanity. I considered myself well-travelled and well read. Yet, as far as Russia was concerned, I was an idiot.

But the fault was not all mine. The Western media has little interest in helping us get to know one another. Rather they seem determined to ensure we do not, by making Russia seem foreboding- even sinister, and not a place we could relate to.

I read a lot of newspapers, online and in print. Over the last few years, I noticed how standards seemed to be slipping to a rather alarming extent. For instance, unattributed quotes are a virtual epidemic in the UK press, and frequently used to pass judgment on individuals, companies, and even entire nations.

I wrote a regular column for the Canadian Globe and Mail for a few years, about data security, hackers and the like. There was no way I would file a story with an unattributed quote. You just didn't do it.

The editor would tell you to get a source to go on the record. Now maybe if I was on a Deep-Throat investigation and the very security of Canada was at stake, I could bend the rules, but it had better be good.

I was not a 'proper' journalist in so far as I didn't go to journalism school. I was freelancing, writing about a topic I knew a lot about. I was proud to do it. Yet, many of the most vociferous Russia-bashing journalists in the UK regularly pontificate about the stark dangers that bloggers and 'not real journalists like us' pose to 'press freedom and standards.'

There might be something in that if there were any observable standards amongst the 'professions,' as opposed to the great unwashed writer masses. On the contrary, based on my lengthy reviews, standards are conspicuous only by their absence. Stories are poorly researched, frequently overtly biased, and little effort made to distinguish comment, conjecture and fact.

After clipping a veritable mountain of negative press clippings about Russia over several years, I got to a stage where I just couldn't stomach reading another formulaic polemic by respectable British journalists about Russia and Russians. The US media was not innocent, but the UK press had the edge with the vitriol and the frequency of the attacks.

It didn't take a genius to figure out that there are always at least two sides to every story and that demonization of subjects is a wholly undesirable practice.

Then the Murdoch 'hacking' scandal broke. I wondered if my astonishment at the UK media coverage of Russian affairs was just a stark example of a far deeper malaise.

Journalism used to attract gentlemen, and even the occasional gentlewomen. These quaint folk, now a seriously endangered species, believed that it was a profession with standards and principles to uphold. Such people understood that what they wrote mattered, and that there were limits to the methods they employed to get the news into print.

Not anymore. If the melt down in the Rupert Murdoch news empire is anything to go by, British journalism is in chaos-an amoral limbo land, where anything goes.

The tawdry revelations that led to Murdoch pulling the plug on the News of the World marked a new low in dishing the dirt.

Hacking the phones of murdered children, soldiers who had died in Iraq and even victims of the 9/11 Twin Towers terrorist attacks was a bridge too far even for the most jaded observer. The appetite of the UK public for sensationalist news did not extend to condoning illegal, insensitive and plain boorish tactics to get it. The boundaries of common decency had been breached.

In a YouGov survey from November 2011, 58% of the British public surveyed indicated they have lost trust in newspapers after the phone-hacking scandal. UK TV networks command more trust (64%) and UK radio (58%) is a trusted source for news. These results suggest that the BBC's influence is still deep, although the Jimmy Saville sex scandal has taken its toll. By contrast, in the US, 44% of Americans still trust newspapers and 42% trust TV.

Someone had to pay for the ensuing outcry. Unfortunately, it was the rank and file *News of the World* staffers (who likely never hacked, or gave the orders to do so, anyone in the lives) who paid the price, when they lost their jobs en masse.

The UK media, but mainly the tabloid press, has always had a reputation for using scorched earth tactics to get the news, so I wondered if the exposure of a seemingly deep immorality in UK journalism might ultimately do some good. There was the potential for some serious debate about the nature of journalism, what it means, and who it serves.

Yet, surprisingly in the Russian context, the tabloids are not the worst offenders. Far loftier media outlets that undoubtedly look down on them are partisan and biased in their coverage of Russian affairs and frequently resort to stereotyping and labelling to add lustre to sordid allegations that would not look out of place in the National Enquirer.

I had high hopes that Lord Leveson's inquiry, set up in the UK to investigate the phone hacking allegations, would remind the UK media, clearly in thrall to the British political elite, and indeed far too close to law enforcement, that they are not omnipotent, and that the strictures of a civil society apply to them also.

In *A Journalist's Creed* by Walter Williams, first dean of the University of Missouri Journalism School, written around 1905, Williams wrote, 'I believe that no one should write as a journalist what he would not say as a gentleman.' This laudable, albeit old-fashioned sentiment is no longer part of the journalist's creed in the UK, if it ever was.

A great number of reports I have read about Russian affairs present a distorted, one-dimensional view of the 'facts.' Commentary about Russian public figures (politicians in particular- and Putin most especially) is often based on scurrilous and damaging quotes from unnamed sources.

An unnamed source cannot be identified as reliable and unbiased, or their assertions challenged. One cannot be even sure the quote was provided by the individual in question.

In my view, unless the circumstances manifestly support and disclose the need for secrecy, a story that is heavily reliant on information from unnamed sources to make damaging allegations or criticisms about named individuals should never make it into print. Yet this practice is routine in the UK media.

Indeed, I have the distinct impression that granting anonymity to sources with something 'colourful' to say about Russia or Russian public figures is a commitment that is rather casually made by UK journalists. Clearly, if a source desires to disparage the reputation of another, there ought to be a very good reason to justify anonymity.

It is a markedly rare occasion in the UK media when a journalist discloses to readers a possible bias on the part of a source, named or otherwise. Indeed, I have read many a story about Russia in the UK press where it appears that the writer was willing to allow an unidentified source 'spin them' for their own purposes, or where the writer was apparently oblivious to being used in this manner.

It is not that there is no regulation of the Western media-but the myriad voluntary codes of conduct that exist lack teeth, and are often, at best, light touch in nature. They have failed in rather spectacular fashion to rein in the worst excesses of the UK media.

At the European Union level, *EU Resolution 1003 (1993), Ethics of Journalism*[5] ('the *Resolution*') affirms certain ethical principles for journalism, and suggests they 'should be applied by the profession throughout Europe.' They clearly are not.

The *Resolution* states firmly that a 'basic principle of any ethical consideration of journalism is that a clear distinction must be drawn between news and opinions, making it impossible to confuse them.'

Furthermore, 'News broadcasting should be based on truthfulness, ensured by the appropriate means of verification and proof, and impartiality in presentation, description and narration. Rumour must not be confused with news. News headlines and summaries must reflect as closely as possible the substance of the facts and data presented.'

Headlines are often used by the UK media to suggest a conclusion or a set of facts (e.g. Putin is evil, corrupt) that the text simply doesn't support. If someone doesn't read the story, but merely glances at the headline (as we often do when we are in a hurry)- he or she will not be able to judge the flimsiness of the material underpinning the headline: The damage is done.

For instance, in December, 2011, the Financial Times ('the FT') ran a front page headline[6] titled '*FT Investigation*' with a photo of Putin in dark sunglasses, captured to look as ominous as possible-with the by-line '*Putin's Russia: The new oligarchs-links between capital and the Kremlin exposed.*'

It was heady stuff. However, the 'analysis' inside was long on supposition, hyperbole, and conjecture. I hope it isn't what passes for proof in the UK nowadays.

The text was riddled with quotes from an insider allegedly with proof to burn, but littered with provisos- 'Some investors allege' (unnamed)...'documents appear to show.'..documents shown to the FT provide 'some' support for these claims...the source had 'no documentary evidence' that the transactions were conducted on Mr Putin's behalf.'

Despite the sensationalist headline, the allegations did not amount to a hill of beans, consisting of a surfeit of 'golly gee' hypothesizing, but finishing with the conclusion that 'the paper trail, however, is relatively scanty...'

The article, in its totality, failed to deliver on the promise of the lurid headline. The best the 'investigators' could come up with was that one of Putin's subordinates supposedly stated he may have called him 'boss' or even 'tsar.'

With respect to the role of the media, the *Resolution* states that 'journalism should not alter truthful, impartial information or honest opinions, or exploit them for media purposes, in an attempt to create or shape public opinion, since its legitimacy rests on effective respect for the citizen's fundamental right to information as part of respect for democratic values.'

To that end, the *Resolution* states that 'legitimate investigative journalism is limited by the veracity and honesty of information and opinions and is incompatible with journalistic campaigns conducted on the basis of previously adopted positions and special interests.'

It also states that the media has 'a moral obligation to defend democratic values: respect for human dignity'- but ought to do so by 'solving problems by peaceful, tolerant means, and consequently to oppose violence and the language of hatred and confrontation and to reject all discrimination based on culture, sex or religion.'

Additionally, the 'media must play a major role in preventing tension and must encourage mutual understanding, tolerance and trust between the various communities in regions where conflict prevails....'

Before the recent Russian Duma and Presidential election campaigns, the UK and Western media threw itself whole heartedly behind a single unified message, a very decided 'special interest'- namely 'regime change.'

The Western media gave huge coverage to allegations that fraud marred the outcome of the Duma (parliamentary) elections, and subsequently the Presidential elections. They compared the peaceful Russian protests with the predominantly violent Arab Spring uprisings and implied that Moscow was on fire. By contrast, when London actually was on fire, the unseemly rioting 'business' was rapidly taken off the front page.

Numerous friends called me to see if I was alright, believing I was in Moscow and in mortal danger. Several articles I read about the protests amounted to thinly veiled exhortations to the Russian opposition to take up arms against Putin.

Emotive editorials in many blue chip Western newspapers demanded change, and relished the prospect of what the Wall Street Journal called the 'Russian Spring.'

Is fomenting revolution in a friendly sovereign state the role of the press?

I believe it is an absurd and dangerous conceit. Yet, the media does not feel constrained to any degree in engaging in what can only be described as overt political activism-more akin to what I expect from the official opposition in government. Indeed, a friend observed that the UK media was arguably more vociferous and more effective in acting as Putin's opposition in the last elections' than the real thing.

Based on my review of hundreds- probably thousands of news clippings and broadcasts about Russia over the past few years - I have no doubt that many British journalists believe it is their job not merely to report the news, but rather to call the Russian government to account, indeed to play a significant role in taking it down.

They were overt in endorsing certain Russian political candidates (about whom highly relevant background information was not provided) - almost as a knee- jerk 'Back any horse but Putin' fallback position. A well-balanced, unbiased, informative analysis of the overall political, economic, historical and cultural context was missing in action.

Their consternation was palpable when Putin was re-elected with unquestionably a strong majority. Even if the results were bumped up by misguided, over-enthusiastic Putin loyalists, there is little doubt he commanded at least 45% of the vote- magisterial by Western standards, as our politicians are routed one by one in elections.

The UK press made itself part of the story. Their outcome, the outcome they had promoted so heavily had failed to materialize. The fact the British press presumes to influence UK politics, but also Russian domestic affairs, cried out for the attention of the Leveson inquiry. Indeed, the presumption extends beyond Russian borders.

On April 9th, 2012, an editorial in the FT proclaimed that 'The world must unite to save Syria.' It urged US and

European governments, failing a 'peaceful transition.' to 'put the options of arming the opposition and creating safe havens for the rebels on the table'-concluding with the ominous warning that in doing so they will make it clear 'that this time they will be serious about them.'

Besides being shockingly naive about the ramifications of arming insurgents who undoubtedly have a smattering of Islamic extremists in their ranks, is it the role of the most influential business daily in Europe to make such pronouncements, and to presume to dictate outcomes, by violent means?

I hope not. The UK press, however, powerful, is not comprised of elected officials. It presumes too much, and too far.

Indeed, the Western media, alongside Western politicians, have openly and naively egged on protesters in predominantly Arab countries to overthrown existing governments. In the process, they have unwittingly enabled a motley crew of religious zealots, extremists and assorted malcontents to seize power from incumbents. The situation in Iraq and Afghanistan is worse, in my estimation, than it was before we interfered.

In very many places where we have raced in, guns and missiles blazing, or provided resources and cover for rebel forces to prevail, we have done so, ostensibly, in a vain and misguided effort to substitute Western values for local culture, ethnic and religious sensibility.

Instead of 'freedom.' we have left carnage, zealotry and misogyny in our wake for the locals to sort out. What is the plight of women in Iraq, Afghanistan, and Libya now that that we have armed the zealots and handed them political power? Have we improved their lot? Have we made the West safer from extremists? I think not.

When we had or have a moral imperative to intervene- to bomb the Nazi death camps, to stop the Rwandan slaughter, to prevent famine and starvation in the poorest places on the planet – we fail to deliver.

We can't take care of business at home. What makes us think we can do a better job in countries that we can never truly comprehend? We think we can bomb them into thinking and acting as we do? And then pack up and leave?

A similar pattern is emerging with Russia. The Western media has been in overdrive trying to throw its weight behind anyone who will unseat Putin. Yet, who do they promote in his stead?

Columnist Seamus Martin in the Irish Times on 13 January 2012, wrote about Putin opponent- 'blogger' Alexei Navalny- routinely described by the UK/US media as a viable, even desirable alternative to Putin: A young, intelligent, eloquent modernist who purports to represent the Russian middle class.

As Martin points out, Navalny is no Renaissance Man- even if he does know how to 'blog.' He espouses extreme right wing political views, including a crass, unsophisticated anti-immigrant stance, and, according to Martin, attends meetings 'with racist skinheads.'

The FT, in particular, through its editorials, is fond of issuing what read as rather insufferable Diktats to the Russian government- about what they 'should' or must' do. Do we not have enough to do at home right now without presuming to run Russia from our armchairs?

The *Resolution* requirement that 'information and opinions must respect the presumption of innocence, in particular in cases which are still sub judice, and must refrain from making judgments'- is also broken with impunity by both the UK and US media, with the support of Western politicians.

In several domestic Russian criminal cases that are at the investigative stage, or open before the Russian courts, the UK and US media have rushed to judgment, ignoring the presumption of innocence, incensing the Russians in the process by high-handed meddling in their affairs.

US politicians are in the process of devising 'ban lists' (and asset freezes) on Russian officials (to prevent them entering the US) they claim are implicated in domestic Russian criminal matters in which they have taken an interest, usually 'causes' adopted by the Western media.

Supposedly UK politicians have circulated similar lists, albeit 'unofficially'-and various wrong-headed EU and even Canadian laws have been suggested to pressurise the Russians on domestic legal matters.

Even the European Parliament got involved, passing a resolution recommending an EU-wide travel ban and asset freeze for Russian officials they allege are tied to the death of Hermitage Capital lawyer Sergei Magnitsky in 2009 while in pre-trial custody in Russia, where he was held on tax evasion charges.

EU parliamentarians cited 'ample evidence' for its stance. Yet, how can they possibly know what evidence exists, against whom, or how it would stand up to scrutiny in a court of law? The EU is far too quick to play 'follow the leader.' We are way out of line.

As a seasoned trial lawyer, I am perplexed at the absurdity of Western politicians and journalists presuming to retaliate against the Russians for failing to convict Russian nationals, without trial, indeed without charge, for alleged criminal offences committed in Russia.

It is certainly audacious, but also quite extraordinarily presumptuous. It presumes to interfere with the judicial process in a foreign country by sanctioning foreign nationals, not all of whom have been charged, let alone convicted of crimes under Russian law. Can one image the outcry if the Russians purported to retaliate against American nationals they alleged were guilty of crimes on American soil?

Our high-minded stance also assumes, quite wrongly, that our justice system is peerless and human rights abuses non-existent. I assure you, in case you need convincing, that there is no shortage of inequity within Western borders. The Russians in their very young democracy have not, by a wide margin, cornered the market in that regard. However, we somehow feel empowered to be sanctimonious where the Russians are concerned.

I used to write utterly hopeless letters to US governors in death penalty states asking them to commute or re-examine sentences of death imposed on individuals in circumstances where innocence was a serious concern. However, according to a June, 2011 Washington Post editorial[7], the US Congress should play chicken with the Russians to try and get them to 'rein in the endemic lawlessness of their regime.'

I was incredulous to read a quote from Senator Benjamin Cardin (D-Md), the Senator who introduced legislation in the US Senate to ban Russian officials the Americans allege are implicated in Magnitsy's death, as 'not an interference in Russia's domestic affairs but rather, an attempt to 'create consequences' for members of an autocratic regime 'who are currently getting away with murder.'

US concerns about human rights abuses in the Arab world, by comparison, have been muted at best, and have not resulted in calls for bans against implicated government figures, or a freeze on their voluminous offshore assets.

In 2012, a Magnitsky bill passed through the US Senate and House of Representatives, forums not short of lawyers, who ought to have some comprehension of its ramifications. It was signed into law by Obama on December 14, 2012, to a furious reaction from the Russians.

Putin called the law 'a purely political and unfriendly act.' adding, 'I don't see why they would sacrifice US-Russian relations in order to get some political dividends.'

The Russians retaliated with a law banning US adoptions of Russian citizens. The measure has received the usual widespread, uniformly negative coverage in the Western media, with no context provided. It is fair to say, however, that the prohibition is not supported by a number of prominent Russian politicians.

However, some Russian children have died after mistreatment by American adoptive parents. These cases were widely publicized throughout Russia, so there has been mixed reaction to the new law from the Russian general public.

It has also been pointed out by Russian commentators and child protection agencies that Russian children are frequently brutalised at home, and that child protection laws and prosecutions for abuse are few and far between.

However, that being as it may, I fully expect that the tide of Russian public opinion will turn firmly against the US-and in Putin's favour, when the Magnitsky act does what it purports to do.

It is as inevitable as death and taxes that the passing of this law will sour relations between the two countries to a very significant extent, a wholly unnecessary and undesirable outcome. Its swift passage through the US legislative process has all the hallmarks of political gerrymandering. It is a huge provocation to the Russians, as it would be to any sovereign nation if the situation was reversed.

As a practical matter, US immigrant law provides ample authority to US state officials to surreptitiously ban anyone they like from entering US soil, without providing any rationale for the decision-a power used in the recent past against several wealthy Russian businessmen.

The law requires the US to deny visas to Russians presumed to be linked to Magnitsky's death in prison and freeze any assets they have that are situated in the US. However, if the sanctions regime is used (under the auspices of the UN) to add their names to official sanctions lists, the ramifications could be global.

Both the finding of guilt and sentence would be imposed without any due process or adjudication in a court of law, in keeping with the modus operandi of the sanctions regime more generally.

These are invidious developments from the perspective of a lawyer, such as myself, who believes that due process actually means something. Obama, a seasoned jurist, is operating on the edge of a very slippery slope in this regard. I am desperately disappointed in him for turning a blind eye to the consequences of running a coach and four through the most fundamental principles of law.

The trial of the former deputy warden of the prison in which Magnitsky died (he is also a physician), Dmitry Kratov, resulted in a recent acquittal. He denied charges of negligence. Magnitsky's death was conceivably caused by acts of negligence on the part of prison officials, or the prison authorities, that fall well shy of criminal culpability.

In July, 2012, an overwrought FT editorial about the Magnitsky bill[8] stated that 'Some crimes are so odious that the culprits should be named and shamed.'

In other words, according to the foremost business daily in Europe, we ought to dispense with the presumption of innocence and a fair trial. Rather we should come to our own determination of the guilt or innocence of people for crimes allegedly committed in their homeland!

Furthermore, we propose turning the thumbscrews on them to prevent them travelling, doing everything we can to undermine their human rights-in order to carry out a verdict rendered by the court of public opinion in the West: Next stop, public lynchings.

God help us all if that is where we are headed. I hope I am long dead before it all goes to hell in a hand basket.

By contrast, I don't recall the same level of consternation in the UK media about the fact that on September 21, 2011, Troy Davis was executed in the US by the State of Georgia, despite widespread public opposition and serious doubts about Mr. Davis's guilt.

His execution was very likely a gross miscarriage of justice, an 'odious crime.' However, many innocent people have been executed in the US over the years, and there are undoubtedly more to come.

Perhaps we should put officials in the state of Georgia who carried out the execution on a similar watch list- devise a European 'Troy Davis bill'? I doubt there would be many takers for that suggestion amongst the Western political elite.

The fact is that the death of a quite possibly innocent black man at the hands of the US state failed to seize the imagination of the Western press to any significant extent. Yet, the recent conviction of three silly girls jumping and screaming on the altar of an orthodox cathedral in Moscow draws the ire of every Western media outlet.

Frankly, I don't know what has come over our press and politicians. The toughest rule book on planet earth applies to the Russians, who daren't look sideways, yet we throw the whole kit and caboodle out the window, seemingly willy-nilly, as it suits us.

Even worse, I get the distinct impression that certain elements in the Western press (egged on by the political elite) will not be satisfied until they see Russia ripped apart by a tiny, violent minority that lacks the support of the vast majority of the Russian people. Such people will not be happy until blood flows on Russian streets.

US businesses, keen to exploit opportunities in Russia have expressed concern at the passage of the Magnitsky law, fully aware of how it is will be perceived in Moscow. They also know that these retributive measures against the Russians are also tied in the minds of certain US politicians to Russia's recent accession to the World Trade Organisation (WTO).

After 18 years trying to join (China was granted entry in 2000 with support from the Clinton administration) - the WTO officially welcomed Russia as a member on 16th December, 2011- the Russians ratified the accession on August 22, 2012.

There are still mixed feelings in Russia as to the merits of joining.

Membership should bring opportunities for Russian exporters, but it will inevitably also mean more competition from abroad, which is currently a major concern to Russian businesses. However, WTO rules permit new member states to protect domestic manufacturers by limiting imports in vulnerable sectors for a period of years; various derogations also exist to protect emerging markets, although not in perpetuity.

In principle, this development should increase economic ties between Russia and the United States, but WTO accession required the US to establish 'permanent normal trade relations (PNTR)' with Russia by revoking a 40 year old, long out-dated Cold War legal provision known as the Jackson-Vanik ('*Vanik*') amendment that tied US trade relations with the former Soviet Union to the rights of Jews and other religious minorities to emigrate freely. Russia has been in compliance with the Jackson-Vanik provision since the 1990s.

Vanik had to be repealed to establish normal trade relations with Russia to help US companies compete in one of the world's fastest-growing markets. General Electric, of Fairfield, Connecticut, reported $1.6 billion in sales in Russia last year, which may triple by 2020 if *Vanik* is repealed.

If it was not repealed by US politicians keen to maintain a 'lever' in reserve against Russia, Russia could deny US companies WTO trade concessions available to other member states. Such action would be hugely detrimental to US business. Old habits die hard, however, and much to my dismay, the repeal of *Vanik* has been tied to the passage of the Magnitsky bill.

I am completely perplexed as to what the US and other nations playing 'follow the leader' expect to gain by such interference in the domestic affairs of a sovereign, friendly, nation. There is absolutely no question that if the boot was on the other foot, that US and UK politicians would take severe umbrage.

The fact is that US politicians with time on their hands do not have to scour Russia looking for miscarriages of justice or problems to solve- the American people are positively crying out for their attention.

I used wonder why the Western media is so Russophobic.

I considered the possibility that journalists perceive a demand for purely negative coverage about Russia and its people. Why else would they run the broken-record stories day after day, always beating the same monotonous drum?

Michael Foley,[9] a lecturer in Journalism at the school of media at the Dublin Institute of Technology, in an opinion piece in the Irish Times on 4th November 2011, discussed what makes a story newsworthy. He discussed various factors noted in academic studies, including 'negativity'-the theory that people like, or are attracted to bad news stories.

If that is true, when it comes to stories about Russia, the British public must feel unusually sated. I, for one, am heartily sick of it. Noting the role of bias in story creation, Foley observed that 'Most would probably accept that what constitutes news is a mix of newsroom culture, subjectivity and probably bias.'

He quotes Alexis de Tocqueville, however, who wrote in 1835 that 'in order to enjoy the inestimable benefits that the liberty of the press ensures, it is necessary to submit to the inevitable evils it creates.'

There is undoubtedly merit in that observation. However, it does not mean, in my view, that the media should be unconstrained in what they write, or always allowed to hide behind the public interest defence, the ultimate 'get-out-of- jail' card for uncorroborated conjecture on 'important issues.'

UK media titans appeared in front of the Leveson inquiry to urge him towards clemency, and to protect their 'fundamental rights.' I had faith that the venerable Judge would not be cowed or held hostage to flamboyant pronouncements about the dire consequences of the UK press being forced to respect human dignity and basic standards as they ply their trade.

The US media, as I will discuss, is also guilty of Russia-bashing, but to a far lesser extent than in the UK. One of the reasons may be that the US has a broad base of media outlets and thousands of newspapers. By no means is Russia always on the front page.

Indeed, it is fair to say that most Americans are not lying awake at night thinking about Russia and Russians.

Surveys suggest they are far more fixated on China, to the extent they even think beyond US borders.

There is, however, far more media concentration in the UK, and unless you live in a cave, it is nearly impossible to avoid the fact that Russia gets an inordinate amount of media coverage- most of it negative. Surveys suggest that such coverage has had an impact, with Britons expressing, not surprisingly, more negative opinions about Russians than Americans, despite the Hollywood factor.

In addition, as a general premise, media standards, at the most basic level, are higher in the US than the UK, where a certain cowboy mentality seems to have taken hold.

Indeed, certain segments of the British press positively luxuriate in their 'verve and vim and fearlessness,' and view it as part of their job to' push against the prissy self-esteem that 'respectable' US journalists revel in.'[10]It's akin to a badge of honour to let it rip.

Even the BBC, as I will discuss further on, has produced and aired shockingly biased programmes about Russian affairs that are presented as impartial and fair-minded. Contributors with a known bias (but not necessarily known to members of the audience) are served up as impartial observers. The personal bias of the writers and producers is made abundantly clear from the outset.

Evidence to support various inflammatory contentions is scanty at best- and in many cases, lacking entirely. No other perspective (that is not tacitly or overtly mocked) is presented: There is only one side to these stories.

This trend is concerning, because surveys suggest that the BBC is still viewed as a credible source of information and news by UK viewers, far less enamoured with the print media.

What is also extremely worrisome is my recent observation, not restricted to the UK media, that many newspapers and magazines (not lacking for lawyers) routinely publish material that is blatantly defamatory. They do so based on what I can only assume is the cynical calculation that the Russian subject will not sue, for fear of making matters worse, or presuming they can depend on the 'public interest' defence to write what they like.

Thus, shocking invasions of privacy and hugely damaging attacks on personal credibility are made on the basis that we have the upper hand; we calculate that the Russian victims will not exercise rights we hold dear in our free and democratic societies.

As I have said, it is open-season on Putin. If the Irish press, for instance, set on David Cameron the way the British press treats Putin, there would be hell to pay.

UK media coverage of Russian affairs shows, by and large, with a few notable exceptions, a marked lack of original thinking and superficial, inaccurate, lob-sided research. Conclusions are drawn from uncorroborated 'facts' that rarely support the underlying premise and are often little more than barely disguised opinion. Accuracy is similarly compromised by opinion masquerading as fact.

The result, in my case, is that I trust little of what I read in the UK press about Russian affairs, with a few notable exceptions. I am frequently left with the niggling concern that stories replete with quotations from unnamed sources are not credible, and, in a worst case scenario, that the references were simply made up. The UK media's unhealthy connection to British politicians is also deeply concerning.

As the FT's editor, Lionel Barber, has pointed out, 'Many members of the political elite in Britain have all worked in or with the media industry'[11]. What is the impact of these close ties? They expose politicians to the suggestion they may turn a blind eye to the media's worst excesses so long as they further the government's agenda.

The perception that the media and politicians are in each other's pockets does little to add lustre to the concept that the media is an important component of the system of checks and balances that is critical in a truly democratic society.

In turn, the UK press, as I will discuss, possibly due to a sense of inviolability instilled by virtue of these warm blanket ties to government (and even the police force), has, I believe, become lazy, spoilt, condescending and sloppy.

In one recent article[12] about a dispute between Russian businessmen, the FT ran a story that contained not one, but four unnamed sources, quoting 'one associate,' 'one banker with knowledge of both men.' 'another banker' and finally 'a well-connected businessman.' The final quote was disparaging about one of the businessmen.

How do stories about serious, not frivolous matters, that cast aspersions on the character and reputation of the subject in question, ever make it into print with so few people (or anyone) prepared to go on the record to substantiate the claims made?

Lloyd Barber has extolled the virtues of US journalism. By his own account, he worked for many years in that country. 'The news prose and lay-out might have been a tad stodgy compared to feisty British rivals, but the spirit of inquiry was indomitable and the commitment to quality absolute.'[13]

The US tradition of separating news from comment arises from a traditional commitment to impartiality. This strict separation is not, however, the norm at UK newspapers- and it shows.

Many UK journalists at respectable papers- not the tabloids- in their coverage of Russian affairs use their positions to hammer home, with tedious regularity, views that suggest a deep ideological agenda.

A paper that publishes a healthy diversity of views makes for interesting and balanced reading. However, in my views, a dangerous tipping point occurs when a paper adopts a single, uniform view on an issue- and all the columnists and reporters at that publication remain 'on message'- all espousing the same ideological perspective.

As a trial lawyer (I have been both a civil and criminal trial lawyer, including a period as a Canadian wiretap and drug prosecutor), it was my job to weigh both sides of an argument, to identify inconsistencies and gaps in the evidence. The more I read about Russia in the media, the more I became utterly convinced that there was bias at play and on a grand scale.

It mattered little who invaded who (the Georgian conflict), or whether there were two sides to the story, or whether the same criticisms could be made with equal force against other nations, often closer to home. No, the Russians were always on the back foot, always at fault.

The media is, however, loath to concede bias, for obvious reasons.

According to a research paper by Prof. David P. Baron[14] in August 2004, titled *Persistent Media Bias*[15], 'The news media plays an essential role in society by providing information to the public for both individual and collective decisions.'

He notes that in the US, the 'news media, however, is widely viewed as biased.' Many Americans believe that the US media has a 'liberal' (Democratic Party) bias. Baron describes a 1999 survey by the American Society of Newspaper Editors (ASNE)[16] that 'revealed that 78 percent of the public believed that there was bias in news reporting.' However, Baron notes that there was 'little consensus on the nature and direction of the perceived bias.'

Baron acknowledges that 'although journalists may have incentives to bias stories, those incentives can be dampened by factors such as professionalism and by controls instituted by the news organization.' In other words, bias is not inevitable.

In examining the many reasons for bias, Baron surmises that bad news may indeed sell, thus, 'Biasing stories may increase the probability that a journalist's story is published or may promote the world view of the journalist.'

He quotes a researcher, John Zaller,[17] who wrote that 'career success means producing stories that make it onto the front page or get lots of airtime on the evening news, from whence flow fat salaries, peer respect, and sometimes a degree of celebrity status'...'If stories about the bad state are more likely to be published than stories about the neutral state, bias increases the probability of being published.'

It may be the case that presenting 'good news' stories about Russia to a UK editor, or stories that offer a different perspective to the 'Putin is An Ogre' prevailing orthodoxy is considered potentially injurious to one's career as an ambitious British journalist. It is certainly an observable fact that far fewer of them make it into print than the formulaic offerings.

As Baron points out, bias can manifest cumulatively over a series of stories, and arise by means of unbalanced coverage of an issue. Another form of bias is simply overemphasis of extreme events.

In the case of Russia, the predilections of the UK media is so obvious that it is usually a straight forward exercise to predict the content of an article about Russia by a particular journalist based solely on the form of the headline.

Baron notes that another source of bias may be that newspaper owners and editors have certain ideological preferences that permeate the output. This is certainly true in the UK and at many prestigious papers in the US.

He observes that to 'create bias a journalist can include in her story quotations from advocates of particular perspectives. The advocates then can present their perspectives, make assertions and allegations, draw conclusions, and argue for particular actions.' As he points out, 'Favouring of groups on one side of an issue is contrary to the journalistic objective of balance.' However, this practice is standard in the UK.

As Baron points out, 'Journalists surveyed overwhelmingly rejected the notion that the media is biased. However, he cites an academic study by Bernard Goldberg,[18] which concluded 'not only that the news media was biased but that it did not understand that it was biased.'

He also quotes a study by Patterson and Donsbach[19] that concluded that 'Indeed journalists typically deny the existence of this bias, claiming that their decisions are premised solely on professional norms. There is, as a consequence, a perceptual gap between journalists' self-image and their actions, and it leads them to reject any suggestion that they are politically biased.'

In 1996, Patterson and Donsbach surveyed journalists in five Western democracies and concluded that bias was present in their reporting. They presented them with news situations and asked them to make decisions about story content and headlines. They correlated the responses with the self-reported political orientations of the journalists.

They concluded that 'When they move from facts to analysis, their decisions are subject to errors of judgment and selectivity of perception- partisanship can and does intrude on news decisions, even among journalists who are conscientiously committed to a code of strict neutrality.'

Baron notes that the ASNE survey[20] suggested that bias may manifest in many forms, such as 'favourite causes' ... 'tenacious beliefs.'.. 'unstaunchable convictions of what's right.'. 'attitudinal mindsets' such as 'self-righteousness, and 'skepticism gone bad to cynicism.'

However, he noted that bias 'means many things to many people.' For instance, the ASNE study found that:

• 30 percent of adults see bias as 'not being open-minded and neutral about the facts.'

• 29 percent say that it's 'having an agenda, and shaping the news report to fit it.'

• 29 percent believe that it's 'favoritism to a particular social or political group.'

• 8 percent say bias in the news media is 'all of these.'

Does it matter if the media is biased?

Baron wrote that bias does matter, because the 'news media bias can affect both public and private politics.' For instance, news ' plays a role in helping individual make decisions in their daily lives that 'could pertain to health, safety, personal finance, product selection, the environment, employment, or other issues about which individuals make purposive decisions.'

It is also reasonable, I suggest, to assume that Brand Russia, its reputation, and that of the Russian people, is negatively impacted by the predominantly 'bad-news' Western media coverage.

In his lengthy pre-election manifesto ('the manifesto') which I will discuss further on, Putin made it clear that he is well aware that Russia's reputation matters on a number of fronts, observing that 'In today's globalized world, it's all about different countries competing for ideas, talent and capital.'

He also observed that Russian efforts to 'foster an accurate image of Russia abroad' is not an area in which they have 'seen great success.' This is a commendable under-statement. He noted that 'When it comes to media influence, we are often outperformed.'

What to do about it?

Putin describes it as 'a separate and complex challenge that we must confront.' In his manifesto, he also wrote, with considerable justification, that 'Russia has been the target of biased and aggressive criticism that, at times, exceeds all limits.'

He wrote that when 'given constructive criticism, we welcome it and are ready to learn from it.' However, 'when we are subjected, again and again, to blanket criticisms in a persistent effort to influence our citizens, their attitudes, and our domestic affairs, it becomes clear that these attacks are not rooted in moral and democratic values.'

These statements are often adjudged 'autocratic' by the Western media, but in many respects, based on my analysis over several years, they are restrained.

Russians often use more emotional, on occasion, even crude (by our standards) language when they react to what they believe is injustice towards them: A cultural difference in how they express themselves does not invalidate their perspective. They have yet to learn how to play us at our game.

Putin describes Russia as 'a young democracy' and that as such, it often defers to 'our more experienced partners.' However, he pointed out that Russians still 'often have something to say.' The Western media, including the FT, characterize this kind of sentiment on his part, in derisory terms, as 'respect seeking'- yet it is a perfectly rational sentiment.

In this book, I will discuss why things are the way they are, and, to a certain extent, examine what, if anything, can be done about it. However, endemic stereotyping, entrenched Western media bias and Russophobia make it a complex problem to solve, as Putin has observed.

What explanations exist for media bias?

As a general matter, Baron tends towards a 'supply-side explanation for the existence and persistence of media bias.....' He acknowledges, however, that media bias 'could also have demand-side explanations.'

By that he means that 'Individuals have a demand for news as entertainment and may have a demand for stories that are consistent with their political or social viewpoints. This may provide an incentive for a news organization to bias stories to cater to particular clientele. Similarly, a news outlet that relies on advertising revenue may cater to high-income subscribers.'

I do not believe, however, that the root cause of the Western media's biased coverage of Russian affairs is on the 'demand-side' – in other words, that Westerners somehow desire it or that it feeds our inherent bias towards Russia and its people.

On the contrary, although colourful stories about wild-spending, immoral Russian mobsters and corrupt politicians and intrepid, beautiful spies are undoubtedly entertaining, I firmly believe that there is an untapped market for news about Russia that doesn't sound like the script for the latest Hollywood B movie. This market is grossly underserved by our 'one-trick pony' Western media.

There may be other explanations for media bias in the US context.

A 1995 US Pew Research four-month analysis of over 7,000 US international news stories[21] confirmed what has long been surmised, namely that Americans are mainly domestically focused, with little demand for international news.

Pew researchers noted that 'the US media carry few international articles that would broaden and educate Americans about the world beyond those hot spots where 'breaking' news, usually about conflict, is occurring, confirming the bad news is news 'rule of journalism' that Barron touched upon.

By contrast, a mere 8% of US media stories dealt with 'cooperation' between the US and other parties, which may explain, to some extent, why Russia's cooperation with the Americans on a host of issues rarely gets an airing.

The Pew researchers concluded that the 'parochial' choice of topics was 'understandable' if 'lamentable.' but they duly noted that 'the overemphasis on US-related stories caters to the self-centred concerns of Americans during this period of rising isolationist sentiment.'

They also noted, however, that the US media is not entirely at fault.

When the popular 'Today' show went to Africa, ratings nosedived. The anchor of the show noted drily that 'the predators at (Murdoch's) Fox (News) would swiftly counter in the same hour with sex and song.'

Sadly, I expect that 'sex and song' likely trumps misery in Africa in many Western countries as well.

However, the Pew team gave Europeans the benefit of the doubt, observing that 'the social norms of what Americans are expected to know about international affairs- i.e., much less than Germans or the British-may explain best why American television rates so low in the information value of its new programs.'

Arguably, that certainly used to be the case, but the success of endless, mind-numbing reality TV shows belies the comforting suggestion that Europeans are more high minded than Americans.

In this respect, Russian TV is no better- with cheap 'entertainment' front and centre and little independent political analysis in evidence. Indeed, the Russian media sector is arguably somewhat embryonic. Russia appears, for instance, to lack experienced news anchors and serious media personalities. If we are not careful, however, they will become equally extinct in the West.

The Pew study is non-conclusive as to whether the media 'leads or just reflects public opinion on the less dramatic issues where public attitudes are rooted in American political culture.'

It noted, however, that the Clinton administration ignored public opinion on the question of military intervention in Bosnia, which Americans 'steadfastly opposed.' Similarly, there was compelling evidence that Americans, across the political divide, were solidly opposed to the $800 billion bailout of the US banks, but the Obama administration bowed to pressure from the lobbyists, and did it anyway.

With respect to US media coverage of Russia, the Pew study concluded that 'Most of the stories with a perceptible tone were negative about Russia as a nation and overwhelmingly negative toward its current leadership, specifically including President Boris Yeltsin. The coverage was also negative in outlook for the current regime and for the current political system there. About the only policy issue regarding Russia on which the coverage was positive was the attitude toward US involvement in that country.'

Despite the fact that US media coverage of Russia during the 1990's under Yeltsin was 'overwhelmingly negative,' it is noteworthy how a revisionist view of history now makes current US politicians hanker for that era.

Pew noted, however, that negative US media sentiment towards Russia 'did not coincide with American public opinion,' as at that time, the US public had the same 'warm feeling' towards Russia as it had towards Israel, according to surveys, with a slight majority (49% vs. 44%) having a favourable view of Russia in general.

In addition, in contrast with the 'very negative coverage of Yeltsin,' Americans felt as warmly towards him 'as toward Bill Clinton,' and a significant majority wanted Yeltsin to remain in power (45% vs. 24%).

By the same token, 'closer to home, coverage was also critical of Mexico, although public opinion is not openly hostile to that country.' This study- and others like it- offer hope that even if the Western media and many Western politicians are incorrigibly biased towards Russia, ordinary people may be reachable.

My concern is that even though the media's stance on issues may not always reflect public opinion, there is a danger that it may shape it over time. The impact of propaganda shows it clearly can do so.

How many negative stories about Russia must a fair minded Westerner read before it has an impact?

Chapter Two

The Formula

The UK media is aware that it has problems, and that standards are not what they should be.

However, they seem to possess the happy knack of being able to acknowledge the issues, while carrying on regardless.

In the FT in July 2008, columnist Gideon Rachman[22] wrote about the differences between the US and the UK media. He referred to widespread fears that Rupert Murdoch's purchase of the venerable Wall Street Journal would decimate standards.

Rachman wrote that his sympathy initially rested with Murdoch, as 'American newspaper journalism strikes me as self-reverential, long-winded, over-edited and stuffy...American journalists, I realised, regard themselves as members of a respectable profession – like lawyers or bankers.'

Rachman worked as a freelancer in the US, and had occasion to attend the offices of the Chicago Tribune newspaper.

He wrote that he was impressed by his American colleagues, noting that when the Chicago Tribune said it was conducting an 'investigation,' it was a painstaking, meticulous process. He contrasted the approach with the UK: 'On the British paper I then worked for, an 'investigation' was something we started on Tuesday and published on Sunday. I was also sure that when American papers used the phrase 'sources say.' there really were some sources. I was not always so confident when that phrase appeared in my own newspaper.'

He described a situation where he found himself defending a British colleague in Thailand against criticism from

American colleagues for using quotes from the Bangkok Post without attribution. The reporter in question subsequently admitted to Rachman that he made the quotes up.

As Rachman observed with alacrity, 'This kind of thing has brought British journalism into disrepute in the US..The Americans are stuffier and more cautious. But they are also more careful and take the idea of journalism as a civic duty much more seriously. Much as it pains me to say this, I fear the Americans are closer to being right than the British.'

Rachman then described a mindset that he believed was widespread in UK journalism. 'Accurate and timely journalism is crucial to public life.'... 'yet British journalists are often curiously unwilling to acknowledge their power. A recent Reuters Institute report[23]on the *Power of the Commentariat* is in no doubt that opinion writers shape politics...But the British commentators reluctance to accept that their scribblings matter also reflects a refusal to accept responsibility.'

He concluded, 'In the end, those American journalists who insist on the civic importance of good journalism are correct. What we write does matter – even if it is sometimes easier to pretend that it doesn't.'

However, barely a month before Rachman wrote this commendable and insightful article, he wrote a piece in the same publication[24] titled *Respect for the law is in Russia's Interests*. In it, Rachman rails against Russia's alleged disrespect for the rule of law, a common theme I will discuss at length.

Rachman quoted an unnamed 'senior Shell executive' involved in a dispute with the Russian state over a stake in a Russian energy project, as comparing the experience to 'eating a polonium sandwich.' The quote presumably refers to the death by poisoning (believed to be the radioactive material polonium) in London, of Russian, Alexander Litvinenko in 1996.

Rachman also refers to a favourite theme at the FT, namely the allegedly rough treatment meted out by the Russians to UK state champion BP and their senior management team.

From my massive trawl through the UK media, I have noticed a trend whereby any perceived slight or problem experienced by a British company in Russia, especially state champions such as BP, are blown out of all proportion by the British media.

In many cases I reviewed, my analysis suggested that the companies in question, rather than being helpless victims, simply lacked strategic vision and the ability to execute in the Russian market. They failed to respect local custom, antagonised the locals, and generally made a bags' out of the whole affair.

Rather than soul searching, however, the media coverage I have read over several years suggests that some British companies that have problems in Russia turn to the UK press to help them spin business failure into victimisation.

The inevitable PR circus may temporarily rehabilitate them at home, but the tactic makes them few friends in the markets they demonize, as BP has discovered, as US energy Exxon Mobil giant recently eat its lunch by sealing a large deal with the Russians that it had long coveted.

I grew weary of reading reports about the plight of Robert Dudley, the Chairman of the TNK-BP Russian joint venture after the very public falling apart of the extremely lucrative arrangement in Russia. BP bought its stake for $8bn and has received $20bn in dividends over the years; its stake was ultimately worth several multiples of its original investment

The FT persistently refers to Dudley 'fleeing the country' or being 'forced' to leave. My sources tell me he did no such thing- his visa simply ran out when shareholders voted him out.

Minority shareholders suggest that Dudley tried to run the TNK-BP consortium as a BP subsidiary and blocked potentially lucrative Asian investments by it as they would have competed with BP's interest in the region; they also indicate that BP charged the Russians a fortune for 'seconded' Western consultants and refused to back down when minority investors complained.

As they say in the vernacular, BP gave the Russians the 'high-hat' every chance they could, despite the fact that the TNK stake was arguably the jewel in BP's crown. When the Russians fought back, Dudley turned up the PR dial.

The UK media constantly imply that long-suffering Dudley was on the cusp of joining jailed Russian tycoon, Mikhail Khodorkovsky in a Siberian jail cell. I believe this allegation had no basis in reality. One was left with the impression, however, that those darn Russians were just beastly to Dudley and BP in general, and that both were hounded out of Russia.

It's a better story than just calling a space a spade: BP botched its strategy in Russia. The impression given by the UK press, rightly or wrongly, that it always went crying to Mammy for help when things got tough, had one obvious side effect- it succeeded in alienating the Russians, an own goal if there was ever one.

BP will, however, hang onto a stake in the highly-lucrative Russian market as a result of recent deal-making with the Russian state. In no small part, this better than expected outcome can be credited to the acumen and proficiency of BP's operational staff on the ground in Russia, who are well regarded by the Russians.

In his FT article, Rachman quotes Rex Tillerson, the CEO of Exxon Mobil as warning the audience at the Russian equivalent of the Davos Economic Forum, the St Petersburg International Economic Forum- that 'there is no confidence in the rule of law in Russia today.' Exxon appears to have had a change of heart.

Rachman's use of the entirely gratuitous and inflammatory 'polonium' quote, from an unnamed source, does little, in my estimation to further or advance any serious debate or to improve perceptions about the standard of British journalism.

Rachman goes on to suggest that Russia has 'an image problem that goes well beyond business worlds.' He refers to disputes with smaller neighbours 'such as Georgia, Ukraine and the Baltic States.' He states that 'the Russian State has a growing reputation for using legal pretexts to justify thuggish intimidation.'

He refers to the Russians cutting off gas to the Ukrainians, another episode the UK media made hay with, without providing an even-handed explanation of the Russian position. The Russians steadfastly maintain it was a commercial dispute based on the fact that below market prices were being paid by the Ukrainians for their gas supply, a situation that wouldn't be tolerated in other countries.

Putin believes the EU is trying to squeeze Russia out of the European energy market. This is true, I believe. In reality, the EU energy market is notoriously monopolistic.

However, Rachman makes light work of the Russian characterization of the action as 'just a business dispute about unpaid bills and pricing.' stating instead that 'The rest of the world, however, assumes that this is politically motivated intimidation.'

I can't disagree with Rachman on this point, but I asked myself why the world would jump to this conclusion in the first place? Could it be that the Western media makes it a foregone conclusion that it does so? Not so. According to Rachman, 'this kind of behaviour-whether in business or in foreign policy-means that foreigners increasingly talk of Russia as a gangster State.'

That wasn't enough. Rachman continued, 'One big Western businessman (unnamed) claims that dealing with the Kremlin is just like dealing with the Mafia.'

I did a double take. As an ex drug prosecutor, I was intrigued and alarmed by the suggestion that 'big Western businessmen' have dealings with the mafia, sufficient to recognize them. Who might that be? There's surely a story in that allegation that's worth telling?

Rachman was on a roll. He suggested that 'a Mafia-Style reputation can be useful in getting your way, in the short term. In the long run, it means that even when Russian has a strong case it will be treated with suspicion.'

A lot of tough talk, indeed, but what strong case was Rachman referring to? A strong case for what? Why should Russia need to make a strong case?

Rachman is right, however, that it is a very rare occasion when Russia is given an inch, even with a 'strong case.' Any such case is treated by respectable journalists with derision.

Russia was isolated from the West for decades under Soviet, communist rule, so it is disadvantaged in 'spinning' its case and hiding behind the justifying slogans and self-indulgent jargon prevalent in the West that our media rarely challenge.

In addition, the fact we know so little about Russians, who remain an enigma to us-makes them easy fodder for Western politicians and the Western media.

The 'gangster state' label is corroborated by Western popular culture that paints Russians as grim faced and taciturn going about their grey lives in their crime-ridden society, run by mobsters.

I abhor the lack of delicacy and empathy inherent in such crass labels as the 'gangster state.' Is that the best the cream of the Western media can do in discussing Russian affairs? For shame I say, for shame.

Indeed, I often wonder what constitutes 'a gangster state?' What are its prerequisites? Could Italy, Mexico, and Columbia qualify? In Ireland, we sometimes, colloquially, refer to Irish politicians who presided over a form of crony capitalism that has nearly bankrupted the country, as a 'bunch of gangsters.' Perhaps that qualifies us as a gangster state too? If not, why not?

Sloppy thinking and sloppy words have consequences, especially if written by people with influence, who should frankly know better.

FT readers go on vacation, and we cannot help but form opinions about particular destinations from what we read. What rational reader would plan a trip to Russia, the 'gangster state' after week after week of reading the diatribes? One would be forgiven for imaging that death was imminent from the moment one left the aeroplane; that thugs and gangsters roam the streets looking for hapless tourists to murder.

Yet, curiously, according to my observations at least, most of the Western media based in Moscow live rather well. They pay very little tax relevant to what they would pay at home. They eat well, send their kids to good schools, enjoy wonderful music and ballet, and suffer few of the indignities that a rational reader of their output might assume to be de rigueur for foreign correspondents forced to live in the 'gangster state.'

On my first trip to Moscow, I felt like the famous explorer Richard Burton, setting off on a perilous journey into a strange and treacherous land. The worse thing that happened to me was being charged 10 euro for a coffee in a plush hotel. A few weeks later I was robbed in Amsterdam.

Russia is not devoid of problems, as I will discuss at length, but neither is it a war zone.

Rachman threw a bone to the unfortunate Russians behind the 'gangster state' label, writing that Russia should 'get serious about the rule of law out of respect for the welfare of its own citizens.' Yet, he fails to recognise the impact that the adoption of glib labels and stereotyping by influential Western columnists has on the welfare of these same people.

The FT is a paper I read daily. A day without 'the brown paper.' as a friend calls it, is a bad day. It now costs me the princely sum of 3 euro. For that price, I expect a premium product, high quality research and writing - not cartoon characters on a page, or the same old tired perspective rehashed over and over.

I read that it has an average daily readership of 2.2 million people worldwide. It is hugely influential. What it publishes, matters. Nonetheless, a big proportion of the press clipping in my vast, Everest sized negative media pile about Russia comes from this publication.

Lionel Barber, the editor, has defined the 'essence' of the FT as 'reaching those people who influence or seek to influence decisions in business, finance and public affairs around the world'- referring to the paper as 'a premium product.'..with 'weight, global reach, and tradition.[25]'

Assuming he is right, the FT has a heightened level of responsibility to ensure scrupulous adherence to principles of objectivity and impartiality. A paper dedicated to these principles will not resort to stereotyping or labelling.

Jonathan Guthrie, in his FT Lombard column on April 18, 2012 (wrongly) discounted the possibility that a Canadian might be made governor of the Bank of England, on the basis that 'In Britain, jockeys are traditionally Irish and monarchs are German. Central bank governors tend to be British.'

The Irish in Britain have occasionally taken time out from the race track for other ventures, such as founding the FT. An Irish man, Brendan Bracken, a brilliant, quixotic, social-climbing rogue, who was a confidante to Churchill for over 30 years has that accolade.

I have read hundreds, probably thousands of examples of Western media bias against Russia. From my analysis, it appears that great swathes of the Western media- most particularly in the UK- adhere to a 'formula'- a kind of cheat-sheet template for all stories about Russia.

For instance, if an editor tells a UK journalist to write about Russia, output suggests that he or she ensures that whatever is written ticks the boxes marked, 'Corruption, Rule of Law, Gangsters, Mafia, Transparency, Bribery, Oligarch.' and so on. The result is the constant regurgitation of the same trite, stale material that relies heavily on labels ('the gangster state') and rampant stereotyping.

There is rarely any critical thinking or analysis in evidence, and there is most decidedly no recognition that the formula impacts real people.

Besides overt box ticking, there are themes that reoccur over and over in pieces about Russia, and that are part and parcel of the formula. The emphasis may vary depending on whether the outlet is American or British, but there are many themes in common.

A common refrain, especially in the US, is the suggestion that Russians, especially Russian politicians, are authoritarian, belligerent, suffer from Cold War paranoia, and hate America.

Part and parcel of this theme is the suggestion that Russians engage in 'empire building' and bully their neighbours as they seek to preserve their traditional 'spheres of influence.' Due to this reprehensible behaviour, Russia must be 'contained' by the Protectors of the Free World, and somehow brought to heel.

In a review by George Walden in the Sunday Telegraph in December 2011 of the book *Spies and Commissars: Bolshevik Russia and the West*, by Robert Service, in his opening paragraph, Walden wrote: 'As a regular visitor to Moscow (I chair the Russian Booker Prize), I am constantly struck by how many educated folk share the official paranoia about the West. Maybe, it's because there was a time, historically, when we really were out to topple the regime.'

Mr Walden apparently doesn't read the UK press coverage about Russia.

Part and parcel of the belligerence theme is the suggestion that the Russians are paranoid to worry about encirclement by NATO or missiles on EU soil that may be pointed at them. They are scolded for complaining or making their case. 'Why do the Russians behave as they do?' is a common US media lament, expressed with all the slippery guile of a velociraptor.

I will deal with all these charges at length in due course, but suffice to say at this stage that the US politicians and media outlets that make them are brazenly impervious to the fact that these allegations could justifiably be made (and have been made) against the US, the UK and other Western nations.

US right-wing Republican hawks are particularly fond of these multi-part accusations, which receive a constant airing from such influential dailies as the Washington Post. Indeed, editorials at this influential paper that deal with

Russian issues are frequently little more than jaw-dropping polemics.

2008 was a real low point for the Western media in reporting about Russia, especially during the Georgian conflict. No allegation was too low. A truly enormous amount of venom was spewed.

Philip Stephens wrote a column in the FT in August 2008,[26] about what he described as Russia's invasion of Georgia.

The Western media automatically assumed that the Russians were responsible for the outbreak in hostilities. A subsequent independent report by the EU[27] found, however, that Georgia launched the attack, although the report was critical of Russia's response. To this day, several UK and US journalists still describe Russia as the aggressor.

According to Stephens in the FT, however, 'Europe stands for a global order based on co-operation, norms and rules.' The current financial crisis, and our chaotic response, would suggest otherwise. However, Stephens maintained that 'Moscow prefers the use of force. Appeasement invites only further contempt.'

He wasn't finished. He compared Russia's stated desire to protect the territories invaded by the Georgians with the Soviet invasion of Czechoslovakia in 1968, and then, most extraordinarily, wrote- 'Hitler used a similar pretext.'

Putin is routinely compared to Stalin, but now, the FT was going out on a limb: Putin had been compared to Hitler! Only for the huge human sacrifice made by Russians in the Second World War (including Putin's father, who was wounded fighting the Nazis), we would have a great deal more to fear from the Germans than austerity measures.

Stephens was undaunted. He followed with a mixed bag tirade of charges, including Russia's alleged desire to dominate oil and gas markets, and its neighbours more generally. He mocks Russia fear of encirclement by Nato.

He moves back to a favourite at the FT, the expectation that Medvedev, while President, might have been a dog that would go to Western heel- (that he would, as Stephens put it, 'temper Mr Putin's belligerence'), but instead he is 'a finger-puppet tucked into the Prime Ministers' (Putin's) breast pocket.' According to Stephens, 'authoritarianism is back in fashion.'

Stephens acknowledges that Russia has riches, such as oil and gas at its disposal, but due to low fertility and high mortality rates, he views the future as bleak, due to the 'crumbling health and education systems and decaying civil infrastructure.' He described corruption as 'rife'- and the 'present political leadership.'..'better described as a kleptocracy, than an autocracy.'

He makes reference to Putin's 'deep sense of grievance against the West.' If Putin reads the Western media- and articles like this one- he would have very good reason to feel aggrieved.

Stephens' also refers to the belief (indeed widely held in Russia) 'that the US and Europe conspired in Russia's humiliation after the collapse of the Soviet Union.'

Stephens makes light work of that assertion. He suggests rather that in the long term the West's 'strategic response to Mr Putin's belligerence' should be guided by a clear-sighted 'appreciation of Russia's weaknesses as well as its strengths.'

In 2008, another FT columnist, this time Chrystia Freeland[28]wrote about Russia, and how the Oligarchs 'could save Russia.' Wealthy businessmen in Russia are frequently described by the Western media as 'oligarchs,' a pejorative term, implying criminal mendacity or shadiness of character. However, we rarely apply the moniker to our own, however dubious their antecedents or unmeritorious their record.

Freeland refers to Putin's 'neo-authoritarian regime'- in the context of the Georgian war. She wrote 'having finally agreed that the new Russia is nasty – and not just to its own journalists and human rights activists – Western leaders are also coming to the view that it may be hard to influence, let alone contain.'

I asked myself, why should we feel the need to 'contain' Russia? Ms. Freeland suggests that the oligarchs, although 'crony capitalists,' are focused on global markets, and as such, with the benefit of Western education, will eventually do things the Western way.

However, with a view to, as Ms. Freeland put it 'hemming in a resurgent Russia,' she recommends that the West use its leverage to continue to deny Russia membership of the WTO and continue to support 'vulnerable' neighbours such as the Ukraine. She suggests that Russia is now a state with which...'we cannot continue 'business as usual.'

Freeland made the usual predictable and yawn-inducing references to BP's alleged travails in the country, and closes by indicating that an (unnamed) oligarch had 'recently told me that Mr Putin's tragedy is that 'he wants to rule like Stalin but live like Roman Abramovich.' She finishes with a flourish-a warning that we 'need' to 'make it clear to him and his business buddies that they cannot do both.'

I found this article smug, patronising and from the Russian perspective, even threatening.

In light of the current financial crisis (that no-one, to my knowledge, has yet pinned on the Russians), and the apparent shift in the balance of power from West to East, many of these press articles from 2008 show a distinct naivety about the moral authority these writers appear rests with Western politicians and institutions, rather than with their poor cousins in the emerging markets. This type of colonial contempt has been exposed as wishful thinking, as I will discuss in Part Two.

An adjunct to the belligerence theme, often picked up by the UK dailies (including by Stephens in the FT- as referenced above) is the 'charge' that Russia feels 'humiliation' having 'lost' the Cold War; that it craves 'respect' and will do anything to avoid further humiliation. This aspiration is routinely mocked.

Articles in the UK business press employ headlines that appear to rejoice in the expectation that Russians, both politicians and business people, will be, or have been ' humiliated'- such as *The humbling of Russia's masters of the universe* (FT- November 27, 2008), and *The humbling of a tsar* (FT December 10 November 2011), referring to Putin.

Indeed, in 2008 and 2009, when the crisis took hold with a vengeance, there was an avalanche of media articles in the UK press crowing about the fact[29] that various Russian businessmen were in severe difficulty. The topic was picked to death, with numerous churlish articles appearing on the topic, sometimes several times in the same month.

Inexplicably, the journalists appeared to derive satisfaction from their struggle to save their empires. They wanted them 'humiliated.'

Why? Had these individuals done them some personal wrong?

As they wrote, Irish, German, British and American businessman, indeed business people all over the Western world were being similarly 'humiliated,' if you viewed the world through such a cynical lens. Several people committed suicide, out of despair and a deep fear that they had been 'humiliated' in the eyes of their peers. Was their trauma something to gloat about? It was disquieting to read these articles.

Companies, many of them significant players, were going bust everywhere, so why this obsession with Russia, and why so mean spirited? Indeed, several of these Russian businessmen displayed considerable courage under fire, and admirable tenacity as they fought the good fight for survival, emerging relatively unscathed – with help from the Russian state, dispensed even more liberally in the West.

However, many of the UK columnists, the same people who gleefully predicted their demise, were begrudging- unprepared to give credit where it was due. I, the reader, was left with a sense of their disappointment that all the gloomy, doom-laden scenarios had not come to pass; Russia was still standing, its captains of industry intact, and by no means over and out.

After the fall of the Soviet Union, Mikhail Gorbachev, not venerated in Russia, but popular in the West for his attacks on the current regime- was quoted as observing that the Americans thought Boris Yeltsin did a great job in the 1990s, despite the fact Russia was left on its knees, its economy in shatters after his tenure, a period the Russians refer to as the 'era of chaos.' Gorbachev concluded that 'It suited the West for Russia to be half dead.'

In an article in The Sunday Times in August 2008, discussing the Georgian conflict,[30] Putin is quoted as saying that Russia is frustrated because 'There's a feeling that the West treats Russia merely as a loser in the Cold War, which has to play by the winner's rules.' The article points out that the Russian hierarchy believe that although they co-operated with the West in the fight against terrorism, Afghanistan, Iran and North Korea, they have received little or no credit for doing so.

A Kremlin official is also quoted in The Sunday Times article as saying 'we cannot endlessly retreat with a smiling face.' Similarly, Russia's ambassador to the EU, Vladimir

Chizhov, has expressed a desire to facilitate closer economic ties with Europe, while also making it clear that Russia deplores condescension towards it: 'It is not the all-knowing EU playing God and descending to earth to modernise the savages. It is a mutually beneficial endeavour.'

In a column titled 'Round two: The West versus the rest.' published in the FT on 17th June 2011, Philip Stephens again wrote about Russia, the rivalry between the US and China, and how the emerging markets are challenging Western domination of the global economy.

He stated that Russia has put itself on the side of the emerging market economies. However, 'curiously for a State that still likes to pretend that it is a super power equal to the US, it (Russia) seems happy to be designated one of the Bric nations.'

He indicates that this positioning arises due to the fact that 'Mr Putin's worldview was shaped by national humiliation after the collapse of the Soviet Union. He is of a generation of Russians that cannot shake off the notion that Russia's natural adversary is the US-led Nato alliance.'

Not so, according to Stephens.

Rather, the 'biggest threats to Russia are internal- economic obsolescence and rapid population decline.' This theme combines two favourites of the UK media- the 'basket case' motif and the 'Russians are dying out anyway' dynamic.

Another favourite Stephens' theme is the bizarre notion that China looks down on Russia- an unwise perspective if true, which I doubt, as the facts belie it.

'China scorns Russia as a declining nation, unable to produce anything useful except oil and gas and slowly but surely drinking itself to death. Even its military technology now falls short of Beijing's ambitions. Russians must know this. A strategic outlet unburdened by emotion would see

Moscow exchange the part of useful idiot in Beijing for economic integration with the West.'

A number of thoughts, including incredulity, occurred to me as I read the piece. 'Useful idiot'? What on earth did he mean? Drinking itself to death? I gave him the benefit of the doubt, and fervently hoped he was referring to oil and gas consumption.

As for integration with the West, that prospect does not look terribly alluring right now, as we totter on the edge of the precipice. The EU remains Russia's largest trading partner, so our respective fates are inexorably intertwined, but Russia clearly has much to gain by ramping up business with the Chinese (as it is doing)- far closer to Russian borders than many Western countries, and with real growth potential.

The notion that China 'scorns' Russia as a declining nation is part of the UK media's love affair with China- granted high indulgences long denied Russia, which ought, by any fair measure, be considered a democratic paradise by comparison.

China has many strengths, but it also has many weaknesses (not to mention the fact it is a communist state), including lack of water, land that can be used to produce food stuff and many critical raw materials, as I will discuss in Part Two.

Stephens, and some of his FT colleagues, are keen on the notion that the US will remain the Big Kahuna on the world stage into the distant future. 'The likely role of the US will be that of indispensible balancing power.' My view on the US's role in world affairs is far less benign.

Stephens' reference to Putin and Russia's 'humiliation' after the collapse of the Soviet Union is, as described, a tedious, recurring theme throughout Western media coverage of Russian affairs.

However, this 'humiliation' that Stephens's refers to, was not an abstract political or economic construct. The collapse of the Soviet Union in 1991 resulted in misery for millions of ordinary Russians-and democracy delivered nothing but chaos and lawlessness.

Russians died in huge numbers during the Second World War to stop Hitler in his tracks. The inhabitants of Stalingrad, blockaded by the Nazis, starved to death and many of them consumed human flesh to try to stave off a painful death. After the fall of Hitler, Stalin brutalized the Russian population some more.

Why do we need Russia to be humiliated? Who suffers but the people? I derive no satisfaction from the prospect. Surely the Russians have suffered enough? What can possibly be gained by such glib condescension and such a profound lack of empathy?

I was very disappointed at the lack of external support for Russia during the 2010 smog and forest fires crisis. It did not seem that that many countries, especially in Europe (close neighbours) offered support, or were as quick as they ought to have been to do so.

If the fires had been outside Paris or Zurich, or London, I suspect we would have been keen to fly in fire fighters and equipment. Instead, the Western media lambasted the Russian government for not having modern equipment or infrastructure to deal with the problem, ignoring how both the UK and Ireland were brought to a halt by modest snow falls.

This lack of empathy for the impact this crisis had on the lives of ordinary Russians (many of whom were trapped in stifling heat in their apartments all summer long) was disquieting.

I recall how Putin was the first world leader to offer sympathy and support to President Bush after Saudi nationals took down the Twin Towers- a fact quickly forgotten when he put Russian interests ahead of those of the US.

The UK media's sarcasm as it focuses on the theme of Russian 'humiliation,' and the manner in which it jeers the desire for respect is tawdry and ill-mannered, to say the least.

What rational individual or nation does not seek respect, or wish to avoid humiliation? Respect is a critical element in building trust, reputation and brand image.

The Irish are a proud and stubborn people. Our current financial predicament is a source of great embarrassment to us. Many Irish people, from all walks of life decry the perceived loss of sovereignty as the European Commission and various international agencies appear to control our destiny.

We too crave 'respect' on the world stage. Every nation desires it, including the UK and the old superpowers, desperate to remain relevant in a New World where the old colonies flex their muscles and financial might. The UK's Falklands war with Argentina: what was that about? Was it not fought to protect a traditional 'sphere of influence, or the long drawn out conflict to keep Ireland in Britain's grip?

Expensive PR campaigns to burnish a country's brand- such as the markedly unsubtle 'Great' Britain brand campaign, developed by ad agency Mother for the UK Government, can hardly claim not to be about, well, shouting out how 'great' Britain is. Is that not 'respect seeking' on a rather grand scale?

Personally, I find the campaign terribly 'naff'- no better than the previous 'Cool Britannia' marketing fiasco. 'Cool Britons'- of whom numerous examples exist- do not need this banal nonsense to make it so. These campaigns are a profound waste of taxpayer money, and makes UK politicians look like a bunch of supremely square nitwits.

I would strongly caution the Russians not to fall into the same ignominious trap.

Let there be no mistake, the old colonial powers loath the prospect of losing respect and influence on the world stage just as much as the Russians- and they will fight tooth and nail to retain it.

Contenders for the US Republican Presidential nomination made no bones about their desire that America be respected; indeed, there is huge consternation on all sides of the US political spectrum at the mere notion that the US is in decline, or losing influence globally.

In 2010, Mitt Romney published a book titled, *No Apology: The Case for American Greatness*. He has also vowed he will 'insist on a military so powerful no one would ever think of challenging it.'

The US is the world's leading arms buyer, spending a staggering $711 billion in the process- compared to Russia's paltry $8 billion. China spends $143 billion in the sector and Europe another $407 billion. All in all, it is a disgraceful amount of money, with famine and extreme poverty still rampant in the world.

Yet, US politicians, and the US media, make no apologies for grotesque levels of military spending and overt 'respect-seeking,' but woe-betide the Russians if they show similar aspirations or demonstrate national pride, or simply endeavour to protect their borders, breached on several occasions in recent memory.

As matters stand, however, the 'Cold War paranoia.' humiliation' and 'respect-seeking' charges are highly effective instruments to trivialize legitimate Russian concerns and grievances with the West. The Western media typecasts anyone voicing such concerns as a sad-sack paranoiac.

By the same token, this biased, self-satisfied, frequently pompous characterisation enables our media assuage any vestige of conscience they may have that there are two sides to the story that merits telling. Above all else, it is an extremely effective pre-emptive strike against any effort by the Russians to fight back.

Another favourite theme, currently much in vogue with US and UK politicians and the Western media alike, is the allegation that Russia disrespects human rights. This charge has become a hot-button issue on Capitol Hill. As explained, it has escalated to the point that it has found expression in bills (laws) tabled before Congress, coupled with allegations about lack of rule of law and 'endemic corruption.'

The basic premise is that America and the UK have the high moral ground on human rights issues, and must therefore work to put things to rights by using legislation, if necessary, to force the Russian government onside. This assumption is flawed.

There has been an enormous fuss about the sentencing of the telegenic 'Pussy Riot' girls to two years in prison for cavorting on the altar of Moscow's main Orthodox cathedral wearing sinister balaclavas, in what was supposed to be an anti-Putin stunt.

American politicians have described the sentence as 'disproportionate.'

In the 1990's, extremely draconian prison sentences were meted out to offenders who ran afoul of the infamous US 'three strikes and you are out' drug laws. In one notorious case[31], Leandro Andrade, an Army veteran with children and a drug habit was sentenced to '50 years to life' for stealing videos from a convenience store. Life sentences without parole were mandatory for a third offence. African Americans were imprisoned under the three-strikes law at ten times the rate of whites.

Such sentences were intended to be disproportionate.

Indeed, European nationals, Britons included, go to quite extreme lengths to avoid extradition to the US, for fear of the severe sentencing laws.

In Britain, Al Qaeda suspects sit in prison for nearly a decade, without charge and without trial. This too is 'disproportionate.' unless merely being charged with a terrorism offence deprives one of entitlement to the basics tenets of a fair legal system, as appears to be the case.

The FT, never slow to seize an opportunity to do its bit for the Russian opposition, wrote the most sanctimonious, self-righteous drivel in an editorial after the Pussy Riot sentencing, grandly titled, *'Putin's fear of the punk iconoclasts.*[32] The editorial piece opined that, 'This is one of the worst perversions of justice in 12 years of Putinism.'

The media savvy women are now Mother Theresa, Aung San Suu Kyi and Martin Luther King all wrapped into one- and positively guaranteed a Western record label deal.

The FT editorial gushed that the girls' defence of their actions was 'eloquent, intelligent....powerful indictments of Putinism.' 'This is more profound punk than the Sex pistols ever offered.' According to the FT, their idiotic antics amounted to 'political art.'

That was too rich for me.

A recent Levada Centre poll in Russia suggested that 44 percent of Russians polled believed the Pussy Riot trial to be fair and unbiased; the group enjoys the support of a mere 7% of Russians. Russians are far more religious than we might imagine. Orthodox believers are thought to make up about 70 percent of the population.

It is also by no means clear (however much the Western press would like to make it otherwise) that Russians will punish Putin for the Pussy Riot storm in a teacup, as many religious people believe they got their comeuppance.

To the best of my recollection, even Madonna, the Empress of Shock, never hurled herself onto the high altar of St Pat's cathedral in Manhattan to do a spirited rendition of Anarchy in the UK. I highly doubt that New York's police constabulary- with a fine smattering of pious Irish lads amongst their ranks-would have been overly impressed. She'd have been dragged off kicking and screaming to her heart's content.

I tried to imagine the reaction if Pussy Riot had plied their wares in a similar fashion on the altar of the Pro-Cathedral in Dublin or at the Vatican in Rome. Undoubtedly, the Catholic clergy would have been appalled by the blasphemy, and had they offered resistance, the pert lassies would have been unceremoniously removed in a paddy wagon to cool their jets in an Irish-Roman prison.

Some of you may recall back in 2003 when Natalie Pasdar, the female lead singer of the popular US country band, the Dixie Chicks, told a London audience that she was ashamed that then President George W. Bush came from her home town, Texas, a reference to her opposition to the war in Iraq.

She was subsequently abused from on high by a large number of her countrymen, and the band was blackballed throughout the US; radio stations took her music off their play lists. Dixie Chicks' CDs were destroyed in public, and the band members received hate mail, even death threats. Pasdar reiterated her right as a US citizen to free speech, but got a crash course in a peculiar American reality: Free speech in the US often comes at a high price.

Radical right wing US Republicans would not have welcomed a Pussy Riot display at one of their evangelical Christian services. The US state may not have intervened- but fringe elements in American society have proven willing over many decades to take the law into their own hands.

However, rather than playing right into the hands of the Russia/Putin haters by giving them a two year sentence, I would have left the band members in an uncomfortable jail cell for a couple of days, and then slapped them with a hefty fine for their troubles. I'd also have sent them on a compulsory course to teach them to respect the feelings and religious beliefs of their fellow Russians.

Around the same time as the Pussy Riot sentencing, the UK government appeared to totally lose the run of itself by threatening to storm Equador's embassy in London to capture WikiLeaks activist, Julian Assange, granted sanctuary by Equador. Had the UK state followed through on this quite extraordinary threat, the repercussions would have been grave.

Putin's cynical view of the West's new-found enthusiasm for promoting human rights in far off places mirrors my own. In his manifesto, he wrote that 'A string of armed conflicts under the pretext of humanitarian concerns has undermined the principle of national sovereignty, which has been observed for centuries.'

Putin wrote that 'the United States and other Western states dominate and politicize the human rights agenda, using it as a means to exert pressure. At the same time, they are very sensitive and even intolerant to criticism.' Second, the objects of human rights monitoring are chosen regardless of objective criteria but at the discretion of the states that have 'privatized' the human rights agenda.

He accepts that 'human rights are more important than national sovereignty,'but views crimes against humanity as the remit of an international court' rather than 'airstrike democracy'- a thinly veiled reference to the fact Russia approval of a UN 'no fly zone' over Libya was used an illegal pretext to cripple it and lynch its leaders.

French and British consultants wasted no time, coming in practically on the heels of the Libyan assault, in doing deals with rebels that favoured their companies, and cut out the Russians and other incumbents. UK Trade and Investment (UKTI) – a UK government organisation that helps UK exporters-has estimated that the 'rebuilding' of Libya could be worth £12bn to UK businesses over the next decade.[33]

Putin has pointed out a fact that I draw attention to in this book, namely that 'no country has a perfect record on human rights and basic freedoms.' He believes that when the 'the older democracies commit serious violations,' Russia should not 'look the other way.'

He is no fool, and notes that 'obviously, this work should not be about trading insults. All sides stand to gain from a constructive discussion of human rights issues.' He refers to Russia's first report on global Human Rights issues- a response to the annual US report that routinely lambasts Russia and other countries, while assuming the moral high ground itself.

He describes this initiative as 'just one aspect of our efforts to promote our international and diplomatic activity and to foster an accurate image of Russia abroad.'

Unfortunately, authored as it is by the Russian state (viewed with suspicion in the West), this report, however meritorious (I echo many of the sentiments in it in this book), has already fallen into the dustbin of history. It was either ignored completely by the Western media, or dismissed out of hand as a 'white-washing' exercise.

Yet the US report, regularly stuffed to the brim with gaping double-standards and moralising, receives little or no critical appraisal from the Western press. To my mind, this speaks only to a deep-seated bias.

US politicians openly discuss the need to maintain a 'lever' (like the Magnitsky law) in reserve to beat the Russians with. Charges of alleged human rights abuses frequently serve as the justification for this interference in the affairs of a sovereign nation. In truth, it is a cynical ploy to keep the old Cold War enemy on the back foot and its reputation in tatters. It is, however, hugely near sighted on numerous fronts.

A very damaging, amorphous charge, already touched upon, centres round the allegation that Russia is a 'mafia state'- a description of Russia used by US diplomats in cable transmissions published by WikiLeaks. The US media love this one-and, as we have seen, 'the gangster state' monocle has been adopted in the UK. It does us little credit that we have adopted such meaningless, but extremely damaging labels to describe a complex country.

Chapter Three

Frogs and Princes

The most idiotic charge levelled against Russia is the suggestion that it is an economic 'basket case.' As already stated, Russian economic fundamentals are very sound, indeed magnificent by current Western standards.

The basket case motif is often coupled with mean-spirited 'jibes' about poverty, income inequality, population decreases, low life expectancy, healthcare issues, high levels of alcoholism, and oil and gas dependency.

By way of example, Sam Fleming in the Sunday Telegraph on January 2, 2012[34], described Russia as 'the ugly sister of the BRIC quartet'- a country that 'should never have been included in the first place, given its dismal demographics, horrendous public health problems and stubborn reliance on oil and natural gas.'

'Dismal demographics' exist in Germany and Japan, to name just two major economies with similar issues. On the healthcare front, many EU countries, including my own, have grappled with 'horrendous public health problems' for decades, with little success, and one in four Americans (about 48 million people) have no health coverage at all[35].

The Gini co-efficient is a measure of income inequality. The CIA World Fact Book rankings[36] place the US in 40th place, with a score of 45 based, on 2007 numbers (the higher the number scored, the more unequal the society), behind Bulgaria and Jamaica. It is likely that this ranking does not reflect the current economic difficulties in the country.

Russia is ranked 52, with a score of 42, based on 2010 data. The EU scored reasonably well-around 30.4 based on 'estimated' 2010 data. However, with very high unemployment and a worsening financial crisis on the horizon, I have grave doubts that this latter ranking reflects the current reality.

The methods used to calculate income inequality vary from country to country so comparisons are not sacrosanct. For instance, the black market economy is not included, which is believed to be huge in many countries, including China, as well as EU countries such as Greece and Italy.

The CIA World Factbook acknowledges that 'Definitions of poverty vary considerably among nations. For example, rich nations generally employ more generous standards of poverty than poor nations.' For instance, only 2.8% of Chinese are deemed to live below the official poverty level- but by Western standards, huge numbers of Chinese live in dire straits.

In 2005, the World Bank suggested the global poverty line should stand at US$1.25 ($1.66) a day. As of 2007, the Chinese official 'absolute poverty' level was set at approximately $90 per year, with the official 'low income' line set at circa $125 per year. By contrast, Israel's poverty line is set at $7.30 per person per day.

The Washington-based International Food Policy Research Institute last year placed India 67 out of 88 countries listed in its global hunger index. The Indian Government has tried to fix the official poverty line at 32 rupees (87 cents) a person per day in cities, and 26 rupees a day in rural areas.

Sadly, poverty is in the eye of the beholder, and expectations differ wildly across the globe-and governments often massage the numbers.

In October, 2011, the Russian State Statistics Service reported that 14.9 percent of the population lives below the poverty level. Shockingly, that still leaves Russia ranked roughly 127th (on 2009 statistics) in global populations below the poverty line. However, the situation in the US is nothing to brag about either.

The US Census Bureau's annual report on income, poverty and health insurance coverage reported that the US's national poverty rate climbed for a third consecutive year to 15.1 percent in 2010, the highest number in the 52 years that the Census Bureau has been publishing poverty estimates.

Russians care about such issues. An August, 2011 survey by the Russian Levada Centre found that 73 percent of the population consider inflation the most serious problem in the country; 52 percent cited concerns about poverty, and 42 percent cited increasing unemployment.

The current subsistence income in Russia is approximately 7,023 rubles ($221) a month for a working adult, 5,141 rubles for a pensioner and 6,294 rubles for a child. Employed Russians' average income is at 23,154 rubles per month — 330 percent higher than the subsistence income. The per-capita income of Russia is twice that of China and about eight times that of India.

Putin has often acknowledged that the gap between rich and poor is too wide in Russia. He has firmly stated on several occasions that 'Russia is a welfare state.' I will discuss his vision in this respect in Part Two.

Can you imagine a US politician making a similar statement? It would be the ultimate kiss of death. Putin's vision of the future for millions of Russians, has, however, much in common with European values, rather than the dog-eat-dog American ethos, so beloved of US Republicans.

The Western media often gloats in an insufferable fashion about the fact that the Russian population is dwindling. Financial incentives to encourage people to have more kids may help, but will not come close to fixing a problem that exists in many Western nations.

Improving healthcare will help reduce high mortality rates, but mass immigration must surely form part of the solution, although Putin is not keen to emphasize the obvious, for fear of stirring up xenophobia in Russia.

Population decline is a problem that Putin is keenly aware of, but not one that I'd expect our media to delight in.

Russia has slipped one place in the rating of the world's biggest countries by population and now ranks eighth with 142.8 million inhabitants, the State Statistics Service said. Women outnumber men by 10.7 million, but mostly due to a large number of early male deaths.

The UN estimates that Russia's population will decline to 125,687.2 million by 2025 and to 104,258.5 million by 2050. The average life expectancy for Russians during 2012 is expected to be 76 years for a woman and 64 years for a man, according to the State Statistics Service.

The root cause of the problem includes the fact that many Russians enjoyed poor health for decades under communism. It is compounded by alcoholism, heavy smoking, the impact of damaging levels of pollution in industrial areas, and the effect of long term stress.

The current Russian government is spending heavily on healthcare. In conjunction with Putin's focus on healthy living, these long overdue initiatives will ultimately have an impact, but it will not happen overnight.

Under the Soviet system, there was no incentive to improve services or the quality of care and equipment became very outdated; providers were rated on the volume of services, not quality. Due to paternalism, people also did not take care of their own health, looking to the state for everything-which undoubtedly impacted life expectancy.

Despite receiving a basic level of free care, reports indicate that they had no right to complain, and no input. In 1994, the average pay of health care workers was only 80% of the mean earnings of the average worker in Russia.

During the 1990's, enforced austerity resulted in hospitals starved of funding using innovative means to survive, in the process violating legislation- often inadvertently (and encouraging corrupt, inefficient practices) as they tried to operate independently, by, for instance, charging for services supposed to be free. Regulations were lacking to govern the sector, and insurance premiums supposed to be paid by employers for workers were often not paid.

People responded by paying 'bribes' to jump queues or just to be seen by a doctor. The more affluent were (and are) taken care of by an expensive, de facto, private system within the system. Lack of oversight, control, responsibility, and standards made the problem worse and encouraged corrupt practices.

As is often the case in Russia, the problem will not be solved simply by throwing more money at it. It requires strategic oversight; increased efficiency and better use of existing resources will go a long way to improve matters. The toughest nut to crack is likely attitudinal change, as people must begin to take responsibility for their own health.

In my parents' generation, only the rich and educated saw a doctor; many poor, rural people died of curable conditions. The Irish have been trying as long as I can remember to 'fix healthcare' to little or no avail. It remains in what seems like a permanent state of crisis.

The legacy of the Soviet system and the era of chaos was that TB and other old diseases, as well as 'new' diseases like aids, are still around, or on an upswing. However, the Health 2020 strategy, which has quadrupled health care spending since 2001 and national campaigns to discourage smoking and drinking- and claim to have increased life expectancy by three years and infant mortality by a third- shows promise while not being a panacea.

The appalling experience in the UK and Ireland with failed government IT projects that promised increased efficiencies and quality of care (e.g. electronic health care records' projects that flopped in spectacular fashion) have cost the tax payer billions. The Russians can learn much from such chronic wastage and mismanagement- and not repeat our mistakes.

Mean-spirited jibes about high levels of alcohol abuse are frequent in the UK media. In this regard, however, the UK has little to crow about.

A UNICEF Innocent Research Centre study of children's well-being in twenty-one industrialized nations[37] ranked the UK and the United States in the bottom third of the rankings for five of the six dimensions reviewed. The Netherlands was top of the table.

GDP per capital is not decisive, as the Czech Republic scored much better in child well-being than wealthier countries. The study pointed to high levels of obesity amongst kids in the UK and especially the US, which is a good predicator of future health problems. The skinniest kids are in Poland and the Netherlands.

In terms of 'risk behaviour,' the UK was also at the bottom of the league table by a wide margin- (defined as smoking, drinking, cannabis use, sex by age 15, and use of condoms). The percentage of UK kids aged 11, 3 and 15 who reported having been drunk more than twice is the highest in the league- a high percentage also reported smoking more the once a week. The Russians kids were placed in the mid range of the rankings, well behind the UK and the US on most dimensions.

This is not to suggest that alcohol abuse is not a serious problem in Russia, especially amongst males, and a factor that negatively impacts health and life expectancy, but binge drinking amongst teens and young women is at epidemic levels in my own country and the UK. We cannot rely on the legacy of communism as our excuse.

Ironically, the fact that Westerners live long lives creates a dilemma for governments that must support them over decades to come. A UN study[38] has estimated that by 2050 437 million Chinese will be over 60.

As James Kynge has observed in his excellent book, *China shakes the world*[39], 'It may be that China grows old before it is rich'- in large part due to the impact of the 1980's one child rule for urban couples; two children are allowed in rural areas. It has also resulted in a huge shortage of women. The same UN study estimates that 26% of Russians will be 60 and over by 2025 (compared to 29.4% of Britons) and 37.2% by 2050 (compared to 34% of Britons).

The Western media also loves to disparage the Russians about deficiencies in so-called 'rule of law.' The UK press writes about it like it was HP sauce that can be dispensed from a Marks and Spencer bottle. If the Russians would just lob the stuff about, they'd solve all their problems.

Most of the time, they haven't an earthly notion what they are writing about as I will explain in Part Three. As I will reiterate throughout this book, I am not suggesting that Russia is Utopia. Far from it, but neither is it the worst place on earth, as much of the Western media would have us believe. It has also made phenomenal progress in a short space of time.

Furthermore, I believe it fair to say that the US governments' keen interest in rule of law in Russia is a relatively recent phenomenon. It turned a blind eye to corruption in the Yeltsin government in the 1990's.

In May, 2011, Alexander Domrin, Head of Department for International Programs at the Russian legal firm, the Pepeliaev Group, wrote[40] about the fact that in the mid 1990s, President Boris Yeltsin was hugely disliked by the

Russian public for his bungled mismanagement of the country.

He was impeached in October 1993 by a parliament that offered armed resistance to his rule. He employed overtly unconstitutional means, backed up with force of arms, to muscle his way back into power, storming parliament, killing 200 people and injuring scores more in the process.

Domrin noted that Yeltsin's strong armed tactics were, however, condoned by US President Bill Clinton as a 'consolidation of democracy in Russia.' One can only imagine the ruckus if Putin ever did likewise.

Domrin observed that one Sarah E. Mendelson, who worked in Moscow in the mid-1990s, revealed that the US Embassy was expecting that the 1996 presidential election (which Yeltsin was expected to lose) would be less than fair. It is widely believed that the outcome was 'rigged' by benefactors of the loans-for-shares fire sale of Russian state assets during that period.

According to Domrin, Mendelsohn 'warned' the Moscow US Agency for International Development (US AID) Mission to keep a 'distance from monitoring efforts that might actually uncover fraud.' Domrin wrote that although 'some Western scholars came to a conclusion that the official results of the 1996 elections cannot be trusted because the Russian 'electorate behaved in a way that was, both statistically and sociologically, unbelievably unlikely.' the US State Department declared them to be 'free and fair.'

American consultants openly 'participated' in the 1996 elections. Despite US rhetoric to the effect that 'the promotion of democracy' was 'a key feature of American foreign policy.' when it was expedient to put such expectations to one side to protect US foreign policy interests, pragmatism took centre stage.

As Domrin points out, the US administration considered Yeltsin, warts and all, as 'our horse' (as he was described by US Ambassador Strauss). Richard Dresner, head of a group of US consultants, was asked 'if he had any compunction about the extent to which the Yeltsin campaign was violating election spending laws by many orders of magnitude.' His answer was 'No.' because 'Yeltsin was for democracy, and whatever it takes to win is OK.' The end justified the means.

The US government openly criticized Russia about the results of the recent Duma and Presidential elections. I expect that if Putin was prepared to roll over, and do what he was told by his American friends, he would have been given the benefit of the doubt.

Domrin wrote that 'Nowadays the Washington Post openly defines Yeltsin as a 'corrupt but friendly drunk' – a new version of Theodore Roosevelt's 'our son of a bitch.' The problem with post-Yeltsin governments of Russia in the eyes of Washington is not that they are allegedly more 'corrupt' than the regime of 'old pal Boris.' but because they are less 'friendly' (read: less submissive and obedient, not a lap dog any more).'

Today, the Washington Post is vociferous in its opposition to the Russian government and wastes no opportunity to twist the knife.

Sadly, the fate of the Russian people in this whole sordid affair was never even considered. One is left with the impression that America's 'friends,' however despotic, are held to fundamentally different standards than those who plot a more independent course.

Domrin also referred to 'the notorious US *Russian Democracy Act of 2003* (2002, as far as I can see)[41] and its preamble, which openly states that US Government funding has led 'to the establishment of more than 65,000 non-governmental organizations, thousands of vibrant independent media outlets, and numerous political parties.'

The Act also states that 'These efforts contributed to the substantially free and fair Russian parliamentary elections in 1995 and 1999 and presidential elections in 1996 and 2000.' Pulling no punches, the Act declares that 'the success of democracy in Russia is in the national security interest of the United States.'

The act pledged 'not less' than $50 million to a series of activities promoting democracy, rule of law and US interests in Russia. It is an eye-opening read and flies in the face of US denials that it interferes in internal Russian affairs and the contention that such an allegation is merely 'Putin's Cold War paranoia.' His recent move to expel NGO, US-AID from Russia is entirely in keeping with his quite rational view that the US actively nurtures (with its pocket-book) dissent in Russia.

A related theme in the UK media centres round a distaste for Russians litigating high-value disputes in London. Certain UK journalists deplore having these frightful Russian chaps with their vulgar 'new, funny money' in their midst.

Even worse-and perish the thought-wealthy Russians presume to pollute the UK's venerable stock exchanges by listing their 'corrupt' companies, dealing corporate governance a potentially fatal blow in the process. We did that all by ourselves-with no help from the Russians.

It is pomposity taken to new heights. Some of the worst offenders are so high up on their respective high-horses that it is astonishing they can find air to breathe.

By contrast, I am absolutely sure that Russian companies and litigants would be hugely welcome in Ireland. Our lawyers and our commercial courts (very efficient) would be delighted to act as a venue. Indeed, I am sure we could throw in a round of golf on our finest courses and a guided tour around the Ring of Kerry for good measure. Wealthy Russians will get no 'sniffy' attitude from our newspapers.

I discuss the role of the UK courts in adjudicating purely Russian disputes in Part Three.

On October 14th, 2011, long after the dust had settled from the Georgian conflict, Phillip Stephens put pen to paper at the FT again. The piece was written after Putin's announcement that he, not Medvedev would run for President in the March 2012 elections (often referred to in the Western media as the 'swop'). That fact alone was guaranteed to raise his ire.

The piece was titled, 'Putin's Russia: frozen in decline.' The opener was that 'The West used to worry about an over-mighty Russia.'

Stephens' was worked up about the London Commercial Court battle between Chelsea football club owner, Roman Abramovich and Boris Berezovsky. The trial was described by Stephen as opening a window 'on A Russia still trapped in the past.'

The trial was about the ownership of assets acquired during the 1990s, under Boris Yeltsin after the fall of communism. No-one, including the protagonists in this expensive litigation, denied that this period was anything but chaotic. As the facts in the court case relate to that time frame, the allegations and counter- allegations were destined to be lurid.

In the litigation, the plaintiff, Berezovsky, basically alleged that Abramovich was his partner in the 1990's, but that he strong-armed him to sell certain assets to him at a huge discount under threat of appropriation by Putin if he did not do so.

Abramovich denied the existence of a partnership and maintains he paid Berezovsky billions of dollars over the years for 'krysha.' literally a 'roof'- essentially protection money for Berezovsky's influence with Boris Yeltsin and people close to him.

In discussing the litigation, Stephens wrote that Berezovsky might be in danger from dark Russian forces, and inferred that the UK security service 'hints' that is the case.

There is no mention of the fact that Stephens could likely wallpaper Buckingham Palace with the names of Berezovsky's many enemies. He employs a private army to protect him that pundits describe as more elaborate than the Queens's security detail.

Stephens, however, in the context of fears for Berezovsky' safety, points to Alexander Litvenenko's fate. According to Stephens, 'The crime carried the footprints of the Russian state.' That was a big accusation for a FT columnist to make, without the benefit of one iota of compelling evidence he was prepared to share with his readers to support it.

However, this type of highly damaging accusation is routinely made against the Russians with casual indifference by the UK press corps, allegations that undoubtedly stick in the minds of readers.

Stephens describes the court case as like a Le Carre novel, but I struggled to get to the bottom of his fascination with it. He wrote that it threw a light 'on the present, and future, condition of Russia.'

His logic eluded me, but it was something to do with Putin.

According to Stephens, the Abramovich trial showed that Russia is 'still trapped in the 1990s.' There is merit in that suggestion, in my view, but not for the reason Stephen's suggests.

He concedes, after a fashion, that Putin restored a 'semblance of order' in Russia after the era of chaos, but characterizes his not insignificant achievement in that regard in the following negative terms- by suggesting he did so 'by concentrating power in the Kremlin and the state security services.'

He describes 'the game' as 'essentially the same.'

What game? According to Stephen.' the 'game' is as follows: 'Wealth is concentrated in the hands of a privileged few, corruption remains endemic and the rule of law is a flimsy pretence. Business leaders, as oligarchs are now called, still pay for political protection.'

He refers to Khodorkovsky as another Putin victim. Stephens lays another vague but startling charge against the Russian state- namely that 'At the Kremlin, there is certain coyness about what fortunes have been amassed by Mr Putin and his close allies. Diplomats (un-named) say they run into many billions.'

Stephens then returns to his 'Russia is a basket case' theme. Although 'Russia is richer now' (but only due to higher energy prices during Putin's term in office)...'on every other economic measure- foreign investment, technology, the pattern of trade, the condition of the national infrastructure, or educational attainment- the clouds have darkened.' Finally, to return to a familiar refrain, 'Russia's population is shrinking fast.'

It immediately occurred to me that if we get lucky the Russians may simply die out and spare us all a mile of ink. There are more churlish references to Russia's 'economic backwardness.' and (to return to a theme) .'..the scorn this attracts in places such as Beijing.'

On a recent trip to China, Putin and his Chinese counterparts announced a deal in which China agreed to contribute $1 billion to a joint state fund that will inject most of the capital into Russia-the value of that investment is, as the Moscow Times pointed out, about equal to the value of all Chinese direct investment in Russia since the Soviet Union collapsed in 1991.

Stephen then goes after Putin again, referring to his preference for 'old enemies' and his feelings of 'victimhood' (little wonder). He points out that the Russian economy is a 10th of the size of the US.' However, it is not neck-deep in debt like either the US or the UK, both mired in recession.

He describes Russia's 'wilful embrace of decline' and says, unconvincingly, that it is nothing for the West 'to celebrate,' as 'American and European interests lie in a modern, stable, and prosperous Russia closely engaged in the world.' He suggests, however, that a 'declining Russia will prefer to seek out enemies rather than make friends. Sad to say, all the signs are that Mr Putin is beyond convincing. Like the oligarchs, he is frozen in time.'

In my view, it is the UK media that is frozen in time.

In his pugnacious article, Stephens described Boris Berezovsky, in peremptory fashion, as someone who fled Russia to the UK after incurring Putin's 'wrath.' No context is provided as to Berezovsky's identity, or the role he has undoubtedly played for nearly a decade in tarnishing Russia's reputation in the West.

Indeed, it is impossible to ignore the role both Berezovsky and jailed Russian tycoon Mikhail Khodorkovsky have played, and still play, in this regard. Their unsavoury past is well documented and should have made the metamorphosis from Frog to Prince a severely challenging endeavour.

However, as Abramovich is reputed to have told Le Figaro, the difference between a rat and a hamster is PR. In this case, a great deal of money has been spent on PR to make two rats into two very fine, even cuddly hamsters.

The fact that the Western press has bought the 'line' is hard to fathom. However, a dangerous seed has been sown that has bore fruit, especially in the UK.

Both Khodorkovsky, from his Russian jail cell, and Berezovsky, from far grander digs in 'exile' in London, have spent a fortune on 'rehabilitation' PR, and an obsessive desire to undermine, even destabilize the Russian government.

Berezovsky cannot escape the fact, however, that he is loathed in Russia where he is a convicted felon. Ordinary Russians, who bore witness to, and were painful beneficiaries of his ruthless indifference to their plight in the lawless 90's are flabbergasted that the UK refuses to extradite him.

Russians got a taste of revolutionary change in the 1990s after the collapse of communism in 1991, and they want no more of it. There was a rapid exodus from Russia to London in 2000 when Putin, newly installed as President, made it clear he intended to clean house.

Putin had the overwhelming support of the Russian people in doing so, who despised the greedy Russian capitalists, men like Khodorkovsky and Berezovsky, who had led them up the garden path, with promises of easy money, and then grabbed as much as they could for themselves, leaving them in the ditch in their wake.

Berezovsky luxuriated in playing the role of King-Maker in the 90's, pulling the strings of power and using his wealth and influence to keep Boris Yeltsin, ever less popular as the economy collapsed under his stewardship, in the Presidential office.

Putin's endeavour to reclaim the state was a terrible shock to Berezovsky. He chose Putin, the unknown bureaucrat, as President to succeed an ailing Yeltsin in 2000 on the tacit understanding that he would not rock the boat. Instead,

Putin capsized the boat. Ultimately, to avoid drowning, Berezovsky fled to the UK, with many more like him.

A huge amount of money moved with them.

Estimates range from $100 to $150 billion over the decade, a phenomenon described by David Hoffman[42] in his utterly depressing, but laudable book on the era, as 'one of Russia's most debilitating diseases in the 1990s.' It was money 'that was needed for investment at home, to rebuild factories and start businesses.'

Instead, as Hoffman wrote, the money went 'on the run'- 'for many reasons: to hide it from taxes, shareholders, investors, creditors; to conceal the pillage of natural resources or stripped factory assets; or just to skirt political and economic upheaval.'

The Yeltsin government hadn't the interest, or clout to stop it leaving, and the Central Bank rules against capital export were ignored or not enforced. Even the government sent huge sums abroad to tiny tax havens.

The appalling facts-and their inevitable consequences for the Russian people-would make you weep.

One of the richest countries in the world was literally being stripped dry. Westerners were right there in the scrum, keen to get our share of the action. If thinking about it makes Putin want to throw up, who could blame him. Men like Berezovsky and Khodorskovky were ringleaders in the desecration. These are the facts.

In many instances, the money was packed into suitcases, and rapidly converted into luxury goods or hard assets. It was manna from heaven for London traders. A blind eye was turned to its origins as free-spending Russians fuelled a vibrant local economy. Meanwhile Putin was at home trying to bring order to chaos.

Unquestionably, some, if not a great deal of the money that flowed into London constituted funds derived from whole scale tax evasion and other illegal activities under Russian law. Attempts by Putin to close the lid on the cookie jar that so many had gorged from in the 1990's amidst the chaotic transition from communism to capitalism, was not, however, well received in the West.

As Mark Hollingsworth and Stewart Lansley have wryly, but astutely observed, in their book, *Londongrad,* [43]'The party was over.' The West wasn't pleased with this unwelcome turn of events, so it turned the West's PR machine on Putin to mischaracterise his efforts to regain control as evidence of his 'autocratic' nature.

There was gargantuan hypocrisy at play.

We were willing to ignore the blatant lawlessness that following in the wake of communism, so long as the pickings were ripe, and we got our share. However, as soon as the well ran dry, deficiencies in rule of law in Russia became our paramount concern. It was not our finest hour. Sadly, the hour has stretched from day to night, and ever onwards.

I have no doubt that if Putin had been willing to leave well alone and feather his own nest, while leaving us our share of the spoils, that the Western media and Western politicians would have portrayed him in a very different light. Furthermore, if he'd been prepared to play US puppet, he would unquestionably have a far different public persona today.

As Hollingsworth and Lansley recount, even Berezovsky, his arch enemy, has acknowledged that Putin wasn't corrupt, describing him as 'the first bureaucrat that I met who did not ask for some money and he was absolutely professional.[44]'Since then, however, he has been more than willing to thrown whatever dirt he can at Putin, in the hope that something will stick.

To add insult to injury, rather than backing Putin's efforts to restore order, Britain instead granted asylum to tax evaders, money launderers and assorted 'gangsters' wanted in Russia for real crimes - whose unsavoury past followed in their wake.

These men were not the Dali Lama. MI5 could have got their measure by speaking to the average Russian on any Moscow street corner. Yet the UK kept harbouring such men even after the Litvinenko murder in 2006 in London, granting them the patina of respectability in the process.

To say Putin was irritated by such lack of support from a 'partner' nation likely does not do justice to his feelings on the matter. I struggle to understand Britain's stance which defies logical analysis.

According to Hollingsworth and Lansley,[45] 'like Napoleon on Elba, he (Berezovsky) began plotting, turning himself into Putin's most bitter opponent, dedicating his days in exile to removing the Russian President from office. Most of his energies and fortune became devoted to one cause: blackening Putin's name in the West and destabilizing him in his own country.'

The authors suggest that Berezovsky regards the Western media as an extremely important ally in the fight to rehabilitate his image outside Russia. They quote him as saying, 'I use the mass media as a form of political leverage.'

As Hollingsworth and Lansley point out, his PR efforts have been remarkably successful, gaining him access to the highest echelons of British society, even appearing on BBC1's Question Time in June 2007, where he railed against Putin.

The Russian government looked on, askance, furious that a fugitive from Russia could receive such a respectful hearing in the UK, allowed to preach on prime time TV what they considered to be sedition against them. He fled Russia for France in October 2000. He applied for asylum in the UK the following year, which was granted in September 2003.

To this day, this sequence of events infuriates the Russians, and they react with fury to lectures delivered by the UK press, UK politicians and even US politicians about their unwillingness (not permitted under Russian law) to extradite Russian citizens to the UK, on charges they believe are concocted by MI5.

The fact of the matter is that Berezovsky has frequently got the better of the Russians with his wily use of the UK legal system, top flight lawyers and covert but highly effective manipulation of the press. At the end of the day, however, his hot-headed and injudicious attacks on the premier of a friendly country have not helped UK Foreign Office efforts to curry better relations between both nations.

According to Hollingsworth and Lansley, in 2004, before the 2004 Russian Presidential election, Berezovsky spent £250,000 on full-page ads in the New York Times, the Washington Post, the Times, the Financial Times and the Daily Telegraph, titled, ' Seven Questions to President George Bush about his friend President Putin'- accusing Putin of genocide in Chechnya, and making various sensationalist and lurid allegations about his avowed enemy.

However, Madam Justice Gloster's recent devastating assessment of Berezovsky's character as she rendered judgment against him in his massive UK law suit against Roman Abamovich[46] may signal a turning point: His luck may finally have run out.

Remarkably, her preliminary judgment states that Berezovsky remains domiciled in Russia for tax purposes. I wonder how that is possible?

The dispute was ultimately a credibility battle between the two men about events long past, primarily the existence and terms of 'four highly contentious oral agreements.'

Gloster J wrote that the 'oral evidence relating to such claims was extremely stale.' However, the 'burden of proof was on Mr. Berezovsky to establish his claims.' She noted that 'very few issues of law were involved' spelling the death knell for any prospect of a successful appeal.

Court decisions on findings of fact are nearly impossible to challenge on appeal, as few appeal court judges will overturn the verdict of a judge who has had an opportunity to observe the witnesses and fully assess the facts over many weeks, even months of evidence.

Gloster J. noted that she found Berezovsky 'an unimpressive and inherently unreliable witness, who regarded truth as a transitory, flexible concept, which could be moulded to suit his current purposes. At times the evidence he gave was deliberately dishonest.'

It really doesn't get much worse than that for a plaintiff. She described his ill-advised tendency when the going got tough in the witness box to blame his lawyers as, 'not convincing.' A fatal blow to his credibility was struck when it was found that two of his witnesses stood to 'gain very substantially' if he won his case- an arrangement he initially denied outright in the witness box.

Berezovsky's shenanigans in her court room clearly made a strong impression on Gloster J. She delivered the penultimate coup de grace in the following manner: 'I regret to say that the bottom line of my analysis of Mr. Berezovsky's credibility is that he would have said almost anything to support his case.'

By contrast, Abramovich, was a veritable knight in shining armour. 'I found Mr. Abramovich to be a truthful, and on the whole reliable, witness.' The Chelsea owner is known to be shy and hates being in the public eye. He will undoubtedly be highly gratified that the man who dragged him into the spotlight got his comeuppance in such a pleasing fashion.

In the course of giving his evidence, Berezovsky described Abramovich as 'not very bright.' although he conceded that he could be charming. On this occasion, it appears that charm prevailed over hubris. In any event, I am highly sceptical that Abramovich lacks grey matter.

After the verdict, Berezovsky, always playing to the crowd, described the blistering judgment against him as something that could have been written by Putin himself.

UK media reports about the judgment lurched from the usual refrain about wicked Russians spending vast sums of 'funny money' in UK courtrooms for justice they can't get at home, to a vague, reluctant realization that Berezovsky, the man they'd deified for years, might not be a boy scout after all.

A Kremlin spokesman expressed satisfaction at the result. At one stage, early in the proceedings, Berezovsky wore a Putin mask in court with obvious glee and was widely photographed in the regalia. I have no doubt whatsoever that Putin had an extra spring in his step when he heard about the verdict.

Berezovsky has agreed to pay his nemesis £35 million in legal costs and will apparently forego an appeal.

Although Berezovsky's star may have crashed to earth like a meteor, Khodorkovsky's allure remains high in the West. The notion that he was imprisoned because he was a born-again humanitarian, aghast at Putin's authoritarianism, is revisionist posturing, with no foundation in reality.

He has shown steely determination and courage during his incarceration and earned a degree of sympathy from Russians as a result, some of whom, but by no means all, believe he has done his time and should be released.

Although his defiance under harsh conditions is laudable, that does not make him a saint, not by a long stretch of the imagination. His continued pronouncements and media interviews show a man who lacks self-awareness and who has come to believe the wholesome persona the spin doctors have created for him. His raison d'être remains exacting revenge on Putin.

Khodorkovsky was probably the wiliest of wily men in the bad old 'free for all' 1990's in Russia.[47]

He doesn't deny it, but he has cleverly reframed his past to make it far more palatable to a Western audience. It has been very well-played by his lawyers and PR maestros.

He displayed massive cunning and no scruples in the ruthless manner in which he acquired state assets for a pittance in the chaotic 90's to build up the vast Yukos empire.

In his ruthless quest to acquire absolute control, he burned his Western bankers and creditors, forcing them to write off his loans-simply by calling their bluff. He used every trick in the book to dilute minority shareholders, and to avoid the payment of tax.

He used Menatap Bank, 'his' bank- to acquire Yukos, and to secrete huge sums of money in complex, offshore vehicles, putting them out of reach of creditors and regulators alike. There are credible suggestions that he used Yukos's own money to buy the company, in a complex sleight of hand manoeuvre.

Regardless, he quickly became Russia's richest man and survived the 1998 crash that wiped out most Russians, as he had secreted his assets overseas.

After tightening his hold on his empire, the penny dropped that he had to clean up his act to expand, possibly even sell his business to Western investors. He understood that in the West, reputation matters. He set to work to acquire one that would pass muster.

The ensuing charm campaign was hugely successful. He spent large sums of money on lobbyists and PR. He duly cast himself in the role of corporate governance champion, the new modern face of Russian business: The West lapped it up. He was handsome and articulate, although his English was poor to non-existent. His pro-American stance went down a treat in Washington.

He made liberal, albeit strategically focused donations to US neo-conservative causes, including a sizeable donation to a charity favoured by Laura Bush, George Bush's wife.

His advisers suggested he create the grandly named Open Russia Foundation, modelled on George Soros's Open Society Foundation. It was extravagantly launched at an opulent venue in London in December 2001, and then in Washington D.C at the Library of Congress in September in 2002, with presentations from such luminaries as James Wolfensohn, the President of the World Bank. Trustees included Lord Jacob Rothschild and Henry Kissinger.[48]

Khodorkovsky, however, just like Berezovsky, made one critical miscalculation as his ego grew larger than his burgeoning fortune. He wildly over-estimated the strength of his power base and forgot to whom he ultimately owed his vast wealth and good fortune.

As he wined and dined his affluent, Western friends, Putin was at home trying to rebuild the economy, and restore some semblance of order. Ordinary Russians brought low in the 1990s struggled to make ends meet. They felt a deep and unabiding hatred for self-interested opportunists like Khodorkovsky-who preached morality and good governance in America, having left them high and dry without a backwards look.

Not seeing the writing on the wall, Khodorkovsky splashed money around in the West, but gave nothing back to the Russian people he'd exploited quite egregiously. Somewhere along the way, he simply got too big for his boots. He made glib and disparaging comments about Putin and rank and file Russians to the British aristocrats he cultivated.

According to Hollingsworth and Lansley,[49]in 2003, he finally lost the run of himself, vilifying Putin publicly in Russia, funding opposition parties, and he 'even acted like a sovereign power, negotiating with the Chinese government directly to build a pipeline through Siberia to China' ignoring the government. He talked openly about his political ambition to oust Putin.

In his mind, Khodorkovsky was the Sun King of Russia. Except for one small fact, Russia already had a Sun King- and a formidable one at that. Putin was not going to stand idly by and watch business, in the form of the pro-American Khodorkovsky, retake the state after all his work to reclaim it from his kind.

At a fateful meeting of the 'oligarchs' with Putin in February 2003, a reckless Khodorkovsky astonished the assembled 'Who's Who' of Russian business by attacking Putin, accusing the state owned energy company Rosneft of paying kickbacks to acquire an oil company he wanted, at below market value[50].

He demanded that Putin investigate, telling the President that his bureaucracy was 'made up of bribe-takers and thieves.' Visibly annoyed, but icy, Putin pointed out the obvious, namely that Khodorkovsky had himself acquired Yukos at fire sale prices and suggested he was guilty of wholescale tax evasion. The fact that Khodorkovsky, an intelligent man, did not see the gaping hole in his argument was remarkable in itself.

Khodorkovsky had publicly dug his own grave, but he hadn't quite stepped into it. That was yet to come. He might have survived the unprecedented public attack on the President from a markedly vulnerable position, had he subsequently eaten humble pie. Instead he upped the ante-sharpening his criticisms of Putin.

In July 2003, his business partner, Platon Lebedev was arrested and warrants were issued for the arrest of other Yukos executives, many of whom fled to the UK. Undeterred, a few days later, without consulting with Putin, Khodorkovsky flew to Washington for meetings with US Congressmen and Energy Secretary Spencer Abraham, apparently engaging in negotiations to sell a large stake in Yukos to US oil giant Exxon Mobil[51].

In my mind, a view shared by Hollingsworth and Lansley, that action may have been the straw that broke the camels' back.[52]

There was no way that Putin would countenance allowing an upstart like Khodorkovsky sell out what was not his to give away, from under his nose, without even consulting him. In Putin's minds' eye, Yukos, a company that pumped out more oil than both Libya and Qatar and comprised strategically valuable Russian state energy assets, was held by Khodorkovsky on trust to manage for the Russian people.

In the process, he had become fabulously rich, but if he wanted to stay that way, he was expected to live up to his side of the Faustian bargain. Khodorkovsky understand full well. He once admitted, 'I don't own anything. I rent it.[53]'

By all accounts, Putin gave him several opportunities to follow his colleagues and leave the country. He didn't budge. He may have thought that his wealth made him untouchable. Some people close to him say he'd acquired a 'martyr' complex[54].

A few months later he was arrested, and charged with grand theft, fraud, forgery and tax evasion. Yukos was declared insolvent in 2006 and liquidated the following year, its assets acquired by state oil champion Rosneft. Khodorkovsky was sentenced to eight years in prison in 2005.

He received a second term after an additional trial on separate charges in 2011. He was due for release in 2016, but was recently given a two year reprieve on his sentence by a Russian court, which could see him released in October 2014.

He remains dogged in his conviction that a great injustice has been done him. He would have been released years ago had he shown any contrition, and had he called off the spin doctors.

Minority shareholders (Russian and foreign alike) steadfastly maintain that his business practices were patently illegal, especially his bludgeoning of shareholder rights, not to mention whole-scale asset-stripping and tax evasion. He openly flouted the law and thumbed his nose at Putin's efforts to restore order.

He also did everything in his power to block legislative changes that would increase the amount of tax payable by Russian oil companies such as Yukos-revenue desperately needed to improve the plight of the average Russian- and, ironically (in light of his subsequent metamorphosis) that would have improved corporate governance in Russia.

The reforms he blocked, once introduced, made a huge difference to Russian state finances and helped put it on a sound economic footing.

Putin is well aware that once released, he will devote his final years (he's still a young man) and his vast secreted, offshore fortune, to undermining the Russian government all over, and burnishing his Gandhi credentials in the West.

Putin will not relish the prospect of his release. He was prepared to pay the very high price exacted by international investors and the Western media alike when Yukos was broken up. Putin believed that there was enough at stake to merit the fallout.

The Yukos case was heard and adjudicated by the European Court of Human Rights in September 2011. The numerous allegations against the Russian state included a charge that the break-up was politically motivated. The court ruled that the Russian state had violated certain procedural rights in the Yukos prosecution, but rejected the claim that the break-up was politically motivated.

Yukos had claimed the sum of $98 billion in compensation, but the court gave both sides time to reach an out-of-court settlement. In its ruling, the court said the Russian authorities had carried out 'legitimate actions... to counter the company's tax evasion.'

Both parties claimed victory.

Khodorkovsky is, however, sticking firmly to the script. In an opinion piece in a Russian magazine, he said that 'Those who made up criminal cases against me and my colleagues simply wanted to take for free the country's most profitable oil company with a market value of $40bn.'

He omitted to mention that he acquired Yukos essentially 'for free' in the first instance.

Khodorkovsky writes a column for the US New Times magazine about his incarceration in which he wastes no opportunity to lambast Putin and burnish his martyr credentials. He recently lambasted the US for not being tougher on the Kremlin-in an outburst that was published in Newsweek on September 25, 2011.

He describes himself as a de-facto freedom fighter- once Russia's Richest Man, arrested in 2003 'after speaking out against the growing power of then-President Vladimir Putin.' He suggested that unless the US force Russia's hand on human rights (peppering his article with the magic bullet buzz words that go down so well with the US press)...it risks losing 'its moral capital — capital that is by no means limitless.'

His view of himself is eye-opening: 'Those of us who continue to believe in and fight for the ideals of freedom will find ourselves fighting an even lonelier battle.'

Like St Paul on the Road to Damascus, I would like to believe that Khodorkovksy has experienced a metamorphosis-from Sinner to Saint. But I do not. Maybe he will prove me wrong.

Ironically, Putin has now done Khordokovsky's original deal with Exxon, but on Russian terms. Under the deal, Exxon will gain access to valuable oil and gas deposits in Russia's Arctic and the Black Sea, while Rosneft will have the right to purchase stakes in Exxon projects in the Gulf of Mexico and Texas; the total investment from both sides could be as high as $500 billion.

BP had done an $8 billion stock swap between BP and Rosneft with plans to jointly develop the same Arctic oil sites- but the deal fell apart a few months later in spectacular fashion. As usual, the UK media assigned blame to the Russians.

BP recently sold its lucrative stake in the TNK-BP joint venture to Rosneft for $17.1bn cash and a 12.84% stake in the Russian oil giant. The rest of the venture's valuable assets were acquired by Rosneft for a hefty $28bn from the AAR Russian consortium with whom BP has tussled over the years, and which played a significant role in derailing the original BP-Rosneft arctic deal.

Putin's approval was crucial. Ever the pragmatist, he was willing to let bygones be bygones and sign off a deal that is demonstrably in the Russian state's best interest. Rosneft has now overtaken ExxonMobil as the world's largest publicly traded oil group. Putin is also likely relieved to see the fraught TNK-BP relationship come to an end. Although BP acquires two seats on the board, it is clear that Rosneft will remain firmly in the drivers' seat.

The Russian deal with Exxon was a big loss to BP, facing punitive damage claims from massive oil spill in Gulf of Mexico, and a hugely costly trial in the US in early 2013. As such, BP badly needed some good news. Maintaining a stake in Russia constitutes good news.

There is still a danger that US Republicans will refer the Rosneft-Exxon deal to the Committee on Foreign Investment, the body that can block foreign investment for security reasons. It has a heavy political agenda.

The deal includes rights to explore on US territory. However, there is a scarcity of rich resources to explore and common sense is likely to prevail.

BP in turn has few friends in the US, in so small part due to its bungled response to the deadly oil spill on US soil. The British CEO, Tony Hayward seemed petulant and spoilt in public- saying he wanted to 'get his life back.' Carl-Henric Svanberg, the Chairman of BP was quoted as saying that 'we care about the small people.'

Another thorn in the side of UK- Russian relations is the Alexander Litvinenko affair.

He was an ex-KGB, organized crime operative. After doing a spell in prison in Russia, he fled to London in November 2000, and with Berezovsky's help, sought asylum in Britain, which was granted eight months later, to a furious reaction from the Kremlin.

Litvinenko died November 23, 2006 after meeting former colleagues, Andrei Lugovoi and Dmitry Kovtun for tea at the London Millennium hotel. After his death, traces of the radioactive element polonium were found in his system. It resulted in a series of tit-for-tat diplomatic expulsions between Russia and the UK. Britain put Dmitry Kovtun on the international wanted list and accused Lugovoi of the murder.

Russia's refusal to extradite Andrei Lugovoi resulted in heated rhetoric from the British side with William Hague, Foreign Secretary 'demanding' that Russia change its law to lift the constitutional ban on extradition. A furious Putin reminded Hague that Russia was not, and never had been, a British 'colony. Lugovoi, who ran a security company at the time of the murder, became a celebrity in Russia after the killing and was elected to the Duma in 2007. He denies any part in it.

Ordinary Russians were confounded and angry with Britain's stance in demanding that Russia extradite Lugovi, in light of the fact it harboured (and refused to extradite) individuals such as Berezovsky, wanted in Russia for serious crimes. There is no such blanket prohibition on extradition under UK law.

The sad photograph of the dying, bald man, poisoned by a rare and lethal radioactive material in the centre of London was global front page news, in no small part due to Berezovsky paying to ensure it got there, and stayed there. It resulted in screaming headlines from the UK press.

Litvinenko, described by some of those who knew him as a 'thug[55]' was reborn as a true Englishman, an innocent abroad, taken down in his prime by Satan himself, Vladimir Putin, the latter tried and convicted in abstentia by the UK press, egged on by an ecstatic Berezovsky.

I have read many reports about the killing. There is no evidence that I have seen that Putin was involved. The idea that Putin would waste time on a nobody doesn't hold water. Even if he was a threat to Russian security interests, would Putin have him poisoned in broad daylight in an already hostile Britain, playing right into Berezovsky's hands?

In turn, the Russians have implicated Berezovsky in the killing.

Who knows where the truth lies. Litvinenko was considered an attention-seeking conspiracy theorist and fantasist by many, and it seems entirely likely that he simply made far too many dangerous enemies over the years.

For instance, many of his ex KGB colleagues considered him a traitor, after a rash episode in Russia during which he publicly accused colleagues (egged on by Berezovsky) of being guilty of a variety of heinous crimes, an allegation that was widely reported by the Russian news media. He may have signed his death warrant right there. An erratic, turncoat spy has reason to be fearful[56].

Recent near-hysterical UK media reports suggest that he was an MI6 spy. True or not, I am inclined to view any MI6 'approved' media respecting Russian responsibility for his death with extreme scepticism. However, if he indeed turned traitor, no quarter would have been given from the Russian side.

In September, 2011, after a five year hiatus, David Cameron was the first British Prime Minister to visit Russia since the Litvinenko murder. He was under pressure to lecture Russia about human rights, and to try to convince them to extradite Lugovoi, despite the constitutional prohibition on extradition.

That was not a winning strategy in dealing with Putin who has referred to the UK's propensity to harbour 'criminals and terrorists.' Many British companies do business in Russia- and they would like to do more. Putin is unlikely to do them any favours. He reputedly met Cameron when he attended the London Olympics. I doubt the reunion was warm.

Indeed, having been on the receiving end of a tidal wave of abuse from UK politicians and the UK press over the past few years, I would not be surprised if there was a 'reckoning' of sorts.

Putin is known to be staunchly loyal to his friends and to those who have shown him a modicum of respect. For that reason, one might expect that the old adage might come into play: You reap what you sow. In this regard, the UK press and certain British politicians do UK business no favours in demonizing the Russian President, although his preference for dealing with businessmen over politicians may be a saving grace.

In one respect, the FT's correspondents are right when they say that Russia is still trapped in the era of the 90's, but not for the reasons they espouse. Rather, it continues to hover over Russia like a black cloud in large part because our media works overtime to keep it right there. The Russian people remain caught in the crossfire.

Neither Berezovsky nor Khodorkovsky care a whit about human rights. The plight of Russian pensioners eking out a meagre living in a harsh climate is of no consequence to them. Rather, it is a boorish, undignified game of revenge, played out over a decade, and showing no signs of abating. Our media are willing dupes in this high stakes PR battle.

Berezovsky has funded rallies and protests in Russia, and generally tried to foment as much trouble for Putin as he possibly can, using civil liberties organisations as front for his battle.

According to Hollingsworth and Lanskey, he has tried to destabilize Russia from his UK base, by 'stirring up opposition in its former satellite states...'funding opposition parties in Ukraine and Latvia. He told a Russian Society at Oxford University on November 2004, that he 'had spent some $25 million' in such countries to weaken Russia[57].

Ironically, the funds used by both Berezovsky and Khodorkovsky for the vendetta were derived in no small part from the fire sale of Russian state assets in the 1990's. In this way, as a result of their obsession to 'get at' Putin, both men will persist in wreaking havoc with Russia's reputation. Sadly, so long as the PR battle continues, the Russian people are suffering twice at their hands.

What is tragic is that Berezovsky and Khodorkovsky are very smart men. Instead of using their considerable wealth and grey matter on PR that only compounds stereotyping of their countrymen, and conceivably makes Russian lives all the harder, they might consider their legacy, and finally make amends.

Berezovsky, a gifted mathematician and scientist, quite probably a genius, once aspired to winning a Nobel Prize for science.

Does he really want to be remembered as the man who spent his life seeking revenge? It's all terribly dramatic, and would make an extraordinary movie, but as Maude said to Harold, in the cult movie classic, *Harold and Maude*, 'Is it enough?'

His mother wants him to give it up, to make peace with his demons. He should listen to his mother.

Chapter Four

Stuck in a Groove

A prominent theme with the Western media revolves around the notion that Putin is a) villain, and b) a bad politician who has not served his people well. I maintain they are wrong on both counts.

An FT editorial on 1st October 2011 discussed Russia's future and stated that 'In eight years as president and almost for years as prime minister, Mr Putin has done little to help the Russian economy become more competitive.'

I had to read this paragraph twice, to ensure I had read it correctly. It is so manifestly unfair and untrue as to barely warrant a rebuttal. However, such commentary from the main European business daily conceivably has a significant impact on investor sentiment and how people perceive Russia more generally.

Putin has helped guide the country from chaos in the 1990's to investment grade standard. Russia has little or no debt, significant upside and low levels of unemployment. By contrast, the UK has a monstrous debt load and high levels of unemployment; the spectre of bloody riots and looting on London's streets is also suggestive of a deep malaise in British society.

The FT editorial made the usual criticism about Russia's over-reliance on the energy sector and the need for diversification, a fact in many resource-rich countries. However, it's surely better to have resources than not. There is a whiff of envy in this wearisome refrain.

Putin can be quite the wit. Like Obama, he is also a fine orator, with an impressive ability to speak without notes for hours on end, recounting details and facts from memory. Referring to Russia's reliance on natural resources, he has observed that despite serious efforts to diversify the economy, the Russian state does 'not, of course intend to kill the chicken that currently lays the golden egg.'

The UK is currently in the throes of a dilemma to satisfy dwindling long term natural gas and energy supplies. No doubt the British government would be hugely grateful to find itself 'cursed' with a healthy supply of such scarce and critical commodities.

The FT editors referred to the old staple, 'rife' corruption in Russia, and expounds the view that 'The biggest obstacle to foreign investment is the country's corrupt court system.'

It is my contention, however, that one of the main obstacles to investment in Russia is the Western media's biased and unfair coverage of Russian affairs.

The Russians market is over-sold, in no small part due to negative Western media coverage that places a drastic over-emphasis on bad news. Russian equities currently trade at the cheapest valuation amongst 21 emerging markets tracked by Bloomberg.

In 2001, Putin implemented a flat tax rate to simplify Russia's complex, outmoded tax system. It was very forward-thinking and despite predictions by naysayers that tax revenues would fall precipitously, the opposite happened: Two years later, inflation-adjusted income tax revenue grew 50 percent. It is likely that the low rate tempted money in the black economy to 'come clean.'[58]

In 2011, Russia's income tax rate is 13%. Compared to many EU countries, including the UK and Ireland, Russians pay very little tax and have high disposable incomes. The standard rate of corporate tax in 2012 is 20%.

By contrast, US companies pay one of the highest corporate tax rates among industrialized nations. Indeed, the net effective rate- circa 40%[59]- will be the highest corporate tax rate in the world when Japan lowers its rate to 35. 64% (currently 38.01%).[60]

However, according to commentators, creative accounting and tax planning to get around the US's byzantine tax laws and regulations have made US multinationals world leaders in tax avoidance. A 2008 US Government Accountability Office (GAO) study found that 55 percent of United States companies paid no federal income taxes during at least one year in a seven-year period it studied.[61]

The US is one of very few countries that taxes multinational corporations on their foreign earnings. However, they can avoid those taxes indefinitely by keeping profits overseas, so they play complex games of hide and seek- moving profits to low tax countries and investing profits offshore. Some experts believe that these manoeuvres cost the US government in excess of $50 billion a year in lost revenue.[62]

By contrast with the US, the Russian tax system is a model of simplicity and lucidity. However, there is little or no prospect that a similar system will be implemented in the US as long as US politicians remain at each other's throats- and US businessmen avoid the payment of taxes like it was a strain of the Ebola virus.

In November, 2011, a Forbes list described Putin as the world's second-most powerful person behind Obama. However, in making the 'announcement' Forbes could not be gracious: 'Assuming that he serves two more terms, the increasingly autocratic Mr. Putin will be in office until 2024. Take that, Stalin!'

In the same breath, Forbes boasted that 'The US remains, indisputably, the most powerful nation in the world, with the largest, most innovative economy and the deadliest military.' Yet, despite this bellicose statement, the Western media is adamant it is the Russians who are belligerent.

Besides denying Putin any credit for pulling Russia out of the mire we helped put it in, the Western media is also, more recently, obsessed with his possible term in office.

The FT described the news that Putin would run again as 'a sad and ominous development'[63] – surmising that Putin may be back for another 12 years. 'A President who occupies power for 20 years would be bad news in any country.' wrote Gideon Rachman.

Ireland's President, Mary McAleese recently stood down after two consecutive terms, having served a total of 14 years. Indeed, Eamonn DeValera and his party Fianna Fail, in tandem with the Catholic Church had a near complete stranglehold on Irish politics from the inception of the Free State in 1922.

When the party (blamed by the Irish people for the crony capitalism that led to the banking collapse) was routed in the last election, the politicians were stunned- there was a strong sense of entitlement and bewilderment that an era had come to an end.

George W. Bush was US President from 2001 to 2009. His father Georg H. W. Bush was President before him, from 1989 to 1993- the Presidency passing from father to son. At least Putin has kept his kids out of politics, indeed entirely out of the public eye. There are no known photographs of his two daughters.

Luxembourg Prime Minister Jean-Claude Juncker is the longest serving EU leader. He is acting Prime Minister since 20 January 1995. He was re-appointed Prime Minister on 23 July 2009. He better retire soon, or face media censure over the length of his tenure. Of course, there will be no similar backlash against him.

Lee Kuan Yew, the ex-Singaporean prime minister (widely admired, but no democrat) was more than 50 years in public office. The mere hint that Putin might enjoy similar longevity on the political stage, however, causes hysteria in the West.

The attacks on Putin are usually inelegant, boorish and generally in very poor taste. He is routinely referred to as an ex-spy, a Csar or Tsar; the Wall Street Journal has designated his government a 'Czarist dictatorship.'

As we have seen, he has been compared to Stalin, even Hitler. It is blithely assumed that such attacks are justified. Members of the Chinese Communist ruling party and the Saudi Royal family inexplicably get kid glove treatment by comparison.

Putin was a KGB operative in East Germany, but moved back to Russia in 1989 when the wall fell with the rank of Lieutenant Colonel. In 1990, his luck turned when his friend Anatoly Sobchak was elected mayor of his home town, St Petersburg. Sobchak made him Chairman of the City Council's International Relations Committee. He was promoted to Deputy Mayor in 1994.

Every credible account I have read about his time as a bureaucrat and Deputy Mayor in St Petersburg describes him as honest, and that Westerners found him fair to deal with.

When Sobchak lost his job in 1996, Putin moved to Moscow and worked his way up to Deputy Chief of Yeltsin's presidential staff. He was appointed director of the KGB's successor- the FSB- in July 1998, having come to Yeltsin's notice as a safe pair of hands after his predecessor resigned over a scandal. In August 1999, he was appointed the fifth prime minister in seventeen months in Yeltsin's revolving door government.

He was a total unknown, but his popularity sky rocketed when he bombed and then invaded Chechnya after a series of devastating apartment bomb blasts killed 246 people in September 1999. Soon after, he was offered the role of interim President by an ailing, deeply unpopular Yeltsin.

Expressing a cynical view of politicians, it is reported that he refused initially, but ironically it was Berezovsky who convinced him to accept. In the 2000 Presidential election, he won 53% of the vote- a landslide victory- the same year that George Bush triumphed over Al Gore by a hairs breath in a bitter campaign that ended up in the US Supreme Court.

As soon as he was elected, Putin set about breaking the oligarchs' stranglehold on political life and the economy.

There was silly, school boy glee in the Western media when Putin was seemingly booed at a pre-election boxing match. A mountain was made out of molehill. Irish politicians have had pies and eggs thrown at them. Newt Gingrich was booed in the US on the campaign trail. Greeks have set themselves on fire in front of the Parliament building.

Attacks on him refer to his 'swagger'- and mock his macho, action-man sex symbol image in the Russian heartland and his 'autocratic' nature. Yet compared to most US Republicans, he is positively left wing. His political and economic views are liberal, even progressive, as I will endeavour to demonstrate.

One only had to look at the Republican slate of candidates for US President to see hypocrisy at play: a revolving door of woeful candidates that appeared to include racists, homophobes, misogynists, proponents of violence against government officials (Rick Perry's threat to Bernanke, the US Federal Reserve Chairman), religious zealots and serial philanders.

Yet the US media remained mysteriously and culpably silent. These folk made Putin look like Beau Brummell. In the recent US Presidential election, dirty tricks campaigns were standard fare-with lawyers and ex-prosecutors running scorched earth 'PR' campaigns against opponents, tactics once described by Bill Clinton as exercises in 'personal destruction.'[64]

Putin is a sex symbol in Russia-and not just amongst middle aged women. In October 2010, The London Times reported that Russian journalism students at Moscow's State University had produced a raunchy calendar for Putin for his birthday, featuring them in their underwear. The Times notes that one of the models wished him a happy birthday with the message: 'You put out the forest fires but I'm still burning.'

I tried to imagine Irish students being so overcome with lust for any of our politicians as to strip and be photographed semi-naked in their honour. The alarming thought brought tears to my eyes. This is not the first occasion, and undoubtedly will not be the last, that scantily clad, attractive Russian women endeavour to endear themselves to Putin, notwithstanding the Western press's antipathy towards him. He remains immensely popular at home.

By all accounts, Putin is highly intelligent. He has a prodigious memory, is very well read, and extremely well informed on foreign affairs generally. This fact alone distinguishes him from the majority of US politicians, especially on the Republican side.

Why can't the Western media accept that a majority of Russians voted for Putin; that they respect him, trust him-and that the protests are evolutionary, not revolutionary, and that they do not, furthermore, reflect the views of huge numbers of people outside Moscow and sections of St Petersburg.

The protesters don't represent rank and file Russians, especially the older generation. Just try suggesting to them the fulfilment of US Republican politician John McCain's blood fantasy that Putin be lynched in public by a mob- and you'd get an earful. Putin is their man –and Moscow isn't Russia, in the same way that New York City isn't America. He is one of them- and is credited with bringing the Money to heel.

The Western media-who rarely wander far from Red Square-utterly failed to comprehend that right wing bloggers, old communists and philandering billionaires simply do not represent the views of average Russians-across its vast territory.

Indeed, many old-school Russians dislike Putin, not because he is an autocrat, but because he is a capitalist with ties to big business. The Western media equate the average Russian to the average American or Briton-a false comparison. Russia is a far more complex country than most Western media outlets and politicians can credit or bother to find out.

After Putin's victory in the Presidential election, it was unclear whether Obama had called him to congratulate him or even acknowledge his victory. By contrast, news reports indicate that Putin was quick to call Obama after his recent election win.

A bland (rather passive aggressive) statement was published on the internet by Washington, congratulating 'the Russian people on the completion of the presidential elections,' without even mentioning Putin by name. Reports indicate that Obama eventually got around to making the call, but undoubtedly the delay in doing so was duly noted on the Russian side.

Any slight to Putin in this regard would have been exceptionally bad form. When US companies beat down his door for growth opportunities lacking at home, one wonders if he will hold back his indignation.

The European Union was equally remiss in not calling Putin as soon as his victory was announced, although individual leaders did so, presumably as the penny dropped that insulting the President of an important trading partner was ill-advised.

The current financial crisis leaves Putin with more challenging times ahead than ought to be the case, in light of Russia's prudent fiscal management. The irony of the fact that this crisis was home grown in the US and exported worldwide- and to Russia's shores- has certainly not escaped his attention, as I will discuss in Part Two.

Furthermore, the fact EU leaders are demonstrably unable to bring order to chaos in Russia's biggest market (the EU) doubtless also irks Putin, forced to endure endless patronising lectures from his EU peers who have not, by any measure, distinguished themselves in recent years.

Another theme that engrosses the UK media, in particular, is an obsession with Russian spies and skulduggery, very much in the Cold War, James Bond tradition. They imagine Russian spies concealed under every British rock, albeit that it was the Russians who found a surveillance bug in 2006 in a rock in Moscow, believed to have been planted by British agents.

Six years after the episode was laughed off by the UK government, Tony Blair's former Chief of Staff admitted that it was true and not far-fetched Russian propaganda, as initially suggested.[65]

However, UK media paranoia and hyperbole aside, if the Russian intelligence community indeed has 'eyes' in the UK, it would be hardly surprising. The fact that Britain harbours individuals wanted for crimes in Russia, who use their ample financial resources and Western PR acumen to preach the violent overthrow of the Russian state, arguably makes it incumbent on Russian intelligence to ensure their fantasies are never realized.

If one-or several of my countrymen (as has happened in the none too distant past) preached the violent overthrow of the British state from a safe haven in the Irish Republic, it is a foregone conclusion that UK intelligence would keep a watchful eye this side of the water, as history attests they have done.

In July 2010, the US and Russia completed the biggest spy swap since the Cold War at Vienna Airport. Both governments insisted that they had got the better side of the deal. US Republican politicians said that the White House was too soft with Moscow. Not to be outdone, Rahm Emmanuel, Obama's then loquacious White House Chief of Staff, remarked that 'it (the spy capture) 'sends a clear signal to, not only Russia but other countries that will attempt this, we are on to them.'

By contrast, many Russians felt that the US had staged the whole affair to sour relations between the two countries. Polls conducted around the time in Russia showed that 53% of Russians believed this to be the case.

In the West, we were agog with reports about glamorous Russian female spies in deep cover in the US suburbs, respectability personified. The most infamous of the spies was the flame haired Anna Chapman, now a minor celebrity in Russia.

The spies gave renewed hope to a whole generation of *Desperate Housewives*.[66]The hit US TV series *Alias* had previously aired an episode in which US intelligence agents unearthed Russian spies living as wholesome US families in a Potemkin Village planted in US suburbia.

Putin and Medvedev were castigated by the Western media for welcoming the spies home and declaring them to be patriots.

However, in an article in the FT in October 2010,[67]Sir John Sawers, the Chief of MI6, the UK's foreign intelligence service, gave the first ever public speech by someone in his office. In the course of the speech, defending the work of the agency, he said – 'secrecy plays a crucial part in keeping Britain safe and secure.'

Sawers was frank in acknowledging the work that secret agents (spies) did for Britain and proclaimed, 'our agents are the true heroes of our work.' He made it clear that the UK does exactly what Russia was derided for doing, and his expression of gratitude to his secret agents was little different than that expressed by the Russians.

According to a Moscow Times article, one of the spies, Vladimir Guryvev, used the pseudonym Richard Murphy as cover. However, according to his academic supervisor in New York, 'Murphy' had a very strong Russian accent, which tended to give the game away.

The Irish Government was understandably upset by the fact that at least a couple of the Russian spies had used stolen Irish passports to masquerade as Irish citizens. It caused a diplomatic incident, and got wide coverage in Ireland. I was intrigued by the suggestion that being Irish was perceived by the Russian intelligence agencies as good cover in the US: A vote of confidence for Brand Ireland.

My countrymen were worried, however, at how easily an Irish persons' identity could be stolen and assumed by the surly Guryvev. However, I heard several local people wryly remark that 'real' Irish people in the US would never have had to resort to such drastic measures as living undercover to get information. 'They would simply have gone down the pub, and asked for it.'

More recently, the charge that the Russians are cyber-criminals, stealing state secrets and sensitive data from Western companies and governments has been tacked onto the formula and has become a reoccurring theme.

I worked in the cyber security field for many years, so this is a subject close to my heart.

A report to the US Congress released Nov. 3, 2011[68] described cyber-espionage attempts by China and Russia as a 'pervasive threat' to the United States, and accused both countries directly of conducting cyber-espionage campaigns against American companies. As of writing, China publicly denounced the accusation. Russian officials had not commented.

This is rather disingenuous, to say the least. Richard Clarke, former cyber-security Czar to President George W. Bush, said at a conference in Washington, D.C that the United States 'doesn't engage in economic cyber-espionage like other countries do.' The facts suggest otherwise.

In 2000, a Scottish journalist Duncan Campbell[69] wrote an expose about the US spy satellite infrastructure 'Echelon' – and alleged that US defence firm Raytheon used information picked up from the top secret US National Security Agency (NSA) Echelon satellites to secure a $1.4bn contract to supply a radar system to Brazil instead of France's Thomson-CSF.

Echelon is a global surveillance system used by the NSA to intercept and analyze communications traffic flowing across the Internet, telecommunication channels and well as faxes and radio signals; it is believed it can do the same with data from underseas cables.

The system was established under a secret 1947 'UK USA Agreement,' which brought together British and American surveillance capabilities. They were joined by the British Commonwealth countries, Canada, Australia and New Zealand. Under the agreement, they divided up responsibility for overseeing surveillance in different parts of the globe. Britain's zone is believed to include Africa, Europe and large parts of Russia.

The Echelon system has Cold War roots and HQ is at Fort Meade, in Maryland, but a main listening post is run by Britain's Cheltenham-based GCHQ (the UK'S NSA) surveillance centre.

The main technical challenge is to make sense out of the huge volume of data generated. Keywords are used to track subject matter and individuals of interest, including terrorists. US civil rights activists and anti-Vietnam War protesters, such as actress Jane Fonda have been targeted in the past.

The French (well-known in the intelligence community for running their own aggressive signals intelligence operations, known as 'sigint') were incensed by Campbell's allegations. According to Campbell, [70] the French have a 'large satellite interception centre at Domme in the pleasant south-Western Dordogne valley, which is almost as large and technically advanced as the site Britain's GCHQ runs in Cornwall for the same purpose.'

Like the Iraq War 'French fries' war of words between the US and France, Campbell reported that 'some irritated British and American spooks' dubbed the French surveillance network 'Frenchelon.'

As Campbell wryly observed, however, 'French double standards are merely as well-nourished as their own. It would be better if they all grew up and stopped pretending that economic and industrial espionage is not now a major part of the intelligence business on both sides of the Atlantic.'

The spectre of US 'Big Brother' helped by 'Junior Big Brother' (the UK Government), spying on EU companies on behalf of US competitors to give them an edge to win deals caused outrage in Europe.

Under huge pressure to get to the truth of the matter, the European Parliament struck a special committee to investigate, and produced a wide ranging report[71] that basically corroborated most of Duncan Campbell's findings and strongly recommended that EU companies encrypt all sensitive traffic to foil the US/UK operation.

The US denied passing on commercial information to individual US firms, but former CIA director James Woolsey, in an extraordinary diatribe published in March 2000 by the Wall Street Journal,[72] acknowledged that the US did conduct economic espionage against its European allies: 'We have spied on you because you bribe,' the ex-CIA boss wrote.

He claimed that such actions were justified as European companies had a 'national culture' of bribery and were the 'principle offenders from the point of view of paying bribes in major international contracts in the world.'

Woolsey acknowledged as 'correct' and 'intellectually honest' information in Duncan Campbell's report to the European parliament - that US communications surveillance was used to prevent Airbus Industries and Thomson CSF winning billion-dollar contracts in Saudi Arabia and Brazil respectively. But 'the fact [is] that the subject of American intelligence collection was bribery.' he claimed. He also stated that 'Most US intelligence data came from open sources, he said. But '5% is essentially secrets that we steal.'

In the Wall Street Journal article, Woolsey, a neoconservative hawk, close to US Republican John McCain, also disparaged EU society and technology, implying that the latter wasn't worth stealing.[73]

He expounded the view that EU companies bribed 'because your economic patron saint is still Jean Baptiste Colbert, whereas ours is Adam Smith. In spite of a few recent reforms, your governments largely still dominate your economies, so you have much greater difficulty than we in innovating, encouraging labor mobility, reducing costs, attracting capital to fast-moving young businesses and adapting quickly to changing economic circumstances. You'd rather not go through the hassle of moving toward less *dirigisme*. It's so much easier to keep paying bribes.'

A finer example of jingoism and national character stereotyping (discussed at length in Part Four) would be hard to find.

Despite the hullabaloo, as Campbell right observed, it is simply a fact that governments spy on each other. They always have and likely always will. It is part of what they do. Only the truly naive believe otherwise. There is no doubt that this spying includes economic intelligence gathering. Many governments don't even bother denying it, while avoiding confirmation of overtly illegal activities.

As Duncan Campbell wrote, 'Under a 1993 policy colloquially known as 'levelling the playing field.' the United States government under President Clinton established new trade and economic committees and told the NSA and CIA to act in support of US businesses in seeking contracts abroad.'

Similarly in the UK, GCHQ's enabling legislation from 1994 openly identifies one of its purposes as to promote 'the economic well-being of the United Kingdom in relation to the actions or intentions of persons outside the British Islands.'

Under the heading 'information warfare.' covert government intelligence agencies are determined to counter what they consider the biggest threat to their operations since their inception- namely the ability of regular people (as well as criminals and terrorists) to use unbreakable encryption to code communications so they cannot be read.

Indeed, the history of modern encryption technology is fascinating. Scorched-earth tactics have been used by the

US government, in particular, against US citizens who developed strong encryption systems for mass use. However, the cat is now firmly out of the bag, and it is unclear whether the US government has regained the upper hand in the ultimate cat and mouse game. That doesn't mean they will stop trying.

Instead, they likely rely to a significant extent on top-secret co-operation from companies on the front-line.

Every so often, there is a suggestion that governments have convinced technology companies and data carriers to embed 'backdoor 'access into software and hardware systems to preserve law enforcement and intelligence community access to communication data. These allegations are always vociferously denied, for good reason, as any suggestion that tech companies are facilitating 'Big Brother' access to consumer data is the kiss of death.

In certain markets, such as China and Saudi Arabia, it is most unlikely that foreign software companies are granted access to local markets if there is any prospect that the interception capabilities of local law enforcement are compromised in the process.

However, the fact is that well-funded independent researchers (employed, for instance, by hugely wealthy Columbian drug cartels) can develop their own encryption capabilities that are not beholden to private sector efforts. This fact has lead to secret but frantic efforts by national governments to build the most powerful supercomputers that can crunch even the most complex data to break previously impenetrable code.

It is currently believed that Japan and China still have the fastest and most powerful supercomputers, but I expect that US and Russian intelligence are keen to bridge the divide, if they have not done so already, as the stakes are huge. Just don't expect to hear about it on the 9 o'clock news.

Under the auspices of the UK government's Communications Capabilities Development Programme (CCDP), UK Internet service providers (ISPs) will be required to gather, store and retain a huge amount of data on users (including email traffic and social networking communications) that would be available to law enforcement and UK intelligence in real time and on demand. It sounds like a major fishing expedition, and may not pass muster under EU law, unless some derogation can be relied upon.

The UK already has a controversial law on its statute books that authorises interception of data, often known as the RIPA Act (*The Regulation of Investigatory Powers Act 2000*)[74].

After the London riots, David Campbell expressed his unequivocal intention to backdoor social networking channels to enable law enforcement shut them down in the event of similar disturbances. Before the London Olympics, with concerns about terrorist attacks omnipresent, it is highly likely that social networking operators and ISPs were put under severe pressure to 'co-operate' on a covert basis to 'protect national security.'

The UK government has indicated that they want legislation in place by June 2015. It will get a fight from UK civil liberties campaigners who helped squash previous plans to do the same. It is thought that GCHQ is concerned its surveillance capability is falling behind that of the NSA.

An American author, James Bamford, is probably the most influential and knowledgeable commentator in the murky cyber surveillance field. He is the author of several excellent books about the NSA, including the aptly named *The Puzzle Palace*[75].

In a recent article in Wired magazine,[76] he stated that 'the blandly named Utah Data Center is being built for the National Security Agency.' The top-secret 'heavily fortified $2 billion center' is expected to be operational by September 2013. Bamford describes it as 'A project of immense secrecy.'.'the final piece in a complex puzzle assembled over the past decade.'

It is intended to play a role in breaking encryption codes as well as being used to ' intercept, decipher, analyze, and store vast swaths of the world's communications as they zap down from satellites and zip through the underground and undersea cables of international, foreign, and domestic networks.'

What does that mean for the US public?

Bamford wrote that the spy centre will scoop up 'all forms of communication, including the complete contents of private emails, cell phone calls, and Google searches, as well as all sorts of personal data trails—parking receipts, travel itineraries, bookstore purchases, and other digital 'pocket litter.' He compares it to a similar failed initiative in 2003 from the Bush era that was abandoned after public outcry.

Bamford, a long-term NSA watcher, observes that 'there is no doubt that it (the NSA) has transformed itself into the largest, most covert, and potentially most intrusive intelligence agency ever created.' and that 'In the process— and for the first time since Watergate and the other scandals of the Nixon administration—the NSA has turned its surveillance apparatus on the US and its citizens.'

He writes that it has 'established listening posts throughout the nation to collect and sift through billions of email messages and phone calls, whether they originate within the country or overseas.' If Bamford is correct, this endeavour is an exponential escalation in US covert surveillance operations and firmly puts paid to any notion that US citizens enjoy any real expectation of privacy. Even worse, as he explains, the clock and dagger operation 'is all being done in secret.'

UK citizens, already living in arguably the world's pre-eminent surveillance society, can look forward to more of the same, although it is highly likely that the UK government will be out-spent to a significant extent by the Americans.

As stated, the British public, and the Americans to a lesser extent, are subjected to a steady stream of hysterical and exaggerated media reports about Russian spies in Britain and the US. I suggest that the real threat to our fundamental freedoms can be found far closer to home. Glamorous and deadly Russian spies are a convenient smokescreen.

It is also commonly suggested that the Russian government censors the Internet, which it does not. In China, by contrast, all web traffic is also routed through the notorious 'Great Firewall of China' with thousands of sites black listed. Of course, the Chinese manage to get around these restrictions.

An editorial in the London Times stated that in Russia, 'Privately funded but State-backers are known to be working to destabilise Western economic interests. In China such activities are more explicitly State-controlled.' As is common in UK media reports, no source was given for this allegation.

Numerous reports from ostensibly independent (although predominantly American) data security companies suggest that cyber attacks on both Western commercial and state interests emanate from China, despite vociferous denials.

There are numerous examples over past decades of Chinese nationals stealing proprietary data (especially R & D intelligence) from Western companies- in what has long been assumed to be a concerted effort by the Chinese to play 'catch- up' with Western competitors.

However, as in all things, as demonstrated with the Echelon expose, it is singularly unlikely that Western nations have clean hands in this regard, and the Chinese may just be a convenient scapegoat.

Cybercrime is a borderless and anonymous crime. It holds special allure to young people in poor countries, where opportunities for advancement are slim. The chances of being caught or extradited are slight and the rewards potentially great. Internet crime laws are simply inadequate to address the global nature of the problem.

Savvy 'hackers' from Eastern European countries, including Russia, with a strong background in mathematics, computing and science have made fortunes from cyber-crimes such as bank card fraud and identify theft.

The leader of one hugely profitable online Eastern European 'bazaar' trafficking in stolen bank card data was believed to have been Russian. He used the 'handle' (nickname) 'King Arthur' – various commentators reported that he made as much as $1 million a week off his illicit activities. To my knowledge, he has never been caught.[77]

There have been other high-profile cases in which Russian nationals suspected of involvement in cyber crime in the West were conned (or 'entrapped.' depending on one's perspective) to enter the US with the lure of legitimate employment, and then arrested by the FBI in a 'reverse sting' operation. In one such instance, FBI operatives obtained passwords from those arrested and used them to hack Russian networks, an illegal activity not guaranteed to improve Russian-US relations[78].

The US is notorious for conducting offshore sting operations that drive a coach and four through both domestic and international laws.

However, despite colourful examples of Russian cybercrime perpetrated by Russian nationals, the fact remains that the US is the hotbed for global cyber threats. Indeed, as a general matter, the cyber threats that impact global consumers and businesses still emanate primarily from the US.

Global (US) security company, Symantec, in its *2011 Internet Security Threat Report*[79] confirmed that in 2010, the United States was the top country of origin for attacks against European, Middle Eastern and African (EMEA) targets, accounting for 36 percent of all attacks detected by Symantec sensors in the region.

In terms of the source of global malicious activity, the US ranked first with 19% of the total (Russia is ranked 10th, with 2% of the total), China ranked 2nd with 16% of the total and the UK was ranked 5th with 4% .

The US also held the top ranking as the primary source of malicious computer code-with 18% of the total (Russia was 10th with 2%). The US also ranked first for phishing hosts (scam emails that invite users to provide sensitive data to fake, but real-looking websites) - with 46% of the total. Russia is ranked 10th with 2%.

The US was also ranked first for 'bots' (armies of infected computers that can be commanded to launch attacks) with 14% of the global total. Russia is not in the top 10. The UK is ranked 7th with 6%. Most of the spam in the world comes from US bots.

An important category is network attack origin: the US is ranked first with 22% (Russia is ranked 8th with 3%; the UK is 4th with 6%).

In 2010, half of all botnet spam detected by Symantec originated in the EMEA region and within the region, Russia was the source of the most botnet spam, accounting for 14 percent of the EMEA total. Globally, Russia ranked third with 7 percent of the total.

One of the main factors for this high ranking is because Russia is a large source of bot-infected computers for major spam botnets. What this analysis suggests is that Russians have a lot of infected computers-they have been scammed into downloading it. In other words, they are victims not perpetrators.

Despite the suggestion, already discussed, that Russia is a cyber espionage hotspot, researchers at security company, Trend Micro have discovered[80] targeted attacks against Russian corporate targets that appear to be instances of cyber espionage.

They have identified a sophisticated cyberspy network geared towards attacking systems in Russia and neighbouring countries. Cyberattacks against Google and attempts to hack into the networks of US defence contractors such as Lockheed Martin and Mitsubishi Heavy Industries have been blamed on China, an accusation the country denies, often alleging it is a victim not the perpetrator of the attacks.

The attacks identified by Trend Micro have, reportedly, hit 47 victims including diplomatic missions, government ministries, space-related government agencies and other companies, with most of the victims in Russia, Kazakhstan and Vietnam. The computer servers running the attacks were tracked back to servers hosted by ISPs in the UK and US.

The spyware used in the attack was hidden in Adobe files or poisoned screensavers and relies on well-known software vulnerabilities, invariably of Western, primarily US origin. Infected systems sent home documents and spreadsheets. Trend Micro was reluctant to speculate on who might be behind the attacks or their motives, but it suggests that the Russians have reason to be fearful of Western cyber espionage operations.

All told, based on independent security analysis, when it comes to cybercrime threats, the Russians, and indeed the rest of the world have good cause to be aggrieved with the US, as it is still the source of most global cyber attacks.

Putin has described the use of the internet and social networks by extremists as 'food for thought' and the need to consider how 'to continue developing the unique freedoms of communication via the Internet and at the same time reduce the risk of its being used by terrorists and other criminal elements.'

The Western media inevitably view this statement as indicative of an autocrat who wants to censor the internet. In reality, every Western government has similar concerns- like David Cameron determined to give British law enforcement the power to shut down social networks after the London riots.

The fact that there is co-operation between the US and Russia with respect to cyber crime gets little media coverage in the West. On July 12, 2011, Howard Schmidt, Obama's then cyber-security chief, reported on the Whitehouse blog that he had 'hosted a Russian delegation, led by his counterpart, Russian National Security Council Deputy Secretary Nikolay Klimashin, for another round of in-depth discussions here in Washington[81].'

He described it as 'a prime example of the 'Reset' in US-Russia relations taking on a new and important dimension.' According to the blog, 'both the US and Russia are committed to tackling common cyber-security threats while at the same time reducing the chances a misunderstood incident could negatively affect our relationship.'

Reports suggest that efforts are underway to establish a hot-line (akin to that existing for nuclear war threats) between the Russians and American to neutralise the possibility of cyber-war threats, both real and imagined causing real war devastation.

Western media attempts to pin cybercrime and cyber-espionage on the Russians-as well as every other ill that besets the planet- is just another example of disingenuous Western bias that has scant respect for the facts.

Reports suggest that the 'Stuxnet' computer 'worm' that targeted Iranian computer systems to sabotage Iranian government efforts to allegedly develop more sophisticated nuclear power capabilities was jointly funded and developed by the Israeli and American governments.

This action opens another front in America's fight against enemy nations.

Targeted cyber attacks can cause physical damage to infrastructure. The New York Times reported[82] that Obama ordered these cyber-security strikes against Iran, and possible other rogue nations, that have sworn to fight back and develop their own counter-strike, even first strike cyber attack capabilities.

This is all very well, but it opens Pandora's Box on a number of fronts.

Firstly, there is no guarantee that the rogue computer code will behave 'in the wild' as intended. These types of attacks still rely on human intervention, such as a willing insider (an unpredictable element at best) to install the virus or worm on the targeted systems. Even when installed, there is no way of knowing with any degree of certainty what the consequences will be.

Furthermore, it is conceivable that the attacker will inadvertently set off a catastrophic chain of events, similar to those which it sought to avoid in the first place. Playing games with nuclear facilities seems most inadvisable.

Finally, it is likely that a cyber attack that is intended to- and does cause actual physical damage, and possibly even death or injury to a target- is an act of war that invites a counter attack. It exposes the attacker to a full scale cyber war against critical infrastructure that is far from secure.

The new trend by which patriotic hackers take matters into their own hands (so called 'hacktivists') to launch sophisticated cyber attacks against enemies also raises the stakes.

The fact that the US is rapidly losing ground in terms of producing students with deep mathematical and scientific abilities, while the Chinese and other emerging markets pump them out, makes the game the Americans appear to be playing in cyber space especially dangerous. Superiority in this context is by no means assured.

Putin has indicated that emphasis will be placed on developing the mathematical skills of Russian students. Recent international surveys, however, do not place Russian students high up the rankings in mathematics, so clearly work needs to be done to reclaim traditional dominance in the field.

Regardless, I have no confidence that we understand the consequences of playing fast and loose with the Western concept of rule of law, It may prove devastating, as I discuss at more length in Part Three.

As soon as we send out the message that the rules of war no longer apply in cyberspace, or in the real world, because we will dispense with them as we see fit, or simply turn a blind eye to patent illegality, we are on the road to perdition.

We have started down that path: We kill 'enemies' with drones and elite paratroopers units, wherever they may be, without recourse to the courts, the law, and without respect for national borders or sovereignty. We unleash computer code that wreaks havoc with critical computer systems and results in all manner of potentially deadly unintended consequences.

In doing so, we invite open season on us all, not to mention the unequivocal surrender of the moral high ground we are so fond of assuming. This theme will be further developed in Part Three.

I have also noted in my analysis over several years a curious and intriguing phenomenon: Several UK journalists are completely wedded to the formula, and they do not let the facts get in their way, especially when it comes to making dire predictions about Russia's economic fundamentals, all the while as they went from strength to strength.

Entrenched views do not die easily. What is interesting about these predictions is how utterly wrong they have proven to be, and yet the journalists in question simply refuse to give up the ghost, perhaps in the hope that it will somehow become a self-fulfilling prophecy if they say it often enough.

I would love to look like Marilyn Monroe, but can I wish it into being? I think not, much the pity.

For years, I have read Ed Lucas in the Guardian and the Economist, endlessly predicting the arrival of the Four Horses of the Apocalypse onto Russian soil. He has written a book called *The New Cold War* and more recently a sensationalist tome, titled *Deception, Spies, Lies and How Russia Dupes The West.'*

In an article by Lucas in the Daily Mail about his book[83], complete with an enormous photo of a leather-clad, gun-totting Anna Chapman, the red-headed Russian spy, he concluded with the following dénouement:

'We are dealing with an adversary who is determined, resentful and paranoid, where we are complacent and trusting. We want to like him. We hope he will like us, and eventually be like us. He wants nothing of the kind. That's the hard truth we must face up to in our relations with Russia.'

I really could not make this stuff up.

However, Lucas is not the only offender. There are a number of UK journalists who have cast themselves in the romantic, buccaneering guise of British Avenger, seeking justice for a down-trodden Russian population, or some such thing that I haven't quite figured out.

Luke Harding, writing in the Guardian, is a prime example. Harding, in his mind's eye, is a crusading James Bond figure, a veritable Daniel Craig, a thorn in the side of the Evil Russian Empire that he will single-handedly bring to, who knows where.

Indeed, he has written a book on Russia, modestly titled, *Mafia State: How One Reporter Became the Enemy of the Brutal New Russia*. The book received a favourable review from none other than Ed Lucas in the Guardian.

Harding, in his courageous James Bond persona, has written alarming articles about dire and deadly Russian conspiracies in which he frequently plays a starring role, stalked and hunted by the Russian security forces, to whom he is the deadliest of foes.

I recall one dense, florid article in which he wrote that his flat had been broken into by Russian security forces. I took umbrage with this account on two fronts-one, that they could be bothered, and two, how did they ever get past his monumental ego?

I fear that Harding is more akin to Johnny English (played by Englishman Rowan Atkinson) than James Bond.

Indeed, when Russia catches a break, a rare occurrence, for instance, when it succeeded in its bid to host Olympic sporting events, the British media went into high dudgeon, rather undermining belated suggestions made half heartedly from time to time, that they really do wish the Russians well.

Russia won its bid to host the 2014 Winter Olympics in Sochi, and more recently to host the World Cup in 2018. These international sporting events create an impetus for infrastructural reform-countries have to build sports stadiums, subways, roads and airports to host the event and accommodate the many fans who will arrive to watch the spectacle.

No matter where these huge events are held, they invariably present enormous logistic and infrastructure challenges; the cost of hosting them is phenomenal, and locals, forced to move, or simply discomforted by the building frenzy, are frequently upset by the upheaval it causes in their lives. The London Olympics had similar challenges, with London commuters and taxi drivers upset over the fuss and bother it caused them.

Jaded Westerners are less enamoured with these flagship sporting events than people in emerging markets or developing countries. Surveys suggest major sporting events attract less viewers in the West than episodes of the X-Factor, MasterChef or Downton Abbey.

By contrast, people in emerging markets are great sports enthusiasts, and delighted when they are chosen to host the events. The 2011 BBC World Service County Rating poll suggests that the year South Africa hosted the World Cup 'the proportion rating its influence in the world rose significantly, from 35 to 42 percent.'

Sports stars are now also moving to emerging markets, for very pragmatic reasons- they can get far bigger sign-on fees and salaries. In the summer of 2011, Cameroon's superstar soccer player, Samuel Eto'o signed a €60 million euro three year contract with FC Anzhi Makhachkala, a soccer club based in Dagestan, a strife ridden region in Russia. Anzhi also appointed Guus Hiddink as manager in February 2012. Anzhi is owned by Russian billionaire, Suleiman Kerimov, who hopes that sport may help bring stability to the area.

Russians love soccer. They will build thirteen world class stadiums and to refurbish three others and to build the necessary roads and railways between events-the total bill could exceed $50 billion US dollars.

Putting on the World Cup is indeed a huge challenge as Russia is so vast and the stadiums stretch from one side of the country to the other, but Russians are more than capable, as history attests, of rising to a challenge. The Russian government is also working to create a visa-free regime to make it easier for people to attend.

These events, guaranteed huge international media coverage expose countries to a global audience-a fact not lost on the Chinese government which spent an estimated $42 billion to host the 2008 Olympic Games, with an eye to improving its reputation and standing internationally.

The knock on effects can be considerable. According to the 2011 Grant Thornton International Business Report (IBR)[84], 2011 is the first year Latin America has led the world on optimism. The survey credits the knock-on effects across the region since Brazil won the right to host the 2014 World Cup, and the 2016 Olympics. It boosted morale in the country as the people look forward to showcasing their county.

Putin rejoiced when Russia obtained the right to host the World Cup in 2018. He said that 'Russia loves football, Russia knows what football is and in our country we have everything to conduct the 2018 World Cup at a very worthy level.'[85]

He expressed his hope that 2018 could shatter misconceptions about Russia, days after a WikiLeaks diplomatic cable exposed US diplomats labelling Russia a 'mafia state.'

Putin said that the Cold War had left an enduring stamp on the world's view of Russia, and this 'flies all over Europe, all over the world, buzzing in people's ears and scaring them...We must show that we are open,' he said. 'People will come and see for themselves. The more contacts, the faster that stamp is destroyed.'

An entirely reasonable expectation, but as I will outline throughout this book, prejudices and stereotypes are tough to shift, especially with the Western media beating the drum to ensure they stick.

I had, however, always imagined the British people to be good sports-a positive stereotype if you like, but clearly segments of the UK media are not.

In an article in December 2010, an article in the FT by Courtney Weaver focused[86] on the possibility that the Russians simply were not up to the task of hosting major sporting events in Russia- writing that .'.serious questions must remain about whether the country will be able to pull off a football contest spanning four time zones.'

It was suggested that the International Olympic Commission 'took a gamble when it awarded the games to a city (Sochi) with virtually no winter resort infrastructure and a lack of decent roads.' The article closes with a quote from a Sochi local in which he describes the 'main problem with Sochi' as 'few roads, lots of idiots.'

What did that even mean? How did it add to the story? We are not short on idiots in the West, as the FT is doubtless aware. Some of them even run entire countries.

The British press is simply incapable of writing a good news story about Russia. They can't help but undermine every Russian aspiration or achievement. It appears almost to be a congenital condition at this stage, it is so ingrained.

A compliment given with one hand is rapidly taken back with the other. On the markedly rare occasion that a concession is made, there is a begrudging surliness to it- and nearly always a sting in the tail.

However, the FT article about Sochi was positively glowing compared to the vitriol that spewed from the UK media when Britain lost its bid to host the 2018 World Cup to Russia.

In an extraordinary piece in The Sunday Times in December 2010,[87] Rod Liddle accused FIFA, the governing body of the soccer championship, of corruption and bribery in relation to the granting of the event to Russia.

The article was a hateful, xenophobic rant from start to finish.

Liddle opens his article with the following paragraph: 'So, the World Cup is to be held in a mafia State and, after that, an authoritarian Islamic desert. That should keep the fans happy.' He is referring to the fact that Qatar was granted the 2022 World Cup.

Liddle points out some of the problems in Qatar, often associated with Arab countries, referring to the availability of women for 'commercial sexual exploitation' and castigates the English fans, by saying they would probably approve of 'cheap whores and poofs in prison – what's not to like.'

Having dispensed with Qatar, he moves to Russia. According to Liddle, 'journalists who delve too deeply into the process that lead to their country winning the nomination are likely to end up glowing like a Belisha beacon, or shot.'

He then refers to the Transparency International report that routinely finds Russia to be in the top rankings of the world's most corrupt countries (a report I will discuss at a later stage, but a favourite with the UK press), and refers to

Amnesty International Reports about alleged widespread racism, etc.

Liddle had nothing negative to say about the loutish behaviour of some British soccer fans over the years, or their reputation for racism. Since then, the appalling behaviour of the UK national rugby squad at the World Cup in New Zealand brought dishonour to British rugby and set a very poor example for national pride.

Liddle is emboldened in his reference to Russia being a so-called mafia state by the WikiLeaks diplomatic cables in which various US diplomats described Russia as a mafia state.

This article was vile, a nasty piece of work even amongst a wealth of contenders for the title.

I thought back with affection on the good old days when the British media wrote delightful satires, far removed from this crude, misinformed, xenophobic drivel. No subtlety, no nuance, no power of suggestion, little wit, just a plain old fist through the face. Journalism is no longer a craft-it has become a brute force activity requiring little skill, and certainly not subtlety.

In a cool headed and laconic response to the jingoism, Liam Halligan wrote in The Sunday Telegraph[88] his view of the whole affair. As Halligan pointed out 'the West doesn't have a God-given right to be rich – or to host major tournaments.'

Amidst all the hysteria about Russia winning the World Cup and out-bidding England, Halligan pointed out that Russia was odds-on favourite to stage the event, well ahead of its rivals in that regard. Although many Britons anticipated a close battle between Russia and England for the right to host the tournament, FIFA's breakdown of the voting showed otherwise.

Russia picked up nine votes out of 22 in the first round, while England only got two and was eliminated. In the second round Russia garnered 13 votes and an absolute majority. Qatar was the bookies choice for 2022.

As Halligan pointed out, the fact that the 2018 World Cup would be the first to be hosted in an East European country is something to be celebrated, rather than derided. The 2022 competition will be the first to take place in the Middle East and the first in a Muslim country.

The host countries will spend a great deal to put on a good show. Doubtless, as Halligan stated, Western businesses, including UK businesses, will be keen to profit by participating in this rare building orgy.

Halligan referred to the consternation and scepticism about South Africa hosting the 2010 World Cup, which it did superbly. He described certain views of these non-Western countries as 'hopelessly out-dated'- now that emerging markets account for 52% of global GDP.

Russia is the world's largest oil producer and has the largest global gas reserves. Qatar, Halligan explained, has the world's third biggest gas reserves. It is also Britain's main liquefied gas supplier- at a time when the UK struggles to satisfy its long-term energy needs. To suggest that the UK can afford to give the high hat to key energy suppliers who can divert supplies destined for the UK to more lucrative markets is dangerous and short-sighted hubris.

Indeed, emerging markets have 87% of the world's oil and gas reserves. In Swiss university IMD's 2012 World Competitiveness Yearbook,[89]Qatar was ranked in 10th place, ahead of the UK in 18th place

Rather than having a right to patronise emerging markets, Halligan reminded us of a chastening fact, namely that the West is now responsible for 90% of all commercial and sovereign external debt. Furthermore, 'in less than twenty years the US has gone from being the world's biggest creditor to the world's biggest debtor.'

Halligan expressed the hope that the fact that large numbers of people will visit Russia for these sporting events (and likewise the Gulf region) will impact Western stereotypical thinking, and that 'Prejudices – about people and places – will be challenged and often broken.'

He is sanguine, however, about the prospect that a few sporting events in 'far flung' places will solve many of the West's problems with energy shortages, but they might have another positive and important outcome, as 'such events do bind the world together, lessening mutual suspicion and trust.'

I do hope he is right. Unfortunately, as matters stand, I see little prospect that we can rely on our media to play their critical role in making it so.

I recall speaking to London cab drivers after the news broke that Russia had trumped England to host the World Cup, and they all told me, perfectly earnestly, that the Russians only won because of bribery and corruption, and expressed the view that there was 'no way' England had been beaten fairly.

Clearly, the UK media had done its job well. I made due allowance for wounded national pride, but it was still indicative of the impact that relentlessly negative media has on at least segments of the UK population.

Chapter Five

False Friends

Besides the formula, all manner of bizarre stories about Russia get press coverage in the West. A personal favourite was the flying donkey saga.[90]The female donkey, Anapka, was sent parasailing as part of a marketing stunt at a black sea resort in Krasnodar, Russia. She died of a heart attack some time later, possibly from post traumatic stress syndrome.[91]

A relative phoned me, knowing my interest in Russia, and told me that 'those Russians are doing cruel things to donkeys.' I remember thinking that if there was a donkey in trouble anywhere in the world, the Western press was sure to find it in Russia. Crazy ad campaigns are two a penny over here, yet one such incident in Russia gets international coverage.

More recently, there was a story about a young girl being slowly devoured by a bear in Russia. I had to point out to several friends that there are many countries in the world, including the US and Canada, where people are attacked by bears.

Strangely, many Russians believe that Westerners think that bears roam the streets in Russian cities. I have actually never met a Westerner who believes that bears are out and about in downtown Moscow, but I recently saw a photograph in the London Times where bears were crossing the street in a Japanese city. In Northern Japan, several people have been killed by bears, even at beach resorts.

As well as adhering to the formula, certain UK newspapers, especially the London Times, appear to have a fascination with finding titbits of news that tend to suggest that Russians are dour or rather odd. Even worse, they frequently give an airing to ugly conspiracy theories that have absolutely no foundation in reality.

In February 2011, the London Times ran a story that suggested that thieves who stole documentary footage about Khodorkovsky, shortly before the film was to be shown at a Berlin Film Festival were acting at the behest of the Kremlin.[92]

The article asserted that this incident raised fears 'that Russian agents could again be active in Western Europe.' It was written in a breathless, 'we told you so' style. It was long on supposition, but completely devoid of anything that might reasonably be considered as evidence to implicate the Kremlin, which, I am sure, has better things to be doing.

Perhaps the ugliest conspiracy theory that has made print in the UK media about Russia over the past few years was published in The Sunday Telegraph's magazine in March, 2011.[93]

This article discussed the very sad case of the air crash in April of 2010 that killed the President of Poland Lech Kaczynski and his wife and entourage in a flight that began in Warsaw and was due to end shortly afterwards in the Russian city of Smolensk.

April was the seventieth anniversary of the notorious Katyn massacre in which a very large number of Poles were murdered by the Soviet secret police. The Polish President was on his way to commemorate their memory. Ninety six people on board the flight were killed. Putin attended the crash scene, and was very quick to express his dismay at the accident.

The article presents various conspiracy theories that arose after the crash, primarily on the Polish side, suggesting that the Russian state had somehow caused the crash. The article gives air time to a particularly vile conspiracy theory that stated that Polish passengers had survived the crash, but were executed by armed Russian police. Footage that was supposed to exist of this heinous crime was found to be a hoax.

Although the author accepted that it was a manufactured allegation (and a nasty one at that) the article and the lurid headline gave it a hearing ostensibly on the basis that the death of Litvinenko was 'widely believed' to have been 'carried out with the full knowledge of the Russian secret service. As always, the article was utterly lacking in proof of any such involvement.

It concluded by stating that there will always be those who believe that there was a (Russian) conspiracy behind the plane crash. The official report about this crash attributed the cause to human error and poor judgment in landing in heavy fog, when Russian ground crew had advised against it. There is no evidence to suggest that the Russian state had any hand in the sad fate of the passengers on board.

What is particularly disappointing about this type of coverage is that it is often the work of fine journalists working at reputable papers who have a following. People pay attention to what they write, and if they read nothing else about Russia, there is a real danger that malicious falsehoods will be all they remember.

Although the formula is frequently used by the US media, US coverage has a few variations, including the notion (echoed by US politicians) that the US is doing Russia a favour by trading with it.

A June, 2011 Washington Post editorial[94] encouraged President Obama to use the so-called reset with Russia to force its own agenda, by using Russia's 18 year long battle to gain admission to the WTO as leverage. Furthermore, it referred, in a high-handed and condescending tone, to the US 'granting' trade privileges to Russia.

Putin has recently referred to the fact that Russia finally concluded 'its marathon accession to the WTO.' He acknowledged his frustration and overcoming the 'urge to walk away.'

It was well known in Russia that he was less than enthusiastic about the benefits of joining. However, he wrote that 'Russia is prepared to meet its obligations' and expressed hope that 'our partners will play according to the rules.' He indicated that Russia has 'already integrated WTO principles into the legal framework of the Common Economic Space of Russia, Belarus and Kazakhstan.'

He credited the fact that 'in the finishing stretch, the Obama administration and the leaders of some major European states made a significant contribution to achieving the final accords.' Ever proud, however, he emphasizes that while he is pleased with the outcome, it is not because of 'the symbolism of Russia's accession to the World Trade 'club'- but rather due to the economic opportunities is confers on Russian business.' In other words, don't expect us to do cartwheels because you eventually deigned to 'let us in'- we enter on our own terms.

The simple fact is that US corporations may need the privilege of trading with the Russians more than the other way around.

We have seen from the recent catastrophic impasse in the US over the attempt to raise the debt ceiling- that the lunatics appeared, at least temporarily, to have taken over the asylum. This debacle is, rather extraordinarily, currently playing out all over again.

US recovery is grossly hampered by such partisan and juvenile in-fighting amongst politicians and a huge mountain of debt. The American people are poorly served by their politicians on all sides of the political divide who appear brutally self-interested and detached from the harsh reality faced by millions of hard-working Americans. US growth is negligible, at best, and likely to stay that way, and unemployment levels remain stubbornly high.

Thus it was ludicrous for the Washington Post to suggest that the US, out of the goodness of its heart, will accommodate Russia by trading with it (leaving aside the fact it must have its support in the war on terrorism, and the move towards nuclear disarmament).

As stated, however, in a further attempt to provoke and infuriate the Russians, US law makers linked the repeal of *Vanik* to 'concessions' they want from the Russian side. Never a chance is passed by to rub salt in Russian wounds.

Things could be worse, however.

Russia's former ambassador to Nato, Dmitry Rogozin (now a Deputy Prime Minister) remarked that if Obama was not re-elected in November 2012, and 'Russophobes' (such as Mitt Romney) come to power, the reset would be in tatters. Obama's victory leaves me hope that the status quo, at least, can be preserved.

However, all efforts to establish trust between the parties was dealt a severe blow when the provocative and ill-conceived Magnitsky bill became law in the US.

Rogozin was apparently infuriated after meeting conservative US Senators, one of whom leaked a supposed military intelligence report stating that the Russians were behind a bomb blast next to the US Embassy in Tbilisi. The Russians vociferously deny these allegations.

Romney has described Russia in bellicose Cold War terms, as the United States' 'No. 1 geopolitical foe.' He downgraded it to 'opponent' on questioning. Such immoderate language gives Russians good reason to be wary of us. Fortunately, it seems that Romney does not have the nation's pulse on this issue.

A February 2012 Gallup poll that found only 2 percent of Americans think that Russia is the United States' main enemy. Iran, China and North Korea were the top three US enemies.

Romney was asked a fair question by an Occupy Wall Street protester: 'You are part of the (wealthy) 1%, what you going to do for the 99% of the rest of us'? He was stumped by it. The best response he could come up with was to tell the person to 'go back to Russia.' When put on the defensive, US Republicans, including a sizeable number of US Democrats, will fall back on stereotyping and Cold War rhetoric.

During the recent US Presidential campaign, Republican hawk John McCain was out and about slamming Putin any chance he got, to anyone who would listen. Putin's decision not to attend the G8 Summit resulted in the inevitable round of chest-thumping by McCain, echoed by the usual suspects in the US media.

If Putin (who sent Prime Minister Medvedev in his place) indeed decided to snub the G8, I could hardly blame him. If I'd been on the receiving end of the abuse he took from many Western politicians and our media in recent months, I would not be tripping over myself to put on the false face and go shake the hands of people who'd bad-mouthed me behind my back.

Ultimately, Putin will, I believe, do what is best for Russia, including making the diplomatic rounds, but he would only be human if he couldn't stomach the charade so soon after his inauguration.

Luckily, for US businesses, captive to irrational politicians with a deep ideological agenda, Putin prefers dealing with business people than Western politicians, many of whom he holds in low esteem. Nonetheless, as growth opportunities are nearly extinct in the West, he will have choice in terms of who he chooses to deal with. Biting the hand that feeds is rarely a winning proposition.

Russian liberals are naive when they say Putin is paranoid to think that Russia has enemies that seek to destabilize the country. Although he may exaggerate the threat, there is nothing benign about the mountain of negative, anti-Russia media that I have read over the past 4 years. If I was Putin, I'd be worried too, at least enough not to take my eye off the ball.

However, the suggestion that there is a vast Western plot afoot to conquer Russia (popular in certain hawkish Russian political circles) is preposterous, mainly for the reason that we are way too disorganized to orchestrate anything that ambitious: we can't co-ordinate our efforts to save the global economy.

Of course, in an ideal world, all the big players would abandon the incessant posturing and sabre rattling- and instead focus on the real threats in the world today.

History has shown us, however, that in business and in politics, our leaders miss the real threats to our way of life, as they come out of left field and blind side us. We are so fixated on old rivalries and problems, real and imagined, that we fail to identify the next wave and plan for the unexpected.

Being 'soft' with Moscow is a stick that US Republicans will happily beat Obama with. Whether the average struggling American cares a whit about helping perpetuate the personal prejudices and entrenched biases of their lacklustre politicians is another matter.

There has been a lot of Western media coverage about the Obama/Clinton led reset in relations between the US and Russia. However, many Russians believe that the much heralded reset means very different things to both sides.

Suggestions from the US media and US politicians that the Russians are not 'reliable' allies translates into 'not always willing to give in' from the Russian perspective- not without justification, in light of numerous concessions made by the Russians over the past two decades for which they have received little or no thanks.

I am acquainted with many educated Russians (and a smattering of well-informed Westerners) who firmly believe that although nobody wants to revert to the Cold War, the Americans are nostalgic for a reset back to the Yeltsin years- a time when Russia was no longer considered an enemy, but was viewed as so backward that it could not possibly be a threat to US hegemony.

A prosperous Russia is an alarming concept for many old school Cold War US politicians.

Photographs of Medvedev having a hamburger with Obama on his trip to the US in 2010 painted a happy picture of improving relations between the two countries.

I want to believe that Obama was sincere when he said[95] that ending the Cold War was one of the most important developments in the past half century. I believed that his relationship with a fellow lawyer and a fellow legal academic, ex-President Medvedev, now Russian Prime Minister, had good prospects. They are both young, former law professors, highly qualified and intelligent men.

It seemed as if there was a genuine desire to come closer. However, Obama, despite his victory, remains on sticky ground at home; he has little room to manoeuvre, surrounded by a radical element that is deaf to rational argument and US Republican domination of the House of Representatives. The re-election of Putin also provides fodder for American hard-liners.

In September, 2011, a New York Times editorial gave begrudging acknowledgement to the fact that Russia has co-operated with the US on a host of issues and noted the need for future co-operation. However, it then echoed a theme that is now part of the formula, namely the suggestion that Obama will 'have to find ways' to work with Putin, while urging him to 'speak out' about human rights issues.

It is always illuminating when the editors weigh in. You get a very clear sense why the coverage, more generally in the publication, is what it is: The cliché-ridden perspectives are front and centre. If this is the editor's view, it is unlikely that the rank and file journalists will have a diametrically opposed view or be allowed express it.

The New York Times editorial warned-in an ominous tone reminiscent of a bad Hollywood movie-'There can be no illusions about who Mr. Putin really is.' Similarly, around the same time, a Washington Post 'Editorial Board Opinion' responded to the news of Putin's run for President in a similar vein.

The news was 'bad news for President Obama, who invested heavily in his relationship with Mr. Medvedev, hoping he would emerge as a true leader. It is bad news for Russia's neighboring countries, such as Georgia and Ukraine, whose independence Mr. Putin views as a temporary and irritating historical aberration.'

The editorial refers to 'stagnation' in Russia. This blind refusal to recognize the fact that the US economy is in dire straits, contrasted with Russia's healthy balance sheet, defies understanding.

According to the Post, abandoning any pretence at impartiality, or level-headedness, Putin seeks 'like Stalin' to 'rule for life.' Then they up the ante:' 'In many ways, Mr. Putin has recreated the Soviet system, down to the ludicrous displays of adulation from the audience at his party congress Saturday.'

Yet, US Republican politicians host rallies than resemble evangelical prayer meetings.

To my astonishment, the editorial wrote that 'Putin has not sent millions to their deaths or to the gulag.' Needless to say there is no mention of Guantanamo. 'He (Putin) showed that the imprisonment or exile of a few key businessmen and the unpunished murders of a couple of dozen crusading journalists could silence their compatriots almost as effectively....Unlike the Communist Party, Mr. Putin pretends to no ideology, other than a kind of snarling, nationalist nostalgia.'

This article was itself quite the 'snarling' piece, positively venomous. It did Putin a grave injustice, but highlights how little even respected publications like the Washington Post know about Russia and its leaders. Little wonder startled politicians on Capitol Hill reading these diatribes over their morning Starbucks coffee regularly give vent to similar sentiments.

The references in many US editorials about the Russians not respecting 'freedom' is particularly jarring- the word is now often laced with menace: It does not imply 'peace, love, food and justice for all.' Rather, it throws up images of Scud missiles and bloody conflict.

Why must we push our agenda on others? We are incorrigible in this regard. Little wonder the pages of our history books are stained with blood.

The Post editorial noted that Putin 'will make decisions based on how he calculates the benefits to himself and his clique.' These commentators seem perplexed that Putin will give priority to Russia's interests over their own. He would be a very poor sort of Russian politician if he did not.

Finally, the editorial demands that the US use the big stick kept in reserve (the lever) to force its agenda on the Russians. 'If the United States makes human rights part of its policy — with legislation such as that sponsored by Sen. Benjamin L. Cardin (D-Md.) that imposes sanctions on the worst abusers — it can affect his (Putin's) calculation.'

In September 2011, the Wall Street Journal[96] weighed in, opining that Putin's return to the Russian presidency...would add to 'already deep suspicions among US policy makers and lawmakers about the country's intentions and direction.' It refers to 'Russia's slide into what many see as a police state.'

The article delights in mentioning the perennial favourite, the WikiLeaks cables that referred to Russia as a 'virtual mafia state.' The writers appear to take almost childish glee in regurgitating meaningless calumny. 'US embassy officials describe Mr. Putin as an 'alpha dog' who calls the shots and Mr. Medvedev as a hesitant figure who 'plays Robin to Mr. Putin's Batman.'

Undoubtedly, Wikileak cables exist that describe US politicians in less than glowing terms.

It is a sad indictment of our political order that bitchy gossip and puerile back-biting form part of the shaky justification for government policy that may have long-term, highly significant consequences for us all. It is easy to trade insults like precocious children in a schoolroom brawl, but to what end? One thing that is absolutely certain is that threats won't work with the Russians, veiled or otherwise.

Although the Western media regularly eviscerates Putin, seemingly with impunity, they tended to treat Medvedev as a bit of a pet. However, I doubt that Medvedev is likewise intoxicated. I suspect that his experiences with the reset over the past few years have taught him a few home truths.

As a commentator in the Ukrainian Kviv Post shrewdly observed,[97]quoting political analyst Nikolai Zlobinas, 'Many Russian leaders since Gorbachev's times had exaggerated expectations with regard to the West and the United States but with time they vanished.

That happened to Yeltsin, and that happened to Medvedev too.'..he 'realizes that Americans are acting primarily in their own interests without taking the interests of Russia into account,' he said. Putin is the ultimate pragmatist in this regard.

According to Fox News, US House Speaker John Boehner said[98] he was troubled that Russia seemed to be slipping back into its Soviet-era ways. 'In Russia's use of old tools and old thinking, we see nothing short of an attempt to restore Soviet-style power and influence,' he said.

Fox reported that Boehner said 'Instead of downplaying Russia's disregard for democratic values and human rights, we should call them on it. ... The United States should insist Russia 'reset' its own policies. If those appeals require teeth, the House stands ready to provide them,' he said.

These childish barbs endlessly directed at the Russians do not help US companies chasing growth outside the moribund US. Coca-Cola Co plans to invest $3-billion (US) in Russia over the next five years. It gets about three-quarters of its revenue from overseas, with emerging markets among its fastest-growing markets.

In a review of Dick Cheney's autobiography in the FT, Richard McGregor[99] referred to the 'Russian invasion of Georgia.' He quoted Cheney- 'We need to make clear to the Russians and our friends and allies that we will be aggressive in expanding the borders of the Free World and that Russia has to make a choice.'

Extraordinarily, the BBC has used Cheney and his inner circle of US neo-conservative hawks, many of whom profited very nicely from the Iraq war, to supply invective against Putin and Russia. I shudder to imagine a world re-created in Cheney's image.

As you may have gathered, my view of the current state of the reset with the US is somewhat jaded. However, there may still be hope, with Obama back in the White House, but prejudices still run deep on Capitol Hill.

At the annual World Russia Forum in Washington, Russians organizers have said that 'for every one event with a positive agenda' regarding Russia, 'there are hundreds of others with a negative agenda.' For example, a recent Congressional Committee on Foreign Affairs hearing was titled 'Time to Pause the Reset? Defending US Interests in the Face of Russian Aggression:' The formula in full flight.

An article in the Moscow Times suggested that 'the image of Russia in the US is still the Cold War or the 'Wild West' of the '90s,' quoting Andrew Somers, President of the American Chamber of Commerce in Russia, who had just returned from a visit to the US capital. 'Nobody is up to date on American business in Russia,[100]he said.'

The article also stated that 'a few members of Congress told Somers that they believe Russia is a major source of cyber attacks on the American government and institutions. Some even believe that there are as many Russian spies in Washington as there were during the Cold War.'

The article confirmed my hypothesis that politicians on Capitol Hill are adamant that ammunition must be kept in reserve to punish the Russians (the 'lever' argument again). Representative Eliot Engel, a Democrat from New York, was quoted as saying that the Magnitsky act 'is a serious effort to address the gap which would be left by repeal of Jackson-Vanik.'

There was a scintilla of hope that common sense might prevail in the end. The Moscow Times quoted Somers as saying that 'Congresswoman Jean Schmidt practically shrieked with surprise and delight when she found out that

Estee Lauder cosmetics are sold in Russia, which is one of the company's top markets.'

A good faith gesture by the Americans towards the Russians, that has real teeth, would be welcome- a sign that relations can move beyond empty talk and sabre-rattling.

For instance, a bilateral deal to introduce a three-year multiple-entry entry visa programme for several categories of travellers (business and tourists) has been under negotiation for some time. There has been a recent breakthrough:[101] It appears that from September 9, 2012, a new Agreement between the Russian Federation and the United States on visa formalities for Russian citizens and citizens of the United States of America will enter into force.

The Agreement provides for the issue of three-year multiple-entry visas allowing a maximum stay of six months for both tourists and business travellers alike. An official Russian government website describes the initiative as aimed 'at creating more favorable conditions for mutual travel of citizens of Russia and the US, as well as the further development of economic, cultural, scientific, and cultural ties between the two countries.'

It is a positive development. I wish I could get a multi-entry business visa for longer than a year in Ireland. The process is also extremely expensive. Russians have considerable difficulties obtaining visas to enter Europe which adds to a feeling of isolation. Negotiations to improve the situation seem to have stalled, so I may be out of luck for some time to come.

By contrast, Hong Kong has been very quick to extend visa free travel to Russians, many of whom have listed their companies on their stock exchanges. Other countries are negotiating similar deals with the Russians.

However, the overtly biased, even polemical coverage of Russian affairs by many prestigious US newspapers undoubtedly fans the flames of prejudice on Capitol Hill and throughout the US. Sadly, the US TV networks are even more blameworthy in this regard.

Ivan Katchanovski teaches at the School of Political Studies at the University of Ottawa in Canada. He has written a number of interesting papers that I refer to in this book. In 2009, he published an analysis of the US media's coverage of major post-communist countries.[102] He reviewed over 1000 news reports for his study.

At the outset, he noted that previous studies had shown that television coverage affects American public attitudes and the US's foreign policy agenda towards other countries. Katchanovski also noted that in the US (as is the case in Russia) that TV has a far bigger audience than the print media.

In keeping with my findings, he also observed, although not his primary focus, that a large number of stories about Russia from major Western newspapers and magazines, including the Washington Post and the New York Times, presented a negative image of Russia.

He noted that studies have argued that the 'US mass media suffers from an anti-Russian bias or even Russophobia.' By way of example, researchers have observed that ' much of the coverage of the two wars in Chechnya in the US mass media and in Western media in general 'has been relentlessly one-sided and relentlessly anti-Russian.[103]'

It mostly focused 'on the effects of the Russian actions on Chechen civilians and it largely ignored or minimized the role of attacks carried out by Islamic fundamentalists, terrorists, and kidnappers in Chechnya in the start of the violent conflict in 1994 and its resumption in 1999.'

Katchanovski's analysis concluded that post communist countries that are US allies, such as Poland and Georgia, receive far more positive coverage on the US networks than

Russia. In addition, between 2004 and 2008, countries that adopted pro-Western and pro-American foreign policies, such as Ukraine (after the 'Orange Revolution' in 2004, and Georgia before and after the 'Rose Revolution' in 2003) received favourable treatment by the US networks.

He noted that legitimate Russian concerns about the placement of US missiles in Poland and the Czech Republic were 'largely dismissed' and that media reports also 'minimized opposition in Poland and the Czech Republic against the missile system which would make these countries potentially targets of Russian retaliatory measures.'

US TV network coverage of the Georgian conflict in August 2008 largely mimicked the print media coverage already discussed by me. As Katchanovski stated, 'Georgia was primarily presented as a small democratic country, which suffered an invasion of Russia.'

He noted that media interviews were conducted with Georgian President Mikheil Saakashvilli in which he falsely accused Russia of 'unprovoked aggression' against his country. In reality, he fired the first shots, resulting in many civilian deaths.'

US media outlets such as ABC World News ran headline stories that stated that 'hundreds, possibly thousands of civilians killed, apartment buildings and military bases destroyed, as Russian bombers and missiles pound Georgia, a US ally.' However, 'In contrast, interviews which represented Russian and South Ossetian sides of the conflict were almost entirely absent.'

He noted that 'while mostly ignoring cooperation on such issues as the war in Afghanistan and international terrorism. Russian foreign policy was frequently distorted as striving to start the new Cold War with the United

States, allying itself with Iran, and bent on restoration of the Soviet Union by military force.'

Katchanovski concluded that 'Major topics concerning Russia included relations between the US and Russia...the poisoning of Alexander Litvinenko in the United Kingdom. Most TV reports dealing with US-Russian relations focused on tensions between two countries on such issues as the US missile system in Poland and the Czech Republic, the Iran nuclear program, the Iraq war, and sanctions against North Korea.'

He noted that 'Extensive television coverage of the poisoning of Alexander Litvinenko....was generally negative and biased against Russia.' with many news programs implicating the Russian security services ' because of his criticism of Vladimir Putin policies and his knowledge of state secrets, such as alleged involvement of the Federal Security Service (FSB) in a series of apartment explosions in Russia.'

Litvinenko had propagated the accusation that Putin was responsible for a series of lethal explosions in September 1999 at apartment buildings in Russian cities, including Moscow. He claimed that Putin used the fatalities and public outrage to justify a military invasion of Chechnya, action which massively boosted his popularity, handing him an easy win in the 2000 Russian Presidential elections.

Putin-haters periodically resurrect these shabby allegations that lack even a scintilla of evidence to substantiate them.

Katchanovski noted that Litvinenko's propensity, more generally, to make lurid, baseless accusations against the Russian state, such as his claims 'about involvement of Russian security services in terrorist attacks on September 11, 2001 in the United States, London bombings on July 7, 2005 in the United Kingdom, terrorist attacks in a Moscow theatre in 2002, and a Beslan school in North Ossetia in Russia in 2004, were ignored in television broadcasts.'

In addition, Katchanovski noted that Litvinenko was frequently 'misrepresented as a former Russian spy even though he was a former officer of the anti-organized crime department of the FSB in Russia and military counterintelligence in the Soviet Union.'

He noted that the use of radioactive polonium to poison Litvinenko 'was emphasized as key piece of evidence of the involvement of the Russian security services even though the same networks broadcast a large number of news reports concerning lack of security of nuclear and radioactive materials in Russia.'

The use of radioactive material to kill Litvinenko in central London was a huge story internationally, for obvious reasons. Indeed, Katchonovski's analysis found that the Litvinenko poisoning was 'the number one topic of television coverage of Russia in the United States in terms of its length over the five-year period from 2004 till 2008.

However, as Katchanovski observed, the US TV networks did not present the case in an impartial manner, and alternative, plausible explanations that did not implicate the Russia state were nigh invisible.

He also observed an obsession with conspiracy theories that accused the Russians of James Bond style skulduggery. The anti-Russia conspiracy theorists came out in force after the poisoning of Viktor Yuschenko, a US ally, during the 2004 Ukrainian Presidential Campaign.

According to Katchanovski, the US networks implied that the Russian government was responsible, to eliminate a pro-Western Presidential candidate. Other suspects, such as Yuschenko's many enemies, were ignored by the Western media, despite the fact that Yuschenko himself named one of his formal allies as being involved in the poisoning.

Katchanovski notes that the assassination in 2004 of Forbes investigative journalist, American Paul Klebnikov in Russia also received extensive US network coverage, and Russian officials were blamed, ignoring strong evidence that Chechen criminals may have been implicated.

Klebnikov, of Russian/American descent, was vociferous in his investigations of organized crime, terrorism and corruption in Russia. He wrote a truly hair-raising book, *Godfather of the Kremlin* about Berezovsky that was highly critical of him. Berezovsky sued Forbes for libel. Forbes settled with him, printing a partial retraction.

No-one has been convicted of his killing. Suspects brought to trial were acquitted for lack of evidence. Certainly, Klebnikov was a fine journalist and a brave man and his family deserve closure, but he undoubtedly made many enemies and unearthing them is likely no easy task.

Katchanovski noted that although the takeover of a Beslan school by Islamic terrorists in 2004 received some positive US network coverage, an interview with a Chechen Islamist rebel leader responsible for the Beslan attack was shown on US ABC Nightline on July 28, 2005, in spite of vociferous Russian government opposition.

This interview was quite extraordinarily insensitive.To the Russians, it was as if the US networks had invited Bin Laden around for a chat on day-time television after 9/11.

He observed that his study 'confirmed findings of several previous studies which reported a prevalence of negative coverage of Russia. The television coverage of Russia and Russians was dominated by negative stories, such as tense relations with the United States, the poisoning of Alexander Litvinenko, crime, and undemocratic developments in the Russian politics.'

Katchanovski concluded that coverage of post-communist countries by US TV outlets is 'significantly distorted.' The images of these countries are either 'idealized or demonized' depending on whether they are viewed as US allies.

He surmised that such 'virtual reality is likely to have real repercussions, for example, in the area of public attitudes towards post-communist nations and American foreign policy towards these states.'

I believe that there can be little doubt that our impressions of other peoples are formed, to at least some degree, by what we read in the newspaper and see on TV; if that coverage is relentlessly one-sided and biased, unless we have the interest and wherewithal to seek out another side to the story, there is a serious danger that we will be influenced by it.

As well as clipping negative articles about Russia over the past few years, I also tried to find positive articles. It was like finding a needle in a very large haystack.

Most of the positive media about Russia concerns Russian entrepreneurs such as Yuri Milner, the canny Russian investor in Facebook and Twitter, who gets quite a number of inches of positive media. There is also the occasional positive reference to Russian artists (broadly defined) and Russian sportsmen and women.

Katchanovski's analysis of the US TV networks coverage of Russian affairs, revealed a similar trend, namely that the only positive stories relating to Russia that aired were mostly confined to topics such as Russian immigrants like Sergey Brin, the Russian born co-founder of Google, Russian sports people, and artists. There was also coverage of vodka's growing popularity- it was acknowledged to be 'a Russian invention.'

The huge discrepancy between the number of positive stories and the negative is not easily explained. Presumably not every Western journalist is biased against Russia. Those who are not and make it into print clearly have deep affection for Russia and its remarkable, resilient people.

In some instances, it was readers who were the voice of reason when the media lost the run of itself.

In August 2008, when the UK media was at its most virulent in its stance against Russia over the Georgian conflict, two letters were published in the letter's page in the FT.[104]

In one of the letters to the editor, the writer from Belfast described the FT's coverage of the Georgia crisis as partisan and misleading and points out that it was indeed Georgian aggression that had lead to the conflict. 'I am not sure how we would justify US action in going halfway across the world to Iraq and killing thousands in the name of finding elusive 'weapons of mass destruction.' and at the same time condemn Russia for trying to protect Russian citizens in its own backyard.'

The writer recommends that the time has come to 'shed our Cold War mindset. We need to accept Russia as an equal partner and look for opportunities to increase economic co-operation. Shenanigans such as the planned 'missile shield' and Georgia can only put the Russians in a corner and an unsettled, isolated Russia cannot be good for the world economy and peace.'

In the same edition of the FT, another writer, this time from London, suggested that the US and the UK are in no position to lecture Russia given their record over the past twenty years. He points out that it was the West who encouraged President Yeltsin to expand and implement overnight 'disastrous and crude free market policies and cronyism which left tens of millions of Russians destitute.' The writer pointed out that just as Russia got back on its feet, we 'threaten it with missiles in its own backyard and encirclement by Nato.'

He wrote that notwithstanding such 'blatantly aggressive policies, we seem to expect the Russians to be partners in solving the world's other conflicts and problems. The arrogance and hypocrisy of some Western politicians are breath-taking and it is particularly depressing to see Mr Cameron, a likely future Prime Minister, adopt a knee-jerk Cold War approach to ignore its history and the complexities of the region.'

I took solace from these letters from readers like myself. I was not alone after all in being infuriated by the tone of the commentary in the British press with respect to Russia.

I have put a lot of emphasis on the Georgian conflict, because it represented a new low in relations between the West and Russia. On the surface, relations have improved since then, but I fear that animosities remain submerged, waiting for the next trigger to ignite them. It doesn't take much.

Clement Crisp is the Dance Correspondence for the FT. In Clements's own words, he positively 'worships.' to the 'far side of idolatry' the corps de ballet from St. Petersburg's Mariinsky Ballet. They toured the UK in 2011, playing the Royal Opera House in London, to rave reviews. In his FT column, Crisp describes the dancers as 'angels.'

Clement Crisp likes Russians, or at least he likes the Russians who dance for the Mariinsky Ballet.

I would love to see the affable, eloquent Mr Crisp move off the ballet beat periodically to do a turn covering Russia political and economic events.

He might be joined by his thoughtful colleagues relegated to the back page in the FT's Saturday's edition- the cerebral Mr Harry Eyres with his beautifully written and observed 'The Slow Lane' column, and Bon Vivant and world traveller, Canadian Tyler Brule. They would probably, like all sensible men, be horrified at the prospect.

Similarly, Isabel Gorst in Moscow for the FT has also written intriguing 'nice' articles about Russians that humanize them. Just far too few of them.

She wrote about a lady who gave up trading sugar to grow rare roses; in the process, we learnt that Russians love flowers and import about $2 billion worth of cut flowers a year, making them the world's sixth largest market.

Indeed, Russians give each other flowers for all manner of occasions. Even men give other men flowers as a gift. Contrary to the stereotype, most Russian men are charming, old fashioned in their attitude to women. Russian women expect their men to treat them as ladies, to hold the door for them, to pay for dinner, and to bring them flowers. Alas, such gallantry from men in the West has become the exception rather than the rule.

From other articles about Russia with a positive bent, I gleaned that Russians like cats and chocolate. US conglomerate, Mars INC sells more cat food in Russia than anywhere else in the world. This is due to the fact that many Russians live in apartments and like their feline companions.

These facts may not set the world on fire, but if we read more of them, perhaps we would feel more affinity with our Russian neighbours. We desperately need more articles that help us recognize our shared struggle for survival and our quest to find beauty and a measure of serenity in the small things in life that make all the difference.

Sadly, the Western media prefers to ply us with grim tidings and cartoon-character depictions of Russians that belong in a Warner Brothers' cartoon.

A few examples of even-handed articles by the UK press are worth mentioning, if only because they are such an anomaly.

In a rare, fair-minded article in The Times from October 2010, [105] Owen Slot wrote about a conversation he had with Alexei Sorokin, the official responsible for Russia's successful bid for the World Cup in 2018, in the context of the suspicion in the UK that the result was fixed.

Sorokin told Slot that it was time for Westerners to drop 'their old prejudices,' and Slot suggested that it might be time to wake up 'to the fact that though every second villain in *Spooks* (a UK Hit TV series) still seems to be Russian, the Soviet union is long gone and Russians deserve a better hearing than one drenched in sepia-tinted bias.'

Sorokin was keen to talk about 'the prejudice he believes Russia faces from the rest of the world.' observing that accounts about Russian affairs are always delivered from the Western perspective- 'You have not read ours.'..'If we do anything, it's apparently bad, or done out of fear or because of corruption.' Sorokin describes the need to 'live with this every day' and to have to 'overcome these perceptions all the time' as 'so tiresome.'

I find it very tiresome, and I am not even Russian.

Although Slot appears initially sceptical, he conceded that the Russians 'have a point.' He speaks to a legendary figure in Russian football, Evgeny Lovchev, a'52- cap international in the seventies,' who recalled his days playing matches around the world. He said that he felt 'mistrust' wherever he went, and ' No matter what we said, people wouldn't believe.'

Slot asked him if he still felt 'that same mistrust now'? Lovchev said that it was 'A little bit less, but it is still there.' Slot asked him about sundry allegations of corruption around the Sochi 2014 Winter Olympics preparation and various other scandals, but the retired footballer was unimpressed.

As Slot observed, with rare insight, 'The media in the West may well have recounted these stories with a little too much relish and a little too much prominence.'

He also noted how hugely important the 2018 World Cup is to Russia-a way to 'relaunch' and to attract tourism and investment. He observed that it also presents an opportunity to tell the story 'the way they insist it should be told, so that we won't come back in 2018 with the villains from Spooks still spitting out do svidaniya (goodbye) in shocking accents before they pull the trigger on another good guy from the West.'

To his credit, Slot took the time to seek out, listen to and report a Russian perspective that did not merely parrot the formula.

In an article in The Sunday Times in August 2008, Peter Miller castigates David Cameron for his aggressive stance towards Russia during the Georgian conflict, in which he assumed that Russian was the aggressor. In Miller's opinion, UK politicians did nothing but display their utter lack of ignorance about history, 'posturing on politico-economic fault lines of which they appear to have barely schoolboy understanding.'

As he cogently observes, 'Russia is a huge country not as far away as we would like, about which our politicians know far too little.'

In an article in the Sunday Times Magazine in August, 2011,[106] Mark Franchetti recounts various conversations he had with young people in Russia and wealthy expats. Some of the young people who remained at home expressed the view that things were better in the Soviet Union; a number of them described Americans as 'brainwashed,' living in a country with 'little culture or history.'

Others told him that they believe there is 'no point turning to the West for help, because the West sees Russia as a rival. It doesn't want us to do well.'

Franchetti often writes about Russia. He shows compassion and affection for his subjects, and makes an effort to get out of his office to mix with real Russians and hear what they have to say.

It was interesting to note that some of the more rational responses to the Georgian conflict appeared in the Irish media. In August of 2008, David McWilliams[107] wrote that 'the people in power in Moscow, despite the naive caricatures peddled by the Western press, are not idiots. Russia has sent out a signal to everyone: 'Don't mess with us in our own backyard.'

McWilliams suggested that 'mutual respect will be much less dangerous than Western condescension towards Russia.'

Around the same time, Sir Ivor Roberts, the President of Trinity College Oxford and former British Ambassador to Yugoslavia, Ireland and Italy, wrote in the Irish Times[108] about the fact that the West was 'prepared to support Kosovo's secession from Serbia and disregard internationally recognised borders' had infuriated the Russians, who then had no compunction in doing the same 'in respect of Georgia by recognizing the borders of South Ossetia and Abkhazia as those of independent states.'

He noted that 'the Russians dislike of encirclement is profound and historical' and fuelled by enlargement of Nato 'to take in the Eastern European countries formerly members of The Warsaw Pact'- Putin regards the 'appearance of a powerful military bloc' on its borders as a 'direct threat.'

He remarked how the ex-Georgian President, US educated Mikheil Saakashvili, 'played a clever game in Washington endearing himself to the foreign policy hawks around Vice-President Cheney"- including then US President contender, John McCain- who were prepared to ignore less positive aspects of his tenure, such as crackdowns on the opposition and the imposition of a state of emergency before Presidential elections.

In recent elections, Saakashvili's party lost heavily to billionaire businessmen Bidzina Ivanishvili and his Georgian Dream Party. The newly-installed Prime Minister, accused by Saakashvili of being too close to Russia, has promised to work closely with his nemesis.

However, the bitterly fought election campaign made it clear that there is no love lost between the two men, who must, nevertheless, attempt to work together until the Presidential elections in 2013. The new Prime Minister has intimated that he will work towards liberalizing trade with his Russian neighbours. It is highly unlikely that the Americans welcome this possible thaw in relations between the two countries.

Roberts surmised that Saakashvili over-estimated the degree of support he had in Washington-believing that the Americans and possibly Nato would support him militarily when he attacked Russian interests, the same way they went to Kosovo's aid in its fight with Serbia- lending air strike support to attack Serbia in 1999.

As a general matter, the language used by the Western media when writing about Russia is often highly politicised. For instance, when FT columnists referred to the ex-Georgian President, they described his harsh treatment and attacks on opposition parties, as 'verging' on authoritarianism.' They minimized his proclivities while exaggerating Russian mendacity.

Roberts wrote that Russia's 'aggressive response to Saakashvili' was partly a reaction to 'its sense of impotence over Nato action in Yugoslavia, and partly an assertion of Russian power' and its desire to show that 'the years of humiliation after the break-up of the Soviet Union are over.' That word 'humiliation' again.

He notes, however, that as a result of Saakashvili's miscalculation, 'It is now the West which looks humiliated and disoriented'- as the Georgians faced disappointment that the US and Nato had ostensibly let them down.

He referred to John McCain's maudlin cry of support for the Georgians, 'We are all Georgians now' and how he tried to use his tough-man persona to make Obama look weak. Roberts, however, agreed with McCain's assessment of Russia's military response as an attempt to 'intimidate other neighbours such as Ukraine for choosing to associate with the West.'

He noted, however, that suggestions from Western politicians that Russia's recognition of the independence of South Ossetia and Abkhazia violated the territorial integrity and sovereignty of Georgia was contrary to UN Security Council Resolutions are off mark.

He pointed out that if you 'substitute the West for Russia and Kosovo for South Ossetia and Abkhazia and the inconsistency in double standards of the West's position are clear.'

In his opinion this is exactly what the West did when it recognised Kosovo against Serbia's will and in the absence of any Security Council Resolution allowing it to do so. He noted that in light of Europe's 'increasing dependence on Russia as an energy supplier.'..'most of the economic measures which the West might take against the Russians will only hurt the Western Europeans more.'

He suggested the need for 'cool heads' and the toning down of 'the megaphone diplomacy (however tempting it is to deploy with a domestic audience).'

Roberts asked the question as to whether Russia was playing 'a neo-imperialist game.' He observed that we are 'are clearly no longer in a uni-polar world.' and that 'The rush to Nato membership by its former satellites and the foolhardy activity of Washington pests like Saakashvili make a paranoiac Russia distinctly unsettled and unpredictable.'

In his view, 'Talking of a new Cold War and building 'coalitions against Russian aggression.' however, risks being self fulfilling. Engaging with, not isolating, Russia is the path to avoiding further confrontation. Be careful what you wish for, says the old adage.'

Similarly, in August, 2008, in the (Irish) Sunday Business Post,[109]columnist Tom McGurk wrote about the Georgian conflict. He noted that 'Russia has drawn a line in the sand.'

He described events in Georgia as being an 'international accident waiting to happen.' as the US had devoted huge foreign policy resources to satellite states around Russia to spread their own influence in the region, making Russia feeling threatened and encircled.

He noted that Nato encirclement of Russia wasn't helping, and that US aid to Poland to 'develop its army.' and the announcement that Poland and the Czech Republic would become part of the US anti-missile shield- to be placed by the US in the Czech Republic and Poland on Russia's borders, all compounded Russian fears.

McGurk expressed the view that the Georgian war, orchestrated by Saakashvali (described by McGurk as viewed in Moscow as 'an unstable political chameleon and a reckless populist') gave the Russians the opportunity to send 'an uncompromising message to the world about its determination to maintain its territorial integrity.'

McGurk rightly noted that the conflict raised 'hugely important questions both for US policy in this region and for the EU as well.' He observed that had Georgia been allowed to join Nato in 2007-a contingency only avoided by Germany's Angela Merkel's opposition (on the basis that Georgia was 'inherently unstable'), we 'could now have had Nato and Russian troops involved in a shooting war, given that Nato members must defend each other.'

A terrifying prospect that undoubtedly looms large in Putin's mind.

McGurk suggested that the European Union ought to do some soul searching, to decide where 'EU influence ends and US strategic manoeuvres begin.' He asked the question whether we are about to be 'sucked into a developing European crisis that is none of our making?'

He maintained- and I would heartily agree- that it is 'high time' – 'not least given the current developing energy crisis in Europe- that we all realise that it is in the EU's interest to have stability and territorial integrity respected in Russia.'

He asked the question, 'What on earth has the EU to gain by the Czech Republic and Poland allowing a US missile system on their territory? Indeed, do they belong emotionally to Europe or to America? Have they even consulted any of us about this decision? And what are its consequences for all of us?'

McGurk wrote that it was time 'we took a new look at the whole area of EU-Russian relations' He noted that the 'Cold War attitude of the Western media towards Russia this week has been extraordinary.'

'After all, it was Georgia who invaded South Ossetia and then the Russians, having quickly established military superiority, accepted a ceasefire, while Moscow went to enormous lengths using all its English-speaking government officials to mount a media offensive explaining its actions.'

McGurk wrote that 'Seemingly there is nothing Russia can do to satisfy some in the West; Vladimir Putin's clean-up of the mafia-dominated mess he inherited from Boris Yeltsin is merely characterised as ex-KGB man authoritarianism. Ironically, as Russia has become more and more stable and economically prosperous under his hand, the level of criticism aimed at him has only increased.'

McGurk pointed out that 'far from hankering after a lost empire' (a common theme), Putin used his time as President 'to fix Russia's pot-Soviet border, signing treaties with every neighbouring country that would agree-including, last month, China.' McGurk observed that the Georgian conflict highlighted 'the instability that the policy of surrounding Russia has created.' noting that in World War Two, in Europe 'essentially a war between Nazi Germany and the Red Army, 27 million Soviet citizens died.'

'Ever since.' as McGurk rightly noted, 'Russia understandably has deep-rooted fears about its territorial integrity and is determined that another war will not be fought on its territory.'

McGurk concluded by writing that the 'whole affair' had 'also highlighted the divergence in policy between what the US wants in Europe and what the EU wants.' He asked how European 'peace and stability' can be maintained 'if there is a determined US policy of surrounding Russia.'

He concluded by suggesting that 'given the huge importance of Russian energy resources, can acquiescence to such a US policy be in our best interests.' He suggested that after the Irish 'no' vote in the Lisbon Treaty (we were subsequently shuffled back to the polls to vote 'yes'), the EU has 'much' to be thinking about.'

The simple fact is that Russia is far closer to European borders than the US, and, I believe, an integral part of

Europe. In his manifesto, Putin wrote that 'Russia is an inalienable and organic part of Greater Europe and European civilization' and that Russians 'think of themselves as Europeans.'

He proposed working' toward creating a harmonious community of economies from Lisbon to Vladivostok, which will in the future evolve into a free trade zone and even more advanced forms of economic integration. The resulting common continental market would be worth trillions of euros.'

I wholeheartedly concur with these sentiments, which are rather generous in light of the way Putin has been treated by his peers in the EU. Rather than sheepishly following the UK's lead by alienating Russia any chance it gets, I strongly believe Europe should accept Putin's offer of deeper engagement and show some respect.

When we run out of natural resources, will the UK provide them? I think not.

Putin makes it clear that 'the prospects of the entire global economic structure depend heavily on the state of affairs in Europe.' Russia is hurting at present as a result of the financial crisis in the EU. There are many politicians in his inner sanctum who believe that Russia should forge far closer ties with Asia (right on its borders) and turn away from Europe.

I believe that would be our loss. Yet, it may happen, not merely as an economic imperative (the lure of China) but as a result of our intransigence and our inflexible attitude to our neighbours' entirely rational desire to protects its borders and the well-being of millions of Russians.

Part Two: From West to East

Chapter Six

The Strong Man

Russians have no love for metro-sexual politicians. They like a strong man who can hold the line- both in terms of dealing with enemies, old and new- and in having a coherent strategy for the future. Russia's economic and social development has been plagued by flip-flopping politicians.

Indeed, Russians give 'long suffering 'a whole new meaning. For centuries, they have been hostage to quixotic, unpredictable, despotic leaders, changing laws, policies, even enemies in the blink of an eye. Being in favour today did not guarantee that you would not end up in the Gulag tomorrow: Endless days and nights marked by scarcities of the most basic commodities, and constant, seismic change.

A long history of capricious rule was ruinous to the Russian economy and damaging to the Russian psyche. Progress takes time and the dogged pursuit of consistent, realizable, long-term goals. Russian leaders, right through to Boris Yeltsin, were imperious and erratic- and life for the general population has been a veritable roller coaster. Getting off wasn't easy, although many who had the wherewithal to leave did so.

Irish people weep into pints of Guinness and bemoan the grave injustices suffered at the hands of our oppressors. There is not a dry eye in the house if 'the Famine' is mentioned- a famine that dates back to the 1830's, but we still haven't got over it. By contrast, in the 1960's under Mao, 30 million Chinese starved to death, and Russians woke to the dawn of yet a new day with quicksand under foot, while middle class Americans admired the new Cadillac on the lawn.

When communism fell in 1991, the US encouraged the receptive Russian government under Yeltsin to embrace 'shock therapy'- a scorched earth, neo-conservative form of capitalism, which they did at breakneck speed.

Russians were sold on the glories of privatization and it was predicted that great swells of foreign direct investment would flow into Russia from the transition. Both assumptions were gravely flawed.

From the US perspective, the old mortal enemy was wounded- and it wanted it to stay that way. An acceptable alternative was for Russia to re-emerge from the embers of the Soviet Union as a Western clone, preferably with a puppet President ensconced in the Kremlin, who could be counted on (as in Georgia) to be a US ally.

Things didn't quite work out that way.

In 1991, during the initial honeymoon period, Russians were reasonably confident that democracy would be beneficial to their lives. A survey conducted in 1991 by the Times Mirror Center, precursor to the Pew Research Center, noted that a mere 7% of Russians expressed 'satisfaction with life' at that time.

They probably assumed that democracy couldn't be much worse than what they had already experienced, and they were prepared to give it a try. The same survey found that in 1991, 51% of Russians professed a preference for democracy over a strong leader. By 2009, a follow up 14-nation survey by the Pew Research Center's Global Attitudes Project found that only 29% of Russians did so. [110]

What happened in the interim?

Contrary to expectations, the 1990s were a dismal period for Russians. Incompetent politicians, the Asian crisis, and a huge drop in oil prices all added to the misery and the rapid downward spiral of Russian economic fundamentals.

In 2001, at the end of the decade, according to the Russian State Statistics Service, about 50 million Russians, 33 percent, were living below the subsistence level. This number improved to 24.5 percent in early 2005, and 14.8 percent in the third quarter of 2007.

Many Russians, especially those over 40, have a vivid memory of these events and firmly believe that naive Russian politicians were lured onto the rocks by the siren song of capitalism. In their view, the US wanted to deal Russia a mortal blow, and would still like to finish the job if given the chance.

Indeed, despite huge progress in the 2000's under Putin, nostalgia for communism is still strong in Russia. According to the 2009 Pew Research survey[111], 'the prevailing view in Russia (and Ukraine, Lithuania, Slovakia, Bulgaria and Hungary) is that people were better off economically under communism.

However, in an apparent contradiction, the survey also found that 35% of the population surveyed, on average, were now satisfied with life-with approval levels around 40% for the younger generation. Older folk were less convinced- only 25% of those 65 and older expressed satisfaction with life, although up considerably from a dismal 3% in 1991 (the elderly were hit especially hard by the crushing recession in the 1990's).

Variations also existed in responses from urban and rural areas. In 2009, 38% of those living in urban areas rated their lives near the top of the ladder, compared with 28% in rural areas. By contrast, in 1991, fewer than one-in-ten Russians in urban (8%) and rural (5%) regions expressed high levels of personal satisfaction.

The Pew pollsters wrote that of all the countries surveyed, a general conclusion could be drawn from the poll's results to the effect that 'Russians express the least enthusiasm for democratic values.' The most accepting were people in the former East Germany, closely followed by the Poles and Czechs.

After decades of economic hardship, the survey noted that 78% of Russians viewed a strong economy as more important than a good democracy. In my estimation, many Russians who lived through the era of chaos equate democracy with starvation, ruin, false promises and duplicitous, greedy Westerners.

However, they are not alone in placing a high premium on economic prosperity. Many other countries surveyed also valued it highly, in many instances more than freedom of speech, freedom of the press, honest elections and a civilian-controlled military.

Even Americans were divided on the issue, with 49% choosing a good democracy, while 44% favoured a strong economy, down significantly from 2002, when 61% preferred a good democracy.

Is this so surprising? People must put food on the table. They want to live life with dignity. That most basic imperative may trump idealism- even in America.

The 2009 Pew survey also found that there was a consensus in many countries that ordinary people have benefited far less from the transition from communism than business owners and politicians. Russian politicians must take note.

Disillusionment with democracy and capitalism is not restricted to Eastern Europe, but can be found now far closer to home, as the Western middle class is hugely squeezed as prices for day to day items go up and wages stagnate or even decrease and enforced austerity measures take hold. Unemployment levels remain stubbornly high throughout the European Union, resulting in a resurgence of attacks on immigrants.

Hard working people watched their savings disappear when bank stocks collapsed and became worthless, while bank chiefs continued to earn million dollar salaries and huge bonuses for a job badly done.

Questions are being asked as to whether we have lost control of capitalism and whether the tail now wags the dog. Indeed, people all over Europe have said to me that they believe capitalism is a giant Ponzi scheme.

The financial services sector hid behind complexity for decades to keep the unwashed at bay. It was an effective ruse to protect old class structures and hide rampant inequities, greed and excess that would make the ancient Roman elite look parsimonious.

Complex, oblique language also served them well. They sold mystifyingly complex products with equally mystifying names that only geniuses could comprehend or explain to mere mortals. They were 'The Untouchables'- an elite whose feathers ought not to be ruffled lest their sensitive dispositions shatter, unleashing Armageddon upon the planet.

The culpability of the large US banks, in particular, for the current crisis is undeniable, yet barely a glove has been laid on them by regulators, excluding the odd low level sacrificial lamb- people financially unable to 'lawyer up' (i.e. fight back) like the Big Boys.

Egregious examples abound of huge US banks pushing heavily deodorized cow dung on clients, re-labelled Chanel No. 5, while betting against them at the back end. They displayed contempt for their customers, the life blood of such institutions: They were there to be 'shaken down,' no more and no less.

Unfortunately, their reach was global so the damage was not contained. There is evidence that such banks sold toxic debt and bad advice with equal enthusiasm to the German and Irish governments – and that Goldman Sachs helped the Greeks fudge the numbers to gain admission to the EU in the first place.

Complex products, complex laws, complex language, all hid a raft of unpalatable and simple facts, most particularly the fact that certain segments of the banking sector had been running amok for decades: The only thing that mattered was making the bonus pool larger.

Clients, the public, the law, regulators, they were all just pawns on the chess board- and the banks and their fleets of lawyers, lobbyists and spin doctors knew all the moves to ensure they won the game. Best of all, there was no referee.

Right now, to mitigate their damages, they are donning the hair shirt, professing regret for past wrongs, promising to do better. As soon as the dust settles, and memories fade, history attests that they will do it all over again.

However, I think ordinary people have woken up and they have started to see through the fog. People are now fully aware that insiders in the financial system have an edge that regular folk don't. Of course, there never was a level playing field (the dices were always loaded) but most people did not know this: Now they do. What they will do about it, however, remains to be seen.

By contrast, Russians have long held no illusions about their place in the order of things.

The ill-judged and mismanaged transition to a free market economy in the 1990s was a proximate and foreseeable cause of the breakdown in rule of law that allowed organized crime to get a firm grip on the country. In addition, forced austerity measures (the quid pro quo for loans from the IMF to try to plug the huge hole in state finances) starved the government of funds to pay for basic social services, with foreseeable results.

The law enforcement sector was demoralized and over-whelmed with the huge surge in crime. Police and ex-KGB officers moved to private security services that filled the burgeoning demand for protection. No-one had confidence in law enforcement or laws- they knew full well that neither would protect them.

Boris Yetsin had devolved power from the centre, allowing regional Governors huge leeway to do what they liked (including writing their own laws, which may or may not have respected Federal law) and withholding taxes, resulting in a catastrophic drop in tax revenue. Attempts to claw back desperately needed state revenue became gun battles with tax inspectors routinely shot and murdered. It was anarchy, pure and simple: Survival of the fittest.[112]

The economy descended into freefall and the ruble collapsed in 1994. Russian state debt of 38 billion had to be renegotiated in 1996. Yeltsin scrapped through to victory that same year, in highly dubious circumstances. Miners went on strike for wages arrears. The situation was grim. Russia was literally coming apart at the seams.

It was starved of inbound investment that never materialized as foreign investors gave the chaotic business environment a wide berth. The US economic miracle was a deadly chimera. The West made hay when the sun shone in Russia, and ran for the exits when it all went to hell in a hand basket.

As outlined in Part One, the decision to fire sale many hugely valuable and strategic state companies to individuals (like Berezovsky and Khodorkovsky) - with no interest in preserving them for future generations- resulted in asset stripping and fortunes secreted offshore.

State assets were used as collateral for loans to government that became de facto outright sales. Khodorkovsky's Menatep Bank got Yukos oil for $159 million- a company estimated to have been worth $7-10 billion. The infamous auctions became known as 'grabization'- a pun on 'privatization'[113].

Russian society, yet again, was brutalized by scarcity, violence, and the arbitrariness and unpredictability of day to day living.

Huge capital inflows from the West helped fuel the ensuing crisis. The Russian State defaulted on 40 billion of T-Bills on 17 August 1998- known as Black Monday- and Russia's credit rating disappeared off the side of a cliff, wiping out stock market valuations and people's savings. The end was hastened by the sudden plunge in oil prices, which sank to as little as 11 dollars a barrel in 1998 during the East Asian financial crisis.

Yeltsin resorted to printing money. Inflation peaked at 127 percent in July 1999 and caused great suffering, with queues for bread and widespread poverty. Lights went out in subway stations and on trains.

Not surprisingly, Yeltsin was hugely unpopular with the Russia people, but he hung onto power for dear life. Fist fights in parliament did not burnish the image of the institution in popular minds.

As the President became more erratic, he appointed a revolving door series of Prime Ministers and cabinet ministers. Wily businessmen, like Berezovsky, used the vast wealth they had acquired from the fire sale of hugely valuable state assets to keep Yeltsin in power. In the process, there is strong evidence to suggest that they took control of the body politic- a phenomenon sometimes called 'state-capture.'

Three month, high interest rate Treasury notes were issued to fund the burgeoning deficit. A World Bank loan couldn't save the situation. Small businesses went to the wall and banks were wiped out. Yeltsin's approval rating sank to 2%.

Under pressure from the IMF and World Bank, huge inflation was tackled with enforced austerity measures and Russia's GDP dropped to third world levels; the country lost its competitive advantage in areas where it had been on the cutting edge, such as aerospace, high-tech and electronics.

Once proud companies were shaved so tight they had to diversify into areas that were low margin and low value; equipment was obsolete and not fit for purpose. The agriculture sector was decimated. Western companies moved in where Russians companies lost out and Russians left the country in droves.

Life expectancy decreased, infant mortality increased, and health levels plummeted. Prostitution was rife and the AIDs infection as well as old diseases like TB took hold or made an aggressive come-back.[114]

For the average person, life was wretched and huge numbers sank below the official poverty line. Wages were often unpaid, in some cases barter was offered for labour (vodka or toilet paper instead of cash[115]) and wages were pitiful in any event. The situation was a perfect breeding ground for a thriving black market economy, in which bribe seeking and taking became an integral part of daily life.

Yeltsin made Putin Prime Minister (the 5th in two years) in August 1999. In my mind, in light of the pitiful state of his inheritance, it is incontrovertible that Putin rose to the occasion in rather spectacular fashion. Without him, it appears entirely likely that Russia would have sunk further and further into the mire.

The era of chaos left a resounding impression on those who lived through it. The fact that it was Putin who brought prosperity and order in its wake has not been forgotten: The Strong Man delivered what raw capitalism and democracy had not.

Putin brought a singular focus and discipline to the role of President that was chronically lacking in his predecessors: Let there be no mistake, the Russia people loved him for it. He'd thrown the drowning, sick (but exceptionally resilient) patient a life jacket and pulled it to shore.

The poorly considered, rapidly orchestrated break-up of the fifteen USSR Republics in 1991 cut Russian companies off from their traditional markets and supply chains disappeared. Imagine the EU breaking up overnight (no longer so unimaginable) with each country going its own way: the USSR's single economic zone was shattered in one fell swoop.

In April 2005, Putin described it as 'the greatest geopolitical catastrophe of the twentieth century.' Polls taken in 2001 showed that as many as 79% of the Russian population similarly regretted the breakup.[116]The 2009 Pew survey found that 58% of Russians agreed it is a great misfortune that the Soviet Union no longer exists. Nearly half (47%) say it is natural for Russia to have an empire.[117]

In the rush to 'democratize.' it appears that little thought was given to the momentous repercussions of sundering an empire apart. The economic impact alone was guaranteed to be severe. However, reason and logic took a back seat to reformist zeal. Veneration of US neo-liberal, free market economic principles positively guaranteed a very hard landing for the beleaguered Russian people.

I should point out that many reputable economists and political theorists hotly dispute this version of events. They argue that there was no alternative to 'shock therapy' as there was a real danger that the communists would regain power if swift action was not taken. They also deny that Western collaborators wanted to see a weakened Russia emerge from the embers of Soviet power.

I am no economist, so it is fruitless to debate the 'right or the wrong' of what occurred from an economic perspective. However, my focus in this book is on the plight of the Russian people, and I believe it is incontrovertible that regardless of the merit or rationale (much disputed) for the manner in which the transition was handled, the Russian people suffered horribly as a result. It is also clear that many wily Russians and Westerners alike made a great deal of money in the process.

As always, the Russian people paid dearly for what I believe was the short-sightedness of the Russian political elite (in tandem with fleets of Western advisors): It didn't seem to matter whether they were Stalinists or democrats: They botched it, over and over again. If Russians are cynical about politics, they have good cause.

Although many separated willingly, millions of Russian had no say in the dissolution of the USSR and approximately 25 million ethnic Russians live outside Russia in the 'near abroad.'

By no means is it the case, as the Western media suggests, that all people in the Republics were desperate to escape the clutches of Mother Russia. Ethnic Russians trapped behind new borders appealed for assistance, and in some cases remain poorly treated minorities, not embraced by their new masters.

Putin has deplored what he believes to be the fact that Russians are deprived of their rights in Estonia and Latvia where they are a sizeable minority but often complain they are treated like second class citizens. Latvians recently voted to refuse the Russian language official status.

Putin's much maligned efforts to restore economic ties in the region are entirely rational; other emerging markets such as Brazil are keen to form local alliances and making concerted efforts to do so.

Russia, Belarus and Kazakhstan have created a customs union with Russia as of July 1, 2011, allowing foreign companies that manufacture in one of the member countries to move product around the customs union duty-free. The union represents circa 82 percent of the former Soviet territory, and, in that regard, is by no mean insignificant.

Putin has described the endeavour as an important attempt to rebuild economic ties severed by the Soviet breakup. Although the Western media have lambasted his efforts, senior executives at several Western manufacturing companies are enthusiastic for pragmatic reasons- the union makes their products more affordable to customers in the region.

The Moscow Times has reported that the transition to paperless clearance by the Russian Federal Customs Service has been a big boon for businesses, cutting down on red tape and bureaucracy. Gaps in the VAT rules and legal lacunae are being addressed. Progress has been unusually swift: The project took just over three years to realize, from its inception in 2007. Western businesses are impressed with the speed of progress, demonstrating that Russia is fully capable of instigating change.

As soon as the USSR came apart, the US wasted no time in marshalling the lost sheep onside, using hard cash and influence to rapidly Americanize the old Soviet Republics, in effect surrounding Russia with pro-American allies, and doing all it could to encourage fledgling revolutions to finish off the process.

Eastern European countries and even the old Soviet republics were encouraged to join NATO, Russia's old Cold War nemesis. On 12 March 1999, the Czech Republic, Hungary and Poland became the first former members of the Warsaw Pact to join NATO. On 29 March 2004, Bulgaria, Estonia, Latvia, Lithuania, Romania and Slovakia and Slovenia followed suit, with Albania and Croatia joining on 1 April 2009.

Bill Clinton administration's most important foreign-policy initiative was NATO enlargement- a concept utterly anathema to the post-Cold War world and deeply alarming to the Russians who view it simply as an effort by the US to encircle them.

More recently, in January 2010, US Secretary of State Hillary Clinton defended NATO expansion, but described Russia as no longer an adversary, but 'a partner.' Her perspective as to how one treats and engenders trust with a partner is markedly different than mine.

She reiterated that the US won't recognize Russia's claims of independence for Abkhazia and South Ossetia (the Russian protectorates at the centre of the 2008 Georgian war) grandstanding with quintessential US flair- 'More broadly we object to any spheres of influence claimed in Europe in which one country seeks to control another's future.'

She made no reference to persistent efforts by the US to do just that. Columbia is but one example. US politicians seem deaf to how arrogant and double-dealing these statements sound to the Russians.

NATO was formed as a defensive military alliance to protect Western Europe against the Soviet threat. When the Soviet Union disintegrated in 1991, it had to justify its continued existence, expanding its remit from defence to include economic development, human rights, territorial disputes- some Westerners view it as newly focused on 'interventionism' rather than defence.

When it bombed Kosovo in March 1999, it did so in breach of its own charter (and notably without approval from the UN Security Council) as the country had not attacked or threatened a NATO member state. NATO argued that it was justified to act on the basis it was an 'international humanitarian emergency.'

The matter was brought before the UN Security Council by Russia, in a draft resolution which sought to affirm 'that such unilateral use of force constitutes a flagrant violation of the United Nations Charter.' China, Namibia, and Russia voted for the resolution, but it failed to pass.

The conduct of the 'war' was less than humanitarian, as it invariably is.

Ugly weapons such as cluster bombs were used and industrial targets- all state owned- were devastated- causing significant economic and environmental damage. The Serbian TV headquarters in Belgrade was bombed on April 23, 1999, killing 16 people and injuring a similar number. Amnesty International described this strike on a civilian target as a war crime.

When the Chinese embassy was bombed in Belgrade, Chinese Premier Jiang Zemin accused the US of a new form of colonialism, describing the attack as a pretext to aggressively expand its influence and interfere in the internal affairs of other sovereign nations. This statement closely mirrored Russian views and certainly frames Putin's view of the West.

Subsequent events confirmed his view as Russia's reluctant agreement to approve the imposition of a no-fly zone over Libya in March 2011 morphed into full scale war. This development was another example of 'mission creep.'

In conjunction with the Kosovo affair, the Libyan war convinced many emerging markets (by no means only the Russians) that the US and its allies will intervene militarily in the affairs of other sovereign nations, as it sees fit, without reference to the rules. The West's interest in 'resolving' the Syrian crisis is viewed by Putin in a similar vein.

The Chinese and Russians also, for good reason, have serious concerns about the upsurge in Islamic fundamentalism in their regions, and a well-founded belief that the West's enthusiasm for 'regime change' merely results in installing extremists that pose a threat to both their borders and business interests. The Russians, in turn, have no love for the Saudis - a key US and UK ally-as they believe that they fund Islamic terrorists in Chechnya.

There has also been an exponential increase in illegal drug flows, as narcotic sales are used by extremists and other criminal elements to fund their activities. This problem is especially acute in Afghanistan- with drug flows pouring across Russian borders.

I have read disturbing media reports that suggest NATO expansion protects us 'in case Russia goes back to its bad old ways.' But when did Russia attack the West or the US? The Russians fought and died with us in droves in World War Two: Russia has been our ally, not our enemy. We seem to suffer from selective memory syndrome. The idea that Russia poses a threat to the West is simply preposterous.

In the West, we are experts at 'talking ourselves up.' Unfortunately, we talk the Russians down with equal enthusiasm. Indeed, from the Russian perspective, nothing seems to suffice to defuse the old hostilities. Trying to emulate us brought them to the edge of financial and social oblivion in the 1990's, so if they have little appetite to become a Western clone, who could blame them?

Actions speak louder than words and to the proud Russians our offers of friendship ring hollow. We keep a big stick in reserve to beat them with- 'just in case.' How can mutual trust emerge from such a warped dynamic?

The fact is, however, that neither the EU nor the US accept Russia as a friend. The UK, in particular, seems focused on confrontation rather than co-operation- a stance that does the rest of Europe few favours.

Some of this antipathy towards Russia has historic roots. As stated by Gregory Freeze in *Russia-A History,*[118] edited by him, 'the media, politicians and even many scholars regard Russia with a mixture of condescension, antipathy and fear.'

Mr Freeze points out that for 'those predisposed to characterise Russia as a threat to Civilisation.'.'the pervasive antipathy is often dismissive of the favourable dimensions of the Russian experience; a Russophobic tone too often becomes the default, reinforcing ill-informed stereotypes of omnipotent authoritarianism, backwardness and alcoholism.'

As we have seen, reputable media outlets constantly reinforce these stereotypes.

Mr Freeze points out that 'these stereotypes have deep historic roots, dating back to the sixteenth-century travellers' accounts, but only come to dominate popular images of Russia in the modern period, which were shaped by anti-Russian diatribes in the mass media of the nineteenth century, and, far more profoundly by the ideological battles of the twentieth century and the Cold War.'

I discuss stereotypes at more length in Part Four. However, Freeze also wrote that until recently, historical scholarship on Russia has done too little to correct politicised stereotypes of Russia, to produce a more balanced, better informed picture. 'Scholarly studies of Russia, in fact, appeared rather belatedly, most of them after the Second World War, and long bore the taint and distortions of the Cold War.'

Max Hastings, in a review in The Sunday Times Magazine of a book by Orlando Figes on the Crimean War,[119]noted that it was the first war in history that was launched to 'appease British public sentiment (media-inspired paranoia) about Russia.'..rather than in pursuit of any 'coherent national purpose.'

I was disappointed, however, to read a recent book review by Hastings in which, as a throwaway line, he describes Russia as 'a gangster state.' The formula has a tight grip on the UK press corps, including highly respected historians and journalists such as Hastings.

Historians advise that there was a significant xenophobic aspect to the Crimean War, as Britain and France sought to contain Russia and protect their 'spheres of influence' in the region- a charge frequently levelled by the UK media against Russia. Yet Britain, in its colonial heyday, made no bones about expanding its territory through force of arms.

In addition, some of the antipathy towards Russia has racist origins, as many Western politicians have long considered Russia an Asiatic power. In 1940, Stalin is believed to have commented that the Russians were an 'Asiatic' people, and in 1941, he is reported to have told the Japanese Foreign Minister, 'You are an Asian, so am I.'[120]

What difference would that make, you might ask?

Racist beliefs about Easterners and other 'non-whites' run deep in the West, ingrained over centuries. These sentiments were used to justify appalling violence and cruelty in wars of colonisation, e.g. the savage aggression displayed by 'civilized' Westerners towards native American Indians, and enabled us assuage our conscience as Europeans massacred and subjugated the native populations of the New World, taking from them what was rightfully theirs.

Racist dogma, pseudo science and a gratifying superiority complex in most every respect allowed Westerners disguise the patently economic imperative for the slave trade and colonial expansion more generally.

In his wonderful, albeit hugely dispiriting book about the Allied battle for the Pacific in the Second World War, US academic, John W. Dower,[121]lays bare the unpalatable fact that the Allies viewed the Second World War as 'a race war'- and disparaged the Chinese even though they were on our side.

Our mistreatment of the Chinese goes back a long way. Chinese –Americans, who built the US railroads, and died in droves doing so, were treated cruelly by white settlers in the late nineteenth century. In 1879, California's new state constitution denied suffrage to all 'natives of China, idiots and insane persons.'[122]

American native Indians fared little better. Dower points out that the US Declaration of Independence 'enshrined the phrase 'merciless Indian savages' and the First President of the US described native Indians as 'beasts of prey.'[123]

Before he became President, in a speech in 1886, Theodore Roosevelt said, 'I don't go so far as to think that the only good Indians are dead Indians, but I believe nine out of every ten are, and I shouldn't inquire too closely into the case of the tenth. The most vicious cowboy has more moral principle than the average Indian.'[124]

Similarly, Roosevelt described the US victory in the Philippines as 'a triumph of civilization over 'the black chaos of savagery and barbarism.' As for Asians, they were the 'Yellow Peril.' Dower describes how Winston Churchill was also 'inordinately fond of the racial slurs that were guaranteed to alienate Asian people. His Chinese allies remained 'little yellow men' to him.'

Lord Halifax, the British Foreign Secretary insulted his Chinese allies by describing the war in the Pacific as 'a struggle to save Christian civilization.' Dower described how a Chinese professor wrote to an American magazine pointing out the obvious- namely 'that the most destructive wars in the world's history have been waged by the Christian countries.'[125]

The enemy- the Japanese- were casually described by the Western media, Western politicians and the general public alike as 'yellow bastards' and 'yellow monkeys.' In American newsreels, they were sometimes simply described as 'the LYBs' – shorthand for 'yellowbellies.'[126] Other labels included 'gooks,' slant-eyed, and 'Slopies'- a favourite GI slur.

However, the belligerent, racist, Western slurs against the people of Asia disguised a deep Western fear that 'the Yellow Peril' would advance on Europe and the Western Hemisphere to dish out a spot of richly deserved comeuppance.

The fact that the Japanese showed technical acumen and military might in the war added to the sense of paranoia; there were fears that the pupil was gaining ground on his master and that he might one day out-wit and out-gun him.

The notion that the Chinese might ultimately 'join the enemy camp' was considered unthinkable[127]. US paranoia, scare-mongering and overt racism towards the Chinese, was, however (as it is now) tempered with enthusiasm for the potential for China to become an economic power-house, and 'the only post-war market for American manufactured goods.'[128]

However, pragmatism aside, fear remained that even in defeat Japan might pose a threat to white, Western supremacy as the potential existed for the Asian countries to combine forces to defeat what they considered (quite rightly) to be racist Western imperialism towards them. Western politicians mused that the Third World War might be a race war that whites might lose.

Even worse, as relations with Russia rapidly deteriorated after the war, it was feared, as Dower described it, that 'the race war and the struggle between Russia and the West, were not in fact mutually exclusive. On the contrary, one could easily envisage the two conflicts becoming one.' There was concern (as there is now, although we avoid overtly racist language in expressing it) that 'white supremacy was imperilled.[129]'

In light of the fact that Stalin himself had reputedly described Russia as an 'Asiatic' country' Western paranoia deepened; there was fear and dread at the prospect that the 'revolt against white imperialism beginning in Asia and spreading to other parts of the globe would receive Moscow's support.'

Dower wrote that 'as World War Two built to its ferocious climax, the vision of a Yellow Peril and a Red Peril began, at least for some observers, to fuse in an absolutely overpowering way.' The spectre of the 'hate-infuriated colored warriors' (equipped with Russian fire-power) determined to 'wreak vengeance for the thousands of injustices heaped upon their people' loomed large.

As matters stand, however, and as I will discuss in this Part, the Yellow and Red Perils (although it is the Chinese who remain both Yellow and Red) - did not have to lay a glove on us to usher in our demise: That, we were well capable of doing for ourselves. Ironically, both the US and Europe are currently authors of their own misfortune, through greed and hubris and looking to the East for salvation.

Writing in 1986, Dower pointed out a singularly unpalatable fact that is remarkably prescient in light of current events, namely that our past does us shame, that we have very little to boast about, or moral high ground to claim.

He noted how the West's huge historical focus on the Holocaust (understandable by virtue of the sheer monstrousness of the evils perpetrated by the Nazis on the Jews and other vulnerable minorities, including the disabled and mentally challenged) has, however, allowed us paper-over our own misdeeds during that period.

He wrote that the critique of Nazi racism 'had a double edge, for it exposed the hypocrisy of the Western Allies. Anti-Semitism was but one manifestation of the racism that existed at all levels in the United States and the United Kingdom.

Even while denouncing Nazi theories of 'Aryan' supremacy, the US government presided over a society where blacks were subjected to demeaning Jim Crow laws, segregation was imposed even in the military establishment, racial discrimination extended to the defense industries, and immigration policy was severely biased against all nonwhites.'[130]

Dower's blunt indictment is unanswerable, yet rarely voiced in our 'free' society. We are far more accustomed, as they say, to dishing it rather than taking it.

He also noted that *Executive Order 9066* signed by Roosevelt on February 19, 1942 caused the internment of 110,000 Japanese-Americans in ten camps throughout the US. These people, including bona fide American citizens were kept in appalling, degrading conditions, in filthy horse stables and pig pens that stank of manure, forced to sleep on straw beds-all because of their ethnicity. The only saving grace, as Dower observed, was the dignified response of those incarcerated[131].

The hacks at the LA Times adopted what Dower describes as 'blood-will- tell racism' to justify this atrocity, writing that 'A viper is nonetheless a viper wherever the egg is hatched-so a Japanese-American, born of Japanese parents, grows up to be a Japanese, not an American.' [132]

After the war, in giving testimony to a Congressional committee, Lieutenant General John L.De Witt, Commander of the Western Defense Command, in charge of the 'evacuation' said that he 'was not worried about German or Italian nationals, 'but the Japs we will be worried about all the time until they are wiped off the face of the map.'[133]

However, back then, our lack of humanity, racism, and flagrant disrespect for rule of law did not go un-noticed. Chinese and Indian people deplored the double-standards inherent in a political stance that found them fit to fight- and die- in the Western cause, but denied them the right to US citizenship. Black folk spoke openly about the inequity inherent in fighting the white man's wars.

The Western media, sadly, were not fearless defenders of the under-classes, the oppressed and the racially stigmatized. No, they stoked the fires of hate. The Hearst newspapers 'declared the war in Asia totally different from that in Europe, for Japan was a 'racial menace' as well as a cultural and religious one.'[134]

As Dower noted, 'Cartoonists, songwriters, filmmakers, war correspondents, and the mass media in general all seized on these images (of the Japanese as apes, vermin, subhuman)- and so did the social scientists and Asia experts who ventured to analyze the Japanese 'national character' during the war.'

In a great many respects, this hostility, this dehumanization of the Japanese by every arm of the Western 'machine' was strikingly similar to Goebbels campaign against the Jews. The imagery used was designed to paint the enemy as 'not human, 'not like us.' thus making him or her, man, woman or child far easier to kill with an easy conscience.

The Japanese, likewise, used propaganda to incite hatred and fear of allied troops amongst Japanese soldiers and the general population, who in some instances committed suicide en masse rather than be taken prisoner by 'demonic' allied soldiers. War is an ugly business and all sides waged a nasty propaganda campaign against the enemy. However, we had the edge in doing so.

As Dower pointed out, the Japanese were far more hated, even before Pearl Harbor, than the Nazis or Germans ever were, as the latter were still white Anglo-Saxons, not savage 'yellow men' of Asiatic descent.

Hence, the enduring concept of 'The Good German,' even as the full horror of the Nazi death camps was brought to light; created and sustained by precise, near military operations on a massive scale not easily hidden from view. The Nazis had the tacit, if not the overt support or acquiescence of a sizeable proportion of the German population. Yet, Anglo-Saxon sensibilities demanded that there be 'Good Germans.'

By contrast, as Western military leaders and politicians were quick to point out, the only 'Good Japs' were 'Dead Japs.' The dehumanization of the Japanese by the Western propaganda machine contributed in no small part to the decision to drop a nuclear bomb on a civilian population, an act that was, in my mind, a war crime of momentous proportions, for which no-one has ever been held to account.

It is rarely even discussed; it's water under the bridge, our dirty little secret, albeit hidden in plain view. Yet, the Americans vigorously prosecuted Japanese prisoners in war-crimes trials in Japan, accusing them of atrocities that arguably paled into relative insignificance when compared to the devastation and suffering wrought by the dropping of the nuclear bombs on helpless civilians.

US historian, James J. Weingartner, has stated[135] that one of the reasons for the US decision to drop a nuclear bomb on the civilian population of Hiroshima and Nagasaki was the dehumanization of the Japanese: 'The widespread image of the Japanese as sub-human constituted an emotional context which provided another justification for decisions which resulted in the death of hundreds of thousands.'

After the bombings, US President Truman stated: 'The only language they seem to understand is the one we have been using to bombard them. When you have to deal with a beast you have to treat him like a beast. It is most regrettable but nevertheless true.'

A fine example of intelligent people using ugly words to justify heinous crimes.

However, the US politicians and censors took no chances, by exposing the American people to images of the aftermath. For decades after the Second World War, American censors ensured that Americans were not shown pictures of the impact of the attacks on Hiroshima and Nagasaki, or told that children were cooked alive where they stood, leaving nothing but the mangled remains of their metal lunch boxes to indicate that they had ever existed.

In his book, Dower noted that technological 'advances' made it easier than ever before to kill vast numbers of people, from a distance without the need for physical contact. Even worse, the old fashioned notion that civilians were not viable military targets quietly disappeared from the lexicon, and millions of Japanese citizens were specifically targeted, with devastating effect.

The 'rules of war' were de facto no more, or lobotomized to a significant extent. Some more old fashioned military commanders did find this an unsavoury proposition, but stereotyping the enemy helped salve the conscience-killing apes and vermin were a different proposition than men, women and children.

I recall in more recent times, media commentary about guided missiles 'reaching their target' in Iraq, and the use of vague but colourful metaphors that completely depersonalized the attacks, and fastidiously avoided any allusion that human beings, often in their thousands-civilians included-had simply been wiped off the face of the earth, or left scarred for life.

One advantage of hand to hand conflict, a harrowing experience endured by millions of Russians who fought the Nazi scourge in Stalingrad- is that looking into the eyes of a fellow human people you must kill, or be killed, concentrates the mind very keenly on the meaning of war, in a way that hitting the button marked- 'self-guided missile' does not.

Now that we have automated war, making it akin to a technological imperative, we lack the crucial connection with consequences that may make us think twice about our actions. This is not progress, whatever spin militarists and defence industry contractors want to put on it. In his book *The Nazi Doctors*, psychologist Robert Jay Lifton observed that 'The unfortunate truth is that people can all too readily be socialised to killing'- even genocide. I do not doubt it for a second.

Some historians believe that the Hiroshima bomb and indeed Nagasaki were dropped by Truman as a warning to the Soviets not to move further into the East, as they planned an invasion of Japan. It was, they argue, a sign of force that started the nuclear arms race that was unnecessary in any event, as the Japanese were already defeated.

As our media and politicians currently agonize about whether the Iranians have, or might acquire the ability to make a nuclear device, I am always struck by the fact that the only country to have ever actually used such a devastating weapon is the US - and that it did so against a helpless civilian population. Ought that fact alone not teach us a little humility?

I do not under-estimate or denigrate Israel's genuine fear of some of its Arab and Islamic neighbours (who deny it the right to even exist), but I fear that scare-mongering, religion run amok, political grand-standing and the West's desire to remain relevant in a new world order, will cast us into the abyss.

Bigotry and racism aside, politicians have rarely showed talent at spotting new threats and planning accordingly. The new global enemy is clearly not Russia- unless we make it so.

The financial crisis has shown us, without any doubt, that complex and poorly understood inter-dependencies exist between nation states and that none of us can go it alone.

Indeed, the new enemy may not be any nation state at all, as outlined in Part One. It likely has no obvious face or leader: It is international terrorism, cyber crime, and a host of challenges, including pandemics, massive food, water and natural resource shortages, climate change, ageing populations, protectionism, sky high commodity prices and inflation, huge unemployment and widespread disenchantment.

Many of these threats, including global terrorism and cyber crime have no borders. International co-operation at a level that we have not seen to date will be necessary to have any hope to stem the tide of terrorism and to address borderless crimes that affect us all. Finger pointing and xenophobia have little place in this modern world.

Cold War thinking and Western colonial condescension towards emerging and developing countries is holding us back. We are still stuck in the past, at a time when we must plan for the future- to ensure we have one.

Russian politicians have good reason to view NATO not as a defensive alliance (that the US can ill afford) but as a body that exists to support the foreign policies of Western democracies- including regime change, as occurred in Libya after the public lynching of Gaddafi- an inauspicious start to ostensible Western efforts to promote rule of law in the country.

US Republican politician John McCain's threat to Putin, to the effect that he better watch his back, or get similar treatment (to Gadaffi) was received with incredulity and horror in Russia. In the circumstances, Putin's response to such extreme and crude provocation has been remarkably restrained.

US hawks such as George Bush's national security advisor, Condoleezza Rice, have been quoted as describing Russia as 'a threat to the West in general and to our European allies in particular.' Yet the likes of Rice and her Cold War cohort are now inexplicably lauded by the BBC as providing substance to demonstrably biased TV reports about Putin and Russia.

As matters now stand in US politics, reason and objectivity are trumped by political triumphalism. However, insulting politicians in emerging markets is not in the best interest of US businesses chasing growth abroad. It is unclear, however, whether pragmatism will prevail on all sides of the political divide

NATO enlargement around Russia serves no purpose other than to makes it geopolitically isolated, which is most inadvisable. We need to embrace Russia, not antagonise or bait it every chance we get for reasons unknown, except sheer bloody-mindedness. I will also suggest that we may ultimately (if we stopped for a minute to consider the matter) need the Russians far more than they need us.

Russia has quite legitimately expressed concern that if a conflict broke out between NATO and Russia, NATO would have a significant advantage by launching an attack against it from close to its borders in NATO member countries, Poland and Hungary.

Thankfully, plans to admit Ukrainian and Georgia are currently on ice. The Ukrainian election of an ostensibly pro-Russian President in 2010 was definitive: For now. The 2009 Pew Research survey found that 51% of Ukrainians oppose joining and majorities in Ukraine (51%) and Russia (58%) expressed unfavorable opinions of NATO[136].

In 2008, both countries were, however, given assurances by the West that they would be eventually admitted.

Since the 2008 Georgian war, the Russians have worried about the fickleness of the West, its 'fair-weather friend.' and noted how they are never given the benefit of the doubt as the West assumed, without possession of the facts (and even after acquiring them) that Russia was the aggressor-the inevitable rush to judgment in evidence yet again.

If Georgia had been a NATO member in 2008, would NATO have gone to Georgia's 'defense'? I, for one, have no difficulty, having read profoundly belligerent Western media coverage of the brief war, as discussed in Part One, in understanding Russia's concern. The precedent set in Yugoslavia and Libya (and possibly now Syria) is hardly reassuring.

After the Soviet Union collapsed, two regions, comprised of non-Georgians with a close affinity to Russia, formed autonomous regions in Abkhazia and South Ossetia. From the early 1990's, with relations tense with Georgia and its President, Mikhail Saakashvili, Russian peacekeepers enabled these territories remain autonomous.

South Ossetia declared independence from Georgia in 1990, affirming its position as a Republic within the USSR, but the Georgians refused to recognize this action. After a bloody conflict in 1991, a ceasefire was called by Georgia in 1992, but tensions and fighting remained a constant threat.

On August 8, 2008, with the expectation of US support, Georgia attacked South Ossetia with tanks, heavy artillery and air support, killing twelve Russian peacekeepers and injuring many more. The Georgian met with fierce Russian resistance, and speedy defeat.

Russia, Nicaragua and Venezuela (and no-one else) subsequently recognized the independence of both South Ossetia and another breakaway region, Abkhazia. The West refused to recognize over-whelming South Ossetian support for independence in a (second) referendum in 2006.

There is compelling evidence (denied in the West) to suggest that the Georgians- helped by the West- have tried covertly and otherwise to make life tough in the breakaway regions, isolating them both economically and politically, and using visa restrictions to choke both trade and travel.

As I have tried to demonstrate in Part One, Russia's defence of both territories unleashed the most vicious attacks on it by the Western media and politicians. The UK's response was little short of extraordinary, frequently descending into hysteria and zealotry. UK politicians were vocal in their support for a 'hard line' with Russia, but fortunately more rational minds prevailed.

The 'colour' revolutions in Georgia, 2003, Ukraine 2004 and Kyrgystan in 2005 were supported by US funded NGOs that brought to power US-friendly politicians that had acrimonious relations with Russia.

In 2005, the US awarded 85 million dollars to a number of Russian based organizations to support 'democratization'- a codeword for regime change, but this time in Russia itself.[137]Putin's dislike of foreign NGOs that surreptitiously work to ferment 'revolution' in Russia is well-known and largely justified.

He has referred to them as 'pseudo-NGOs, agencies that 'try to destabilize other countries with outside support.' The Western media dismiss this charge as mere paranoia, but Western (mainly US) NGOs played a significant role in replacing governments in the Ukraine and Georgia with US allies, donating not just moral but financial support to 'the cause.'

Putin views such actions, denied by the US - although frequently conducted in plain view- as hostile acts. Putin's move to restrict and regulate their activities is described by the Western media as evidence of his authoritarian tendencies, yet such blatant interference in the affairs of a sovereign would never be tolerated in the West.

Proselytizing democracy is viewed by Putin as a form of Western colonialism and cover for the promotion of vested interests. Certainly, many Western politicians seem more concerned about democracy and rule of law in Russia than they are about similar issues at home.

Putin has repeatedly stated that Russia will determine its own fate and the pace and nature of democratic change, and it will not be dictated to. No Western nation, similarly provoked, would take it kindly. The Russians, however, are expected to always turn the other cheek.

The Russian Foreign Minister, Sergei Lavrov told NATO that there would be no progress on NATO-Russia relations as long as NATO does not listen to Russia's concerns. The NATO-Russia Council established in Rome in 2002 was a half-baked attempt to mollify the Russians. The whole enlargement issue has been a disaster for Western-Russian relations. We only have ourselves to blame.

Gallup polls conducted in 2008 and 2009 found that nearly 50% of Russians and Belarusians consider NATO a threat to their countries as do countries with traditionally close ties to Russia.

Encircling Russia wasn't enough, we had to twist the knife a bit deeper, with the US insisting it would deploy a Star Wars style national missile defence (NMD) system-an idea concocted in the 1980's, in NATO member countries, purportedly to counter threats from 'rogue' states believed to be developing nuclear weapons.

As US historian Gregory Freeze has pointed out[138], NMD 'not only violated the 1972 Anti-Ballistic Missile Treaty.. but also created the spectre that subsequent developments could neutralize Chinese and ultimately Russian deterrence.'

The US's insistence to plough ahead with NMD and to place it in Poland and/or Czechoslovakia- close to Russian borders is madness. I am perplexed as to why Europe is so quick to facilitate the Americans in this fashion. It also undermines, possibly even jeopardizes serious achievements to date in the sphere of nuclear disarmament-most of the world's nuclear arsenal is held by the US and Russia.

Medvedev indicated that the Russians may upgrade Russian air and space defences to counteract such a threat. The Kremlin maintains that the action threatens Russia' defences and has sought a legal guarantee that the missiles will not be directed against it.

The Moscow Times quoted Medvedev as saying that assurances that the system is not aimed against Russian nuclear forces must be 'affirmed not in a friendly chat over a cup of tea or a glass of wine but in a document.'

'No one has explained to me why we should believe that the new missile defence system in Europe isn't directed against us,' Medvedev said at a security conference. NATO has expressed the desire to cooperate with Russia on the issue, but has rejected Moscow's proposal to jointly run it.

Russian Deputy Prime Minister Dmitry Rogozin (previously Russian ambassador to Nato), cut to the chase with commendable logic, according to the Moscow Times, observing that 'Those who are smart know that the defensive arms race is no better than the offensive arms race. Strengthening of the shield entails strengthening of the sword.'

These provocations were not subtle, despite the spin put on them by the US and EU media and Western politicians. However, on September 19, 2009, in a welcome policy U-Turn, Obama announced he was scrapping the initiative.[139] Medvedev described the news as 'positive.' Putin said it was a 'correct and brave' move. It seemed to spell hope for the reset- although US Republicans such as John McCain predictably described the decision as 'seriously misguided.'

However, incredibly, in 2010, tensions rapidly resumed when the US Secretary of State, Hillary Clinton, signed an agreement with Poland to use an airstrip near the Baltic coast as a missile defence base. I was utterly baffled by this turnabout. It undoubtedly seems like a betrayal to the Russians, who feel they were 'had.' Clinton said the door was open for Russia to take part in the US's missile defence plans, but indicated that the Russians had not 'responded positively.'

To stick the knife in even further, reports indicate that the Americans are interested in Poland's shale gas deposits, intimating that if the Poles find rich reserves, it might allow Europe to 'diversify' away from Russian gas. Clinton has also been quoted trying to inveigle the Ukraine to join NATO.

In retaliation, Russia commissioned a radar system in Kaliningrad in the Baltic, capable of monitoring and responding to missile launches from Europe and the North Atlantic. To the Russians, what the Americans give with one hand, they rapidly take back with the other.

Where this silliness will end is anyone's guess.

Not surprisingly, Putin intends to equip the Russian military to ensure it can protect Russia, with an allocation of 'approximately 23 trillion rubles for these needs over the next decade.' It is doubtful that such large amounts of money will be spent at this juncture, but Putin won't abandon the armed forces.

The Western media deride his aspirations in this regard, on the basis that no threat to Russia exists. If that was true, and the world really was a safe place, the US and China would disarm. I imagine that eventuality will not occur any time soon, and it would be reckless folly for him to assume it will.

He also refers to the Arctic region (brim full of natural resources) and notes that 'The leading military powers have intensified their activities in the Arctic, which forces Russia to secure its interests in the region.'

This is an accurate statement of fact. Putin clearly views himself and Russia as under siege- an impression we in the West have done little to dispel. On the contrary, we have given him good reason to take every precaution. Our media's enthusiasm for a 'Russian Spring' (the Wall Street Journal) that would inevitably tear Russia apart was bald-faced, with ferocious personal attacks on Putin de rigueur.

As well as current threats to Russian national security, Putin believes that Russia must look to the future- to 'estimate threats for 30-50 years ahead.'

In response to ex-Finance minister Kudrin's concern that the initiative to rebuild the military will be too costly, he writes 'I strongly believe that we have enough resources and we can afford it.' He believes that 'more delay cannot be tolerated to compensate for years of underfunding, with 'officers unpaid for months.'

He affirms his commitment to increase military wages, social benefits and improve military housing, to grant military retirees privileged access to further education, and to reform military education in partnership with the private sector.

He pays tribute to the armed forces and admonishes those who insult servicemen and the institution. He considers insults to the forces as 'a real moral crime and an act of betrayal.'..'you must treasure the Armed Forces. You have to strengthen them; otherwise, you will have to 'feed somebody else's army' or even be enslaved by bandits and international terrorists.'

Tough talk, but by US Republican party standards, such patriotic utterances are positively lame. His candour will resonate with many Russians, especially the older generation.

From the time he was first elected in 2000, Putin expounded he view that patriotism is the glue that holds Russia's huge territory together, especially in hard times. He has spoken of 'national pride and dignity' as essential components of Russia's national identity.

Chapter Seven

The Western Sickness

The Western media often treats Russia like a special case, belittling it when it expresses frustration with the West. However, Russia is not alone in feeling hard-done by. This sentiment is shared by emerging and developing countries, including China.

What are these sources of irritation, besides our history of bigotry, racism and colonial aggression towards many of them? Currently, the issue of Western double-standards looms large.

A current source of rancour is the fact that the US created the current financial crisis and then exported it around the world. Yet the US media, and US politicians, behave as if the whole mess has nothing to do with them, even lecturing the EU on getting its house in order, a stance that infuriates EU politicians, grappling with one of the worst crisis in memory.

The fact the US seems oblivious and uncaring about the harm it has caused ordinary people around the world has not gone unnoticed. To make matters worse, that fact that US politicians wasted no time in throwing the rule book out the window in dealing with the crisis at home has made a strong impression on emerging markets, long accustomed to US criticism that they lack safeguards and mechanisms to prevent 'moral hazard.'

When Lehman Brothers collapsed, however, US fears about moral hazard (roughly speaking, the notion that no entity should feel they will be bailed out come what may) were instantly forgotten. This reaction to a domestic crisis is viewed as a good example of US double-dealing and hypocrisy.

Emerging markets have not forgotten old 'humiliations' suffered at Western hands.

As I have highlighted, the Western media routinely mock, and even seem to derive pleasure from Russian feelings in this regard, but the sentiment is genuine and deep. The fact remains that when emerging markets and developing countries experienced economic hard times, analogous to the current crisis, they received very different treatment from the West than US politicians have dished out at home.

Ironically, this dichotomy may not apply to Europe. Austerity measures that would never pass muster in the US are now being doled out to Europeans by the IMF and EU Institutions (the so-called Troika), similar to those used, with disastrous results, during the 1982 Mexican crisis, the Asian crisis in 1997, the Russian default in 1998, and the Argentine meltdown in 2002.

In all these cases, people suffered cruelly as politicians accepted extraordinary loan terms from international organisations such as the IMF. The Chinese and Indians have avoided the IMF and prospered. However, Asians countries that did not, recall the pain the West inflicted on them as a quid pro quo for loan packages.

In many instances, the Western cure was worse than the disease. Mexicans refer to the 1980s as 'the lost decade, and the Russians, as stated, call the 1990s the 'era of chaos.' However, the balance of power has shifted. The Chinese own circa $1.16 trillion of US government debt.

These dogs will no longer go to heel. The Chinese hoard cash when we need them to spend it, determined never to be dependent on the West for help.

Emerging markets demand a seat at the table and a meaningful say in global affairs. They will, as has already happened to an extent, pool their collective resources to gain the level of clout they believe they deserve at the helm of organisations such as the IMF and the World Bank.

The BRIC Nations have criticised the West for its poor handling of the financial crisis. Brazil's President said the crisis 'started in the developed world' and accused the West of causing 'monetary Tsunami' with policies such as 'quantitative easing' (QE) – printing money- that have 'led to a currency war, and have introduced new and perverse forms of protectionism in the world.'

They also expressed their continued frustration with the fact the IMF and World Bank are still dominated by the West. The West will not relinquish control gladly. They will cling onto traditional spheres of influence for dear life.

The IMF was created after the Second World War in 1946. A deal was done under the table that America allows Europe run the IMF while it in turn controls the World Bank. All ten managing directors since then have come from Western Europe and all eleven World Bank Presidents have been US citizens.

According to Liam Halligan, writing in The Sunday Telegraph[140], this 'old world stitch-up.' is not mandated by the IMF's constitution. The voting structure is also highly skewed towards the old world.

As Halligan points out, emerging markets have good cause to be irritated by the 'stitch up' as they now account for four-fifths of the world's population and almost half of global GDP. Even the busiest container ports, crucial to move important commodities around, are no longer located in the West.

When IMF President Dominique Strauss-Kahn resigned after his arrest in the US, a number of emerging market candidates came to the fore, but they could not agree on a consensus candidate. As a result a Frenchwoman and lawyer, Christine Lagarde, assumed the role, according to custom. Whether having a woman at the helm of the IMF will soften its very hard edges remains to be seen.

The World Bank Presidency recently came up for grabs by an American, according to 'custom.' Obama recommended an Asian-American, Jim Yong Kim, with a healthcare background for the role in an attempt to mollify the BRIC and developing countries.

Candidates in Columbia and Nigeria made a strong play to be considered, but they were wasting their time. The Chinese reacted to Obama's proposed candidate with guarded (but tongue in cheek) approval- as a step in the right direction.

It may be that they would prefer to promote their own version of these Western institutions within the BRIC framework. They may simply be pragmatic (as they tend to be) about their chances of breaking through the glass ceiling. Obama's choice prevailed after initial spats with US Republicans.

Mr Kim has made an encouraging start, at least ruminating on increasing efforts to eliminate world poverty. With the best will in the world, however, I doubt that he will be allowed make a real difference.

The BRICs continue to flex their muscles. Indeed, reports indicate that they held talks in New Delhi about creating a new development bank that would improve access to capital for poor nations, and, presumably not impoverish them in the process.

In addition, China has been saying for years that the dollar should be replaced with a global currency. BRIC countries are increasingly using their own national currencies- rather than the US dollar- to trade with each other. Intra-BRIC trade is a burgeoning market.

In late 2010, Putin and Chinese Premier Wen Jiabao agreed to use their own currencies for bilateral trade. It is by no means clear that the US dollars' future as the world's reserve currency is secure. Pundits believe its reign will come to an end within the next ten years. Local currencies are also being used to circumvent US-led sanctions against trading partners. Reports indicate that China and Iran are creating a barter system by which Iranian oil will be exchanged for Chinese imports.

China is not prepared to stop importing Iranian oil. China and the United Arab Emirates (UAE) have also announced a deal by which they will use the Yuan for oil trades. Similarly, Russia and Iran have agreed to use rubles to trade. Russia has joined China in opposing US sanctions against Iran.

It is entirely likely that countries targeted by the US will increasingly ring fence their economies, to the extent possible, to avoid the US dollar and US financial institutions- the hammers used to push in the nail in the sanctions battles. They will use innovative means- and strategic partnerships – to minimize the impact of such measures.

The fact remains that once-poor countries we used to patronise no longer hold the West in high esteem and countries targeted by economic sanctions feel hard-done by. There is a lot of resentment out there. They certainly no longer look up to the West, or aspire to being like us.

Respect has been lost. The West has been adjudged seriously wanting in too many crucial respects to be worth emulating, although the Western media fights back hard to fuel our delusion that nothing has changed, while hinting that we may yet deign to let the rest of the world in, doing them a major favour in the process.

However, the underdogs are now wealthy, relatively debt-free, and fast learners: They will play us at our own game in the fullness of time. The Chinese will buy what they lack-assuming they are allowed do so (not a foregone conclusion, as we will see) or, if reports are to be credited, they may, on occasion, steal it, probably with little conscience about doing so, believing we did likewise to them for centuries and thus only getting our just desserts.

We are living on past glories as the Chinese, in particular, plan decades out. The Russians are disadvantaged with the Western media all over them, but the fact remains that they have- in abundance- all the crucial natural resources that many countries (and even the Chinese) lack, rich land, water, minerals, oil, gas, as well as a literate, educated population base.

Western politicians seem to believe we must keep the Russians down as long as possible, which is hugely short-sighted, but we are ill-served by self-interested politicians who rarely think further out than a single term in office. In reality, I believe we are running scared, no longer buying our own PR.

There is reason to believe that many Westerners are sick of politicians who have lost touch with those they were elected to serve. Elections seem increasingly meaningless, with low turnouts as people head to the polls with a heavy heart to vote for a mediocre slate of candidates.

Once elected, people feel powerless to prevent catastrophically poor decisions making on issues that will impact them and their families for generations. Western politicians have no concept of the level of resentment bubbling beneath the surface. They have sacrificed their own people to bail out private creditors and to paper over ineptitude and corruption in policy making.

Yet no-one, in most all cases, has been held to account. The people, however, are expected to be 'good sports.' to roll over and take a severe beating.

In Europe, even if Greece splutters through without an 'official' default,' there is a serious possibility that a two tier Europe will emerge, if it hasn't already done so. Cameron and the UK are not in the club anymore- having opted out of the new fiscal union, and threatened to opt out of the European Court of Justice, after it made various rulings against the UK.

New regulations to avoid a repeat crisis are already neutered- like eunuchs at the court of the old elite. All the sanctimonious lectures to emerging markets about the need to follow our example and address shortcomings in rule of law, corruption and poor corporate governance are now little more than a bad joke.

As one writer wryly commented- 'Those dogs didn't bark.' Not even a whimper. Our much vaunted rules were easily gamed by the players and proved to be little better than a face saving facade-an edifice that came crumbling down at the first sign of pressure.

Insider trading is an epidemic, and although efforts are underway in the US to tackle it, despite noises elsewhere, little has been done. Whole sectors of the global financial markets are unregulated and effectively 'owned' by market participants. Attempts by various countries to regulate 'shadow banking' are doomed to failure due to the global nature of business.

Politics demand that regulations needed to regulate a global market are developed in silos, with little or no co-ordination between them. Indeed, it is commonplace for them to contradict, even neutralise each other, adding to a dizzying level of complexity and cost in attempting to enforce them.

Global companies that conduct cross-border business are especially challenged in attempting to do so, wasting scarce resources and countless hours in the process that could be put to far better use. Banking sector lobbyists and lawyers scour through the fine print of complex regulations to find loopholes they can exploit.

The alternative is to use a 'principles' based approach to legislation, where every contingency isn't put into writing for lawyers to pick apart, but rather depends on the players following the 'spirit' of the law. However, such an approach is stymied in a market where market participants lack observable principles, and regulators lack the experience and the initiative to apply the law in a consistent fashion, resulting in unpredictable, inconsistent outcomes.

It is abundantly clear that overly complacent Western regulators took their lead from politicians unwilling to put the brakes on a party that looked like it would never end. Relationships between auditors and clients were way to close, resulting in rosy reporting that did not reflect reality.

More generally, the accounting profession made widespread and creative use of balance sheet tricks that kept the donkey off the lawn, most of them perfectly legal. I was always especially astounded by the fact that US corporations, including banks, could write off regulator fines against taxes-little wonder that the prospect of fines did not act as a deterrent.

In any event, wishful thinking apart, it is clear that what we have at present hasn't worked to rein in excesses and sharp dealing on the part of Western market participants. There is no reason to be confident that the future will be any better as we merely tinker about the edges.

Emerging markets have noted that only one group has emerged unscathed from the crisis- namely the Western elite. They now know that not only are Western politicians prepared to throw them under the bus in their hour of need (through the auspices of the IMF), but they have no scruples in doing the same to their own, setting a very poor example in the process.

When push came to shove, US politicians assumed $800 billion in debt to save the banks- despite the fact the US people were solidly opposed: The lobbyists convinced them that the will of the people was less important that protecting the banks. According to a Wall Street Journal reporter, Stephen Moore, capitalism is more important than democracy. So it seemed.

Westerners have lost all around. As Nobel Prize winning economist Joseph Stiglitz put it in his book *Freefall*,[141] 'the deckchairs have only been re-arranged on US Titanic.'

The disjointed, chaotic response to the crisis by Western leaders has been noted in emerging markets used to negative comments about mismanagement and incompetence in managing their own affairs. Indeed, capitalism has rarely looked uglier- the current crisis has been a Dorian Grey moment, like the character in Oscar Wilde's novel of the same name.

In many emerging markets, our example also begs the question as to whether democracy in its current incarnation is effective as an instrument of the will of the people.

Stiglitz has also stated that emerging countries view the IMF and the World Bank as 'mere instruments of post-colonial control'- suspecting that US free market rhetoric (which brought chaos to Russia during the Yeltsin years) was simply a cover-up for commercial interests and a means for the US to spread its influence throughout the world.

He observed that emerging markets realize that although they need America to recover, they 'view the free and unfettered market ideals American seems to hold' as 'ideals to run from, rather than embrace.' They associate democracy now with an American form of crony-capitalism and believe that corruption is deeply ingrained in US society, but that political accountability is non-existent.

Stiglitz fears that this view that capitalism is inherently warped could throw developing countries into the arms of totalitarian regimes. Another (more optimistic) outcome may be that they develop their own form of capitalism- that has a heart. However, in Europe (supposed to be the bastion of capitalism with a social conscience) – with austerity on the menu for some time to come- a swing to the far right is by no means inconceivable.

Certainly, Western politicians face a weary, cynical electorate in the short term. It is likely that Putin's much maligned approval ratings in the recent Russian Presidential elections will seem ecstatic by comparison.

Emerging markets could indeed be forgiven for thinking that democracy sucks and that our 'free press' is in thrall to Western politicians. The Western media certainly gave the US an easy ride over the fact it caused the current financial crisis.

On October 2008, as the US banking crisis set off a meltdown in global financial markets, Putin called a spade a spade- 'Everything happening now in the economic and financial sphere began in the United States.'

The impact of the crisis on Russia was swift and devastating: Oil prices sank from $147 in July 2008 to less than 40 dollars by the end of 2008. Rainy day money in the well-funded foreign exchange fund had to be used to try to prop up the falling ruble (which sank to 1998 crisis value levels) and to rescue huge businesses in imminent danger of collapsing. The Russian stock exchange went into free-fall, and once impressive annual growth stalled.

Under Putin, Russians had become accustomed to a hefty annual increase in their standard of living, but with oil revenues in the doldrums, and government revenues hugely diminished, life suddenly got a whole lot tougher for the Russian government, through no fault of its own.

Surpluses turned into deficits overnight. The unpalatable truth was clear - the 'Western Sickness' had got a strong grip on the once healthy patient.

Putin and Medvedev refused to instigate tough austerity measures and risk alienating the population. Instead, they and their financial team showed courage under fire, using their ample resources to pump enough money into the economy and ailing businesses to avoid the kind of hard landing seen in the West.

Medvedev had the bad luck to inherit the crisis when he took the reins as President from Putin when he stepped down in 2008 (contrary to Western media reports that Putin was desperate to hang on, he resisted calls to amend the constitution to allow him do so).

Medvedev was not amused. All the years of hard work and careful, fiscal discipline brought to nought by the old enemy still inclined to lecture Russia with wearisome regularity.

Medvedev showed no inhibitions in assigning blame- 'The US economy...pulled financial markets all around the world down with it in its fall'- adding for good measure that the Americans 'did not listen to the numerous warnings from its partners (including from us).'

As we have seen in Part One, unlike Westerners, Russians have little or no debt as Russia is still, by and large, a cash economy. Mortgage and credit card debt is miniscule by Western standards. In addition, few Russians own stocks, probably as few as 3%. Russia is better positioned to weather the storm than many Western economies. The amount of debt that existed at the beginning of the crisis has been massively played down or maturity dates on debt extended and interest rates reduced.

Putin needs the price of oil to stay high. In light of the seemingly endless hostilities with oil producing nations, followed by the usual round of US-led sanctions and tit-for-tat retaliations (that invariably result in higher oil prices), not to mention finite global supplies of natural resources, he has reason to be optimistic. In 2011, the average price of oil was $111- a record high, and 40% higher than in 2010. Sanctions on oil-producing nations may be significantly neutered by global demand for their scarce products.

Nonetheless, it is unquestionable that the current, far from resolved crisis has wounded many emerging markets, Russia included, and resentment is deep. The EU is Russia's biggest trading partner- a sustained recession in the Union would hit Russian business hard.

The EU's pleas to the Chinese for financial assistance were politely rebuffed, and widely reported. By contrast, a Russian offer to contribute 10 billion USD to the IMF to help out was ignored by most of the Western media. A Chinese refusal to lend a helping hand was more newsworthy than the Russians agreeing to do so.

At a recent meeting of the BRICS' leaders, however, held on the sidelines of the G20 Summit (a group that includes Brazil, Russia, India, China and South Africa), the leaders of these countries reiterated their commitment to contribute an additional $75 billion to IMF coffers..

In his speech at the St Petersburg International Economic Forum in June 2012, Putin emphasized that Russia keeps 'a large part of our international reserves' in Euros and promised not to 'take any unilateral steps that could complicate the already difficult situation for the European currency.'

He said that he was aware that 'today the prosperity of the whole world to a large extent depends on the actions of the Euro zone leaders. Therefore, we support our European partners on the basis of our shared long-term goals.'

His support and magnanimity is more than we deserve.

The Chinese, however, with huge holdings of US debt, are not keen to buy more potentially worthless paper instruments-and are shopping for hard assets instead, extending cheap credit to Africa to help fund infrastructure building, with the proviso that Chinese companies get a piece of the action-a small price to pay compared to the kind of savage terms de rigueur at the IMF.

Indeed, to many emerging markets, based on painful experience, resort to the IMF must be avoided at all costs. However, as matters stand, the options available to bankrupt nations are grim. They can default, with often horrendous consequences, including severe reputational damage, which they avoid assiduously, or, as most do, they eventually turn to the IMF for a bailout. Both options are almost equally unpalatable.

The IMF acts as the lender of last resort to insolvent nations. It also functions as a debt collector for private creditors, primarily large banks that invariably play a significant role in dictating loan terms, as private debt is rolled up under sovereign debt guarantees.

The current situation, beget with fractious, complex, even erratic negotiations, suits the banks just fine as they are (at first glance) considerably better off in dealing with insolvent nations than in the traditional debtor-creditor situation, where bankruptcy looms large. Insolvent nations cannot go bankrupt so they are nearly always forced to accept the IMF nuclear option: as such, private creditors know they will get paid.

By contrast, an individual debtor or corporation has one important escape clause: If the debt load gets too big or the loan terms prove too onerous, bankruptcy is usually an option.

A prudent lender will factor this contingency into its loan terms and price accordingly. Bankruptcy allows for the orderly resolution of an unsustainable debt load: the creditors take their losses subject to well-defined rules, and the debtor, if an individual, pays what he or she can, without the fear of being rendered destitute in the process.

Bankruptcy law in most countries permits individuals to keep their principal residence and enough income to pay for the basic necessities of life, such as food and clothing. The debtor is then free to start again.

Sovereign nations do not have this option: There is no bankruptcy regime for nations. It is high time there should be, as Ross P. Buckley extrapolates in his prescient 2009 article in the American Bar Associations' publication, The International Lawyer.[142]However, to date, both the IMF and the banks have strongly resisted any such initiative.

As emerging markets, including Russia, are painfully aware, widespread layoffs, cuts in critical services, and mass privatization of state assets (often sold at an under-value, with corruption and damaging cost-cutting commonplace occurrences) are all standard fare on the IMF bailout menu.

Thailand was bailed out in 1997 during the Asian crisis. Harsh IMF terms resulted in a resurgence of the Aids virus and forced food subsidies led to starvation. Interest rate increases were mandated in Indonesia, and local politicians were prohibited from bailing out banks resulting in a total meltdown. Pakistan was not allowed fund schools, so children went to schools controlled by fundamentalists, with results that we are still reeling from today.

Stiglitz has pointed out that the fact the US has maintained hidden subsidies and barriers to entry into the US market is another source of friction with developing countries. For instance, poor farmers in Africa, South Africa and India are prevented from importing cotton to protect the well off cotton farmers in the US, using tariffs that were in violation of international trade law.

Europeans have done likewise. We encourage poor countries to open their markets, but baulk at reciprocating. The West has refused to open its markets in agricultural products to the Third World, but did not hesitate in forcing them to eliminate subsidies whilst providing massive subsidies to our own farmers.

During the flash Celtic Tiger years, it was by no means uncommon to see young Irish farmers driving about in large, expensive jeeps and living high on the hog, by virtue of earning 100,000 Euro and more, entirely off EU farming subsidies. It is clear that there was huge, almost criminal wastage at the EU level that convinced many Europeans, so to speak, that 'the living was easy.'

Not anymore. We should not, however, expect emerging countries to cry over our plight. Indeed, they view our double standards towards them as exploitation; they have noted that Western requirements that they privatise state assets in return for foreign loans have resulted in foreigners buying them at fire sale prices.

As Stiglitz has observed, some of the same officials who doled out mediocre advice in Asia (and Russia) are now at home 'giving out handouts' to their friends in the US.

The simple fact is that IMF creditors don't care how insolvent governments get the money to pay them back, once they get paid. There is a callous indifference to the plight of the people behind the politicians, who are forced to repay debt they never assumed, in marked contrast to a typical bankruptcy where the debtor at least is responsible for his or her predicament.

This harsh reality raises interesting questions.

Can politicians bind the government and its people to loan terms, however injurious to the human rights of citizens? What, in essence, are the limits of executive power?

I expect we may hear more about these issues over the coming months and years as rebellious Europeans refuse to don the Troika hair shirt, possibly into infinity. It was one thing to dish out harsh medicine to poor people in faraway lands, but it's quite another to do it at home.

As I write, around 39% of Irish people (around 600,000 homeowners) have not paid a 100 Euro household (property) tax before the deadline, despite government warnings about fines and prosecutions if they fail to do so.

People are aware that the Troika has mandated deep cuts as part of bailout terms, but the fact that all aspects of the negotiations are less than transparent deepens public suspicion that the full extent of the austerity measures have not been revealed.

Up to now, the Irish people have been extolled as Poster Children for 'sucking up and putting up.' The fact that several hundred thousand people won't (so far) pay the small charge is possibly the first shot across the government's bow. The Irish people blame politicians for the debt crisis and do not accept that they must suffer as a result of political ineptitude, and to repay private creditors who refuse to accept losses on seemingly 'risk-free' investments.

Based on numerous conversations with Irish people from all walks of life, it appears that this inequity strikes them quite profoundly, and they are loath to accept it, or to trust politicians to give them 'the straight goods.' In this respect, the recent conclusions of the Mahon Investigatory Tribunal that political corruption was rampant in Ireland in the 1990's has angered people further and conceivably hardened their resolve to take a stand.

However, that being said, a large proportion of Irish people are prepared to knuckle down and accept our current economic predicament (up to a point) because they know they lost the run of themselves during the hedonistic, Celtic Tiger years. They feel guilty.

The then (now largely discredited) Irish Prime Minister, Bertie Ahern, set the tone, by extolling the Irish people to spend (by borrowing huge sums of money, relative to earnings), spend, and spend some more. In a moment of temporary insanity, he even suggested that commentators who warned of the imminent crisis should 'commit suicide.'

In a country with high suicide rates, this was an even more extraordinary statement. However, not all Irish people danced the light fantastic. Many were prudent and lived well within their means. Yet these people will also bear the brunt of the austerity measures coming down the track. Continued forbearance by one and all is by no means assured.

The lofty goal of the European Union- its 'raison d'être'- was the solidarity of EU nations. We have seen little solidarity to date. Some German politicians wanted poorer countries like Ireland to fly their national flags at half-mast in Brussels to show contrition for debt burdens and wealthy EU nations demanded collateral for debt relief: The Finns wanted cash, the Germans gold.

Yet, the wealthier EU nations must share the blame for current events. In 2003, Germany and France broke the 3% EU ceiling rule on the national budget deficit, but refused to enforce the fines procedure against themselves. This cavalier attitude to the rules process set a bad example and sent a signal to the rest of the Union that there was in effect no fiscal discipline.

Before the US crisis hit Europe hard, most EU countries were solvent. Rhetoric from US Presidential hopeful Romney and US Republicans to the effect that the EU is broke because it was too generous to people is without foundation. However, EU regulators and politicians imbued with false confidence, promoted a flow of cheap and easy credit that precipitated wild spending.

As matters now stand, although Greek meltdown has temporarily been avoided, it is clear that there are choppy waters ahead.

Unemployment levels in the EU are very high. Low unemployment levels in countries such as Germany and the Netherlands are partly the result of concerted action by companies to keep employees on their books. With an aging population, companies had less leeway to fire workers in bad times, as they knew they would have no-one to replace them with when the economy picked up. Many companies, with good relations with strong unions put workers on short term schedules.

Numerous studies show that the mass firings so popular in the US have devastating consequences for individuals (despair leads to spiralling suicide and crime rates) and a severe knock on effect on the greater community. Yet US Republicans laud business leaders who trim the balance sheet by decimating communities with callous and short-sighted layoffs.

EU countries with low unemployment levels tend to have strong and profitable manufacturing sectors that are actively selling into emerging economies including China and Russia. They were not reliant on the construction sector as in Ireland.

EU citizens in heavily indebted nations are unimpressed with the performance of their politicians. Confidence and trust in them is at record low levels. The repercussions of this fact for the Union will not be revealed overnight- but to my mind, the damage is already done.

I suspect there is a fracture at the core, with, for instance, poorer Southern countries at loggerheads with their wealthier northern neighbours. EU countries facing inbound immigration from poor African countries have already defied the centre and restricted entry, which is against the spirit and the letter of EU law.

Even in the UK, an EU outlier, various surveys have pointed out that as well as losing trust in banks, people, especially the young, have lost trust in all businesses and would not trust large companies to be open and honest about their behaviour unless they were forced by law to do so. It is also by no means clear that the current slate of European leaders have the pulse of the electorate. I suspect not by a wide margin.

After a short-lived period of introspection, marked by carefully worded expressions of contrition for past mistakes, including lip service to considering the 'social impact' of 'conditionality' (jargon for harsh terms attached to IMF loan terms), the IMF has reverted to type.

The IMF fixation on enforced austerity measures as a condition for obtaining loan financing is not shared by other international institutions[143].

A 2010 International Labour Organisation report *Recovery with growth and decent work* warned of 'the economic and social dangers of imposing fiscal consolidation in the midst of an ongoing recession, especially when spending cuts and tax increases primarily hit people on low and middle incomes.'

UNICEF posted a desk review of the IMF country reports from 86 low-and middle-income members. It noted that 'in two thirds of the countries reviewed, the IMF has advised to contract total public expenditure in 2010 and further fiscal adjustment in 2011 for all but a few countries.'

It viewed the approach as undesirable in light of the fact that 'social impacts of the economic slowdown are still felt in terms of rising poverty levels, unemployment, mortality rates and hunger.' However, after complaints from the IMF, UNICEF removed the offending text.

The IMF takes no prisoners in enforcing its terms.

After extending a loan to Sri Lanka, the IMF refused to release additional funds when the country failed to meet tough targets with measures that included selling off public companies (an endeavour that rarely works to the benefit of the people) and cutting public salaries, pensions, and farming subsidies.

Europe now faces similar constraints. This time, however, the IMF's austerity quest- in tandem with the EU Commission and the European Central Bank- is boldly going where it has not gone before - right into the EU heartland, with consequences that remain to be seen.

Europeans from severely indebted nations realize that their options are few and far between. In the absence of a global bankruptcy regime that would facilitate the orderly and equitable bankruptcy of nations, resistance to harsh IMF terms may be a futile endeavour.

In an extreme situation, creditors could, presumably, move to get judgment against a defaulting sovereign state and enforce it with the sale of state assets. It is most unlikely matters would ever get that far. However, cornered rats have been known to fight back. I am not convinced that Europeans are prepared to roll over and play dead.

As well as the clear-cut moral and ethical imperative, there are, I believe, compelling legal arguments that could be advanced to challenge the status quo. Global banks are very quick to produce lobbyists and high-priced lawyers to fight the counter-assault against any attempt to bring right to might, but they may face more formidable adversaries as austerity takes a bite out of the old world.

This determination to collect, come what may, even if it means crippling an entire nation is unethical, but also ridiculously short-sighted. Politicians focused on re-election and short term solutions that will temporarily paper over the cracks in state finances are often willing accomplices, ensuring a poor outcome for the people they represent.

The West cannot lecture anyone about human rights in face of its determination to persist with a system that equates the impoverishment of entire countries with economic progress, which I deem a form of institutionalized corruption.

It is now clear that sovereign nations can, and will, go bankrupt with increasing frequency. An alternative to default or bail-out is needed, and one viable alternative is to establish a bankruptcy regime for nation states. It would not happen overnight. Negotiations to create cross-border, legally binding institutions, tend to be tortuous, but we must start somewhere.

The alternative is unpalatable, namely that the global economy is constantly battered with one crisis after another, defeating any real prospect for sustainable growth and a bright future for all the people on this planet.

Everyone makes money when times are good- even banks suffer when they are not. Banks need to stop viewing these debates (about the best way to resolve a crisis) as a zero-sum game in which they either win or lose in the here and now, and instead try to look out past the next quarter. Shareholders must bear a sizeable portion of the blame for putting pressure on management to focus on short term gains.

In this respect, and many others, Putin's world view, and his vision for Russia, is far more modern, and more in keeping with the expectations of millions of Westerners than the views espoused by our own politicians.

The difference is that he has the money and the resources to realize a good proportion of his people's dreams. Our politicians do not. Yet they seem determined to sunder Russia apart- one of the few bright sparks on a gloomy continent. Why? Perhaps misery really does love company.

A great deal of lip service is paid in the West to so-called 'corporate social responsibility,' but much of it is 'box-ticking.' Although they exist, truly ethical businesses are thin on the ground.

Putin recently reminded one of Russia's top banks, Sberbank of its 'social obligations.' He is not friendly to the West's scorched earth approach to business- he saw its impact in the 1990s and spent the 2000's fixing it.

Chapter Eight

A Just Society

Based on numerous surveys, Putin's vision of the future reflects that of the majority of the Russian people. He is rarely out of step with them on fundamental issues. Recent survey results in Russia suggested his popularity rating is still high, although statistics vary.

A Pew Research survey from May 2012 suggested what while some Russians may have doubts about the results of the March 4th Presidential election, roughly 72% have a favorable opinion of Putin.

The survey noted that while his 'base of support is broad...he is especially popular among women.' A recent Russian Levada survey suggested that as many as one in five Russian women would marry Putin in a heartbeat. Many others would give it serious consideration.

Russians ages 30-49, and Russians with less than a college education also widely support him. Medvedev, now Prime Minister, is described as 'also widely popular.' as two-thirds of Russians have a favorable view of him.

However, despite Western media hype about Putin's opposition in the elections, the Pew survey suggested that of all the Presidential candidates. 'Putin is the only one viewed favorably by a majority of Russians.'

It noted that veteran politicians such as Communist Party head Zyuganov, Just Russia's Mironov, and Liberal Democratic Party leader Zhirinovsky had negative ratings- at 52%, 51% and 66% respectively. Views were 'similarly negative for billionaire and man about town, Mikhail Prokhorov: Roughly half (48%) have an unfavorable view of him.

The West's favourite, Alexei Navalny, a prominent organizer of anti-government protests, was 'unfamiliar' to

54% of Russians. To the extent he was known at all, he was viewed more negatively than positively (31% vs. 16%). The West's love affair with the Russian opposition is plainly not shared by the Russian people, although you would be forgiven for imaging otherwise from even the most cursory read of our media.

The false impression is also given that Russians are not allowed to protest in public. This is simply wrong. Permits are required for large gatherings, but otherwise, protesting is alive and well in Russia. If you start throwing stones and taunting police, you may get dragged off by them, but that can happen in many Western countries as well, including the UK.

Putin, despite his popularity, is not, however, entirely out of the woods after the election. He clearly struggles to understand the aspirations of some segments of the emerging middle class. It is obvious that he considers many of them pampered and spoilt, unlike their hardworking, rather more stoic parents.

During his election campaign, it was a shock to him that the middle class was not uniformly behind him. He initially scorned the protesters as an elitist, Western-influenced intelligentsia, but over time, his rhetoric became more inclusive.

In his pre-election manifesto, he acknowledged that 'our society is very different from what it was in the early 2000s. Many people have become more wealthy, better educated and more demanding.' He implied that he must get credit for the fact that a middle class now exists.

He acknowledged that the new middle class have 'very high expectations, very high demands on their work.' He has described meeting these expectations as 'a positive challenge.' His big challenge will be to break down barriers with them and to get them engaged in a positive way that doesn't involve manning barricades or throwing stones.

Most of Russian business did not support the protestors, despite Western media hype that would suggest otherwise. They criticized naive, incoherent demands, dubious leaders and unrealizable aspirations; there were widespread fear of anarchy, chaos and a return to the 90's.

There were also disputes about the size of Russia's middle class- with protestors estimating that 60 percent of Moscow's population is middle class, but not militant, and others suggesting it is no more than 15 percent, and shrinking.

Regardless, the middle class is growing, but it is highly likely that they are not a homogenous group, and their aspirations likely differ to quite a significant extent, depending on geographical location, ethnicity, religious beliefs, and a host of other factors.

In trying to keep all Russian society onside, Putin has a difficult challenge. He is also chasing the same rabbit as nearly every other Western nation and emerging market in looking to the high-tech sector to deliver on meeting middle class expectations, while preserving and growing traditional sectors.

He wants the 'share of high-tech and intellectual sectors in GDP' to 'increase by 2020 by 1.5 times and high-tech exports from Russia to double. It won't be easy, nor will his promises to deliver on huge numbers of jobs.

Surveys suggest that Russian business and the Russian State need to spend a great deal more on research and development to even catch up with traditionally high investors such as Japan, the US, and China. Indeed, China will soon eclipse, if it has not done so already, the US in terms of R & D spending.

As part of his Presidential election campaign, ex-French President Nicolas Sarkozy pledged to help the unemployed, stating that 'We don't want a society where if you lose your job, you live in a trailer home like in the US.' That was a trifle disingenuous, as many French immigrants live in abysmal conditions within sight of the grand Parisian boulevards, but the sentiment is shared by the vast majority of French people.

Sarkozy had to face down severe competition from the extreme right wing opposition, primarily from Marine Le Pen's National Front party. Le Pen, like Western favourites such as Alexei Navalny, tried to make a silk purse out of a sow's ear by hiding old racist, xenophobic views behind a new economy exterior.

Putin had a hard-scrabble upbringing, a long way from the privileged Oxbridge background of many of the British political elite and its media. For the vast majority of working-class Russians, however, he is 'one of the people'- one of them.

For that reason alone, the supercilious, frequently peevish, public school-boy attitude of many British politicians towards Russia is positively guaranteed to irk him, a sentiment that many Russians (a proud people) undoubtedly share.

I have mentioned it elsewhere, but Putin's vision for the future was set out in his pre-election manifesto. Contrary to Western media reports, which suggested that most Western journalists hadn't actually read it, the lengthy document is clearly the output of a quick, inquiring mind, and not the ravings of an autocratic lunatic. However, the devil is in the details, and it will be a colossal challenge to implement it.

For Putin, social policy should 'support the weak.' He acknowledges the challenges that a knowledge based economy will create for workers, but he berates company owners for mistreating workers- a theme that undoubtedly resonates with his blue collar base with no love for money-makers or big business. His views in this regard, however, create a conundrum for business owners.

Putin appears to desire that Russian companies emulate the German 'social contract' model as he points to Germany's largely successful experience with 'work councils'-expressing the view that 'Together with labor unions, we should consider what laws we can adopt in order to give workers more control over their companies,'- to create a 'worker aristocracy' in Russia.

In recent time, there have been strikes at Frankfurt airport in a tough battle between unions and management. It is by no means clear- especially if the current crisis takes a bite out of the German economic miracle- that the German model (where unions and work councils have huge sway over corporate decision making) will inevitably endure.

In addition, Germany is a very different place than Russia. SMEs-the so-called German 'Mittelstand'-are integral to German manufacturing success and excellence; high levels of vocational training and education give them an advantage that Russia won't emulate any time soon.

Putin acknowledged that small business 'is at least half of jobs in the economy'- but his manifesto was relatively scant on details as to how he proposes helping them out. Comparisons to Germany will remain wishful thinking while Russian SMEs languish without the necessary impetus and support to grow the sector by leaps and bounds.

However, the Germans don't always get it right, and there may be surprises around the corner. For instance, the decision to abandon nuclear power after the Japanese nuclear meltdown is, I believe, short-sighted. No sensible, cost effective alternative has been promoted as yet, leaving aside wishful thinking about giant leaps in solar and wind technology.

Russia has a meagre base of SMEs for a variety of reasons, not least of which was the fact they were decimated in the era of chaos, but they are also handicapped by poor infrastructure, high rents, lack of access to affordable credit, huge bureaucracy, and corruption. International studies suggest that a huge number of Russian companies still pay significant sums for licences that aren't legally required (and take time to acquire); they also suffer disruptive and often illegal inspections that local authorities ought to prohibit.

As a general matter, the cost of capital for Russian businesses (the interest rate charged by banks to borrow money) is high by Western standards.

In addition, the fact that 'business' is not exactly lauded in present day Russia likely lessens its allure more generally. Decades, even centuries of purges against small business owners, including enterprising farmers, have also left a mark.

Russians, however, are hugely resilient people and the younger generation is far more willing (as are women) to determine their own fate. State intervention, and corruption, is far less problematic in 'new-economy,' knowledge- based companies that attract the young.

The general manager of Boeing in Russia,[144]Sergei Kravchenko, told the Moscow Times that the notion that 'everyone emigrated, everything stagnated and all the scientists and schools aged and retired, is actually not true. We always had and still have more proposals and interesting opportunities in Russia than we can work on.'

He also said that although people say Russia is 'very corrupt, it's not transparent and it's difficult to do business,' he has never encountered corruption in his sector. He suggested that the fact that high tech businesses are 'people' rather than 'capital-intensive' may explain it.

Nonetheless, big capital intensive businesses, as in the West, play an enormous role in Russian society, creating and sustaining huge number of jobs across a massive terrain. As well as the cost of creating or upgrading creaking (or non-existent) infrastructure and dealing with severe weather conditions, Russian big business owners face challenges their Western colleagues do not.

For instance, they are often expected to keep bankrupt, non-viable businesses alive in one- industry towns that have no other employer. In Ireland, and certainly the US, such moribund companies, however harsh the consequences-will inevitably go to the wall. Government efforts usually centre on re-skilling and attracting alternative and viable businesses to the region to fill the gap.

Official figures suggest there are 335 single-industry towns in Russia, half of them with fewer than 20,000 inhabitants, but it is likely the number is much higher, possibly as many as 800. Many of them are already in dire straits- some reports state that these towns would require an infusion of close to 1 trillion rubles ($34.45 billion) to reinvigorate them and put them on a sound economic footing.

In his manifesto, Putin moots the concept of such towns becoming a kind of testing ground for 'practicing municipal democracy.' He writes eloquently about political structures in small towns and how they can be improved. However, he is no fool and acknowledged that these 'small towns, which are home to a significant share of our population, represent a separate and often a very troubled issue.'

He notes that they often lack 'sustainable sources of income and are forced to live off subsidies from the regional budget.' However, empathy apart, he clearly has no magic wand solution to lack of employment opportunities in such regions.

There is also a serious problem in Ireland with huge unemployment in many rural communities, but it is a far more complex problem to solve in a country with Russia's vast scale. It is complicated further by the fact that many communities are effectively cut off from the outside world, due to lack of transport options and gaping holes in infrastructure. The Stalin era, in large part, created the problem- and subsequent politicians have failed to solve it.

Putin will struggle to do so, but he knows full well that voters in such towns are a loyal and important part of his base, and they expect him to save them. The fact that Russian society, sired on communist principles, is not accustomed, or inclined, to 'pull itself up by its bootstraps'- poses a difficult dilemma. It is also difficult for workers to relocate, as there is a chronic lack of housing for them to live in.

It seems unlikely that Putin can, or will, prop all these towns up, but in turn, private industry cannot be expected to run them indefinitely at a loss. These harsh political decisions are very tough to implement in a traditionally isolated and paternalistic Russia-where society demanded that the state took care of its workers. It did not leave you high and dry. This is especially true amongst older members of society with little interest in learning new skills and no desire to leave communities they have lived in their whole lives.

Putin acknowledges that many big business owners play a critical role in the economy and have modernized their operations and created jobs. However, he fires a shot across the bow by issuing an implicit warning to them- by referring to the 'social responsibility of business.'

His expectation that business will deliver jobs and the modernization of the Russia economy while being 'socially responsible' is a tall order.

It risks leaving many Russian business owners in an invidious position; required to walk on eggshells at home while competing aggressively on international markets against companies who merely pay lip service to such lofty principles as social responsibility. The danger is that they will be left at a serious competitive advantage unless the state supports the paradigm with its pocket book.

As few as 3% of Russian companies export their goods or services compared to about 15% of their Western counterparts. What does it matter? Companies that compete internationally tend to have the impetus to innovate and benchmark heavily against global standards, increasing productivity and efficiency in the process.

Russian exporters, however, are hampered by traditionally Byzantine customs laws and bureaucracy, and have difficulty recovering VAT on exports. The standard of business education is also frequently cited as an issue, as well as lack of foreign language skills, especially at middle management level.

Considerable efforts are being expended in fixing these problems, but more needs to be done. However, there is potentially huge upside to doing so. A top down approach is, however, by no means optimal.

An examination of regional differences has shown that several regions across Russia's vast terrain have had considerable success partnering with local industry and research facilities and encouraging specialisation in sectors that create jobs and opportunities for far flung communities.

Putin's emphasis on social justice is very much part of the current zeitgeist, and it will inevitably strike a chord with

Russians. However, the problem is how to have it all- jobs, companies that are globally competitive- and social justice.

Putin believes in supporting state champions such as Gazprom, currently facing scrutiny by EU anti-competition authorities. Undoubtedly Putin believes that state owned Gazprom is being targeted unfairly- as part of the EU's desire to keep the energy market in EU hands- and also due to paranoia on the EU side about Russia's ambitions in the sector.

Europe relies on Russia for about a quarter of its gas consumption. Finland, Lithuania, Latvia and Estonia rely on Russia for essentially all its consumption.

Putin has suggested 'more extensive cooperation in the energy sphere, up to and including the formation of a common European energy complex.' He describes the 'Nord Stream gas pipeline under the Baltic Sea and the South Stream pipeline under the Black Sea' as important steps in that direction.'

In a direct response to suggestions that Russia is an unreliable energy partner, he has written that 'Once the pipelines start operating at full capacity, Europe will have a reliable and flexible gas-supply system that does not depend on the political whims of any nation'- a position he believes 'will strengthen the continent's energy security not only in form but in substance.'

However, he notes that 'The Third Energy Package, backed by the European Commission' is 'aimed at squeezing out integrated Russian companies' and 'frankly not conducive to stronger relations between Russia and the EU.'

He quite rightly points out that the kind of partners the EU has brought on board to help fill the competing Nabucco pipeline (at truly massive cost) are not stable and that the plan (rather than protecting EU energy supplies) merely aggravate 'the systemic risks to the European energy sector.'

The EU, in attempting to reduce its dependence on Russia, is building a new link to a pipeline beneath the Caspian Sea- dubbed the Nabucco Project; its goal is to build a pipeline 2,400 miles from Turkey to Austria. The gas will come from Azerbaijan- far from being a bastion of democracy, it is a virtual dictatorship.

There has been a lot of in-fighting and jockeying for position amongst Western companies with respect to the construction of the pipeline, and it remains to be seen whether it will ever go live, let alone realise its potential to compete with Russia. It will cost a fortune-estimates suggest a figure of €7.9 billion Euros, but in all likelihood, the actual cost will be exponentially more.

To fill the pipeline with enough gas to satisfy European needs, it needs not just to get gas from Azerbaijan and Turkmenistan, but also from northern Iraq. To get access to the Iraqian oil, the Kurdish region would have to get permission from its own government, which it is unlikely to get as they are always at logger heads. There are also disputes about whether Russian territory would be breached to build some of the pipelines necessary to conclude it.

All in all, it seems a colossal waste of time and money. The Russians have proven to be reliable partners; disputes with the Ukraine, although the Western media would portray them otherwise, are the result of uneconomic terms that are not commercially viable for the Russians.

I have grave concerns, however, that when it comes to the energy market in Europe, we may cut off our noses to spite Russia's face. Some European Eastern bloc countries, traditionally hostile to Russia from Soviet occupation days, as well as old world nations with state energy champions to protect, may yet drive the bus over the cliff.

Indeed, I worry that Western powers will do business with the devil himself rather than deal with the Russians. Paranoia, stereotyping, and age old prejudices have made us blind, and fully capable of acting against our own best interests.

Meanwhile, Russia's Nord Stream pipeline will be able to carry enough gas to supply 26 million European homes when it is fully functional. It is the first direct link between Western Europe and Russia, and part of the goal of the project is to bypass the Ukraine. Disputes with Ukraine over gas prices effected gas supplies to European customers twice since 2006.

'We are slowly and surely turning away from the dictate of transit states,' Putin said.

Gazprom and its predominantly German partners are building the pipeline in stages. Russia's dominance in gas markets won't disappear overnight, but there is significant competition, especially on pricing, on the immediate horizon. Putin is keenly aware that Russia can't rest on its laurels.

In recent times, countries such as Israel have discovered potentially huge gas deposits they are eager to exploit. The threat posed by shale gas-abundant in the US-(the extraction process, however, poses serious environmental concerns over and above the norm) all focus his mind.

However, as matters now stand, EU leaders appear less focused on solving Europe's imminent energy crisis than in indulging old prejudices against Russia, whom many still view in Cold War terms.

Certainly, Putin does not believe that Russian companies get what the Australians call 'a fair go.' Putin has noted that 'We have yet to learn, as many Western partners have, how to lobby for decisions that favor Russian business in foreign international forums.' He believes that Russian businesses have 'been getting a raw deal abroad'- as 'restrictive trade and political measures' have been used against them.'

He suggests that double standards are in operation, that while 'We are opening up the most attractive areas of our economy to foreign investors, granting them access to the 'juiciest morsels,' in particular, our fuel and energy complex.'..'our investors are not welcome abroad and are often pointedly brushed aside.'

He provides the example of the Russian-Canadian led bid to save Opel in Europe. Despite German government support, it was somewhat mysteriously derailed. However, as Opel now struggles for survival, and cannot count on jobs being saved by the US parent, the Europeans may yet regret the outcome.

Putin believes that Russia needs to do much more to support Russian businesses abroad. He could learn from Ireland in this regard, and France in promoting French film abroad.

Many Western leaders, especially the French are quite overt in promoting state champions.

However, Putin acknowledged a longstanding complaint from Russian business that huge Russian state companies eat everyone's lunch, and leave nothing over for them. For that reason, he wrote that 'Whales,' so-called, should not interfere with the normal development of private businesses in their sectors.'

There is a clear need, however, to drive out corruption and gross inefficiencies from these state bodies, and to ensure that competition laws (and the regulators) are up to the task of preventing and censuring monopolistic behaviour on their part. If they are left unchecked, they will stifle small and medium sized businesses, and act as a destabilizing, negative force that chokes the air the former needs to breathe and thrive.

Observers will watch with keen interest to see how this promise is realized. I have no doubt that Putin will create state champions where he can, as other developing markets- such as China- are determined to do.

Putin recognizes that another major challenge for Russian business is low productivity; he noted that workers in developed countries are 'three or four times more productive than Russian workers, which makes business uncompetitive.'

However, he hits out at any suggestion that Russians are merely lazy. .'.the point is not, as some pundits say that our people cannot, do not want to work.' Rather, he believes they are severely disadvantaged as they 'are engaged in outdated, inefficient workplaces.'

There is little reference in his manifesto, however, to the huge environmental issues Russia faces. Pollution negatively impacts life expectancy and damages the health of people who live and work in areas dominated by heavy industry. A healthy workforce is critical to delivering on the promise of a modern, innovative economy. They will not deliver if they are choking to death, as evidenced by China's abysmal example.

Another significant challenge is that fact that Russians are long accustomed to heavily subsidized energy prices. Russia is hugely energy inefficient.

The Russian state provides some of the largest energy subsidies in the world. The International Energy Agency (IEA) estimated that Russian subsidies for the sector were US$34 billion in 2009. Other estimates place the subsidies at closer to $40 billion.

Russian consumers pay about 77 percent of the full cost of energy prices, well below international market prices. The approximate 'price gap' between domestic and international prices was estimated to be US$19 billion for gas and US$15 billion for electricity in 2009.

Research suggests that subsidies actually encourage higher consumption and chronic wastage at the consumer level. In turn, energy companies have little incentive to spend on R & D to improve efficiencies or encourage innovation, or to focus on reducing very high pollution levels.

Communities even suffer energy outages, extraordinary in such a resource rich country-and businesses complain about the hugely unreliable and inefficient electricity grid; corruption also appears to be rampant at the state and regional level. Russian companies frequently complain about difficulty getting an electricity connection.

Even the gas sector suffers from out-of-date pipelines and lack of investment. Industry has long borne the brunt of the consumer energy subsides, eating into profit margins.

Energy-hungry resource companies complain that high energy costs make it tough for them to compete internationally, even in cases where they own the energy assets in question, as they must sell power they generate to the state first and then buy it back at market prices. In other words, they can't put their own assets to work for them.

The Russian state is liberalizing the energy markets, in stages, with the goal of bringing gas and electricity prices to market prices by 2014. However, industry will continue to heavily cross-subsidise consumer prices for several years, at least. Huge state monopolies also control much of the gas and electricity markets, creating further problems.

Experts believe that the huge cost of subsides would be far better invested in infrastructure building, education, housing, healthcare, helping SMEs and generating tangible, enduring value.

As matters stand, the subsides, although hugely popular with the public, deliver negligible, if any, return on investment for the state, and indeed, do little to improve the lives of the people in the grander scheme of things. Clearly, Russia must put its vast resource wealth to work for the people and industry. If it is taken for granted, it will inevitably be flittered away.

However, it is also a fact that due to the extremely harsh climate and high levels of poverty, especially in rural areas, that many Russians depend on subsidies to survive. Surveys rate energy costs as a major source of anxiety.

For that reason, great care has to be taken to ensure reducing or eliminating energy subsides does not literally result in people freezing or starving to death, as they save on food costs to stay warm.

Fighting inflation remains a serious issue for Russia and other emerging markets, and it will be a significant challenge in the West with oil prices on the rise. However, Russian politicians will be careful not to alienate the public by tackling energy inefficiencies with tough measures that people will hate.

So long as oil prices keep rising, Russia is better positioned to carry the can, at least in the short term. The deregulation of the Russian energy sectors will happen over time- and in this regard, the EU, for instance, is no flag bearer, with progress pitifully slow as incumbents and their lobbyists fight tooth and nail to hang on.

In turn, Putin knows full well that touching pensioners can be fatal as they are a huge demography in Russia. Pension reform is a hot potato issue in Russia, although it is firmly on the Russian state's agenda going forward.

In a recent OECD [145] *Review of Labour Market and Social Policies in the Russian Federation*, it noted that although reforms are likely to 'eradicate' poverty among pensioners, as measured by official benchmarks'- there remain questions about 'the long-term financial sustainability of the private pensions system.' This same comment could be made about practically every Western nation.

Few Western politicians dare touch pension benefits. In the UK, the government has simply kicked the can down the road by failing to address a huge short fall in pension provisioning. Even the UK Treasury keeps huge pension liabilities off its books. Short of an economic miracle, this chicken will inevitably come home to roost, with devastating consequences.

The OECD report noted that rapid population ageing creates a need to increase the pensionable age, which in 2012 is 55 for women and 60 for men. Putin has introduced legislation into the Duma that would increase the retirement age for top officials from 65 to 70- a reversal of Medvedev's efforts to attract the young and phase out older workers. According to the Moscow Times, it is common for Russians to work past the retirement age; about one third of Russia's pensioners are still in paid employment.

It is believed that Putin views older workers as more stable, disciplined and reliable than the young; surveys suggest the latter favour the civil service for perceived opportunities to take bribes.

The peculiar social dynamic that exists in Russia leaves Russian politicians between a rock and a hard place. Convincing Russians that capitalism, even in its most benign form, possibly more akin to the Scandinavian model (currently in 'vogue' with UK PM David Cameron) has something to offer them, will require seismic cultural changes that will not occur overnight.

The young, well travelled and tech-savvy are already converted, to an extent, and keen to do business and make money, but their values are still not the same as those of Americans by a wide margin. It is a hugely complex dynamic which the Western media fails to grasp, even at a very superficial level.

In his manifesto, Putin acknowledges that issues such as affordable healthcare and housing are things that many people took for granted in Soviet times. He recognizes that nostalgia for these times may persist, and that 'A decrease in the affordability of housing is exactly what many of our fellow citizens regard as a sign of deteriorating living standards in Russia compared to the days of the Soviet Union.'

In Soviet times, the state, albeit despotic, provided for basic needs. Putin's (Russia's) challenge is to somehow soften the blow that inevitably flows from reliance on a free market economy (as occurred with the initial 'transition' in the chaotic 1990's)-without spending like a drunken sailor to do so, or creating wholly unrealistic expectations as to what the future can hold.

He acknowledges that spending wildly won't suffice and that there must be an emphasis on efficient use of finite resources.

To create his 'Just Society.' Putin and his successors will have to increase wages for professionals such as doctors, teachers and academics- paid a pittance by Western standards. Putin's manifesto promised significant hikes, doubling wages in some instances, starting from September 2012.

Putin is pragmatic about the need to support education and improve the quality of Russia's universities-that rank poorly in Westerns surveys. Addressing grade escalation and the kind of corruption that allows unmeritorious students gain admission by paying a 'fee' (bribe) will help.

Efforts to introduce standardised testing have been controversial and not necessarily effective, although well-meaning, but these challenges are by no means unique to Russia.

Putin believes that Russia should focus on what it does best by setting a goal to 'make our school education in math the best in the world in 10 years' time' in the hope it will give Russia a competitive edge. The fact that maths grades are appalling in many Western nations – the US included- makes that a reasonable goal, despite the fact that Russian students appear to be losing ground in that area in recent years.

The West's nostalgia for the 1990's is a peculiar phenomenon that does not show us in a particularly positive light. Putin certainly sees the universe through the prism of the disastrous events of that decade, as experienced by ordinary Russians.

In his manifesto, he wrote that the people's experience of 'democracy' in the 1990s was so negative that it 'poisoned Russia's transition to democracy and a market economy, making many Russian people wary of these very concepts – and unwilling to participate in public affairs.'

Indeed, a key premise for him seems to be the need to get people re-engaged. He is obviously well aware of pre-elections surveys that suggest Russians feel they have no voice in politics- and that politicians do not listen to them. Westerners are similarly jaded with politicians.

The recent protests were not representative of the views of Putin's wider base, but nonetheless, it is quite clear that Russia must look to the future, and not belabour the past. In the manifesto, Putin implicitly takes the credit for pulling 'our country out of the mire'- and restoring 'the peoples' sovereignty, the foundation of genuine democracy.' There is merit in that boast, but there are many new challenges ahead.

He is well aware that Russians are unwilling to compromise on certain fundaments, primarily 'the right to work (the possibility to earn a living), the right to free healthcare, the right to education for children.' Western politicians have not delivered, to any impressive extent, on these fundamentals.

His focus appears to be on creating ongoing, iterative forms of dialogue between the Russian people and the state, rather than restricting democratic input to election time: Polls suggest that Russians are not in fact overly impressed with elections. It is arguable that Westerners now feel similarly.

He also writes extensively about measures to increase transparency- with the important, but highly elusive goal of producing 'trust, constructive dialogue and mutual trust between society and the government.' With trust levels between Western citizens and politicians at an all time low, he shares this rather Herculean task with most of his Western counterparts.

How will he achieve this lofty goal?

He wrote that 'Citizens and professional and public unions must be able to 'beta-test' all state documents' to improve decision making, noting that 'the language of legislation must be improved. It should be made at least understandable by those the regulations are aimed at.'

He also recognizes the need for 'development of self-regulatory organizations, whose powers and capabilities must grow.' He expects 'self-regulation to become a cornerstone of Russia's strong civil society.' He believes that Internet driven 'crowd-sourcing' initiatives may engage the public to provide input generally- with respect to lawmaking and other matters.

He notes that initiatives that collect one hundred thousand or more signatures on the Internet can become law in the UK – he views such initiatives as ways the Russian people can have a voice. My reading of what he wrote is that he is responding to criticisms of autocracy by saying, in essence: 'You want a say, well, come and get it.' In a way, he is putting it up to the Russian people to get involved, assuming he delivers on promises to allow them the opportunity to do so.

Some commentators on Russian society believe that Russians are too passive and couldn't be bothered- they simply expect leaders to deliver, with minimal participation. Time will tell. Certainly the protestors are keen to be heard although lacking a cohesive mandate.

Putin believes that in order to get Russians engaged in the political/democratic process, they need experience, and the best way to get it is through exposure to grassroots, local politics. He writes that 'Local self-governance educates citizens in responsibility....It is also a kind of a vocational school for aspiring politicians.'

Putin recognizes the need to drill government down to the community level. He views giving people the right to judge the performance of unelected local officials, such as 'the head of the district police station after his first year of work.' 'the head of the local housing and utilities service' and the 'justice of the peace.'

Putin understands full well that sunlight is the best disinfectant, but it would take a brave Russian right now to publicly tackle local police or utility chiefs- journalists who have done so have been beaten, even killed.

As I will discuss in Part Three, if 'Name and Shame' is to work, the media (often the source of allegations of corruption or mismanagement in the West) must be protected. Regular citizens cannot realistically be expected to 'out' possibly dangerous officials if they see that journalists who do so pay with their lives.

Putin's manifesto is a nuanced and sophisticated analysis, with a formidable grasp of detail and how things work on the ground, but execution is where the rubber will hit the road. He writes that 'municipalities should become entirely self-sufficient and autonomous, in financial terms.....and end their addiction to handouts from higher authorities.'.. He confirms that the direct election of governors will be re-introduced after he eliminated the practice in 2005.

However, he makes it clear that federalism reigns supreme, and that 'the President of Russia will retain certain instruments of oversight and management, including the right to dismiss governors.' In his view, a balance must be struck: 'Neither centralism nor decentralization should be followed blindly as a fetish.'

There is a strong body of evidence collected in the West, confirming that a centralist government is essential for strong, successful government. Certainly, Yeltsin's attempt to create decentralization was a disaster that only resulted in corrupt practices, fiefdoms and crippled state finances as tax revenues dried up.

As a general concept, undoubtedly responding to critics, Putin envisages 'public opinion playing a major role in deliberations.' He is keenly aware that 'Russia's various territories are diverse in terms of social and economic development' and that 'People's lifestyles are determined by their specific traditions, customs and models of behavior.'

As a religious man, Putin notes Russia has 'certain assets of unquestionable value, namely the powerful consolidating factors such as the Russian language, the Russian culture, the Russian Orthodox Church as well as Russia's other customary religions.'

For all these reasons, he reiterates that 'Russia needs a strong, capable and authoritative federal center, which plays a key stabilizing role in the framework of inter-regional, inter-ethnic and inter-religious relations among the various communities that make up our country.'

Russia remains a secular society despite the fact many Russians espouse deep religious convictions. If the Church starts to impede in significant ways in day to day life, it is likely that there will be a backlash.

Putin's manifesto is erudite and cerebral, but he is also a gifted populist and understands that most politics is local and that the issues that infuriate and engage people are rarely the big issues.

He made, as politicians invariably do, various pre-election promises, such as turning back the clock to restore winter time in Russia. Medvedev scrapped it in 2011. People complained that they are in perpetual darkness, and soccer fans miss EU matches on TV.

Before the Presidential election, the Chicago Tribune quoted educated voters as saying that if Putin brought winter time back, they'd 'happily vote for him.' Clearly someone did. Supposedly Putin is not an early bird.

A major irritant to Moscovites is the frightful traffic and the fact that government officials use police sirens to navigate ferocious Moscow traffic- shutting it down for hours to allow Putin's entourage through. I will discuss the 'Blue Buckets' movement further in Part Three as it has a more serious aspect to it.

I recall with some amusement reading that the Goldman Sachs CEO, Lloyd Blankfein, on a trip to Russia to drum up business, recently describe Moscow traffic as the biggest impediment to inbound investment into Russia. I hope he was joking.

I have sat in abominable traffic jams out of Manhattan on many occasions-the inevitable tailbacks to enter the tunnel system have legendary status. I suspect that Blankfein, however, rarely takes a cab when he heads out to the Hamptons for a spot of R & R.

That being said, if Putin can 'fix' Moscow traffic, he will surely achieve overnight Sainthood status.

Infrastructure gaps are a huge problem in Russia. Putin wrote that the state will 'support major infrastructure projects'-to ensure reliable communication with the regions of Siberia and the Far East- and to rebuild local roads.

He pointed out a very salient fact, namely that 'in Europe, America, Japan and Korea, you can build a house or factory anywhere in the 50, even 80 miles from a major city.' However, in Russia, barely 20-30 miles out from cites, there are 'no roads, gas, water and electricity.' so the land is worth nothing, because it simply cannot be used.'

He acknowledges that 'development of the Russian territory have to start from the land around major cities' and that the huge cost will require a public-private partnership.

Opportunities exist for foreign companies as he declares Russia is 'ready to hold international competitions and widely engaged as operators and contractors prominent foreign companies'- manna from heaven for cash-starved Western construction companies.

He also realizes that infrastructure building will 'help the quality of life of rural workers and SMEs.' and help the agricultural sector to become self sustaining. It will cost a fortune, but ignoring the problem isn't an option.

A key challenge for Putin is to keep a handle on the state purse strings in face of generous promises made pre-election on vastly increased military and social spending.

Well-respected, liberal-leaning Finance Minister Alexei Kudrin (who kept a tight rein on purse strings when the crisis hit) fell out with Medvedev and quit over the cost of such initiatives.

However, Kudrin and Putin have been friends for decades, and Kudrin will inevitably make a come-back, in some guise. The two men are unlikely to be permanently estranged.

Russia and other emerging markets are fully aware that the current crisis also presents them with opportunities to go bargain hunting.

As Western banks and businesses languish, it is a good time for them to go shopping. The Japanese are doing likewise. Nimble operators with technical acumen will threaten the hegemony of tired, old world institutions, many of which have out-dated, even hazardous IT systems.

The Chinese are certainly flexing their considerable muscle in the economics realm. Like the Russians, they are not shy about assigning blame for the current crisis. As well as shopping for bargains, the crisis has revitalized plans by emerging markets such as China to develop a super currency to displace the dollar. The Chinese may indeed have ambitions for the renminbi itself to do so.

The Chinese Dagong Global Credit Rating Company lowered the United States credit rating to 'A Plus' in November 2010, long before US credit agencies followed suit. The Chinese took a dim view of the US Federal Reserve's determination to keep printing money, while lecturing it about devaluing its currency- not an easy matter as many Chinese manufacturers have razor thin profit margins for commodities that do not attract a premium, and could be wiped out with rapid currency appreciation.

The Chinese are within their rights under international law to determine the value of their currency, yet they are pilloried by the US for doing so. Indeed, the IMF's own watchdog has pointed out that a high level of groupthink contributed to the crisis, which it manifestly failed to pinpoint, let alone avert. Inadequate, narrow assumptions were pumped into computer software models- that are only as good as what it put into them.

The IMF's obsession with Chinese exchange rates (at the behest of the US) meant they failed to spot real threats to global economic stability. Back in 2005, the IMF's chief economist, Professor Rajan, issued warnings about the threat of widespread financial meltdown, but he was ignored.

He has been quoted as characterizing the IMF's obsession with Chinese exchange rates as 'an unmitigated disaster'- a stance that also fed the longstanding view in emerging markets that the US dominated Fund is biased against them.[146]

Indeed, Chinese rating agencies have accused Western (American) rating agencies of applying double standards in the way they rate US and Western companies (unduly favourably) and have called for an independent player in the ratings field, a view shared by the Russians.

EU regulators want to mandate more diversity in the credit ratings arena in Europe- a move hotly contested, for obvious reasons, by the US incumbents who have long dominated the sector. There can be little doubt that US rating agencies were asleep at the wheel in rating toxic US assets as virtually risk-free. They were also cowed by their clients, who paid for positive ratings, not bad news. So long as no-one broke ranks, the game played on.

On August 5th 2011, Standard & Poor finally downgraded US treasuries from AAA to AA, the first downgrade of US debt in over seventy years, causing uproar and a rout on global financial markets. The Chinese official news agency was quick to point the finger, suggesting that in order to 'cure its addiction to debts.' the United States must adhere to the common sense principle that one 'must live within one's means.'

After the downgrade, the US Securities and Exchange Commission (SEC) announced with fanfare an investigation into S & P's role in the crisis. National pride had been wounded.

The timing of this investigation left many with the cynical impression that US regulators had turned a blind eye as long as the rating agencies played ball. It stank of retribution, despite vociferous denials and statements that the investigation predated the downgrade.

The ex-chief of Citibank (a consummate insider) was installed as S & P's new chief to mend wounded relations with Capitol Hill- a tacit admission that rating agency independence from political influence is a mirage.

Russia is rated BBB by Standard & Poor, two grades above junk status, even though debt-to-GDP is infinitesimal by Western standards. The Russian Finance Ministry has decried this low rating in light of these marginal debt levels, compared to many other developed countries.

The Russian Finance Ministry's website pointed out that the debt-to-GDP levels for Mexico is 42.7%, and yet it has the same rating as Russia. Putin has described the low rating routinely given to Russia by the US credit rating agencies as an 'outrage.'

By comparison, other countries, such as the US and the UK have debt-to-GDP ratios in the stratosphere. There is little rationale for the enormous discrepancy with political/sovereign risk now front and centre in the US and the EU, except for Western bias and markedly poor analysis.

I have long been perplexed as to how economists rationalize bottom-feeder credit and economic ratings for countries in surplus or with negligible debt- but give glowing rating to essentially bankrupt Western nations.

China is rated AA- (stable) by Standard & Poor. Russia is BBB, stable. Fitch's has the same mediocre rating for Russia. The UK, inexplicably, has an AAA negative rating. Dagong, a Beijing based agency, rates Russia A stable. I struggle to make sense out of any of it.

I have not heard a compelling explanation yet. Various gloomy, End-of-Days contingencies are factored into ratings for emerging markets-while far rosier, unreasonably optimistic assumptions are made about the prospects for Western nations-the same assumptions that got us to where we are today.

The US credit rating agencies are currently fixated on the potential impact of falling oil prices on Russian finances-using the possibility as a rationale for cutting the country's outlook to stable from positive. I have no confidence in these 'forecasts' that demonstrate a narrow perspective and lack rigour on a number of fronts.

Russian news outlet RIA-Novosti reported that the Kremlin's economic adviser Arkady Dvorkovich told a news conference that if oil prices fall and 'remain steadily low over a long period of time,' they would 'first use the reserves we have and then adjust to the lower prices.

He foresaw Russia's sovereign debt rising to no more than 20 percent of GDP in the future, from around 10% at present. He pointed to the incontrovertible fact that Russia's debt is one of the lowest in the world, stating that 'we have no intention of going beyond a threshold that seems risky.

He adding pointedly that that the rating agencies 'don't take into account 'the stability that Russia's economy has reached.' while stating that they 'have no reason to worry' about Russian fundamentals. Dvorkovich also added that Putin and Medvedev had decided to put oil and gas windfall revenue into reserve funds, a budget rule that was set aside to deal with the financial crisis that struck in 2008.

These agencies often cite Russia's population decline, lack of competition and the low quality of infrastructure as reasons for the abysmal rating. Yet Western countries that face similar challenges ahead- but lack Russia's obvious advantages, inexplicably get stars in their copy books.

The US borrows about forty cents of every dollar it spends. It will not dig itself out from under this mountain any time soon.

The baby boomer generation is starting to retire, with the associated huge cost to government health care and pension programmes. Despite obliging Western media reports that the US economy is on an upsurge, there is little cause to celebrate.

The US's national debt situation is potentially catastrophic- and totally unsustainable over the medium to long-term: It stands at around $16,000bn (circa 102pc of GDP) at present. The US runs a staggering annual budget deficit of $1,200bn.

However, there is no immediate risk that the county will be unable to pay its debts, as it pays its debt in dollars, and can print them to meet its obligations- so-called' quantitative easing' or 'QE.' QE lowers the value of the dollar, which helps US exporters.

QE also imposes losses on creditors (including sovereign nations with huge US holdings) at home and abroad, while propping up bankrupt businesses, most especially the banks. Low interest rates cause problems for pension funds (with interest rates in negative territory) and liquidity problems as investors chase better returns, buying commodities and foreign currencies causing prices to surge.

Both the Swiss and Brazilians have suffered in this latter respect.

South Korea, China, Russia, India and Mexico have been big gold purchasers as a hedge against the dollar and currencies weakened by QE. They are also stockpiling oil, trying to lock in prices in the face of worries about scarcity and high prices.

However, in reality, the S & P's US downgrade reflected market perception of heightened political risk in the US rather than any serious concern that it wouldn't have the money to pay its debts any time soon.

The bitter enmity between US politicians about raising the debt ceiling was inauspicious. It suggested that the best interests of the country had become hostage to political in-fighting so deep that US politicians might do the unimaginable, and choose not to pay US debt. Negotiation is currently underway to avoid a repeat performance in the here and now. It is unclear whether enduring lessons were learnt first time round.

An article in the Canadian Star newspaper, pointed out that the American people were markedly unimpressed by the performance of US politicians on both sides of the political divide during the last fracas. Reports indicate that Americans described the standoff over raising the debt ceiling as 'frustrating.' 'childish.' 'disgusting.' and a 'joke.' They expect more from their politicians as they struggle to make ends meet.

The major source of wealth for most Americans, namely the equity in their homes, has now all but disappeared. Many people who have retired have had to return to work to pay the bills, making it difficult for young people to get a foothold in the labour market. Various studies suggest that ordinary Americans approaching retirement age have less than one-quarter the funds needed to maintain their standard of living in retirement.

In addition, as many as four out of five US households struggle to pay off their mortgages and have withdrawn funds from pension accounts and continue to re-mortgage their homes to get by. America needs poor 'creditor' countries like China to spend more. The Germans have also been chided for not spending more, much to their annoyance. The fact is that everything and everyone is inter-connected.

Political risk has long been associated with the Russian market, but it has come finally home to roost in the West, as Western politicians appear increasingly inept and self-interested. With Putin now firmly in control, this risk should dissipate in Russia. However, relentless negative Western media scaremongering will, conceivably, continue to rattle investors and the general public alike.

Chapter Nine

What's Yours is Mine

Americans are notoriously optimistic and perennially convinced that the US is the ultimate Big Kahuna. This conviction, however, has taken a beating over the last few years.

Incessant media coverage about the financial crisis, reports that China will inevitably overtake the US as the world's biggest economy, and the realization that China owns much of US debt, have made an impression.

According to a 2011 Gallup poll,[147]52% of Americans view China (rather than the United States at 32%) as the leading economic power in the world today. Gallup also asked Americans to rate whether what happens in various countries is vitally important to US interests. In 2011, 70% thought China's importance was paramount- only 36% said the same about Russia (46% thought Russia important, just not 'vital').

The Chinese, however, believe that Westerners are over-indulged and lazy, and paid way too much to produce too little.

In his book, *China Shakes the World-The Rise of a Hungry Nation,*[148]previously referred to, James Kynge wrote that the EU has a subsidy of $2 a day for cows- 'more than the average daily income for 700 million Chinese.' The cow subsidy may be in jeopardy now- with budgets pared back to the bone, but the point is well taken. The Chinese work ethic makes even Americans look like slackers.

Despite the fact that the Chinese Communist Party is in firm control, Kynge observes that 'China today is a great deal less socialist than any country in Europe.' pointing out that the approximate 120 million migrant workers 'receive no welfare at all.' In many respects, the Chinese are the world's most fervent capitalists.

In this regard, they have advantages: The absence of meaningful labour laws in China made it possible for Chinese politicians to lay off 25 million workers from bloated state enterprises in 1997. Even in the US, that would be a tough sell.

The Chinese have other advantages: They are not religious, which gives them (and Asian cultures more generally, with a Buddhist, non-corporeal sensibility) an edge over the US and other Western nations in scientific fields such as stem cell research. US research has faltered in the face of religious opposition to using embryonic stem cells in cutting edge research.

The financial crisis has had other consequences in the West that may ultimately inure to the benefit of emerging economies. One example is a backlash in the US-and to a lesser extent in Europe-against white collar occupations.

A book written by American motor cycle repair man, Matthew Crawford became a US best seller (*Shop Class As Solecraft: An Inquiry Into the Value of Work*). 'Shop Class' is the American term for trade courses like welding or woodwork.

Crawford extols the virtues of 'a real man's job' in which one uses one's hands. Crawford has a Ph.D in political thought and worked at a think-tank that dealt with the oil industry. He hated the work and set up a motor cycle shop and was quoted as saying that 'there was more thinking going on in the bike shop then in the think-tank.'

He also stated that he found his previous work to be demeaning- and not 'befitting a free man.' James Dyson, the UK hoover (vacuum cleaner) entrepreneur in the UK has also said recently that he would like Britain to go back to being a place 'that makes things again.'

A similar debate has raised its head in Russia.

According to the Moscow Times, Putin's campaign manager, Stanislav Govorukhin, called liberals the 'filth of the nation'- a quote from Lenin about the Russian intelligentsia. Govorukhin, a very old-school Russian, suggested that the label 'creative class' should belong to engineers and labourers, and not to' the office plankton.'

He suggested that only those Russians who 'build underwater cruisers, who construct pipes along the floor of the Baltic Sea' deserve the designation. In other words, the only people who are creative are those who 'make things, or use their hands.'

To create an 'innovative (a hugely over-used word that is often nigh-meaningless) 21st century society, everyone should have a role to play, and feel valued. That being said, it is likely that the future will, for better or worse, be high-tech centric, with the value of intangible assets out-stripping physical asset valuation, and increased automation inevitable.

We have an aging population we have made no provision for and can't support and who can't support themselves- unlike the case in Japan where society takes charge and everyone pays for elder-care. Not so in the UK, US, or Ireland where frail old folk, after lives working their hearts out, die from the cold or are brutalized in old people's homes run by the criminally negligent.

This huge growth in the aging population in many Western and Asian countries will impact society in ways we cannot yet comprehend, but it will undoubtedly create opportunities as well as challenges, with health care and elder services likely to be a burgeoning market. However, the potential exists that the working classes will merely exist to service the aged, wealthier rich, with few prospects for advancement.

The collapse of the banks has made many Westerners question the value of the financial services sector. In his book *Freefall*, Stiglitz wrote that 'the sad truth is that in America's financial markets, innovations were directed at circumventing regulations, accounting standards and taxation.'

This perspective was echoed by Lord Turner in the UK who questioned the utility of so much talent consumed by financial markets – smart people working for the banks, pursuing seemingly futile endeavours that contributed little to society. This tart observation did not, however, lessen Lord Turner's enthusiasm for acquiring the top job at the Bank of England, recently lost by him, most unexpectedly, to a Canadian, Mark Carney.

Despite the possible merit of some of these observations, people in Asian countries, China included, have no romantic illusions about manual labour or time for navel gazing. The Chinese, in particular, are as hungry as we in the West are tired, and will eat all our lunches if we fail to look to the future and revert to Dickensian values instead. Crawford may have a future fixing Asian robots, but to do so, his Ph.D may prove useful.

Like the Chinese, Russians have a strong respect for advanced education. Every second Russian I meet over 40 seems to have a PhD in the hard sciences-often more than one. There is a high level of literacy in Russia, ranked 17 in the world-with 99.4% of the population literate. China, by comparison is ranked 101, with official statistics believed to be high, especially in rural areas and amongst women. India is ranked 171- with 61% literacy levels.

A survey held in December 2012 found that nearly two-thirds of Russian families who have children from 13 to 20 years are prepared to make considerable sacrifices to acquire a university degree for them- especially households where parents are similarly educated. Wealthy Russians also send their kids to UK schools and to UK and US Ivy League universities.

The Chinese, like the Russians venerate education and learning; families will pool meagre resources and make great personal sacrifices to send their kids to good Western schools. Like the Russians, they favour the UK in this regard.

The Chinese are also learning English in huge numbers. By contrast, Britons, and many Westerners, have poor language skills. Russians are good linguists, but English language skills need a great deal of improvement.

By contrast, many Irish people learn several languages at school, and are proficient, enthusiastic linguists. This gives us a competitive advantage in attracting US multi-nationals to Ireland that wish to use Ireland as a hub for doing business throughout continental Europe.

By contrast, simple economics have made Americans question the value of education in light of the huge cost to acquire it. It used to be part of the American Dream to own a house- an aspiration that is becoming increasingly unattainable- further education may fall into the same category.

Reports suggest that the US middle class fear-quite legitimately- that they will never be able to repay the debt they would incur to get a university education.[149]Clearly, if the American middle classes decide against sending their children to university, this will impact education levels in the US, already in decline.

In addition, short-sighted decisions by both the US and UK governments to deny visas to foreign students is creating a situation where future entrepreneurs are simply returning home upon graduation-a loss to both economies, as immigrants have played a crucial, often unsung role in creating truly innovative companies in both countries. Our loss will be their homelands' gain.

New jobs will favour highly educated and technology savvy workers. Yet US society is being progressively 'dumbed down'- with Republicans chiding Obama for snobbery for suggesting that American youth should aspire to a college education. Republicans question basic science and climate change at a time when US kids show poor scores in science and maths subjects, increasingly in high demand.

There is little or no investment in education in the US and a backlash against it in any event.

In US Republican circles, intellectual rigour and academic excellence is replaced with religious fervour and the cult of 'positive thinking.' If Americans simply smile broadly and often enough, God and 'American values' will see them through. If only. The Chinese and the Russians are under no such illusions. If the US gets dumber, as China and Russia gets smarter, it will make for interesting times ahead.

Whatever way you look at it, pitting the beleaguered working class against the 'intelligentsia' (in the case of Russia, but a non-existent class in the West, except maybe in France) or, more broadly in the West against white collar workers-is short-sighted and divisive.

What we need is a world where everyone has a role to play. Neither wishful thinking nor the Opium of the People will make this so. On the contrary, more education, not less, is likely essential, but far more closely correlated to actual workplace needs, both now and into the future.

However cathartic it may be to attribute blame for the crisis to the US- the fact remains that we face a new reality that is tough for Westerners to swallow: dwindling resources, fewer jobs, benefits, longer work days, longer work life and pensions that may never materialize.

Despite the many indulgences granted it by the Western media, for all its many strengths, China is clearly not a democracy, or about to become one any time soon. Neither is it a socialist, workers paradise.

Kynge describes a corrupt culture in which appalling violence against women is widespread and female suicide a virtual epidemic. Present day Chinese culture- as Kynge describes it- does not exactly place a premium on morality. However, in this regard, the West currently has little to crow about.

From the perspective of the Chinese people, one might imagine China is the worst of all possible worlds, neither Socialist nor capitalist, as we understand the concept. Yet surveys suggest the Chinese are far more optimistic about the future than almost anyone else. Do they see the road wide open ahead of them, with every extra dollar made a step up the ladder? Or do they simply believe official propaganda?

Meanwhile, we watch the clouds darken on a once prosperous continent and fear that our entitlement complex is about to run out of road. Our media and politicians are fixated on China, while inexplicably giving Russia the high-hat.

Yet, Russia is far closer to us in nearly every respect than China or even the US, with whom it shares many characteristics. Russians have no desire to go it alone to realize the American Dream. They still expect the state to look after them, to a significant extent.

Despite our many commonalities, Russia is looking ever eastwards. Russian rail, pipeline and resources companies are gravitating toward Asia, with a view to getting closer to the end customer-the mighty China, on Russian borders.

However, the Russian Far East region is inhospitable with severe weather conditions and poor infrastructure. It won't be easy to entice people to move, unless they have an intrepid disposition.

However, with jobs very scarce in many parts of the world right now, it would not be difficult to encourage immigrants to move, or Russians living in areas with high unemployment.

A 2,300-mile oil pipeline from Siberia to China is in the works. Bloomberg reported that the size of the deal has resulted in China overtaking Germany as Russia's largest trading partner. Russia also plans to ship Siberian gas to China, but the devil is in the details, with pricing still contentious. Russian power companies also hope to develop infrastructure to deliver power to China from Siberia.

The Chinese and Russians share a border, trade relations and a number of grievances towards the West. The Russians are quick to point out that they have never been a Western colony. The Chinese resent the fact they were, and Chinese politicians rarely miss an opportunity to remind the Chinese people about the many humiliations they suffered at Western hands. They relish the prospect of gaining the upper hand.

The Americans still enjoy needling the Russians with claims they 'lost' the Cold War- even though that is not an accurate synopsis of the situation. Both countries have been disadvantaged by US/Western tariffs and subsidies that aim to keep them out of Western markets. Both have retaliated. Both lack soft power: The Chinese are out and about trying to buy it; the Russians are unsure how to go about it.

Putin has described China's economic growth as 'by no means a threat, but a challenge that carries colossal potential for business cooperation – a chance to catch the

Chinese wind in the sails of our economy.' He has made it clear that Russia will 'seek to more actively form new cooperative ties....in order to develop the economy of Siberia and the Russian Far East.'

He has also thrown down the gauntlet to the West.

'China's conduct on the world stage gives no grounds to talk about its aspirations to dominance. The Chinese voice in the world is indeed growing ever more confident, and we welcome that, because Beijing shares our vision of the emerging equitable world order. We will continue to support each other in the international arena...'

Old enmities are being set aside; 'We have settled all the major political issues in our relations with China, including the critical border issue' He notes, however, that the relationship is not friction free- and writes that Russia will 'closely monitor immigration from the People's Republic of China.'

In reality, Russia needs immigrants, but pre-election, Putin dared not risk raising the spectre of a Russia over-ran by Chinese, a fear held by many Russians of my acquaintance. However, he clearly views the BRICs collective strength, now accounting for more than 25% of world GDP, as ultimately a foil to US hegemony. Russia will chair the G20 in 2013.

Russia has many advantages that China does not. The one child rule has caused a drastic shortage of women in China, with a thriving illegal trade in brides. By 2020, according to the Chinese Academy of Social Sciences, twenty three million Chinese men will have to live without women.

Russian has the opposite problem, a surfeit of women- a happy situation for my Russian male friends who tell me they 'have their choice.' Russia, however, as stated, has a shrinking population as Russians have few children. The Germans have a similar problem, with one of the lowest birth rates in Europe and a greying population. Germany is considering a tax on income to off-set increases in social-security costs as people retire.

Kynge believes that trust in Chinese society is as scarce a commodity as women, as 'poverty and the competition for scarce resources impinge on it.[150]Its absence shows up in 'rampant piracy' and 'identity is an item to be bought and sold.' One can buy fake credentials, indeed a whole ID makeover 'with a Ph.D in rocket science' for less than $100: A quick way to move up the ladder.

Huge numbers of Chinese impersonate police and military officers and journalists take bribes. A huge underground economy exists that Kynge describes as 'almost institutionalised,' quoting a Chinese scholar who estimated it might be as much as one-third the official economy.[151]Underground banks provide financing mainstream banks won't- like the Mafia in Italy and 'Tax evasion is endemic all over the country.'

With such a brutal struggle to survive, and a government that rules with a rod of iron, it is hardly surprising that creativity is also a scarce commodity. The Chinese state, realizing that future growth and soft power is not acquired without a creative class, has tried to mandate it. Not surprisingly, this approach has not worked.

However, as Kynge explains, the biggest problem the Chinese face, is that it is an 'environmentally exhausted nation' as 'the extreme frailty of its physical environment contrasts with the prodigious strength of its human capital.' Kynge writes about the 'mismatch between the size of its population and resource base,' caused by 'decades of wasteful exploitation and disrespect for the environment that characterized the era of communism.'

These problems exist in profusion in Russia as well, making complacency very ill-advised. However, they tend to be swept under the carpet. If they are ignored long-term, catastrophe is inevitable.

Kynge wrote that huge water shortages in China, with streams and rivers dried out, have created a situation where '400 out of 668 large Chinese cities are short of water,' and forced to ration it. The lack of a conservation mentality has resulted in the fact that 'China uses between seven and twenty times more water to generate a unit of GDP than the developed countries of the world.'

Lack of water is also a serious problem for Chinese resource companies who need water to generate power. The Russians are striking deals close to Chinese borders to provide this critical resource to its neighbour.

Fixing the environmental problem won't be easy or cheap for the Chinese.

According to Kynge- 'The cost of patching up China's wounded nature are only just starting to be realised.' Pollution is a grave issue. 'On the World Bank's list of the twenty most polluted in the cities in the world, sixteen are in China.' Acid rain falls over 30% of China. Many rural communities are 'a dumping ground for toxic waste,' as multinationals manufacturing in the regions have helped turn it into' the rubbish tip of the world.'

The Chinese need for resources has had a severe impact on the rest of the world, as rainforests are cut down to satisfy voracious demand for timber and pulp products, including boreal woodlands in Siberia (licenses to log there can only be obtained if the ancient forest has been damaged by fire, so criminals supplying the Chinese set them on fire).

According to Kynge, 'Places known as the 'lungs of the planet' for their role in turning carbon dioxide into oxygen, are disappearing at unprecedented rates to satisfy Chinese demand.' The Chinese environmental crisis has resulted, as Kynge explains, in contaminated water and food, new pandemics like SARS, horrendous air pollution, and animal and bird extinction.

The Chinese are critically dependent on oil imports- they have imported the shortfall since 1992. The state oil company, the China National Petroleum Corporation buys oil assets where it can to reduce supply side vulnerabilities, but it still owns way too little to secure supplies.

Buying is not as easy as it might seem. Another big Chinese oil company, the China National Offshore Oil Corporation (CNOOC) got a rude awakening when it tried to buy a mid-tier US oil company Unocal in 2005. It was to be largest overseas acquisition by a Chinese company. However, the US was at war with Iraq, and a media backlash characterized the bid as the Chinese stalking a strategic US asset (which it was not).

Similarly, Huawei, the Chinese telecoms equipment maker was blocked from making acquisitions in the US due to strong resistance from the US defence industry, which accused it of industrial espionage and being an arm of the Chinese government, keen to gain access to sensitive US technology.

CNOOC was also accused of being an arm of the Chinese communist party. Yielding to pressure, President George Bush referred the bid for a 'national security review,' at which stage the writing was on the wall, and the Chinese withdrew. The crushing defeat resulted in CNOOC's Chief Financial Officer stating that political prejudice had been used to deny China access to the energy it needed.

At a news conference, Kynge reports that he said that the rout amounted to a human rights violation: 'What are human rights? I'll tell you what it means. It means having guaranteed access to energy. It means having petroleum to run your car.'

CNOOC may succeed in a bid for Nexen, one of Canada's biggest energy companies, although the acquisition has also resulted in tough negotiations in Canada, and Canadian government approval is essential and by no means a sure thing. A bid for approval also had to be made in the US, as Nexen has operations in the US Gulf of Mexico. Chinese companies have succeeded in buying other US assets, not deemed sensitive or strategic.

Petrol prices are a hot button issue in the West. People who care nothing for politics will make their voices heard when prices soar at the pump. Petrol prices recently went through the roof in the EU and US-with a threatened oil tanker driver strike causing panic buying in the UK.

The Saudi's tried to put the brakes on, but US insistence on sanctions against Iran will cause price to rise, on worries about supply constraints. Paying more at the pump stokes latent anti-Arab hostilities in the US: the Saudis are keenly aware of this fact, but oil prices will remain high as the Middle Eastern countries need them to remain above $100 a barrel to break even on their budgets and to keep social unrest in check. In addition, supplies are not infinite.

I have heard reports of working class Americans grumbling about the price of gas at the pumps and blaming the Saudi's for hiking prices to buy more 'gold plated limos.' As I reiterate throughout this book, when the going gets tough, stereotyping and scapegoating invariably take centre stage. Politicians usually play along, happy to distract disgruntled voters.

As Kynge pointed out, if the US starts to view China as 'an enemy in prospect,' protectionism (and tacit racism) will again rear its ugly head and the old anti-Beijing arguments will be regurgitated, namely 'that it is an unfair trader, a manipulator of its currency value, a pirate of intellectual property, an exploiter of its own workers, a beneficiary of subsidised financing from its state banks.'

The latter argument no longer holds any water in light of the huge bailouts given to moribund Western banks. However, history suggests that we are still quite capable of making it.

Russians are also used to cheap energy and petrol. Indeed, protests about rising petrol prices are far more common than those that decry election irregularities, and, in my estimation, far more worrisome for Putin and his advisors. As I have stated, a great many Russians are ambivalent, at best, about democracy, but they have strong opinions about petrol and energy prices.

Russians are fortunate to have huge energy resources at home, but they need inbound investment to exploit them, especially after years of neglect when times were tough. Resource extraction, especially in harsh terrain, is an expensive business, so they will partner up with governments and companies they trust, who treat them with respect.

By contrast, the Chinese must safeguard the safe passage home of critical oil supplies, and host of other essential commodities. China's claim to Taiwan, lost in 1895 after war with Japan has deep emotional as well as practical significance. It is situated in the South China Sea lanes that lead to Japan, making it of great strategic and trade importance.

Chinese oil supplies come from the Middle East through the Strait of Malacca. The Chinese are aware that if there was a dispute with the US over Taiwan, supply routes might be disrupted. To counter this threat, the Chinese are forging alliances and building naval and communications capabilities along these routes home to monitor and protect them.

In 2005, Donald Rumsfeld, the US Defence Secretary expressed concern about China spending money on its military, questioning its need to augment its military defences- not a challenge the US will allow when it comes to doing the same thing in Europe on Russia's borders.

On a recent trip to the region, Hillary Clinton infuriated the Chinese by criticizing their efforts to secure their interests in the hotly contested South China Seas, believed to be rich in natural resource deposits, as yet undiscovered, to which everyone, including the Chinese, will inevitably lay claim. The Chinese recently established a naval base in the region.

The Chinese told Hillary Clinton to essentially mind her own business and also accused the Americans of fuelling hostilities between them and the Japanese, an old enemy, closely allied with the US.

Climate change is causing the melting of ice in Arctic regions, allowing the Russians and neighbouring countries with a claim to the region to drill for natural resources. The phenomenon may create new sea passages for ships, alternatives to the Suez Canal and possibly change the existing power axis.

Russian oil executives have said that Russia could 'double' oil reserves by tapping its Arctic deposits. Rosneft and Exxon Mobil- with experience of similar conditions in Alaska — as indicated, have signed a deal drill for oil and gas in the Russian Arctic in a project that could cost double-digit billions.

The impact of climate change- denied by many US Republicans- is unclear. How will it affect indigenous fauna, flora, animal life, peoples in this region? Nature will adapt, as it always does, but there may be unforeseen consequences. However, Russia may gain access and ownership to even more scarce natural resources in the process.

Kynge writes, with great prescience, about the 'geopolitics of scarcity.' a concept that is highly relevant to Russia and other resource rich countries. He observed:'Although trade increases the mutual economic dependence of the countries that engage in it, it does not make the peoples of those other nations any fonder of each other'- possibly leading to resentment and loss of goodwill. China's acrimonious relations with Japan are a case in point, with politicians in both countries unwisely stoking the fires of xenophobia.

Whatever Russia's vulnerabilities may be- other than those created by a hostile Western media- lack of natural resources isn't one of them. This abundance of riches undoubtedly concentrates the minds of Russian politicians. History suggests that when you have something of great value that others crave, there will come a point in time when they consider taking it from you.

Fortunately for the Russians, history also speaks to the fact that military incursions onto Russian soil tends to end very badly for the aggressors. In addition, Russia's huge arsenal of nuclear weapons makes engagement undesirable, except for the most insane-or desperate- of foes.

Ever the pragmatist, Putin has predicted that 'The probability of a global war between nuclear powers is not high, as that would mean an end to civilization.' 'As long as we keep the 'powder' of our strategic nuclear forces, produced by the hard labor of our fathers and grandfathers, dry, nobody will dare to launch a large-scale aggression against us.'

In other words, we are not a sitting duck target like Libya. He predicts that space-based weapons systems will play a great, if not decisive role in armed conflicts- a profoundly depressing thought.

African countries with abundant land also make attractive targets for water and land-starved regions, currently on a buying spree for such assets, leading to charges that the purchasers are engaged in new forms of colonialism.

The Amazon is being decimated by Brazilian farmers cutting down the forest to grow soybeans for the Chinese. The Chinese are aware they must preserve their frail environment and devise alternative fuel and energy sources (there is interest in GMO crops, for instance, to increase yields). We must hope that the world's most precious natural resources are not decimated and stripped dry before that happens.

The UN Food & Agricultural Organisation forecasts that global food demand will jump by 70% between now and 2050. Drought and bad weather make the challenge all the greater.

This scenario has caused a surge in the value of companies that produce potash used to produce fertilizers to grow food. Many of these producers are in Canada, Russia, Belarus and Israel.

Potash shortages and burgeoning demand has resulted in a flurry of activity as players attempt to dominate the lucrative market. China is short of potash and must import a great deal of it.

Russia is well positioned to dominate the global trade in this valuable commodity. Russia also has the advantage of producing low cost nitrogen fertilisers from an abundant gas supply.

Russia is also the world's third-largest grain exporter. The Russians still remember with chagrin, the fact that in the early 1990s food shortages forced them to turn to the US for food aid, notwithstanding the fact that they have extremely rich land.

A serious drought caused the Kremlin to issue an expert ban on wheat in 2010, to preserve local supplies. Food prices rose as Russians with a very strong memory of Soviet-era shortages, hoarded supplies.

It is one of Putin's goals to revive Russians supremacy as an agricultural producer. He is determined to end what he has described as a 'humiliating dependence on foreign bread.' However, a lack of investment in the farming and agricultural sector has meant that there is much to be done to modernise operations to attain this goal of self-sufficiency.

Russia has the world's fourth largest expanse of arable land and huge potential to supply the world with commodities such as wheat. Indeed, Siberia has some of the world's richest land. However, its full potential is not even close to being realized, hampered by the vast distances involved in transporting goods and a lack of investment in modern equipment.

Westerners have moved to the region and the Ukraine, also blessed with rich, unexploited land, in an endeavour to bring Western agricultural practices to Russian food production. An article in the Wall Street Journal in 2008 [152]stated that 'the untilled, arable land of the former Soviet Union could generate 115 million metric tonnes of wheat a year.'

The Chinese and Russians have many reasons to co-operate and many shared grievances with the West to mull over. However, that does not mean that they lack grand, even futuristic ambitions. They are not wedded to the past. They also look to the skies for inspiration.

The Chinese, like the Russians, are interested in space exploration, for pragmatic military as well as scientific reasons. The US has militarized space and used its 'civilian' GPS system to facilitate space weapons- a move countered by the Russians and Chinese by developing their own systems. The US leveraged its space-based weapons systems to eradicate Saddam Hussein's military during the 1990-1991 Gulf War.[153]

As indicated, China is determined to try to keep the US out of its backyard, warning it not to become involved in disputes, for instance, with Vietnam over the South China Sea. Enhanced satellite capabilities have given them the ability to move the Chinese fleet around at short notice- to enable their navy reach any hotspots before US battleships do so.

The prospect, however remote, that America might use its traditional military and naval domination in the region to 'starve China out.' is viewed as a serious threat that must be neutralised. Chinese reconnaissance satellites have quite conceivably reached the point where they match the US capability to observe from space.

The Chinese also have a growing space programme, while the US has grounded the space shuttle and decimated funding in that area, despite the recent successful landing of the NASA 'Curiosity' robot on the surface of Mars.

Both the Russians and Chinese realize that they lack soft power in the world. To that end, they fully understand the allure and symbolism of space travel.

Space travel, like great art, fuels our imagination, rekindles our childish sense of wonder about the universe. Obama made a mistake abandoning the US space program-ceding it to self indulgent billionaires. The Russians are serious about space.

In March, 2012, Russian news outlets reported that Russia's Federal Space Agency, Roscosmos, had submitted an ambitious space exploration strategy to the government, for completion by 2030.

Reports indicate that it envisages conducting several space exploration missions, including 'a piloted flight to the Moon with landing on its surface and sending probes to Venus and Jupiter.' In cooperation with foreign partners, it also 'plans to deploy a network of permanent research stations on Mars.'

A very position endeavour is mooted- namely the removal of 'space junk' orbiting Earth. Contrary to Hollywood's histrionic and outmoded view that Russia is a danger to the planet, it envisages protecting it from asteroids and comets. A new agency may be created to coordinate the programme.

Putin, with his usual colourful turn of phrase, has made it clear that the extent of Russia's ambition in space extends well past playing 'international space ferryman' – referring to its role in ferrying international astronauts to and from the International Space Station.

I still recall the thrill of watching the US Apollo mission blast off, waiting for That Voice to say the magic words: 'Houston, we have a Go'- and then the count-down. It was phenomenal TV. Then the collective sense of grief when it went badly wrong, and an astronaut was killed- right before our eyes in many cases. The astronauts were special people-our pioneers, our very own space travellers.

The idea that there may be someone or something else out there, and that we might find them, made us believe what we no longer believe, that anything is possible, that there is hope for a grand, even fantastical future.

Not anymore.

Instead, billions are wasted in fighting wars that don't concern us-decimating young lives in the process, and leaving thousands of soldiers maimed and desolate- billions we might spend doing something worthwhile- something grand.

Americans can no longer even project their dreams into space. They must focus instead on the fact that times are really tough, and will only get tougher. It is little wonder they are turning to religion in their droves.

When do Western politicians give the people something to celebrate? Instead, whenever they can, they pit regular people against one another. Russia has become something of a fall guy in this respect.

Fully aware of this fact, with the mighty, albeit flawed China on its door step, Putin is likely to embrace the adage, ' Keep your friends close, and your enemies closer.' With friends in short supply, that recommendation may have more profound implications that we currently imagine.

Part Three: Rule of law

Chapter Ten

Throwing the First Stone

When did you last read anything about Russia that didn't refer to problems with rule of law and corruption?

These problems are usually described as so serious and pervasive as to be a serious impediment to Russian efforts to attract foreign direct investment (FDI). International organisations frequently add fuel to the flames with reports that highlight the bad news and minimise or ignore the positive. The Western media is more than happy to play along.

There is a gross lack of proportionality in this coverage, which usually ignores the historical antecedents of the problem and its complex nature. It also sets a higher standard for Russia than we can meet ourselves.

In truth, Russia, barely out of communist shirt sleeves, has made remarkable progress in a very short period of time and corporate governance has taken centre stage. Indeed, investors active in the Russian market for well over a decade point out that many of the worst corporate governance transgressions were perpetrated by Western media darlings such as Khodorkovsky and Western companies.

In Q1, 2013, Russian public companies will be required by law to report their financial results according to internationally accredited IFRS-GAAP accounting standards. In addition, anti-bribery and corruption laws in the UK and the US apply to foreign companies with UK and US business interests.

However, these laws were only recently passed in the UK after years of criticism from international organisations about Britain's poor track record in prosecuting corruption.

Complaints were also made about lack of transparency in doing so.

The most cogent example of these deficiencies arose from the infamous BAE case, which had highly significant ramifications for the British justice system, the separation of powers, and the independence of the prosecutorial authorities.

Between 30 July 2004 and 14 December 2006, the UK's Serious Fraud Office (SFO) carried out an investigation into allegations of bribery by BAE Systems (BAE) in relation to military aircraft contracts with the Kingdom of Saudi Arabia. On 14 December 2006, the SFO Director announced that he was ending the investigation.

The UK High Court, at the behest of two public interest groups heard a request for judicial review to determine the legality of that decision.[154]The decision was rendered on April 10, 2008.

In October 2005, BAE's solicitors sought to persuade the Attorney General (AG) and the SFO to stop the investigation on the grounds that it would adversely affect relations between the United Kingdom and Saudi Arabia and prevent the United Kingdom securing what it described as 'the largest export contract in the last decade.' Initially, despite significant pressure brought to bear, the SFO Director and the AG stood firm.

However, in July 2006, the SFO was on the verge of obtaining access to pertinent Swiss bank accounts. At that point, according to Lord Justice (LJ) Moses' narrative in his High Court decision (sitting with Mr Justice Sullivan), persons described 'discreetly as 'Saudi representatives' made a specific threat to the Prime Minister's Chief of Staff to the effect that if the investigation was not stopped, 'there would be no contract for the export of Typhoon aircraft and the previous close intelligence and diplomatic relationship would cease.'

According to LJ Moses, the Government contended that the Director 'was entitled to surrender to the threat' as 'the law is powerless to resist the specific and, as it turns out, successful attempt by a foreign government to pervert the course of justice in the United Kingdom, by causing the investigation to be halted.' The court was urged to 'accept that whilst the threats and their consequences are 'a matter of regret,'they are a 'part of life.'

Even Prime Minister Tony Blair intervened. He was at pains to explain 'how the help and confidence of the Saudi authorities is critical to success' (referring to the UK's work for peace in the Middle East), and how recent developments 'are throwing that cooperation into jeopardy.' He wrote that it was 'very clear' in his judgement 'that the continuation of the SFO investigation into Al Yamamah risks seriously damaging Saudi confidence in the UK as a partner.'

He also emphasized national security concerns and wrote 'The Defence Secretary endorses what is said earlier in this letter about the impact on Defence interests and both he and the Foreign Secretary share my overall view, as expressed here, on the damaging impact of the SFO investigation.'

LJ Moses made reference in his judgment to the OECD's Convention on Combating Bribery of Foreign Public Officials in International Business Transactions 1997 (The Convention), and set out the terms of Article 5:

'Investigation and prosecution of the bribery of a foreign public official shall be subject to the applicable rules and principles of each Party. They shall not be influenced by considerations of national economic interest, the potential effect upon relations with another State or the identity of the natural or legal persons involved.'

He cogently observed that 'If the investigating state depends upon good relations with the foreign state whose public official it seeks to investigate for its own national security, Article 5 seems to have little, if any, utility. It is all too easy for a state which wishes to maintain good relations with another state whose official is under investigation to identify some potential damage to national security should good relations deteriorate, all the more so where that other state is powerful and of strategic importance.'

Furthermore, he observed that 'Self-interest is bound to have the tendency to defeat the eradication of international bribery. The Convention is deprived of effect unless competitors are prepared to adopt the same discipline. The state which condones bribery in its economic or diplomatic self-interest will merely step into the commercial shoes of the states which honour their commitment.'

There was no 'specific admission' of the Saudi threat by the UK government, noted LJ Moses, but upon further enquiry of counsel for the government, he was satisfied that 'The significant event which was soon to lead to the investigation being halted was a threat made by an official of a foreign state, allegedly complicit in the criminal conduct under investigation, and, accordingly, with interests of his own in seeing that the investigation ceased.'

The AG had expressed concerns that halting the investigation 'would send a bad message about the credibility of the law in this area, and look like giving into threats.' He had also indicated that he was 'extremely unhappy at the implications of dropping it now.'

SFO officials observed (as did in fact happen) that even if they pulled the investigation, the US might 'take up the case,' and the Swiss might decide to conduct a probe of their own.

LJ Moses noted that he had been advised by the AG that BAE 'has always contended that any payments it made were approved by the Kingdom of Saudi Arabia.' In short, they argued that they were lawful commissions not bribes. This contention was never tested in a court of law in light of the way the allegations were handled.

LJ Moses was not amenable to the suggestion that the court had no right to intervene in the circumstances at hand. He observed that when a threat 'involves the criminal jurisdiction of this country, then the issue is no longer a matter only for Government, the courts are bound to consider what steps they must take to preserve the integrity of the criminal justice system.'

Furthermore, 'in the instant application, the Government's response has failed to recognise that the threat uttered was not simply directed at this country's commercial, diplomatic and security interests; it was aimed at its legal system.'

He wrote: 'That threat was made with the specific intention of interfering with the course of the investigation. The Saudis knew what was proposed: the SFO intended to inspect Swiss bank accounts. Those who uttered and adopted the threat intended to prevent the course which the SFO wished to pursue. It is unlikely that so blatant a threat would have been made had those responsible not believed that it might well succeed.'

LJ Moses clearly held the view that the UK government had a duty to disabuse the Saudis of that notion. He observed that 'Had such a threat been made by one who was subject to the criminal law of this country, he would risk being charged with an attempt to pervert the course of justice. The course of justice includes the process of criminal investigation.'

He underscored the principle that .'.public authorities must beware of surrendering to the dictates of unlawful pressure groups.'..emphasizing the courts' 'responsibility to protect the rule of law'- noting that 'The surrender of a public authority to threat or pressure undermines the rule of law.'

Counsel for the government 'warned that to invoke the rule of law adds nothing to the argument in this case.' It is noteworthy, however, how frequently the UK government (and the media) invoke rule of law as capable of 'adding to the argument' when Russia is in their collective sights.

Although LJ Moses wrote that 'There continues to be debate about the meaning and scope of the rule of law.' he observed that 'At the heart of the obligations of the courts and of the judges lies the duty to protect the rule of law'- observing that rule of law is recognized as 'an existing constitutional principle' under UK law that recognizes 'the 'relationship between the independence of the judiciary and the rule of law.'

He described the rule of law as 'nothing if it fails to constrain overweening power' and quoted the Honourable J.J Spigelman AC, Chief Justice of New South Wales who described judges and lawyers as: 'boundary riders maintaining the integrity of the fences that divide legal constraint from the sphere of freedom of action.'

He wrote that 'the courts patrol the boundary between the territory which they safeguard and that for which the executive is responsible.' This rather poetic description would likely appeal to Russian lawyers and the Russian judiciary.

He wrote that a line 'of well-established authority demonstrates how the courts protect the rule of law by ensuring the independence of the decision-maker, free from pressure and threat.' He was singularly unimpressed by the Government's rather extraordinary argument that 'the courts are powerless to assist in resisting when the explicit threat has been made by a foreign state.'

No judge worth his salt could let that go. LJ Moses was not about to.

He described it as a 'dispiriting submission.' which captured my reaction to the letter. He described it, however, as revealing 'the extent to which the Government has failed to appreciate the role of the courts in upholding and protecting the rule of law.'

He aptly noted that 'Surrender deprives the law of any power to resist for the future.'. Surrender merely encourages those with power, in a position of strategic and political importance, to repeat such threats, in the knowledge that the courts will not interfere with the decision of a prosecutor to surrender.' He observed that the Saudis likely included this supposition in their calculation when making the threat. They knew it would work.

On the other hand, 'Had they known, or been told, that the threat was futile because any decision to cave in would be struck down by the courts, it might never have been uttered or it might have been withdrawn.'

LJ Moses concluded that the UK government was rather quick to accede to the threat and that the facts, as he knew them, did not support any suggestion that necessity or duress informed the decision to demur to the Saudis: 'There was no specific, direct threat made against the life of anyone.'

He also noted that there was 'no evidence whatever that any consideration was given as to how to persuade the Saudis to withdraw the threat, let alone any attempt made to resist the threat.' He would not assume, as urged to do, that these considerations had informed the decision to cease the investigation: 'It was incumbent on the Director, once it was alleged that he ought not to have succumbed to the threat, to satisfy the court that he had not given way without the resistance necessary to protect the rule of law.'

LJ Moses was clearly unnerved with the actions of the state in the case:

'No-one suggested to those uttering the threat that it was futile, that the United Kingdom's system of democracy forbad pressure being exerted on an independent prosecutor whether by the domestic executive or by anyone else; no-one even hinted that the courts would strive to protect the rule of law and protect the independence of the prosecutor by striking down any decision he might be tempted to make in submission to the threat.

If, as we are asked to accept, the Saudis would not be interested in our internal, domestic constitutional arrangements, it is plausible they would understand the enormity of the interference with the United Kingdom's sovereignty, when a foreign power seeks to interfere with the internal administration of the criminal law. It is not difficult to imagine what they would think if we attempted to interfere with their criminal justice system.'

However, as I have observed in Part One, and reiterate throughout this book, Western governments, in tandem with the Western media, do not hesitate to intervene with the internal administration of the criminal justice system in Russia, or to understand the enormity of the interference with Russia's sovereignty when they choose to do so.

LJ Moses was not persuaded that the UK governments' feeble response to the Saudi threat was born out of a belief that resistance was in fact futile:

'The reason no attempt appears to have been made to persuade the Saudis that the threat could not succeed is not difficult to find.'.. 'too ready a submission may give rise to the suspicion that the threat was not the real ground for the decision at all; rather it was a useful pretext..'

'It is obvious, in the present case, that the decision to halt the investigation suited the objectives of the executive. Stopping the investigation avoided uncomfortable consequences, both commercial and diplomatic. Whilst we have accepted the evidence as to the grounds of this decision, in future cases, absent a principle of necessity, it would be all too tempting to use a threat as a ground for a convenient conclusion. We fear for the reputation of the administration of justice if it can be perverted by a threat.'

In a marvellous paragraph,[155]he observed: 'Let it be accepted, as the defendant's grounds assert, that this was an exceptional case; how does it look if on the one occasion in recent memory, a threat is made to the administration of justice, the law buckles'?

He notes that the UK's Government Legal Service 'has every reason to be proud of its reputation for giving independent and, on occasion, unpalatable advice,' but questions how it can 'be maintained if in exceptional cases, when a threat comes from a powerful and strategically important ally, it must yield to pressure?'

He noted the obligation for the UK to lead by example, to 'provide support and encouragement to those in a less happy position. How do they do so, if they endorse surrender, when in Uganda the courts are forced to resist when those whom they have released on bail are re-arrested on the court-room steps by armed agents of the executive, or when the Chief Justices of Fiji and Pakistan are deposed by military rulers?'

In this regard, he observed that the 'Director failed to appreciate that protection of the rule of law demanded that he should not yield to the threat,' and concluded that his submission to the threat was unlawful.

In his conclusion, LJ Moses wrote:

'The court has a responsibility to secure the rule of law. The Director was required to satisfy the court that all that could reasonably be done had been done to resist the threat. He has failed to do so.'...' No-one, whether within this country or outside is entitled to interfere with the course of our justice. It is the failure of Government and the defendant to bear that essential principle in mind that justifies the intervention of this court.'

He adopted Tony Blair's assertion in 2006 that 'this was the clearest case for intervention in the public interest he had seen' (justifying his desire to stop the BAE investigation) as the logic for the High Court choosing to save it. Accordingly, the court quashed the Director's decision and remitted it to him for reconsideration.

The decision was, of course, appealed to the House of Lords by the UK government.[156] The main issue in those proceedings was, as the Law Lords' observed, 'not whether his decision was right or wrong, nor whether the Divisional Court or the House agrees with it, but whether it was a decision which the Director was lawfully entitled to make.'

The Lords ruled in favour of the government on these very narrow grounds, namely that the Director was entitled to rule as he did.

The judgement of LJ Moses and Mr Justice Sullivan in the High Court is a heartening read. It provides a useful backdrop to the rest of the discussion in this Part.

The US government was decidedly more vociferous in investigating the various allegations against BAE, a company that is very active in the US defence market. Under a 2010 settlement with the US Justice Department, BAE paid a $400 million fine and pleaded guilty to one count of conspiring to make false statements about having an internal program that complied with US anti bribery laws.

That same year in the UK, BAE pleaded guilty to an accounting violation for failing to properly record commissions in the region of £8m paid to a middleman involved in the sale of a radar system to Tanzania in 1999. The plea bargain deal absolved it from wider corruption and bribery charges.

As part of the deal with the SFO, BAE agreed to pay £30m to the Tanzanian people. UK MPs subsequently discovered that the money had not been paid directly to the Tanzanian people, and the company was criticized for purportedly dragging its feet in making disbursements. [157]

The entire affair was an ugly business from start to finish. It is clear that the facts never got a public airing. No-one emerged from the sorry business covered in roses (except for the UK High Court) - and most decidedly not the UK government. The case created the impetus, in no small part, to finally create an anti-bribery and corruption regulatory framework that has teeth.

However, the 'resolution' of the BAE case does not imbue one with confidence that should a future UK criminal investigation yield a connection to the all-important Saudis, that it will be vigorously prosecuted on the merits. The Saudis, at least, have reason to be cheerful. The UK public does not.

That being said, now that new anti-bribery and corruption legislation[158] is in place in the UK, prosecution is far more likely (in non-'exceptional' cases) and fines and penalties for offences are severe. A transgression can also result in severe reputational damage, making non-conformance a potential expensive proposition.

The SFO and the World Bank recently settled with an unlikely offender- the Oxford University Press- fined £1.892 million for bribery allegations involving the sale of school books in east Africa.

In February, 2012, Russia joined the OECD's Anti-Bribery Convention. To do so, amendments were made to Russian criminal and administrative laws to bring them into line with international anti-corruption legislation.

'From now on, not only people who give bribes will be called to account, but also those who promise foreign officials money and other property in exchange for services.' Medvedev said, according to RT News. Bribery of foreign officials has been illegal in Russia since May 2011.

Joining the Convention is a pre-condition to enable Russia join the OECD proper. Medvedev's advisor, Arcady Dvorkovich, envisages Russia joining within two years. Russia must pass a lengthy series of reviews to gain entry.

In December, 2008, the Group of States against Corruption (GRECO) conducted an Evaluation Report on the Russian Federation and its efforts to clamp down on corruption.[159] GRECO was established in 1999 by the Council of Europe to monitor member states compliance with Council of Europe anti corruption standards.

According to the report, 'Corruption is a widespread systemic phenomenon in the Russian Federation which affects the society as a whole.'

GRECO representatives were told by Russian officials that 'corruption has escalated since the breakdown of the Soviet Union. The authorities acknowledge that corruption not only poses a danger to the functioning of the State institutions but also exercises a negative impact on business in general as it undermines competition between market players for goods and services and makes the Russian economy less attractive in respect of foreign investment.'

GRECO noted, however, contrary to the view expressed by most members of the Western media, that 'There is no doubt that the Russian authorities take these problems seriously and consequently, the fight against corruption is recognised as a priority at the highest political level.'

In his plenary address to the St Petersburg International Economic Forum in June, 2012 (Russia's equivalent to the Davos Economic Forum), Putin said that 'Unfortunately, corruption is without exaggeration the biggest threat to our development,' describing 'the risks as even worse than the fluctuation of oil prices.' He noted that 'people are tired of everyday corruption, bribery in the state bodies, courts, the judiciary and state-owned companies.'

GRECO referred to the fact that a Russian Presidential Council on Counteracting Corruption was established in May 2008 'as the overall co-ordinating body' and that (then) President Medvedev approved a National Anti-corruption Plan (NACP) in July 2008, 'which further strengthens the political commitment to act rigorously against corruption.'

GRECO observed that 'there appears to be a strong consensus among officials for the need to introduce substantial measures against corruption beyond the mere issuing of declarations, programmes and legislation of which there is no lack.'

It acknowledged, however, that fighting corruption is a major challenge in such a vast country. It was recognized, as a practical matter, that corruption is greater (as is unemployment) and harder to eradicate in battle-scarred regions such as in Russia's Northern Caucasus.

GRECO noted, however, that progress has been made. 'The existing Constitutional and legal framework clearly establishes independence from the legislative and executive powers.' GRECO indicated, however, that the principle of judicial independence needs to be 'strengthened further in practice' highlighting the need for 'systematic introductory and in-service ethics training to be provided to judges of all levels and ranks.'

A significant concern is the fact that the Russian Constitution and federal laws permit a 'comprehensive system of immunities from criminal proceedings and detention concerning a large number of categories of officials.' GRECO recommended, quite rationally, that 'these categories need to be reduced to the minimum required in a democratic society.'

Officials with immunity from prosecution clearly can act in a corrupt and unethical fashion with a sense of impunity, an undesirable state of affairs.

The so-called 'Blue Buckets' movement in Russia arose from a practice that drives regular Moscovites crazy- senior government officials abusing a special privilege that allows them use blue police sirens they can stick on top of their cars to speed through traffic.

Abuse of the privilege is rampant, and photos have been taken of women using the sirens to race to beauty salon appointments. In some cases, other drivers have been killed in accidents involving reckless driving by speeding 'bucket' drivers.

Putin, reacting to public anger at the practice, has reduced the number of bucket permit holders by half, but wryly observed that he expected the numbers of permits in circulation to increase no matter what he does. Truly horrible traffic congestion in Moscow is a major irritant to just about everyone who drives.

I recall uproar in Dublin when the controversial CEO of Ryanair, the hugely successful Irish budget airline, bought a taxi plate (licence) in 2003, allowing him to make the 108-mile round trip from his country home to Dublin airport in the dedicated taxi and bus lanes.

The quintessential O'Leary stunt is legal, provided his journeys are metered and the taxi cab has a driver. It's fair to say that sympathy to his plight is scarce to non-existent amongst Dubliners stuck in traffic as he whizzes past.

The blue buckets phenomenon infuriates most Russians, understandably. Putin is well aware of this fact. Russians know that political insiders have an edge on them, but they don't like their noses rubbed in it. If Irish cognoscenti tried a similar ruse, I doubt they'd make it out of the 'bucket' cars alive, or there would be huge black market demand for the sirens.

GRECO also expressed concern about lack of access to public information, and the need for Russia to make significant changes to meet European standards in this regard.

More generally, it stated that reforms must be implemented with proper regard for 'civil society concerns,' recommending 'broader representation in order to better reflect the interests of the regions as well as those of civil society,' noting, with concern, an overtly 'top-down' approach to reform.

It emphasized the need to ensure that 'civil society is in a position to provide input to, and to make its views known.'

GRECO recommended that 'whistleblower' protection legislation be introduced to protect those who report suspicions of corruption in public administration, in good faith, from adverse consequences and to provide systematic training to all staff concerned.'

This measure is a tough sell in Russia where journalists who expose corruption are routinely beaten within an inch of their lives or murdered. The rank and file civil servant can hardly be expected to step forward without convincing assurances that they will not meet a similar fate for doing so.

However, recent reports on the Russian Internal Ministry website suggest that a new program will facilitate the payment of up to 3 million rubles in monetary rewards to people who provide information that helps to solve crimes.

Concern has been expressed that the well-meaning initiative (huge whistleblower payments are becoming common in the US) could allow unscrupulous business people and those with a grudge to punish their enemies-a practice long established in Russia. Clearly the information provided will have to be carefully vetted to prevent such occurrences.

Putin has mooted giving 'social movements.'..'the right to file lawsuits to defend the interests of their participants'- in essence he appears to contemplate class actions that allow vulnerable individuals to 'resolve a dispute with a governor, for example, on behalf of a large social organization, not on his own.' In this regard, he appears alert to the reality that 'naming names' is still a very hazardous activity in Russia.

In all, GRECO made 26 recommendations to the Russian Federation. In December 2010, [160] GRECO published a follow- up report to assess the measures taken by the Russian authorities to comply.

It concluded that the Russian Federation had 'implemented satisfactorily or dealt with in a satisfactory manner just over a third of the 26 recommendations' contained in the original report.

This result does not sound overly impressive, but GRECO duly noted that Russia had 'received a vast number of recommendations in the Joint First and Second Evaluation Round,' and that 'some of the recommendations require fundamental measures, including the creation of a clear basis for the National anti-corruption policy, far-going legislative reforms and organisational changes in public administration, law enforcement, the judiciary as well as in relation to civil society.'

Clearly, Rome wasn't built in a day. GRECO officials conceded the obvious:

'It goes without saying that this is an immense task to accomplish in only 18 months. GRECO is therefore pleased that the Russian authorities have addressed a large majority of the recommendations even if only just over a third of them could be considered as implemented in full.'

'The adoption of a National Anti-Corruption Strategy and the accompanying accompanying National Anti-Corruption Plan 2010/2011 for the implementation of the strategy are obviously an important achievement and so is the adoption of general legislation on access to documents and information in various fields of public administration.'

That being said, concern was expressed that 'a large majority of the recommendations need further attention by the authorities, in areas dealing with the criminal immunity of public officials and the independence of the judiciary,' noting that such measures 'appear particularly critical matters..' It also noted that part of the challenge is 'that many recommendations are about implementing legal norms, rather than adopting new legislation or rules.'

The central role played by the prosecutorial authorities in fighting corruption was described by GRECO as having a negative aspect to it, namely the fact that 'Such an approach conveys the message that a rather strong repressive approach to the fight against corruption prevails in Russia.'

This finding flies in the face of statements made by Putin rejecting a draconian approach to fighting corruption. Imposing solutions on a wary public simply will not work. Change must be accepted by society at large. A square peg never fits into a round hole.

GRECO was again at pains to stress that 'more emphasis needs to be placed on preventive measures outside the criminal justice sector, such as training of employees of the civil service. It reiterated that anti-corruption measures introduced in various sectors would benefit from being complemented with 'more input from civil society representatives, such as international non-governmental organisations with an anti-corruption agenda.'

In my view, it is Russian civil society that must provide this input, as there is considerable suspicion in Russia- often for good reason-towards many Western anti-corruption bodies and Western NGOs. In any event, these are Russian issues that only Russians can ultimately solve.

Russia has made considerable progress in fighting corruption in other areas.

In 2008, the Financial Action Task Force (FATF), the international body tasked with setting and monitoring global efforts to counter money-laundering, reported on Russia's efforts to conform to international obligations.[161]It made a number of recommendations for improvements.

In April 2012, FATF reported on progress made.[162]

A major findings of the report was that Russia has 'in a short time (since 2003) implemented and enhanced its AML/CFT (counter financing terrorism) system and has done so in less time than many other countries.'

The central body in Russia tasked with compliance, Rosfinmonitoring, was commended for performing the traditional tasks of such a body 'in full compliance with the FATF Standards, as well as many other tasks, including serving as the central responsible agency for AML/CFT matters.'

FATF noted that many important facets of Russian anti-money laundering measures were 'generally sound and in line with the FATF Standards.' Improvements suggested are not out of line with outstanding issues in many developed countries.

It noted, however, that the supervisory authorities in Russia lacked 'an adequate level of (sanctioning) powers-noting that 'criminal ownership of financial institutions is not specifically prohibited.'

Alarmingly, the report noted, that 'some banks are in fact still believed to be owned and controlled by (suspected) criminals and their front men.'..observing that Russian supervisory authorities 'need more legal powers with respect to preventing criminals from controlling financial institutions.'

FATF commended the Bank of Russia, however, 'for performing its tasks at an acceptable level despite the lack of legal tools' and it observed that 'International co-operation by the Russian Federation is generally sound, based on practical mechanisms and supported by numerous treaties.'

Despite all this emphasis on corruption in Russian society, things are not nearly so bad on the ground. Hundreds, probably thousands of deals are done in Russia every day by non-Russians, without incident.[163]

The annual World Investment Report from the UN Conference on Trade and Investment has reported that FDI inflows into Russia were $52.9bn in 2011, in ninth place behind the US ($226.9bn), China ($124bn) Belgium ($89.1bn), Hong Kong ($83.2bn), Brazil ($66.7bn), Singapore ($64bn), the UK ($53.9bn), and the British Virgin Islands ($52.9bn).

There is clearly much room for improvement. However, the numbers reflect the world's continued love affair with China, despite the fact that it has problems with rule of law and corruption that eclipse those in Russia by a wide margin.

Much has been written about doing business in Russia. I cannot begin to do the vast subject justice in this book.

Suffice to say that in the business context, successful, lucrative deals can be sealed with Russian companies and the Russian state without sacrificing one's principles or lowering ethical standards. One must do one's homework first, however.

In its 2011 annual 'Deal Drivers' survey, international law firm, CMS Moscow reported that inbound M & A activity remains strong in Russia. In 2011, 70 deals worth Euro 21.2bn closed. US investors were particularly active. UK companies were also in the top ten investors in Russia.

Survey respondents, however, cited legislation, bureaucracy and corruption as 'significant roadblocks for foreign investors.' These issues are problematic, but Russia is rarely given credit where it is due.

In many cases, the problems that Western investors experience in the Russian market are due to lack of due diligence and lack of local knowledge. As is always the case with doing business abroad, knowledge, appreciation and sensitivity to local laws, culture and norms is essential for success. Russia is not unique in this regard.

Going in blind is ill-advised. Acquiring local partners in Russia is usually critical for success. Joint venture (JV) arrangements are popular, but in keeping with the trend globally, they tend to crash and burn quickly- one side needs control or bickering is inevitable, as occurred with the BP and TNK joint venture. When that deal was originally struck, Putin warned that a 50-50 arrangement would be unworkable.

It is entirely possible to do business in Russia without paying bribes or engaging in other corrupt practices. However, having and adhering to ethical principles of one's own is necessary in the event a request is made for the payment of bribes.

It is also advisable to have a long term strategic commitment to the market: Russians tend to view Westerners as inveterate 'takers' who give nothing back to the greater Russian community.

Western companies that have prospered over decades in Russia have contributed to local schools, third level institutions, and generally worked hard to win the trust and respect of local communities and politicians. There is nothing revolutionary in such a basic concept, but it is remarkable how frequently it is ignored by Western companies entering the Russian market.

Corruption, in the form of bribe seeking, most often arises in situations where licences or permits are required-where bureaucracy is at its greatest. The rules of engagement (zero tolerance) need to be made clear from the outset, without condescension: In Russia, one sucks and blows at one's peril. Consistency is key. It is not uncommon for Russian businesses to 'test' one's resolve in this respect.

Russians, traditionally with low expectations of Westerners, often express pleasant surprise, even incredulity when they meet 'honest 'Westerners. It hardly bears repeating, except for the fact the Western media ignore it, that Russians lack experience with 'ethical behaviour.' They have seen little of it throughout their fraught history. We are hardly awash with it in the West either, but we at least can talk the talk.

At the risk of stereotyping, in my observation at least, it appears to be a quirk of the Russian personality that Russians rather despise perceived weakness in business partners. For instance, in business negotiations, adopting an American slap on the back, 'win-win' strategy is a sure-fire losing proposition, as one will be perceived as a turkey ripe for plucking. Making concessions early on, or being 'too nice' will backfire, at least until you are a known and trusted commodity.

Indeed, it is worth observing, despite the rather naked generalization, that Russians are the toughest people I have ever met. Many of them seem to have steel at their core. They can appear inured to suffering after enduring decades of precarious living and the need to remain constantly on high alert.

It is a saying in Russia that one (however successful) should 'never say no to poverty or prison.' For that reason, Russians tend to live for the day, on the assumption that tomorrow may never come, or, if it does, that calamity will follow in its wake.

This somewhat jaded ambivalence to everyday existence is tempered with the most laconic sense of humour, deep sardonicism, and a beguiling tendency towards hedonism. These are outrageous generalisations, so take them at face value.

Issues with corruption and bribery exist throughout the world. Such behaviour is part and parcel of the human condition, and will remain so. In many countries, including Western nations, corruption takes many forms and has cultural underpinnings. We are far from paragons of virtue.

Despite various attempts at legal definitions in legislation, corruption is hard to pin down and attitudes to it vary. Behaviour considered corrupt in one culture may not be viewed as such in another.

Russia's image (and that of its people) suffers each year when various Western 'Holy-Cow' surveys are published by OECD, Forbes, Transparency International, etc. Russia invariably finishes close to rock bottom.

I do not suggest, as I reiterate throughout this book, that serious problems do not exist on the ground, but to suggest, year after year, that Russia is the bottom of the pile is simply not an accurate reading of the situation.

These 'surveys' do more harm than good, and are especially damaging to the people behind the lurid headlines. They frequently present a narrow, siloed approach to a multi-dimensional, highly nuanced and complex problem. However well-intentioned, they are misguided in the extreme.

For instance, in 2011, the notorious Transparency International (TI) 'Corruption Perceptions Index' (CPI)[164] ranked Russia 143rd in 2011, with Uganda, and Nigeria. Russia's current ranking is an improvement on its 154th place in the Berlin-based anti-corruption watchdog's 2010 list.

The UK ranks in 16th place and the US, 24.t.h.Ireland is ranked 19th. Extraordinarily, Saudi Arabia is ranked 57th. The rankings are based on interviews and workshops with supposed 'experts.' It is a highly subjective process, and thus susceptible to all manner of personal bias. The exact methodology used to gather and correlate the results is remarkable in itself for its lack of transparency.

According to a number of folk I have met in developing markets over the years, in certain instances, the data for the TI in-country results is supplied by vociferous opponents of the ruling party. Such a scenario raises the prospect of political bias, and should be disclosed up front.

Several countries that are ranked higher than Russia have issues so significant that they are de facto closed to tourism, and controlled by warlords, drug cartels or Saudi princes in countries where women cannot drive, vote or work in the professions.

It also appears nigh impossible for wealthy Western countries to score poorly, even when large Western corporate entities (often State champions) from these same nations have admitted to corrupt activities in the very countries that rank leagues beneath their home states. Their corruption drags down the rankings of the countries they do business in.

I have reviewed these surveys for years, in conjunction with well-publicized and confirmed incidents of corruption and fraud by Western companies, and I could make no sense whatsoever out of the rankings, which appear hugely skewed towards a Western, primarily neo-colonial world view, intentionally or otherwise.

TI is described as 'non-partisan,' but is a self-appointed guardian of the free world in the battle against corruption, and is funded by many Western State agencies and government bodies.

Senior representatives of the TI organisation in the UK make no bones about their animosity to the Russian market-and the Russian state in particular. I have attended meetings where such persons equated Putin with Robert Mugabe, and casually observed that it is impossible to do business in Russian without paying bribes.

Preposterous nonsense, but alarming, nonetheless, from an organisation that has influence with global investors.

Upon close examination, however, TI's Corruption 'index 'delivers exactly what it says on the tin.

What is it after all? It is a 'perceptions' index. How can it account for the potential for bias? Whose perceptions are assessed? About what, when and where? How are the 'facts' that underlie these perceptions corroborated? By whom?

How does one gauge the veracity or accuracy of a 'perception'? Is the 'perception' of parties with a contrary view taken into account, and, if so, where are they documented, and why are they discounted? The index demonstrably lacks academic rigour and is, at best, a window into Western perceptions of countries not in the inner sanctum.

Why does it matter? Surely its limitations are obvious at first glance.

It matters a very great deal on a number of levels. Many investors are hugely influenced by these studies, given massive coverage by Western media outlets every year when they appear. They negatively impact fledgling efforts to attract inbound investment and to grow the tourism sector.

Of course, the intent is to shame countries into 'doing the right thing.' That is all very well if we had the high ground. We do not. Indeed, in my estimation, Western countries ought to be receive penalty points- a severe handicap- at the outset, before the 'rankings' are compiled, for failing to eradicate corruption after decades, even centuries purporting to do so.

Let the bookies devise a number. The current rankings are akin to a spin on the roulette wheel in any event. Right now, however, the dices are clearly loaded against emerging and developing markets. We have, however, a far higher tolerance for corruption at home and in emerging markets that play ball with us than for those countries that demonstrate an independent streak.

The TI survey, in particular, is given a free pass in the West. It is presented as having a nigh divine origin. It is another depressing example of how standards of academic rigour and critical thinking are at an all time low, when entire peoples are judged by such markedly deficient criteria. It is also used by various independent bodies to compile country risk rankings for the financial services sector.

These surveys/indices merely ingrain Western prejudices and stereotypes about countries at fragile stages of development. It may be that we wish it so. Regardless, the cliché that 'perception is nine-tenths reality' is particularly apt in the West, and thus, the damage done is likely all the greater.

The impact of such 'surveys' is conceivably heightened when combined, as in the case of Russia, with relentlessly negative media coverage of the country.

However, as noted, powerful, wealthy emerging nations such as China have started to cry foul about Western dominance, for instance, of the credit rating agencies, as they perceive a bias towards them. Emerging markets and developing countries need to make their voices heard in fighting back against the silly level of media coverage and credence that these annual, highly divisive surveys receive in the West.

Rolling over and taking the inevitable beating is a fool's game.

The Forbes 'Despotism Index' is another example.[165] In 2010, Russia was ranked second last- 83rd out of 84 entries. Russia is the second most 'despotic' (whatever that means) nation on the planet?

I find that preposterous. Columbia is ranked 58th, Mexico, 56th, Bulgaria 64th, China 48th, and Saudi Arabia in 44th place. According to the Forbes website, the 'Index' measures 'corruption, property rights and the legal framework of the country, and cites its sources as : 'IMF; CMA DataVision; Moody's; S&P; WEF Global Competitiveness Report; Transparency Int'l; Int'l Property Rights.'

It is important to note that corruption in the West occurs despite decades, even centuries of democracy. It is deeply ingrained, despite the fact that we have so-called rule of law coming out of our ears.

In recent times, huge fines have been paid by US companies to regulators such as the Securities & Exchange Commission (SEC) with respect to the payment of bribes, and lengthy prison sentences have been handed down for insider trading abuses and fraudulent activity generally by corporate executives and titans of industry.

Barely a day goes by without a new scandal on the front pages, challenging our incredulity that capitalist markets play fair. The giant US retailer, Walmart, is currently embroiled in a scandal over bribes allegedly paid in Mexico to secure permission to open more stores in that country. An internal probe is investigating similar claims in India, China and Brazil.

Part of the problem is that the bureaucracy involved in setting up retail operations is so cumbersome, involving multiple levels of government and state approvals, that it presents numerous opportunities for bribe seeking by low level officials.

Closer to home, Italy still battles corruption, bribery and entrenched Mafia elements. The unfortunate inhabitants of Naples had to live with mountains of festering garbage for extended periods as a result of a standoff between local mafia and ineffective politicians.

Italian police have made many arrests of significant Mafia bosses over the past few years, particularly in the South of Italy. In March, 2012, Naples police arrested 47 people, including 16 tax judges, tax officials, accountants and a lawyer, in an anti-mafia sting operation that targeted ostensibly legitimate businesses that prosecutors allege acted as front operations for the vicious Camorra mob. Assets worth over one billion euro were also seized.

Italian prosecutors allege that the judges were involved in a 'vast web of corruption' and facilitated an 'illicit trade of court verdicts' – one female judge may have acted as a group accountant for the mob's operation.

Small businesses in Naples and across southern Italy must constantly deal with mafia 'requests' for 'Il Pizzo'-

protection money. Brave folk who have refused to pay have had their shops fire bombed and been shot at. Roberto Saviano, the heroic writer who exposed the ferocious Italian Camorra mob in his best-selling book (made into a movie) 'Gomorrah'- is forced to remain in hiding under constant police protection.

Although not as infamous as the Sicilian Cosa Nostra, the 2008 turnover of Italy's most powerful mafia clan, the Ndrangheta, from the Calabrian region, has been estimated at Euro 44bn, or 3% of GDP. The clan is a leading player in the global cocaine trade, with tight connections to drug lords in Columbia, Latin America and Mexico.

Calabria is a poor region and local police and prosecutors are completely out-gunned and out-manoeuvred by the savage criminals. Gang members have blood ties, meaning that 'pentiti' (informants) are very rare, as turning state's evidence involves betraying family. In some mob-ridden towns, police patrols have had to be reduced to save petrol and police cars are barely road worthy.[166]

It's impossible to attract quality judges and prosecutors to the crime-ridden area as the best candidates can choose their postings. Those who get what is considered a hardship post in Calabria rarely last long.

There have been suggestions, by no means far-fetched, that the clan takes a keen interest in politics and has close ties to the Church as well as infiltrating Italian politics and law enforcement at the highest levels.

Their operations are now fully diversified, with interests in extortion, human trafficking and even arms dealing- they have alliances with Chinese gangs and other international crime syndicates to assist in laundering their spoils, often through legitimate front businesses.

In September 2009, the Ndrangheta mob was accused by a former gang member of sinking dozens of ships loaded with radioactive waste off the Italian coast and of shipping radioactive waste to developing countries for dumping- similar to the plot of the *Transporter 3* movie starring British action hero Jason Statham.

In January, 2011, a WikiLeaks cable was released in which a US diplomat said corruption in Calabria involved corrupt politicians, corrupt port officials and woefully unmanned prosecutors' offices. The cable, one of five Mafia-related documents released, dated from December 2008, before the Italian government began a crackdown on the crime syndicate.

The US cables criticized the federal government in Rome for failing to support and resource local law enforcement to enable it fight the mob. It called the Italian justice system 'dysfunctional' – complaining that prisoners are freed early due to prison overcrowding, and trials take so long that they are dismissed when the statute of limitations expires.

'If it were not part of Italy, Calabria would be a failed state,' one cable began, noting that the 'ndrangheta's drug trafficking, extortion and money laundering activities accounted for at least 3 per cent of Italy's gross domestic product.

In everything but name, Calabria was described as a 'mafia state.'

Since the cables were written, the Italian government has arrested around 300 mob suspects in northern Italy and a small number of informants have been unearthed. In addition, the federal government has sent police and soldiers to the region to protect prosecutors who have a very scary job, and require a great deal of courage to do it.[167]

It is clear, however, that the battle to wrench Italy back from the mouth of the mob is by no means won. Some battle-scarred veterans believe it is too late, and that the war has already been lost.

I love Italy and fervently hope that verdict is wildly premature. Nonetheless, I am conscious that Italy's problems closely mirror those in Russia.

Compared to the rough treatment meted out to the Russians, the Western media is, however, very indulgent towards Italy; you don't read gleeful references to 'the (Italian) mafia state' every day in the main Western business dailies.

It is crystal clear that Russia is treated as a special case, despite the unpalatable fact that sophisticated European democracies (like Italy), literally on our doorsteps, still fight pitched battles with crime lords and vicious criminal syndicates that are so bedded down in society that they threaten the very legitimacy of the state. These are not minor problems.

As has been the case in Italy for decades, similarly, in Russia, in the 1980s and 1990s, many legitimate Russian businesses were forced to pay off organized crime gangs to stay alive and to protect their holdings. Those who refused to pay were killed.

As David Hoffman wrote in his book, *The Oligarchs*, previously referred to,[168] 'The city (Moscow) was rife with protection rackets-virtually every business had to employ a *krysha*, or roof, for protection in the early 1990's- and several large organized crime gangs thrived. Bribery, kickbacks, and secret overseas bank accounts were common, and disputes were settled with car bombs and contract murders.'

High ranking, corrupt Russian politicians used bar-room brawl tactics, assassins and the legal system to crush opponents. Libel suits were common to silence those who tried to expose what Hoffman described as the 'corruption sickness that befell all Russia.' Street vendors trying to eke out a meagre living were extorted by 'anyone with a badge,' often forced to surrender a month's pay as a 'fine' for a manufactured infraction.[169]

A ruthless and insatiably greedy cast of characters employed a curious, but deadly mix of violence, extortion and ostensibly legal means to amass and keep the vast riches they had stolen from the Russian people, with state officials acting as enthusiastic co-conspirators.

It's not that people don't fight back.

Many Italian judges and lawyers have been murdered over the years as they sought to bring Mafiosi to justice. Courageous prosecutors such as Giovanni Falcone, his wife, a magistrate, and three police officers, were blown to bits in their car in a massive explosion on a motorway near Capaci, Sicily on May 23, 1992.

A mere 57 days later, his friend and fellow judge, Paolo Borsellino was killed in another explosion on July 19 1992. Both men knew that they would likely die for their convictions, but they carried on regardless, with wit and gallows humour, a remorseless thirst for the truth and justice, and a phenomenal work ethic.

I commend a fine book about the Sicilian mafia and the campaign to eradicate it, by Alexander Stille, titled *Excellent Cadavers*.[170] The book gives both men, and more like them, their fair due. I recall hearing the tragic news of their deaths while living in Toronto, Canada. My heart sank.

The huge outcry in Italy- and internationally- that followed in the wake of the murders created the impetus for a huge campaign by the Italian government to take the fight to the thugs. Sadly, the battle is far from won. Undoubtedly, the blood of more good men and women will be spilled as time moves on.

Falcone was quoted as saying" The Mafia is a human phenomenon and thus, like all human phenomena, it has had a beginning and an evolution, and will also have an end.' It is a tenacious, resilient beast, however, and has proven extremely difficult to eradicate. However, lack of political will and links between Italian politicians, the Catholic Church, and the mob undoubtedly explain its longevity to a significant extent.

It is a common occurrence for Italian prosecutors to charge sitting Italian politicians, even government ministers, with having mafia connections. The world weary Italian public tends to assume the worst about its politicians.

In 2006, an Italian government advisory body, CNEL, estimated the value of the usury black market in Italy at €12.5 billion. Many Italian families, particularly in the South of Italy, do not have access to credit and are therefore easy targets for the mob loan sharks.

The Chairman of the European Central Bank and previous Chairman of the Italian Central Bank, Mario Draghi gave testimony to the Italian Central Bank in which he indicated that the crisis has proved to be a boon for Italian organised crime, making a fortune out of charging usurious rates to small businesses. He intimated that the mob is filling the void that the traditional banks are no longer filling, charging as much as 500% interest.

Although the image we have of Italy is predominantly positive, notwithstanding the number of Godfather movies that are pumped out by Hollywood, it has a seedy underbelly that I am sure the Italians are happy does not get more press. Fortunately, the lure of Italy, with its fine food, wine, art, history, and friendly, creative people, is enough to keep the tourist revenue flowing.

I do not presume to gloat over the Italian situation, however.

Fifteen years after it was first established, the Irish Mahon tribunal investigation into planning irregularities and corruption in Ireland (named after Judge Alan Mahon, the final chair of the tribunal) was published in March, 2012. [171]

The lengthy report concluded that 'Corruption in Irish political life was both endemic and systemic. It affected every level of government from some holders of top ministerial offices to some local councillors and its existence was widely known and widely tolerated.'

It noted that 'those involved operated with a justified sense of impunity and invincibility. There was little appetite on the part of the State's political or investigative authorities to take the steps necessary to combat it effectively or to sanction those involved.'

There have been numerous comments in international agency reports over the years about Ireland's hugely lacklustre approach to fighting corruption. Only in very recent times has comprehensive corruption legislation been tabled to address the problem. Most people- and businesses- are totally unaware of it.

Reports of such endemic corruption have, as noted in the Mahon report, seriously undermined the Irish public's faith in democracy and in its public officials. The report notes that corruption 'thrives in shadows and darkness,' and suggests that efforts to combat it must focus on 'ensuring transparency and accountability in public life.'

Ireland has been a functioning democracy and Free State since 1922. We don't lack tools and instruments to establish and maintain rule of law; we have long had a sophisticated common law system based on English law.

In other words, we have had 90 years to 'get it right.' to iron out the wrinkles. Yet, as the Mahon report makes tragically clear, we have a long road to travel before we can assume the moral high ground or look down on our neighbours.

In the US, powerful right wing corporations dominate law making, in some States literally writing laws that are passed word for word which promote a corporate agenda that discriminates against the poor and disenfranchised. Privatisation is a special agenda item for them, persistently lobbying to have critical public services, from the prison service to education, outsourced to member companies. Invariably, the American public suffers.[172]

Such a warped dynamic, kept very much in stealth mode, is also a form of corruption-the corruption of democracy. Ironically, one of Putin's biggest concerns is that Russian big business might once again succeed in usurping the democracy process, with a view to 'owning' the state. Arguably, that battle has long been lost in the US.

Yet, as we have seen, the US media and US politicians routinely patronise Russia for shortcomings that exist in profusion at home.

Countries such as Italy that have fought the Mafia for decades have much to offer Russia in terms of expertise, and indeed simple bravery in facing down the criminals. Yet, the battle is far from won. It is very unrealistic that our expectations of Russia are so elevated, when you compare it to the situation in many sophisticated, longstanding democracies far closer to home.

Bulgaria and Romania were admitted into the European Union in January 2007 over the objections of many people who felt that the degree of corruption and crime in both countries was such that they could not meet the requirements for entry. Organised crime in Bulgaria is endemic and reaches deep into everyday society.

Romania, an ex-communist country has similar problems. Great effort is being made in both countries to improve matters, with varying degrees of success. In Bulgaria, it has been reported that corruption has undermined the judicial process with allegations of bribery against investigators, lawyers and judges commonplace.

Both the Romanian and Bulgarian public express deep concern about corruption in their respective countries and there is widespread support for tackling the issues, but the public is sceptical that progress has been made. According to a Eurobarometer survey from February 2012, 67% of Romanians consider that corruption has increased in the last three years.[173]

The EU budget has provided over Euro 12m to Romania to fight corruption and to support judicial reform. Large sums have also been given to Bulgaria.

According to a recent EU Commission report on Bulgaria, 'organised crime is still described by independent observers as a fundamental challenge for the state and the society'- a view described as 'shared by public opinion.'[174]

The EU crime agency, Europol is quoted as considering 'Organised crime in Bulgaria as unique in the EU to the extent that it exercises considerable influence over the economy which is a platform to influence the political process and state institutions.'[175]

Europol statistics are provided that suggest that 'the annual turnover of the twelve most important organised crime activities in Bulgaria is estimated at 1.8 BEUR or 4.8% of GDP annually.'[176]Contract killings are common and Bulgarian citizens and foreign investors alike have filed complaints with the EU Commission about 'judicial inaction and alleged collusion with organised crime on local level.' particularly in the Black Sea region.[177]

Both Romania and Bulgaria are still subject to monitoring by the EU regarding their efforts to reduce high levels of corruption and to bring their judicial systems into compliance with EU norms.[178] Yet, we do not read about these issues- in the heart of the EU- except as a tiny footnote in the business press.

However, all kinds of accommodations towards other nations are made by Western politicians when it suits them. In seeking entry to the Euro, certain countries, such as Greece, were less than candid about the state of the country's balance sheet. EU officials, keen to expand membership, turned a blind eye. Those chickens are now coming home to roost with a vengeance.

It is unlikely that Russia will seek membership of the EU any time soon, or ever, but I expect that should it choose to do so, we would not pave the way as we have for Bulgaria, Romania and Greece, despite Russia's very superior balance sheet, and problems with corruption and bribery that are no worse than in many EU countries well within the fold.

Russia is constantly told that 'better regulation and rule of law' will alleviate, if not solve, most of its problems. This is disingenuous in the extreme.

As we have seen with the case of Bernie Madoff, the former Chairman of the US NASDAQ Stock Exchange convicted of running a $50 million dollar Ponzi scheme, regulation will not eliminate fraud, insider trading or corrupt dealings between companies and individuals.

There is no 'magic bullet' regulatory model that will ensure that a capitalist economy is squeaky clean or that all participants will play fair. We are long accustomed to lobbyists and lawyers exploiting loopholes in whatever laws or regulations are drafted to try to ensure a level playing field.

In the organized crime arena, mafia figures infiltrated the US capital markets in past decades, and they still have a strong hold on certain sectors such as the US ports, where their influence has been described by US prosecutors as 'pervasive.'

In January, 2011, the FBI carried out its biggest-ever mob bust. More than one hundred alleged mobsters were arrested, following allegations of racketeering at US ports – the kind of activity portrayed by Marlon Brando in the 1954 movie, 'On the Waterfront.' Sixty years later, little has changed.

There were so many arrests that the detainees had to be processed at an army base. The indictments show that the busy ports of New York and New Jersey remain compromised and that extortion rackets in the ports greatly increase the cost of doing business.

An FT article on the problem[179] quotes Stephen Taylor, Director of The New Jersey Attorney General's Division of Criminal Justice, 'This (the arrests), reinforces the understanding that organised crime is still a problem and that it is so entrenched, it is difficult to uproot.' There have long been allegations that various waterfront officials, paid very large salaries, upwards of $400,000.00 a year, have been complicit in Mafia extortion and other corrupt and illegal practices.

Organized crime is also deeply rooted in Japan with a home-grown version of the mafia playing an ostensibly open role in society. They are known as the Yakuza and are believed to be the largest organized crime group in the world.

They operate quite openly, with offices and Yakuza symbols on their doors. Many members are covered in tattoos they like to show off. They run a vast criminal operation with fingers in every pie, including prostitution rings and human trafficking.

Yakuza also engage in corporate extortion rackets known as 'sokaiya.' They threaten to disrupt shareholder meetings unless they are paid and use access to trade secrets and/or embarrassing company secrets as additional leverage. They provide what in the West would be considered PR, or investor relations services to protect 'clients' from negative publicity they would happily generate.

Kohei Kishi, director of the organized crime division of Japan's National Police Agency, said in an interview that 'Organized crime is threatening Japan's entire economy,'...'And they have deep roots in construction.' Clauses now exist in construction contracts that void them if contractors are found to have yakuza ties. The country's finance ministry has also increased scrutiny of financial transactions to halt money laundering and lending to yakuza.

Corruption scandals in Asia are two a penny. Insider trading abuse is so entrenched amongst the political and business elite in India that it is virtually impossible to eradicate. Similarly in Japan. The President of Indonesia has stated that corruption 'jeopardises the nation's development.'

Russia is frequently criticized for have a corrupt public sector. Yet, corruption in the public sector is by no means uncommon in the West. Corruption in the public sector in Italy is believed to cost Italy Euro 60bn a year.

Public sector corruption raised its ugly head in rather spectacular fashion in 1999 at the highest levels, when the EU Commission under Jacques Santer resigned en masse as a result of serious corruption charges raised by a whistleblower, after individual members refused to resign.

Scandals around state procurement contracts are especially common in the West, and throughout the world: The pickings are usually good, the competition fierce and insider abuse commonplace. In South Africa, officials at a government special investigations unit advised parliament that up to 20% of the government's procurement budget is routinely lost to corruption and general incompetence.

To counter (legitimate) charges of corruption in the Russian State procurement process, Putin has extolled a new law that promotes transparency in the process, describing it as having 'already become a powerful counter-corruption mechanism.' Activists disagree, but it is early days, and a step in the right direction.

In my view, 'privatisation' of State assets - a favourite topic of the Western business press and UK politicians, nearly always ends badly- at least for the people the process should ultimately serve. Important state assets are sold off for below market value to buyers focused on short-term gain. Once in control, they frequently milk the assets as a cash cow with little interest in the concept of providing quality service to the public- or even ensuring safety in critical infrastructure sectors such as transport.

I firmly believe that the State should maintain a healthy majority interest in important State assets and critical infrastructure- to ensure they are managed in the public's best interest. Recent studies suggest, contrary to longstanding orthodoxy, that State controlled companies often produce a better return on investment than the private sector. Much depends on the calibre of management.

Outside the US and European Union, corruption in all sectors is endemic. Organized crime gangs and kleptocrats control many resource rich countries.

In China, seven hundred million people drink contaminated water containing human and animal faeces, leading to as many as sixty thousand deaths each year. In January 2009, the former chairwoman of a Chinese dairy company, Sanlu, was sentenced to life in prison and three other executives received death sentences as a result of a tainted milk scandal that killed at least six infants and sickened nearly 300,000 others.

In July, 2010, 40 people were killed in a high-speed rail crash in China which caused public outrage, resulting in uncharacteristically forthright media coverage and a freeze on subsequent projects.

The former Chinese minister of railways was dismissed in February 2010 as a result of corruption charges. A one-legged fruit seller was recently beaten to death by corrupt Chinese city government officials, in broad daylight, resulting in mass riots.

The death penalty in China is extensively used, even for relatively minor crimes. China executes more people than any other country. In 2008, Amnesty International reported that at least 1,718 people were given the death penalty. Mobile death units (execution vans) exist to carry out the sentence of death.[180]However, in 1986, the US State of Delaware similarly purchased a mobile lethal injection chamber.[181]

The exact number executed each year is unknown as information on the death penalty remains a State secret. According to Amnesty international, capital punishment has been used to 'send political messages, to silence opponents or to promote political agendas in China, Iran and Sudan' and is often applied 'after grossly unfair trials, and used disproportionately against the poor, minorities and members of racial, ethnic and religious communities.' This latter criticism, however, could be used with equal conviction against the US.

In August 2009, the BBC reported that the China Daily newspaper had conceded that executed Chinese prisoners provided two-thirds of all transplant organs in China.

Saudi Arabia is a country we are keen to accommodate. The Kingdom is hardly a bastion of democracy or human rights.

Western media criticism of Saudi Arabia, is, however, relatively scanty. Yet, rebukes to Russia, a poster-child for democracy by comparison, remain stupendous in number. The truth is that we are more than a little afraid of the Saudis.

What the US, Japanese and Italian experience shows is that when corruption is culturally ingrained, it is extremely difficult to eradicate it. The fact is that we haven't succeeded in doing so in the West.

One of the reasons is that capitalism begets greed. That is its nature.

The sole purpose of many large businesses, despite grandiose mission statements, is the pursuit of profits. Thus, unless they have laws to follow, leaders with integrity, or external pressure is brought to bear, as evidenced in the spate of 'corporate social responsibility' projects at major companies, they will follow the money.

During the current recession, US warehousing giant Costco laid no one off, and refused to cut back on workers' health benefits. I recall that over the years, the Costco CEO, Jim Sinegal, a very decent man by all accounts, was repeatedly chastised by Wall Street for treating his staff too well, paying them a living wage, and providing health care.

More surprisingly, he was also criticized for being too solicitous of customers. It was said that if he only was tougher on both, Costco could be even more profitable. Jim Sinegal stepped down from his position in January 1, 2012, resulting in one less good man in US business.

The far more common 'scorched earth' approach to doing business in which people are little more than inputs to the machine, to be gobbled up and spat out, is especially prevalent in the US, and has bred a ruthless survival of the fittest ethos that permeates many sectors. It does not breed a culture of integrity.

Thus, with worker abuse and disregard of community interest widespread, it is extremely naive to imagine that a great many Western companies care about ethics, except as a PR angle. Yet, we seem to care a great deal about it when the problem is in Russia.

Western companies and Western governments, including my own, literally trip over themselves to do business with China. The fact a poor person convicted of a minor crime in China can be executed after a speedy trial in a mobile execution 'van' and then have his or her organs ripped out for sale on the black market, is not an impediment to making money.

This is an entirely pragmatic attitude. Western companies have piled into Africa to chase down natural resources, notwithstanding the fact that West Africa, in particular, has become a hot bed for cocaine trafficking. The drug trade in many African nations is worth a significant portion of GDP.

Politicians share this pragmatic attitude despite hectoring the Russians from an assumed position of strength that is illusory at best.

The Western world is a cynical place and all manner of alliances, covert and otherwise, are forged for purely economic reasons and political expediency. There are winners and losers, and sadly 'justice' rarely prevails.

History is riddled with such examples. However, that being said, it is a rare day when the Russians are fairly treated by us or by our rapacious media, always at the ready to hang them by their petard for the slightest transgression that would be tolerated at home.

Mexico routinely scores much higher than Russia in the TI rankings (it ranked 100 in 2011). However, many Western drug prosecutors believe that the drug cartels own Mexico. Mexican politicians have been similarly candid.

Attempts have been made to increase salaries and perks for police officers to make the job more attractive, to eliminate financial need as the impetus to engage in corruption and bribery, and there are efforts being made to create more transparent jury trials. However, extreme violence is rampant and public shootouts and kidnapping commonplace.

In August 2011, Monterey, traditionally a relatively wealthy city, was embroiled in gun battles between cartel gangs. Over fifty two people died when drug cartel members stormed a casino and set it on fire, trapping everyone inside.

In another episode, a blood stained, half naked body was hung from a pedestrian bridge in the centre of town,[182]reminiscent of medieval Tudor executions adjacent to Tower Hill in London. Headless bodies have been deposited on public sidewalks. The bodies of 35 people, men and women with suspected links to organised crime were dumped under a highway bridge in eastern Mexico near the once quiet port city of Veracruz.

It would be decidedly out of the ordinary for such an eventuality to occur in Russia, although contract killings are still problematic.

The ex-President of Mexico, Felipe Calderon (Enrique Pena Nieto was recently elected President in a campaign marred by ongoing allegations of vote rigging and fraud, issues little reported in the West) is on the record demanding that the US take responsibility for the influx of weapons that move across the US border into Mexico. It is known that the drug cartels use the porous border to acquire high velocity weaponry, exploiting the US's lax attitude towards the purchasing of weapons.

Carlos Slim, Mexico's telecoms magnet, the richest man in the world, has been quoted as saying 'it is unfair that the drug-producing countries get to keep all the problems, and the consumer nations, all of the profits.' Calderon fought the incredibly wealthy cartels for over five years, with limited success. The war on drugs is not being won and the battles for supremacy have spilled out into the public domain. In 2010, Forbes Magazine named Joaquin Guzman, the head of Mexico's Sinaloa's drug cartel as the sixtieth most powerful person on the planet.

This very cursory overview of organized crime and corruption issues in the West, and elsewhere in the world, is simply to demonstrate at the most basic level the extent of the problem and how little success we have had in tackling it.

Chapter Eleven

Sunlight

The examples of corruption in the West outlined in the previous chapter also show severe lapses in rule of law. However, the concept is poorly understood by Western politicians, and not at all by our media. It is a necessary, but insufficient prerequisite to establishing 'a just society.' We keep trying, but, to our eternal shame, we still haven't come close to realizing that most basic goal for all segments of our population.

As previously indicated, Russia emerged from seven decades of communism in 1991. In my estimation, our support for US neo-conservative, free market policies almost certainly ensured a poor outcome for the Russian people. We must bear a measure of guilt for our lack of foresight in this regard. Humility and contrition, rather than condescension ought to be the order of the day.

Sight was lost of the plight of the people on the ground- rank and file Russians, the life blood of a proud country. How would the grand political-economic experiment impact them? The human element was ignored.

As time moved on, and Putin restored order and gave his people hope for a better future, criticism from the West came fast and furious, and currently shows no sign of letting up. To many Russians, it appears that we have one set of rules that we play fast and loose with at home, but a zero tolerance policy as far as they are concerned. It smacks of hypocrisy.

Indeed, instead of the wearisome clichés, the relentless stereotyping, we should take our collective hats off to the Russian people, who have endured so much, not just in historical terms, but in the very recent past. They have maintained their dignity, keeping their heads held high during periods of calamitous change. By contrast, many of us in the West are spoilt and self-indulgent- and worst of all, decidedly lacking in empathy.

Under Stalin and the Soviet regime, Russians were accustomed to the arbitrary and coercive exercise of State power. You could disappear for decades for no reason, forced to do hard labour in a gulag camp, or shoved into a psychiatric facility on the vaguest of pretexts. The terrifying capriciousness of the system taught people not to trust anyone, especially the law.

No one protected you from the State with its powers and laws. At the same time, Soviet propaganda drilled it into your head-, like George Orwell's novel 'Animal Farm'- that 'four legs were good, two legs bad'- or 'communists good, capitalists bad.'

In the 1990s, under Boris Yeltsin, the State became a casino, and certain sure fire winners emerged. Berezovsky, the ringleader, believed that business should dictate to government, and keep it on a nose ring. Blinded by his own genius, he espoused a kind of social Darwinism, in which he and his kind would inevitably prevail. The fate of the Russian people was of little consequence, when empires and vast fortunes were in the making.

As David Hoffman wrote in his book, *The Oligarchs*,[183]'Coal miners, pensioners, teachers, and nurses went without pay because the 'authorised' bankers- the tycoons- who were supposed to distribute their pay on behalf of the State used the money instead to make a quick windfall.'

'Sadly.' as Hoffman wrote...'In the enfeebled condition of the new Russian State, which could barely muster a pauper's salary for militiamen and bureaucrats, money bought power.'

He noted, quite rightly, that the lack of a democratic tradition in Russia made the situation far worse, as the people were complete innocents when it came to recognizing scams and pyramid schemes.

Westerners are routinely scammed by fraudsters in situations where we really ought to know better, as consumer protection agencies and law enforcement repeatedly us to be vigilant. Yet, time and time again, Westerners are taken to the cleaners after ignoring the inner voice that tells us, 'If it seems too good to be true, it usually is.'

With the collapse of communism, Russians work up to the dawn of a new era in which the orthodoxy they were raised on had disappeared. They were veritable lambs to the slaughter.

Glossy advertisements told them that Western riches could be virtually plucked from the clear blue sky. In reality, their unscrupulous fellow countrymen (with Western 'advisors' in hot pursuit) were doing all the plucking and setting them up to be fleeced, exploiting their greed and naiveté.

They had no point of reference by which to assess the promises made to them; they took it all on face value. They believed the rogues and charlatans, because after years of hardship and deprivation, they wanted to believe that a miracle was possible.

The Russian people were pawns in the blood lust for money and power.

Once the dust settled, and the winners retreated from the battle front to count the spoils, the people took stock. They'd been had. It was true what the Soviets had told them- capitalism and democracy really sucked.

Commentators suggest that as many as 25 million Russians were swindled of their investments in this period- and possibly as many as 37 million Russians sold, or exchanged for vodka, the vouchers they received that were expected to give them a share in privatized Russian companies.

The loans-for-shares scheme also yielded little or no financial dividends for the Russian state- not even tax revenue, as the new 'owners' of strategic state assets avoided assiduously the payment of any taxes, focused entirely on milking the cash-cow dry. It was an ugly business- decidedly not mankind's finest hour.

All this hustling and mendacious self-interest had an enduring effect-the brutalizing of Russian society. It set an appalling precedent that still resonates today, as many regular people loath and fear big business and have a markedly low opinion of the legal system.

Many Russian people understandably lack confidence in state institutions and laws, which people have described to me as 'toothless, and not worth the paper they are written on.' They lack legitimacy in the eyes of the people.

Throughout its fraught history, Russians had never known the 'rule of law' in the Western sense. In addition, as Hoffman astutely observed, the legacy of the Soviet hostility to capitalism and business/entrepreneurship in general, created a dangerous situation in which law enforcement, such as it was, felt no compulsion to protect business or businessmen.

As noted in Part Two, the contrary was the case: Law enforcement saw business men as the enemy, to be shaken down, at best, definitely not to be protected. The 'business man' was a murky figure, associated in the public consciousness, after years of Soviet propaganda, with sinister US capitalists, intent on the subjugation of Mother Russia. Business was decidedly not your friend.

Even honest businessmen could not count on police protection or public sympathy. They employed private armies to protect them instead, creating a State within a State, an 'Us-Against-Them' mentality that persists to an extent to this day.

They had little choice. If you didn't protect your business, someone would take it from you, usually by violent means. They might also kill you, your family and your staff in the process. Contract killings, kidnapping and ransom requests are still a threat to wealthy Russian businessmen today.

The somewhat implacable attitude to business and making money that many Russians share is a hard concept for us to grasp in the West. We admire people with money and we aspire to making it.

Many Russians are sceptical about democracy, equating it with the raw hucksterism they observed in the 1990's. However, a 2009 Pew Research survey[184] that I refer to elsewhere, found that Russians prize 'a fair judicial system' above all- with a large majority (69%) deeming it of paramount importance, but only 19% believing the system was actually fair. These findings equate with my own observations.

Most Russians I know did not protest about rigged elections, nor are they lying awake at night worrying about it. However, they are sick and tired of the constant 'shake-down' as they go about their lives, as Putin has acknowledged.

As soon as you leave the outer ring in Moscow, it is accepted that you will be stopped by traffic police for violation of some hitherto unknown road traffic law and requested to pay a 'fine.' It is a tedious business and the further out you go, the more pervasive the practice seems to be.

According to accounts that I have heard, some police officers have to pay quite a large bribe to get into the police force in the first place, so they use these 'fines' on motorists to offset that expense and their low wages.

Medvedev cut 20 percent of the 1.2-million-person police force, increased salaries and changed the name militia to police. Reports indicate that senior officials have been fired and attempts are being made to improve the quality of recruits. However, police forces the world over tend to close ranks in such circumstances and change will doubtless be resisted.

Increasing police wages reduces the motivation to seek or take bribes-a living wage is critical to stem corruption, otherwise people will, rationally, supplement their paltry income anyway they can. There will still be an incorrigible minority who will never do the right things-that's where checks and balances, audits, zero tolerance and oversight are critical.

According to a report in the Moscow Times, a 2011 Russian State poll suggested that public trust in the police may have jumped 20 percent since 2009, although 61 percent still see them in a negative light-but other (non State) polls, indicated a mere 6 percent of those surveyed expressed satisfaction with the police.

The police are regarded in a very poor light by many Russians of my acquaintance. However, the French are not enamoured with the French police either, with many derogatory slang words used to describe them. That being said, for reasons I will outline, it is critically important that law enforcement generally is not regarded as 'the enemy' by citizens and businesses alike in Russia.

There are also continued reports of Russians being roughed up, even tortured by police. Clearly, the people will not trust the police if they are considered barbaric and out of control.

Similarly, attacks on journalists are a shamefully regular occurrence.

The Committee to Protect Journalists (CPJ) has an annual 'Impunity Index.' It was first published in 2008, and identifies countries where journalists are regularly murdered and crimes remained unsolved. For the 2011 index, CPJ examined journalist murders that occurred between January 1, 2001 through December 31, 2010, and that remain unsolved.

Among the 13 nations on the 2011 index, CPJ noted that Russia has 'made measurable progress.[185] Senior investigative officials reopened several unsolved journalist murder cases after meeting with a CPJ delegation in 2010, and, in April, prosecutors won convictions in the 2009 murder of a young reporter Anastasiya Baburova in Moscow.

CPJ Executive Director Joel Simon said that 'Convictions in Russia are a hopeful sign after years of indifference and denial.' He noted, however that 'Mexico's situation' was 'deeply troubling, with violence spiking as the government promises action but fails to deliver.'

However, there is little cause to celebrate in Russia.

Threats were recently reported against Sergey Sokolov, deputy editor of the independent newspaper *Novaya Gazeta*, purportedly by Russia's top investigating official. If true, this is not an encouraging development, as orchestrating change is in no small part engineered by 'tone from the top.'

Sadly, *Novaya Gazeta* has made many enemies in Russia over the years as a result of its investigative journalism: Five of its journalists have been murdered. In 2010 alone, eight journalists were murdered and forty assaulted in Russia.

The most dangerous assignment for Russian journalists is in Chechnya. Investigations by Russian news organisations into the killings in the war-torn region suggest that local security and law enforcement officials are implicated.

The Republic's President, Ramzan Kadyrov, has made no secret of his hatred for the media and the news organizations they represent. He has been quoted over the years making statements that I can only describe as blood curdling.

No doubt Putin would justify Kadyrov's position (he is viewed as Moscow's man in the region) on the basis that there is no point in sending in sheep to herd wolves. Be that as it may, brutality merely breeds more of the same. It is a medieval construct, also common in the US war in Afghanistan.

Indeed, the very brutal war in Chechnya, which has seen appalling atrocities on all sides, has created a toxic mix, which journalists enter at their peril. The battle–scarred, fiercely poor, but proud local population is bereft of hope for the future, and thus, easy targets for Islamic terrorist recruiters and vigilantes of every stripe.

The country has been turned into a simmering cauldron of hate, a virtual wasteland, after decades of war and scorched earth counter-terrorist operations by Russian forces and terrorist attacks.

The conflict has traumatised and brutalized the local population, and, it should be said, Russian troops sent to fight pitched battles in what can only be described as hell on earth.

There is an urgent need to rebuild infrastructure and to begin the long road to peace. Until that process begins in earnest, journalists will continue to die in order to cover the conflict and the people will suffer indignities and degrees of want that no human being should endure.

Russian parents will do nearly anything to acquire the bribe money necessary to ensure their sons are not sent to fight in the region.

Sadly, however, a Russian journalist does not have to go to Chechnya to cover a warzone to put him or herself in harm's way. It is perfectly possible to do that in broad daylight in downtown Moscow covering a commercial dispute.

In November 2010, two unidentified assailants awaited Oleg Kashin, a correspondent for the Russian business daily Kommersant, near his home on a central Moscow street, a 10-minute walk from the Kremlin. He was beaten 56 times by steel rods hidden in bouquets of flowers. His injuries were so severe that doctors medically induced a coma for two weeks.

Journalists from various, often competing publications came together in solidarity after the vicious attack and held a vigil in front of the Interior Ministry in Moscow, calling for better protection of journalists.

Medvedev has vowed to solve the murder, but concerns exist that those implicated have senior government connections and are untouchable. No-one can be untouchable in a modern, just society.

CPJ has concerns that the Russian government, inadvertently or otherwise, helps facilitate a climate of impunity. As they observed, 'Government statements and expressions of sympathy are simply not sufficient. Arrests, prosecutions and convictions are what are urgently needed.'

Oleg Kashin came into conflict with a pro-Kremlin youth group, Nashi, associated with the political party United Russia. This organisation, with friends in high places, has been accused of inciting violence against journalists they don't like. Certainly, the group has a sinister, crude, even thuggish right-wing element.

Putin has supporters who revere him with a fervour verging on religious mania. To such folk, anyone 'against' their man is a traitor, a heretic, only fit for burning. The cult of personality is alive and well in Russia. Putin needs a strong sense of irony and self-deprecation to rise above it.

Nashi is a case in point. The group called Kashin a 'journalist traitor' for his coverage of a dispute between residents over an attempt to build a highway through protected woodland near Moscow.

It is unclear whether the perpetrators of the assault on Kashin will ever be brought to justice, a disquieting fact in itself, as the investigation seems to have stalled with seemingly efficient prosecutors taken of the case in concerning circumstances.

One thing is clear, however, covering disputes that in the West would not be considered particularly controversial can be extremely dangerous for journalists in Russia-a deeply unsatisfactory state of affairs.

Many Russians have told me that attacks on journalists are often facilitated by local government officials. The fact that Russian journalists appear to be sitting- duck targets for predators, thugs and contract killers hardly imbues the Russian people with confidence that change is on the horizon. Doubtless, these harsh realities have a sobering effect on morale. The time for talk has long passed.

The simple fact is that the Russian state must do a great deal more to protect journalists-not by posting armed guards at every journalists' home, but by sending out a message, backed up with vigorous investigatory and prosecutorial powers, duly exercised, that those who harass, injure and murder them will be brought to justice.

The role of the media needs to find its proper place in Russian society. It must not be treated like a pariah, an enemy of the state. There must be an acknowledgement that Russia needs a free and fully functioning press corps to help catapult it firmly into the 21st century.

Innovation and creativity simply cannot thrive when the media cannot cover commercial matters without risking a shot to the head or a beating with steel bars in downtown

Moscow. Publications and web sites that expose instances of corruption in public life should also be left alone. Censorship is not the answer.

It may, however, take time for the media's role in Russia to shake out as it should. There are many reasons for this fact. The 1980's and 1990s were so bloody and anarchic- and the transition from communism to democracy so botched- that it will be a while before the muddy tap water runs clear.

As matters stand, people in business and in politics are far too much in dread of 'payback time'- a reckoning for past crimes, both real and imagined (or simply for having prospered while millions starved) to welcome a bright light shone in their direction. That will change: Time, and the young (and untarnished) will change it.

As discussed in Part One, much has been written in the Western media about the fate of Russian lawyer Sergei Magnitskly. His death has resulted in US legislation and 'ban lists' on Russian officials allegedly implicated in his death.

He was 37 when he died in 2009 of what appears to have been heart failure. It was reported that he was abused in prison and denied medical care to force him to drop allegations of a $230 million tax fraud by Interior Ministry officials.

He spent almost a year in pre-trial detention. 'The failure to provide Magnitsky with adequate medical treatment was a direct cause of his death,' a Russian Investigative Committee has stated.

As a fellow lawyer, I mourn his death, and support the cause to ensure such things do not happen again. Medvedev has decreased the number of offences, previously large in number, for which pre-trial custody is obligatory. Previously it applied to any number of what we would consider to be white collar crimes, including allegations of tax abuses.

It goes without saying that people in pre-trial custody should not die from lack of medical attention, or be beaten to death in prison as the Russian government's own investigation suggests may have occurred.

As already stated, my deep revulsion at the circumstances of his death does not, however, imbue me with enthusiasm for the kind of vigilante justice that is so in vogue with great swathes of our Western media and our politicians. These are issues for the Russian government to address, as I believe it is well capable of doing.

Human rights abuses do occur with depressing frequency in Russia, as evidenced by the high number of cases taken to the European Court of Human Rights (ECHR) by Russian nationals, who appeal to the court as a last resort, having exhausted all remedies at home.

Russia had 1212 judgments rendered against it by the ECHR between 1959-2011,[186] a number only eclipsed by Turkey with 2747 such cases. However, Italy also had 2166 judgments rendered against it.

On closer review (the statistics cover the Soviet period as well, which skews the results overall for the post communist period), there have only two recorded complaints from Russian litigants about breaches of the Right to Free Elections (compared to 16 in Italy), but a hefty 456 Russian claims relating to property rights. There were 611 such claims from Turkey and 310 from Italy.

The more concerning claims are those that dealt with respect for the right to life (202 claims from Russia) - and 422 claims with respect to the right to liberty and security. A large number (570) of related claims from Russian nationals dealt with the right to a fair trial and issues respecting harsh detention conditions.

The ECHR has a web page[187]that breaks down more recent judgements against states that is useful. The court has a pilot programme that tries to facilitate the court in rendering opinions that pinpoint systemic problems in particular jurisdictions, enabling it to make suggestions for reform.

Such an approach is sensible as it tries to eradicate the situation whereby cases appear before the court over and over on the same issues, as appears to occur with Russian litigants.

Russia contributed over EUR 24m to the Council of Europe's budget (which helps fund the ECHR) in 2011. Clearly, there is much work to be done to improve human rights protection in Russia, but Putin and Medvedev are well aware of this fact.

I do note, with concern, however, that Russian lawyers, like journalists, can easily end up in harm's way though little or no fault of their own-sometimes simply by being in the wrong place at the wrong time.

Svetlana Bakhmina, deputy head of the legal department at Khodorkovsky's company, Yukos, was arrested in 2004 on charges of tax evasion and embezzlement and sentenced to six and a half years in prison. She served over half that sentence.

The charges against her appeared extremely weak, and one was left with the impression that she was targeted simply as the last 'man' standing, after the more senior officials fled the country.

She was granted early release in April 2009, much to my relief. In the last few years of his Presidency, Medvedev expressed regret at the brutal deaths of a number of lawyers and journalists, in what can only be considered to be a positive development. However, the time for talk has past.

Russia's prison system is known for harsh detention conditions and poor health care. According to the Moscow Times, Russia's Prosecutor General's Office reported that 4,423 people died in custody in 2010, a 9 percent year-on-year increase. More than 90 percent of prisoners have chronic diseases, including 410,000 with HIV, tuberculosis and other life-threatening diseases.

This is a situation crying out for attention. I am hopeful it will get it. Conditions in Irish prisons are no picnic either, and US prisons, outsourced to private 'contractors' are equally open to harsh criticism. Indeed, the sad fact remains that many prisoners, the world over, are simply warehoused like animals once the gate slams behind them. Out of sight is out of mind.

However, on the other side of the fence, Russia undoubtedly has problems that need urgent addressing.

One high-priority item is, as indicated, the fact that Russians must constantly grapple with the reality that they have to pay 'backhanders' for services that should be free or subject to a set fee, based on transparent, predicable pricing.

The inevitable cat and mouse game with bureaucracy and law enforcement is undignified and saps vital energy that ought to be spent devising new business ideas or simply enjoying life.

Putin is well aware that the 'petty corruption that people face when dealing with police, courts, housing and utility services, medicine and education' must be addressed, or the State risks losing legitimacy, and that matters cannot remain as they are.

Russians are used to paying bribes to get basic medical services, a child into university (however gifted) and to crooked cops and bureaucrats generally. As indicated, they also fear for their sons with the army draft and hazing that can lead to death. Putin has noted the need for reform, without directly mentioning hazing and brutality (often leading to death) with respect to new army recruits and conscripts.

He promotes, however, the establishment of 'A new law enforcement body, military police.'..to ' monitor discipline in the army' and expresses the need to 'engage civil, veterans.' religious and human rights organizations to help educate servicemen, protect their rights and interests and build a healthy moral environment in the army.'

To that end, he writes that 'Chaplains must be deployed at every military unit.' presumably hoping that their presence will discourage such degrading and dangerous rituals as hazing.

Putin clearly wants a professional army, but he has no intention of eliminating conscription'- 'We cannot abolish the notion of the honorable military duty for the male population. They must be ready to stand up to defend their homeland in the time of danger.'

I firmly believe that we ought to introduce conscription in the West, to include women and the academically gifted. It might make us more invested in decisions (now blithely made for us) to wage wars willy-nilly on suspect grounds in countries that don't concern us.

Right now, especially in the US, it is the young and the indigent who fight wars chosen by the rich. This harsh, patently unjust and inequitable reality must change. It would concentrate the minds of war mongering politicians if young Johnny at Harvard or Princeton was conscripted (with no 'out') to go fight the Taliban or whoever the 'enemy de jour' may be.

Putin has acknowledged that 'the current conscription service is fraught with social inequality' and that draftees are 'mainly teenagers from poor working or farming communities, those who did not make it into a university or college and could not use the right to a deferment.'

He does not mention rampant bribe paying by families to avoid service and gain access to university, but he is surely aware of the widespread practice. He believes that young people should regard their duty to serve as 'a privilege, not an obligation.' Clearly, that is a long term goal.

The fact remains, that every bribe paid by ordinary Russians to avoid the draft, or to get basic services, is a ruble less in the real economy- and simply serves to fuel the already vibrant black economy. In such a system, the state is not your friend- it is the enemy of business and the small man alike. It is an obstacle to progress and modernity.

In June, 2011, the Economic Development Ministry reported that Russians paid at least 164 billion rubles ($5.6 billion) in bribes in 2011 to teachers, traffic police and others officials in 'everyday' situations- more than double the amount paid in 2010.

In the business community, the size of the average bribe in Russia more than tripled in 2011, the Interior Ministry's economic security department reported, indicating that 'The size of the average bribe and commercial payoff in reported crimes increased more than 250 percent to 236,000 rubles ($7866),' it said in a statement.

Putin has written that he will 'remove the fundamental causes for corruption and punish particular officials.' However, he consistently refuses to label everyone as corrupt. 'We will boost motivation for those who want to serve Russia in good faith. We have always had plenty of such people, and they will be given a chance.'.... people 'who've been toiling all their life just for the salary in federal and municipal agencies.'

He surmises that 'they are offended when journalists label every official a corrupt one.' He also makes the salient point that such labelling discourages Russians from entering the public service.'

He has expressed optimism for the future-'We have defeated oligarchy, and we will defeat corruption.' Opponents mocked his words, pointing to endless debates about defeating corruption that have led no-where. However, defeatism will not work either, and it is always possible to teach a donkey new tricks. In addition, as we have seen, international organisations do accept that progress has been made.

Putin is under no illusion about the extent of the problem, however, one of the few areas under his previous tenure in which few improvements were made. Medvedev, in his previous role as President, described 'legal nihilism' and corruption as endemic in Russia, and a threat to progress. Medvedev described the battle to fight corruption as 'this large-scale, systemic battle.' He acknowledged that the fight had only just begun.

Medvedev has described himself as a lawyer 'to my bones.' He is known to be meticulous and precise and people close to him advise that he is committed to the idea of imbedding the rule of law in Russian society. Medvedev has described Russia as a country 'where people don't like to observe the law.' In Part Four, I write about this notion that Russians are somehow incorrigible. I do not accept that hypothesis.

Reputable surveys, and the historical record, show that although Russians are sick of paying bribes, they differentiate between them as to how they are characterized. When it comes to getting treatment for a sick child, or paying for a son or daughter to enter university, they do not consider such payments wrong, immoral or even corrupt. It is simply the way things are done.

In the Soviet era, having or acquiring 'blat' – 'influence'- was key to survival. Blat is still important in Russia. It did not always involve money changing hands. Rather it was couched in terms of having 'friends.' well-placed friends who could smooth the way. A favour given was paid forward.

This kind of dynamic is entrenched in Irish, Italian, and Greek culture and throughout much of continental Europe. By no means is it peculiar to Russia, but communism gave it additional layers of complexity.

Putin has written, with some irony, that 'Red tape and bureaucracy have never been a source of national pride in Russia,' citing 'a conversation between Tsar Nicholas I and his chief of secret police Alexander Benckendorf, when the former announced he wanted to stamp out graft, and got the following question in return, 'Do you think there will be anyone left around you?'

Putin has acknowledged that throughout Russian history, 'there've been attempts to curb corruption through repression.' He professes not to be a fan of that approach, recognizing that 'the problem is much more profound – it comes from the lack of transparency and accountability of government agencies to society....These are the areas that present enormous challenges.'

Putin is well aware that he can't just put the whole country in jail. In a clear rebuke to his foes, domestically and externally, he has remarked that fighting corruption is not a 'a matter for political speculation, an object of populist Statements, political exploitation, a goal of short-term campaigns.'

Furthermore, 'Primitive decisions, like a call for mass repressions, are not a solution...for the reason that those who 'demand retribution fail to comprehend that in a corrupt environment, repression could also become subject to corruption. And the scale would be horrific.'

He is clearly no fan of the draconian methods employed by ex-Georgian President Saaskavilli to address allegations of corruption amongst State officials, such as resorting to mass firings of police officers.

However, as indicated, international organisations such as GRECO have described anti-corruption measures in Russia to date as overtly top-down, even repressive, and lacking in input from society at large. The discrepancy between talk and action needs to be resolved or the people will make their voices heard in increasing numbers.

Putin observed that that while teenagers in the 'turbulent' 1990s 'dreamed of becoming oligarchs.'..'now they opt for State official, according to opinion polls.' because 'many view public service as a source of fast and easy cash.' In other words, they view the civil service as a way to make easy money off bribes. Putin remarked that if 'people join public service not to serve but to live off it, then any purges would be useless – exposed thieves would be replaced by others.'

So what to do in the fight against 'systemic corruption'?

Putin wrote that 'we need to divide not just power and property but executive power and the system of checks over it.' He gives a few examples, such as ensuring the right people become part of the official audit process and noted that 'it's high time for members of the State Duma to make the practice of parliamentary investigations an effective procedure.'

Time will tell whether such policies are actually implemented. Putin has proposed that there be 'new principles in our staff policy – in the selection and rotation of officials and their compensation' with the ultimate rational goal of making 'reputational, financial and material losses so great that corruption would no longer pay.'

With a view to putting flesh on bare bones, he gave concrete examples of what can be done, such as identifying 'corruption-prone positions both within the executive power and the management of State corporations. An official in charge of such a position should be eligible for a high salary but should agree to absolute transparency.'

In June, 2012, at the St Petersburg Economic Forum, Putin announced the appointment of a Presidential ombudsman vested with special powers to defend the rights of company owners and directors. The new ombudsman, Boris Titov, was previously the head of the Business Russia lobby group. He is an ally of Presidential hopeful Mikhail Prokhorov, and a well-connected businessman and entrepreneur in his own right.

In his speech, Putin said the ombudsman would represent foreign and Russian investors in legal cases and go to court to block officials whose actions were harming their interests. The new position will enjoy a special relationship with the Prosecutor General's Office, Putin said.

Elsewhere, Putin has written that Russia 'should consider introducing some of the anti-corruption measures adopted in Europe.' recognizing that 'they have great expertise in that area.' Putin is fully aware Russians need input and help addressing the rule of law and corruption problem in Russia.

There are numerous important lessons, however, that the Russians can draw from the current financial crisis, home-grown in the West- primarily the example of how not to do things. Acres of regulations (regulations that Westerners have criticized Russian businesses for not adopting) did not prevent financial Armageddon.

Putin has a keen eye and ear for a flagrant contradiction, and he has almost certainly observed how impervious morality and ethics in the West have been to rule-making.

As international organisations have noted, there have been positive developments on the ground in Russia with respect to the court system.

The judicial decisions of the Russian commercial arbitration courts are now online and judgments must be signed on line by presiding Judges. The project is viewed as a success and is technologically advanced by Western standards. It helps eliminate potential for various undesirable practices, such as the making of retroactive changes to judicial decisions and will most likely lead to more consistent decision making.

Russians lawyers, however, claim, quite rightly that there is a drastic need for this system to be expanded to include all courts, including the work-horse courts that deal with day to day civil and criminal matters, i.e. the courts that most Russians and small businesses have dealings with. Putin has acknowledged the need.

Russian lawyers describe the elite commercial courts as using an entirely different language than the lower courts, which they believe are still in the 'dark ages.' The calibre of judges on the lower courts is also highly variable, although that complaint can be made about many Western countries.

However, there are several reports that suggest that the practice of so-called 'telephone justice' - an official calling a judge and telling him how to rule - has got worse in recent years, noting that judges have become so paranoid about ruling the 'wrong way' that they check with officials to seek ahead of time to seek instructions. Since April 2010, judges have had to disclose their incomes, real estate assets, and other kinds of property that they and their spouses and children own.

There are also reliable and disturbing reports that defence lawyers are routinely harassed by authorities and subjected to searches and other forms of pressure. Such primitive practices must be eradicated.

The standard of lawyers varies enormously in Russia, which in turn impacts the quality of the judiciary. A lot of litigation and community legal work is undertaken by non-lawyers, known as jurists. Pretty well anyone can hang out a shingle as a jurist. The sector is entirely unregulated, and there are no reliable estimates that I have seen as to how many jurists operate in the Russian market.

Advocates, by contrast, are regulated and must possess a level of legal training analogous to that in the West. I have heard estimates from reputable sources that suggest there are around 65,000 advocates in Russia.

Foreign lawyers employed by big US and EU law firms operating in Russia are rarely qualified as advocates, but they are usually subject to strict oversight by their own bar associations, so running riot isn't a viable option. These firms are, however, worried that changes in the provision of legal services will negatively impact a lucrative business model.

There are efforts afoot to streamline the regulation of the legal profession in Russia, but it is no easy matter. Jurists, needless to say, resist change. They do not even have a body that represents members-so there is no-one to negotiate with, just a disparate cast of characters out and about doing their own thing.

There was a somewhat similar debate in Canada when the Canadian law societies took on the huge job of regulating 'paralegals'- non lawyers who performed many quasi legal tasks.

Paralegals resisted strongly, but eventually cooler heads prevailed, and they were brought under the umbrella, and are now regulated. It appears, however, that Russian jurists routinely perform tasks that were solely the rubric of lawyers in Canada, although I am sure there were many grey areas.

I expect that jurists perform many valuable services in the community, and, as such, cannot simply be removed from the equation. That being said, it is clearly the case, based on experience in the West, that the quality of legal training impacts output. It is surely no different in Russia.

It is also equally clear that a sophisticated legal system that conforms to Western norms cannot emerge from a situation where legal services to large numbers of Russians are provided by entirely unregulated, non-lawyers. Various criminal offences, including money laundering, can also be facilitated by lawyers and, I presume, by jurists. As such, the latter must be regulated and accountable.

With a view to increasing transparency, Putin has mooted the idea of 'making online broadcasts of court hearings.'.' to enable them 'assess the performance of every judge and track contradictions in decisions taken on similar cases but involving different parties, and to identify decisions which have not been guided by plain logic. He also noted that 'elements of the precedent law (judicial law making) will help to ensure the constant evolution of the court system.'

He affirmed the 'need to revive legal journalism to debate the legal issues facing society more widely, to improve the level of legal awareness.' In this respect, it is not just legal journalism that needs to be revived, but the role of the media in general in Russia.

Putin has observed that businesses in Russia often prefer to register abroad. He refers to 'a systemic corruption' that adds unpredictability and additional costs to business and distracts them from increasing 'the economic efficiency of their businesses.'

Unless the legal and business climate improves in Russia, Russian companies will continue to incorporate offshore-

and use foreign/UK law in their deals and to litigate disputes. This trend decreases the incentive to develop local law and to streamline and modernise the court system. It also deprives local lawyers and judges of opportunities to gain much needed experience at home and to develop their skills.

Entry into the WTO may be a boon for the Russian legal community, as businesses struggle to become compliant with international trade laws, and to address complex tariff issues. However, I expect that foreign lawyers, especially from the UK, will flock to Russia's shores to fill any gaps in local knowledge.

Not everyone is pleased about WTO accession. Many Russian lawyers and business people believe that far too many concessions were made by weary Russian diplomats, sick of the overtly political process, which was monstrously drawn out. They believe that these concessions will ultimately hinder, even damage vulnerable local industry, and point out that Russian lawyers were not included in the official Russian delegation that conducted the often fraught negotiations, to the detriment of the outcome.

The Russian Economy Minister, Andrei Belousov, recently told Duma deputies that accession would cost Russia as much as 445 billion rubles ($13.49bn) in losses in 2013 and 2014, but he suggested that these losses will, conceivably, be offset by a significant growth in trade.

There have been protests in parliament and on the streets about the issue as many ordinary Russians believe that WTO membership will hurt the Russian economy. Putin was never a big WTO fan although he is gamely out and about now selling its merits.

Much has been written in the Western media about capital flight (money leaving Russia).

Russians do park way too much money abroad-official estimates suggest as much as $80bn rubles in 2011- but far less (circa $50bn) in 2012. The UK and American media outlets have tried to blame the continuing problem on Putin taking office as President.

More rational commentators, however, have observed that the problem has nothing to do with Putin, as skittish investors simply move money around to try to find a safe haven amidst the deepening global crisis.

Indeed, on that basis, a country with little or no debt and a strong leader, capable of making a decision and sticking with it, ought to be reassuring to investors worried about political risk and economic fundamentals in Europe and the US.

It is not uncommon for Western businesses to try to diversify risk and optimize tax and profits by off-shoring. Obama is grappling with the issue at present, trying to force US multinationals to repatriate profits to the US, and to pay more tax at home, involving, unilaterally, foreign states in an effort to identify and penalise Americans with bank accounts outside the US.

The hugely unpopular Foreign Account Tax Compliance Act ('FATCA') is a case in point, a US statute that purports to force foreign financial institutions and foreign governments to become US tax inspectors, driving a coach and four through local privacy and consumer protection laws in the process.

Various governments are striking individual and collective deals with the US Internal Revenue Service (IRS) to ameliorate the worst effects of this heavy-handed extra-territorial law, but some countries, such as Brazil bluntly refuse to co-operate on the basis it is a violation of Brazilian sovereignty.

These US laws, often devised and created for perfectly legitimate purposes (i.e. clamping down on flagrant tax evasion) are a PR nightmare for the Americans, who appear oblivious to the impact on sentiment towards the US.

Putin is aware that the fire sale of Russian assets to a few wily insiders in the 1990s still rankles with many ordinary Russians, who would like nothing better than to see such folk get their comeuppance.

However, the negative reaction of the international community and the Western media to the breakup of Yukos and the imprisonment of Khordovsky means that he cannot afford a repeat performance or any action that smacks of retribution. There are currently signs, however, that certain players may, nonetheless, be called to account.

Putin wrote that many people 'say that the privatization of the 1990s, including the mortgage auctions, was unfair. And I totally agree with that.' However, stripping them of assets would 'lead simply to stop the economy, paralyzing business and a surge in unemployment.'

He also wrote (a huge relief, no doubt, to many incumbents) that not all Russian big business owners are similarly tainted, and he observed that 'many current owners of these assets are formally bona fide purchasers. They do not violate the laws...' He acknowledged that many big business owners play a critical role in the economy and have modernized their operations and created jobs.

Indeed, the perception in the West that Russian business is uniformly corrupt is a stereotype that irritates Russian business owners and entrepreneurs of my acquaintance, who resent being pigeon holed in this fashion.

Putin intimated that he will chase corporate tax revenue and close tax avoidance loopholes, pursuing companies with offshore operations that deprive the state of revenue.

Ireland, Italy and Greece are similarly keen to claw back tax revenue where they can-especially with the IMF/Troika breathing down their necks to get blood out of the stone.

However, as stated, huge numbers of large, successful Russian businesses are incorporated offshore, for a variety of reasons, and what constitutes tax evasion (a criminal offence) versus avoidance, perfectly legal in most Western countries, is often a very fine line.

The danger here, as I see it, is that there cannot be any hint that the Russian tax laws will be used as a weapon for a round of purges against businesses that are out of favour, as has happened in the past. This pattern must be broken. To create a truly modern, just society in Russia, it is absolutely essential that there is a reasonable level of predictability and consistency in the application of Russian laws- across the board-accepting that Western systems of justice are by no means a standard of perfection.

As will be clear in this book, I have sympathy with Putin's view that the West must stop lecturing Russia and let it find its own way. However, in this regard, I do not believe there is much room for debate or manoeuvre. The arbitrary exercise of state power, through the manipulation of the law is simply anathema to the concept of a just society.

Putin suggested, pre-election, that business owners who received a windfall in the 1990's might be required to pay a kind of once-off 'penance' payment (my term). This suggestion no doubt plays to the crowd, but would be severely retrograde. He also averted to the issue in his recent address at the St Petersburg International Economic Forum.

He described the 'corrupt' and dubious deals' done in the 90's that 'involved the abuse of power at markedly low prices, and often with the state's own funds,' as having 'corrupted entrepreneurial motivation, had a long-term negative effect on business ethics that led to profound systemic problems, including on the psychological and mental level.'

He said 'I am sure you will agree that it is difficult to demand public respect for property acquired in corrupt deals,' making it clear that the state's current privatisation plans 'must be a fundamentally different privatisation.' The subject of the 90's 'loans-for-shares' debacle clearly rankles him, as it does millions of Russians who suffered terribly during the period.

However, this is not an occasion, in my mind, to play to the crowd, however gratifying it would undoubtedly be. A line has to be drawn in the sand under this period. Digging up bodies long after the fact and trying to determine who pays what could easily have the appearance of a witch-hunt, the last thing the Russian market needs right now.

There is, however, likely some mechanism by which the original goal of the Yeltsin reformers, namely to make ordinary Russians part-owners of valuable Russian state companies, might yet be realised. The current owners of such entities (many of whom acquired them in the 90s fire-sale) would invariably battle any attempt to dilute their interest or to force them to relinquish control.

However, forcing them to 'share the spoils' has a certain intellectual and moral appeal. Others have suggested the creation of an amnesty for anyone who bought assets at less than fair value in the 1900s' (pretty well everyone) but who has not been charged with or convicted of an offence arising from these events.

I have not looked at the ins and outs of the Statute of Limitation in Russian law-but that arena may also be a fruitful area to investigate-to try to close out the potential-in Russia at least- of endless litigation relating to the period.

It would not stop protagonists running to the UK courts to settle old scores, but the international courts might be persuaded to do the right thing and support Russian State efforts to draw a line in the sand. I wouldn't bet on it, however, as the UK, in particular, now views UK law and the UK courts as a cash cow.

Nonetheless, I view this prospect as the better of two evils, and far and away preferable to the undignified wrangling, litigation and negative Western press reaction that will inevitably occur if penance payments are meted out.

A formula might, conceivably, be devised to calculate the size of a 'voluntary contribution' – to be paid into the Russian state reserves/pension fund, or given to a reputable charity, but it could be a divisive process. Making shares available to the public- by some equitable means, however, might be feasible.

Regardless, it is not the chaotic 1990's in Russia anymore, although the FT frequently suggests otherwise. There are laws, regulatory bodies and institutions aplenty in Russia that have long established the fundamental precepts of rule of law.

Some of the legal framework was put in place by Gorbachev. However, many of his fledgling efforts to wean Russians off the planned economic model they'd grown up with, were subsequently exploited by unscrupulous factory owners and other factions under Yeltsin to acquire hugely valuable state assets for little more than pocket change.

Half-formed laws can be more dangerous than none at all, especially if compounded by lack of enforcement.

The Yeltsin reformers did create a new judiciary and they passed a new constitution in 1993. They also introduced an independent Central Bank, an antitrust agency and other regulatory bodies. However, there were serious gaps in rule-making and most particularly in enforcement.

After the crash in 1998 and the subsequent bailout by international creditors and the IMF, harsh conditions attached to these loans decimated law enforcement budgets and did significant harm to efforts to re-establish order.

As we face a similar economic crisis in Europe today, it is worth noting that creditor demands for a pound of flesh from sovereign nations that require aid are usually self-defeating in the long run and often do far more harm than good, resulting in all manner of unintended consequences, including a resurgence of the black economy and criminality, as money moves underground.

Russian regulators who tried to rein in the worst excesses (there were a few brave folk who tried), often risking their lives in the process, were out-manoeuvred and out-resourced by wily man such as Khodorkovsky and Berezovsky, who ran rings around them.

As a result, the Russian people's suspicion of business and laws is deep-seated, and results in low expectations of the justice system.

Chapter Twelve

Cinderella

Despite the anti-Russian rhetoric in the UK, affluent Russians still flock to British shores, especially London. They have propped up the high-end London property market for years, and spend vast sums on luxury goods and send their kids to UK public schools. They also prefer UK law to their own, and choose London courts to adjudicate commercial disputes-even in cases that have no connection to Britain.

Sadly, even Russian lawyers in Russia favour UK law and hearings before UK courts, in preference to their own. I attended an American Bar Association event in Moscow where nearly 60% of the Russian lawyers in attendance choose UK law over all other systems of law, and UK courts to adjudicate purely Russian disputes.

In some instances, they are compelled to use UK law and courts on major deals. For instance, international banks financing deals may insist they do so. However, when asked, over 50% of the attendees at the ABA event indicated that despite progress in reforming the Russian legal system, they were not optimistic they would choose Russian law over UK law in the foreseeable future.

The Russian lawyers simply lack confidence in their own legal system. The Russian government must give this problem serious attention. Russians must grow to trust their legal system (a trust that will have to be earned), and, additionally, as an adjunct, not routinely replace it with UK law for exclusively Russian disputes.

I find it depressing and ironic that many Russian lawyers reject their own law and legal system in favour of the law of a country that is routinely Russiaphobic. Litigating disputes in a third country is also extremely expensive and should be unwarranted in domestic disputes.

Ireland was a reluctant part of the British empire for many a long year and inherited its legal system. However, over past decades, we have adopted our own gloss on UK law that reflects Irish culture and norms. We, too, use UK law on occasion, especially in large international deals, but not out of any sense that Irish law is inferior.

The UK and US legal systems have evolved over centuries, keeping pace with the colonial aspirations of both countries, and have been integral to the development of international trade and commerce. They are rich with legal precedent, and inherently flexible systems- both systems frequently act as an anchor in stormy seas, mediating disputes between a motley cast of characters.

As such, UK and US law will not be displaced any time soon as the governing law of international contracts, and both countries will remain places that business people the world over choose to fight their court room or arbitration battles.

However, a country the size of Russia-with its wealth of assets and aspirations to be a truly global player- cannot, in my view, accept long term, a situation where its legal system is so distrusted, both by Russians and foreigners alike, that the law of a third country, namely the UK (not even a 'friend') holds sway over its affairs.

The scenario is not helped by the fact that the UK legal system actively courts foreign disputes- the UK commercial courts have done so for decades. They do so from a deep-seated, not entirely unwarranted, but overblown colonial sensibility that UK law (and the UK legal system) is the best there is. Thus, it is entirely understandable that foreigners (and various colonials) flock to their shores for a taste of British justice.

It is not just national pride that is at stake. There are advantages to using local law in international instruments;

the Greek government was able to force a debt restructuring deal on recalcitrant bondholders as the majority of Greek bonds were governed by Greek law. Reliance on one's own laws helps preserve national sovereignty.

In some instances-and wealthy Russians tend to fall into this category-there is even a snob factor to litigating in London- it has cache to do so. As a result, London has become the epicentre for many commercial disputes (like the Berezovsky v. Abramovich trial, mentioned in Part One) that rightly belong in Russia.

UK judges are unquestionably accomplished, experienced jurists, and extremely adept at managing huge, complex cases. They are generally unafraid to call a spade a spade. They are relentlessly polite, patient and occasionally witty and sardonic, which makes for great newspaper copy, and sometimes even grand theatre.

I confess that some of the happiest days of my life were spent in dusty law libraries reading English judgments-some of them written over 150 years ago. However, it is fair to say that British judges have had a lengthy head start to acquire erudition.

On occasion, the UK courts have shown a willingness to disregard the concept in international law of 'comity of nations' (respect for the law and legal system of sovereign States) by openly criticizing Russian courts, and making a determination, in purely Russia-centric disputes, that litigants can litigate in the UK as they would not get a fair trial in Russia.

These pronouncements, needless to say, do not promote increased harmony between the UK and Russian government, a relationship that is fraught at best. Indeed, senior Russian judges have intimated that foreign judgments made against Russian litigants in the UK may not be enforced in Russia. The Russian judiciary is understandably aggrieved that UK courts accept jurisdiction in purely Russian disputes, while casting aspersions on the fairness of the judicial process in Russia.

The US courts have been far more circumspect in this regard. They have sent most of these Russia-centric disputes back home for adjudication, and usually refuse to enter the fray by commenting on which legal system is best, or making disparaging comments about the Russian legal system.

In recent times, however, US courts have become more willing to emulate the UK and accept jurisdiction in cases that have little or nothing to do with the US, for instance allowing foreign companies to use the US bankruptcy courts and laws to shelter them from creditors, provided the debtor can show the slightest connection to the US.

In some instance, foreign debtors in foreign insolvency disputes have been able to claim the jurisdiction of the US courts by merely showing that they had instructed US lawyers and placed small sums on retainer with them. Much to the annoyance of Irish authorities, Irish property developers are similarly flocking to UK shores to exploit its generous bankruptcy regime to avoid the far more draconian system that exists in Ireland.

There is nothing new about 'forum shopping'- and the fact US judges may be more willing to accede to requests to accept jurisdiction may simply represent economic pragmatism in the midst of a global economic crisis.

I do not envisage, however, that US judges will abandon legal precedent (judge made law) by welcoming predominantly Russian legal disputes onshore purely on the basis that Russian law and the Russian courts are not up to the task. I expect that argument will continue to receive a far more sympathetic hearing in the UK.

However, all is not entirely well with US-Russian legal relations. A recent decision by a New York District Court judge to impose a daily fine of $50,000 against the Russian state for failing to comply with his earlier order to return ancient religious texts and manuscripts claimed by a US-based, Orthodox Jewish organisation, Chabad-Lubavitch, hasn't helped matters. The Russians have prohibited lending Russian government-owned art to US museum and art galleries for exhibit for the past two years, as a result of fears that the very aggressive American litigants in this dispute will seize such works on US soil.

Another recent decision by a US District Court judge has also ruffled feathers in emerging markets. It held that stubborn and litigious US creditors owed money by Argentina from the time its economy collapsed in the early to mid 1990's, are entitled to equal treatment (in terms of debt repayment) to creditors who accepted a severe 'haircut' on their loans, has caused outrage in Argentina.

Claims have been made that US courts are undermining Argentina's national sovereignty and putting all debt restructuring by bankrupt nations in serious jeopardy. The decision could indeed have severe implications. An expedited appeal court hearing is set for early February, 2013.

The US government has weighed in behind the Argentine government in this instance, as many of the creditors who accepted a hefty haircut on their loans are large US banks-aghast at the prospect that deals struck nearly a decade ago might unravel at this juncture.

I tend to view the debacle as yet another reason why an international bankruptcy regime needs to be established-both to protect bankrupt nations from immoral actors who would bleed them dry- and to clarify and protect the rights of creditors competing for their piece of what is left of the pie. As matters now stand, it is a chaotic free for all, with no binding rules in place to determine process or outcome.

Regardless of the outcome of the Argentine debacle, it is clear that there is a battle of sorts being waged by many countries to attract complex and expensive litigation to their shores, especially now that times are tough.

The Qatari government has ambitions to become an international arbitration centre, as do many other countries, including my own. It is no easy matter to displace the traditional centres of excellence in London, New York, Stockholm and Paris, which have presided over such disputes for decades. UK judges and lawyers are advising the Qataris about rule of law to help bolster the country's reputation in that respect ahead of the 2022 World Cup to be held in the country.

The Qataris will undoubtedly try to ensure that local law governs international contracts related to the event. The Russians also wish to develop and promote Moscow as an international arbitration centre.

The UK's 'all legal disputes are welcome here' approach has created a smorgasbord of opportunity for UK lawyers, many of whom have made fortunes from Russian disputes, litigated or arbitrated in the UK by protagonists with deep pockets.

The fact that so many large Russian companies incorporate offshore practically guarantees the use of foreign, probably UK law, in contracts and incorporating documents involving these entities. There are many perfectly legitimate reasons to offshore Russian companies, not least of which is the fact that Russian law is in early stage of development and not always 'fit for purpose' for companies with extensive foreign dealings.

English law and US law (indeed the common law (Anglo Saxon) system generally) is more flexible and less formalistic than the law in civil law systems, which are based primarily on written laws rather than on judge-made law. Civil law applies throughout most of continental Europe and hybrid common law/civil law systems exist around the world.

There is a considerable bias against civil law systems in the West. As such, many of the criticisms routinely made about Russian law could be made against civil law systems generally.

This fact, combined with endemic bias against Russia in the Western media (in predominantly common law countries) means that there will be a disproportionate level of criticism about the Russian legal system for some time to come, no matter what changes are made.

However, even if one compares like-with-like, sufficient time has passed in most European continental legal systems for issues that need addressing to have come to light, and many wrinkles have been smoothed out over time. Russia simply hasn't had that kind of time, so there is inevitably much room for improvement.

The fact that the Russian legal system is so new also means that legal precedent is still relatively scanty and undeveloped, compared to the situation in the UK, where judicial decision making has evolved over hundreds of years.

It is simply ludicrous to expect a post-communist country to clone the UK's experience (or that of European civil law systems) overnight. We are still grappling with gaps and inconsistencies in our own laws after centuries trying to refine them.

However, plans for a radical reworking of the Russian Civil Code, adopted first in 1994, have been underway for some time. Much time and effort was expended on these discussions.

Concerns were initially expressed by the Russian business community, and savvy Russian lawyers with international experience, that too many old-school Russian legal academics, with no real world business experience dominated the redrafting process. The fear was that the new Code would be no improvement on the old.

It appears, however, that changes adopted by the Duma on December 14, 2012 were relatively minor. Radical change was rejected in favour of a more incremental approach, which is arguably better than throwing the baby out with the bath water.

In any event, many legal practitioners believe that existing civil law is adequate, and that problems result primarily from a lack of enforcement.

Regardless, there is a long road ahead. Russian lawyers and judges need the opportunity to develop their skills to gain the confidence necessary to interpret Russian laws in a less rigid and formulistic fashion than is currently the case. To allow them do so, market participants need to do their bit for the cause by using Russian law in their deal-making.

In my experience, bargaining power usually dictates outcomes. With the West in crisis- and opportunities aplenty in Russia, Russian companies may find themselves able to mandate the use of Russian law in deals with Westerners hungry for growth opportunities lacking at home.

Whether they choose to do, however, is entirely another matter. Appealing to their patriotic duty may hold little water. The Russian love affair with the UK and its legal system is unlikely to fade overnight.

In turn, the UK government is very keen to protect its turf.

In September, 2011, UK Justice Secretary Kenneth Clarke launched the Legal Services Action plan aimed at promoting London as the legal capital of the world.[188] He has called 'the rule of law' one of the UK's 'greatest exports,' touting its 'national genius for legal services.'

Clarke wants to promote 'UK law wherever and whenever possible'- stating that 'The UK can be lawyer and adviser to the world and my plans are all about promoting that.' He described the sector as 'an overlooked Cinderella ' that 'generated nearly 2% of UK GDP in 2009 – a rather healthy £23 billion.'

He described the UK's competitive advantage in grandiose terms as reflecting 'many things: our open market, the unrivalled quality of the UK legal profession, our record of judicial independence and the plain good sense of English common law, amongst others. People turn to us because they understand that a decision from a UK court carries a global guarantee of impartiality, integrity and enforceability.'

It is clear from his pronouncements that the UK government will try to head off various EU legal initiatives that seek to harmonise contract law, ostensibly to preserve freedom of choice, but really to protect the UK's dominance.

Indeed, with a view to ensuring that as many lawyers as possible draft contracts under English law, influential UK lawyers want changes made to the length of the training programme that solicitors must undergo to qualify in Britain. They believe that US lawyers have a competitive advantage as they can qualify faster.

I am not sure this makes any sense as a proposition, but it certainly demonstrates the level of competition for legal services globally, and the perceived advantage that UK law offers to British lawyers over international colleagues, an advantage they are desperate to preserve.

Bizarrely, as discussed in the media section, the UK media frequently disparages the tendency of wealthy Russians to litigate disputes in the UK, referring sarcastically[189] to Russian law being 'outsourced' to Britain. In this respect, they are markedly out of step with the UK government and the British legal professions very rational desire to keep Russian money flowing.

There are alternatives to Britain. Although geographically less appealing than London, Russian litigants are assured a fair trial in the US. US commercial courts are of a very high standard and tend to be egalitarian and non-parochial.

Despite the EU stereotype that Americans are unrefined Neanderthals without passports, ignorant of international affairs, Americans do understand the kind of frontier mentality that still exists to an extent in Russia, and they certainly understand pride in country. American attorneys are also formidable, skilled advocates.

US judges will also do their utmost to be fair and impartial in international disputes.

With the increased internationalization of trade, and the global nature of business, 'forum shopping' is likely to become more prevalent. It is common in cross-border disputes, where deep pocketed litigants basically shop the Western courts system to get the hearing and outcome most favourable to them.

Forum shopping is not illegal, and, in some cases, strategically desirable. The advantage one country may offer over another may simply be an oblique legal, technical rule that nonetheless is important to one side in the dispute. Very complex and often contradictory international legal rules govern the analysis and process.

In Russia, however, lawyers complain that cases that began in Moscow, for instance, are suddenly mysteriously moved across the country- and the suspicion is that the litigant 'arranging' the transfer, has reason to be optimistic that the new court will rule in its favour (the implication being that this court has been bribed, or is corrupt). This practice, if common, is not 'forum shopping' in the 'legitimate' sense.

Indeed, many illegal, highly complex glosses on existing (primarily legal) Western practices have emerged in Russia.

US lawyer and resident legal adviser at the US Embassy in Moscow, Thomas Firestone, often writes about legal corruption in Russia. In an article in the American Bar Association publication, the International Lawyer,[190]he writes about many of the elaborate scams and shenanigans used to acquire companies and annihilate the competition- a practice known as 'corporate raiding.'

In essence it is corporate identity theft.

The Russian civil and criminal law system is inadequate to outwit extremely wily players. It lacks certain tools that Western law enforcement agencies rely upon for arrests and convictions.

Estimates vary as to the number of raiding attacks that occur every year in Russia. They range from figures of several hundred to several thousand incidents. The phenomena, has, however, entered the lexicon of popular culture in Russia, spawning TV shows, popular novels and self-help books that provide advice as to how to fend off attacks.

It is a remarkably creative crime that requires creative solutions.

Its hallmark is fraud, forgery and extortion, facilitated by corrupt bureaucrats at State agencies, judges who grant court orders based on forged or flawed documentation and false testimony, corrupt law enforcement agents and tax authorities. By no means are the judges all corrupt: many are simply dupes- lied to in court by unscrupulous lawyers and their clients.

Russian law is very formalistic. For instance, as is common in many civil law countries, many official documents must be notarised using an official seal. It is also predominantly paper-based.

Both facts compound the problem as insufficient attention is paid to ensuring the integrity of critical legally binding documentation that establishes title to property and assets, or that provides evidence as to the ownership structure in a company. Attackers exploit this vulnerability in the system.

Corporate identity theft is not unknown in the West. Many Western Law Societies, including the Law Society of New South Wales in Sydney, Australia, have issued member alerts warning, for instance, that the land registration service has become aware of scams in which land transfers are made and mortgage loans granted, using illegally obtained title documents, with the result that the mortgagor acquires the title of the registered owner.

In such cases, the fraudster (the mortgagor) produced a valid Certificate of Title obtained by applying for a replacement title certificate by claiming the original was lost. Devious as this may be, Russian corporate raiders take the concept to a whole new level, mainly by virtue of the fact that state agents are complicit.

In that regard, it is not that difficult to identify the weak links that facilitate the crime. Raiding was not adequately defined (as a crime) to facilitate prosecution up until recently. Medvedev has taken an interest and gaps are being filled.

In Russia, if an attacker can, for instance, steal or acquire (through court order, such as a validly issued search warrant) a company's share register, forged entries can be made that enable such a person to hijack the ownership structure. A forged power of attorney can also wreak huge damage.

Sometimes, company owners are falsely accused of crimes, locked up, and, in the interim, court orders obtained to access the company headquarters, at which time computers and sensitive documentation and data is stolen. Search warrants are often executed with the 'assistance' of heavily armed security men and corrupt law enforcement officers.

In some cases, intrepid employees with management have physically fended off such attacks: Not the average day in the office in Dublin.

As soon as ostensible ownership to stolen assets is established through fraudulent documentation, court orders are obtained to freeze and move them off shore, or they are sold to 'good faith' purchasers, where, under Russian law, they are out of the reach of the legitimate owners.

By the time the real owner is released (assuming that happens), the damage has been done. In many cases, owners do fight back through the courts, and they are vindicated, but it is too late.

One way to deal with the problem, which I am sure has been considered (in the West, we tend to believe that we always know something the Russians don't. In my experience, however, that is rarely the case) is to transition paper-based registration systems online, and to use the most stringent security procedures to protect such databases, in the same way that passport and drivers' licence records are protected (with varying degrees of success) in the West.

Australia and Canada have sophisticated systems that might provide a benchmark, as, no doubt, do many civil law countries. The problem, highlighted in the Australian title document scam, still remains, of ensuring that one's identity, corporate or otherwise, is legitimately established in the first instance.

These are very complex problems, but by no means unique or insurmountable. I believe that a smattering of common sense combined with a dose of ingenuity and the assistance of well-established technology, would, eventually, deal the raiders a mortal blow.

Medvedev signed an anti-raiding law into effect in July 2010, introducing criminal charges for activities associated with raiding. He also spoke about the misuse of criminal investigations for raiding at the St. Petersburg International Economic Forum held in June, 2011.

He also signed into law a bill that criminalizes several ways of setting up a legal entity, such as using stolen personal identification papers.

The fact that such scorched earth tactics are used by Russian operators against competitors, arguably explains to a significant extent why Russian businessmen and women (they do exist) are so much more cynical than their pampered Western peers. If they are in their 40's, or older, and they survived, even prospered, during the era of chaos, they are usually as tough as nails.

Capitalism was never pretty (never less so than now) and hostile takeovers are two a penny in the West. Indeed, the term 'corporate raider' is not especially derogatory in the West- it is often applied to old-school predatory tycoons such as Ron Perlman and Carl Icahn, but their methods seem old-fashioned, even quaint by Russian standards.

In Russia, if a company had debt, bankruptcy laws (since changed, making the tactic far less attractive) allowed raiders to get judgment and bankrupt a company, often for miniscule amounts.

There is nothing new about such tactics. Remember the plot of Alexandre Dumas's classic novel (also made into many movies), written in 1844, *The Count of Monte Cristo*?

The hero, Edmond Dantes, an innocent man, escapes from years of incarceration in a brutal prison that his enemies connived to put him in. Dantes uses his newfound wealth to exact a lethal revenge; he buys intelligence to learn his tormentors' weaknesses, manipulates the stock market and forges documents to create crippling losses for them, and generally sets a precedent for methods beloved of latter day Russian raiders.

The phenomenon of 'Kompromat' is also deeply ingrained in Russia. It is basically the art of digging up dirt on one's adversaries- and publicizing it. TV has always been a favourite medium for doing so, as most Russians have a TV and get their news from it.

It's rather a blunt instrument, but a highly effective means to destroy the reputation of one's enemy, often involving manufactured 'evidence,' such as forged photographs or video evidence of one's nemesis in various compromising positions, often of a sexual nature.

The bottom line is that huge intellectual capital is wasted on devising devious, even diabolical schemes to get the upper hand in business in Russia. Mr. Firestone provides a long, depressing list of methods employed to do so, but he also identifies legal loopholes that could be relatively easily plugged, that would go a long way towards eliminating many of the more obvious scams.

For instance, the civil and criminal courts operate largely in silos, and an action in the criminal courts can easily derail a related proceeding in the civil courts, and vice versa. The raiders exploit these jurisdictional issues to thwart proceedings against them, as they go no-where, trapped in a kind of limbo land. Alternatively, they play jurisdictional games that muddle matters to tie the courts up in knots.

It has become a self-fulfilling prophecy that if 'everyone is doing it.' everyone is forced to follow suit, so even people who want to play it straight feel unable to do so, for fear of appearing weak and thus easy prey for the unscrupulous. Dog eats dog, eat or be eaten.

As part of the 'Russia is a basket case' theme that I have previously outlined, Western commentators are fond of allegations that the Russia state meddles in business to an excessive degree, stifling innovation and progress in the process. There is truth in this charge.

I wholeheartedly agree that Russian state agencies need far more autonomy to be effective, and that they should have transparent ownership structures. However, I do not subscribe to the popular, 'nothing will ever change' fatalism that permeates Western analysis of the Russian market.

Another popular view of Russia is that property rights will remain insecure indefinitely because the State (usually referring to Putin) likes it that way. In effect, the allegation is that the State likes to maintain a lever of sorts over business, to keep it in its place.

In Russia, after privatization and the chaotic transition to a capitalist economy, as previously discussed, a few winners took all. To a large extent, they were chosen in advance by the reformers – as savvy operators, with money, connections and the experience and gumption to run large, strategically important operations.

The result was that power and wealth was concentrated to an unprecedented extent in the hands of a very few. That wealth, to date, has not created as much wealth as one would have hoped. These men, led by the likes of Berezovsky and Khodorkovsky usurped, to a significant extent, the power of the State to govern.

They used their media assets (mainly TV) to attack each other, the state (if it got in their way) and to maintain control- one reason why Putin is so leery of the Media. Berezovsky used his TV stations to lambast Putin's record in Chechnya and criticized his role in the Kursk submarine tragedy. It was widely reported that Putin did not return from vacation to deal with the crisis, which received international media attention. Putin thought Berezovsky had targeted him unfairly.

These men took, or were effectively given, companies (worth billions by today's valuations) for a fraction of their true value. Manna from heaven, you might say. Yes, but up to a point only. There was a quid pro quo- a sting in the tail: The 'grand bargain' – a kind of official 'nod and a wink'- a precarious foundation upon which to build an empire, although many did.

The fact was that the necessary legal and State infrastructure to legitimize the massive transfer of ownership of State assets into private hands was lacking or incomplete. The result was that when Putin succeeded in large part in getting the upper hand, and re-establishing a vestige of order, the winners' legal entitlement to what they controlled was not unassailable.

Lacking the security of uniformly demonstrable, declarable and enforceable property rights (coupled with the fact that the path to ownership was often murky at best) meant that many newly minted capitalists were now beholden to the politicians and ruling elite to an undesirable extent. Conflicts of interest were endemic within State agencies and businesses were exposed to rampant State corruption and the need to grease palms in order to be left alone.

As Firestone states, the legacy of the property rights vacuum created in the 1990's was a situation whereby 'almost any property is subject to a challenge that it was illegally acquired' (from State owned farms to commercial property). He quotes Dmitri Larionov, the director of Peasant Front, 'an organization dedicated to protecting landowners against raids.' as saying,' I can find a legal flaw in any privatization deal.'

Capitalism, in order to function, relies on the existence of secure property rights. Without that most basic foundation, the whole concept comes apart at the seams- and the rule of law takes a severe body blow. You cannot kind of own something- you either do or you don't. If, however, instead of secure property rights, you are at the mercy of the largesse of a higher order, such as the State, or powerful elite, you live in a feudal system, in all but name.

The problem is fixable-but it is highly complex. Putin has no magic wand that he can wave to put everything to rights. However, it requires something akin to a leap of faith on his part to make real progress. He must put his fears to one side that giving business an inch will only result in it taking a mile.

Surveys suggest that wealthy Russians think short-term, and plan only 2 years out. They are not planning, as is common in Europe, to pass their businesses onto their kids; they intend to keep their money off-shore, and to send their kids to British schools.[191]

They have a deep fear of losing everything, and a strong belief that there is no need to take risks and be an entrepreneur in Russia to make money: They have seen corrupt bureaucrats do so with little or no effort, just the right connections. Their fear is not irrational: They have most likely seen enough to have good cause for concern.

Yet, they are very young- the 'first of their kind' in a sense- and pessimism runs deep in the Russian psyche. However, Putin must tackle this fear factor head on, or his 'Just Society' will remain little more than a beguiling chimera: If you believe you have quicksand underfoot, you will not plan generations out. You must believe in the future to plan for it with any conviction.

At its core, there is a lack of trust and understanding on all sides. The older generation's dislike of business doesn't help the complex dynamic. Making money still isn't quite respectable in Russia, a concept utterly alien to the average Westerner, and positively treasonous to an American. You can't realise the American Dream without money, preferably lots of it.

I am no psychologist, however, so it's best not to take this hypothesis too seriously, even if surveys do back it up, to a limited extent. A great deal of rot is written about Russia on a daily basis and I have no desire to add to it. Either way, Putin, the Russian government, the opposition – and most of all, the people of Russia-must decide how it will all play out, and how best to unlock the potential of this extraordinary country.

But what potential!

Putin is a cynical man: that fact I do not dispute. He is, however, as we have seen, often described, most unfairly, as a virtual dictator, in part because of the perception that he subscribes to the notion that the Russian people are too impetuous to be allowed freedom, but rather crave and desire a strong hand- his hand.

Such a perspective has indeed been the hallmark of many a true dictator, a personal creed used to justify a kaleidoscope of monstrous acts. However, I believe that Putin is far too complex a man to be branded in such a trite fashion. He is quite capable of confounding his critics, as he has done many times in the past.

He has held the line for many a year now, while enduring all manner of insults from the West, and receiving little or no credit for his achievements.

How would any of us have reacted if we were plucked from obscurity and installed overnight as the leader of the world's biggest country? We would like to think, I imagine, that our best instincts would surface, that we would rise to the occasion with dignity and aplomb, desiring nothing more than to serve the best interests of our people.

But we cannot be sure of that. Instead, we might be consumed by ego and hubris and devoured by the monster within, in the same way that we do not know whether we would be a coward or hero when faced with situations of great adversity that test our courage under fire. These are hidden depths that most of us, mercifully, need ever plumb.

Yet Putin was forced to plumb them, to face the ultimate test of character.

In my estimation- and that of the vast majority of the Russian public, he did 'step up.' he has delivered. His challenge is that he must continue to deliver, now that the dust has settled and new challenges loom, all the while belittled at every turn by his Western 'allies.' He has turned the other cheek, to a quite remarkable extent, considered the provocation.

A key premise of this book is that we ought not to push him too far.

I feel sure, however, that if matters are put to rights, and all the time, money, and effort currently spent on 'working' the system was instead diverted into legitimate business practices, that Russia would truly be a force to be reckoned with. The return on investment for success would be great indeed. However, I remain fearful that if Russia addresses one problem, the West will find another stick to beat it with.

Even if the unruly corruption beast is grappled to the ground, organized and disorganized crime will still flourish, as it does everywhere else, but at least legitimate business people would have the option to focus exclusively on the serious challenge of building world class companies and jobs for generations of Russians.

It is the case that Western laws that target new crimes, such as cybercrime, rarely keep pace with the ingenuity of the attackers. Law enforcement, the world over, plays 'catch-up' in the fight against crime and are invariably several steps behind the bad guys. So it is likely to remain.

Small and medium sized businesses, lacking in Russia, but the backbone of many Western and Asian countries, will not emerge and flourish in the current context. Leaving aside the purely economic drivers to enable them grow (grants, tax breaks, and incentives successfully employed elsewhere to develop the critical sector), SMEs are sitting ducks for predators.

A Russian friend told me that in many cases, if a successful Russian business person covets your business, he can, and likely will, take it from you, unless you have nerves of steel and the wherewithal to resist. Business is tough enough without the added worry of watching your back 24/7.

It has to be the case, that as long as you incorporate your company properly and pay your taxes and obey whatever regulations apply to your industry, that you should be simply left alone to do business, create jobs and provide stimulus to the local economy.

This is not to suggest that Western companies always play fair. Not by a long shot. I have been involved in many cases where unscrupulous companies hacked into their competitors databases and stole valuable intellectual property, schematics, customer lists, and so in.

However, in the scheme of things, 'raiding.' Russian-style, is above and beyond what one would expect to encounter in the West in terms of routine 'dirty dealings' between companies. Mr. Firestone describes it as 'a novel form of crime.' and it is hard to quibble with his assessment, although similar issues exist in Japan amongst organized crime syndicates that are deeply embedded in corporate structures.

Chapter Thirteen

Jack in the Box

Reading the West's media coverage of Russia, if you didn't know any better, you would assume that our legal system is flawless. Of course, it is not. It can't be: Humans run it.

This is especially the case with the criminal justice system. There is always an element of discretion: The police and prosecutors can choose to arrest and prosecute, or not, to file more charges, or less, to bury or manufacture evidence, or to produce it. To agree to a reduced penalty, or to insist on the maximum. Judges often have leeway on sentencing- to be 'tough on crime.' or more lenient.

Their prejudices and personal biases, their upbringing, even their religious beliefs, can impact the outcome in a significant way.

I attended a recent event in Dublin about Ireland's new insolvency laws (our laws are very out of date, draconian, and rather backward) in the context of the European financial crisis.

A Greek lawyer, who works with debtors and the disadvantaged in Greece, pointed out that certain schemes put in place in Portugal and Greece to help debtors have failed as many members of the judiciary have taken too hard a line with people in trouble, appearing to lack empathy for those whose plight is so far removed from their own. As such, regular folk avoid the courts.

Judges, prosecutors, civil servants and lawyers are all frontline operatives in the process of adding substance and meaning to the lofty concept of rule of law.

If they are weak, corrupt, or uniformly biased, the system festers from the ground up. If they are poorly paid and can't make ends meet without taking bribes, that's what many of them will do to survive.

Even if they do their jobs as fairly and dispassionately as they can, their supervisors in the complex web of checks and balances necessary to keep the whole system functioning, may not. They may undermine them, force them to press cases with no reasonable prospect of success, for political reasons, or simply not back up their subordinates when they make judgement calls.

In the US, district attorneys are elected. This fact means that some individuals have political ambitions that may predispose them to favouring cases and dispositions that garner the most publicity, and make them look good on TV. Senior prosecutors elsewhere, who are appointed rather than elected may be pure political appointees and not deserve their job, or have the necessary qualifications.

In some Western countries, it is not uncommon for ex-chauffeurs to be appointed justices of the peace by their city government bosses- a reward for good service. Standards may thus vary amongst adjudicators, as non lawyers do jobs that ought to require legal training.

The system must be relatively transparent, ideally the punishment should fit the crime and there must be accountability. There are, however, many places and ways for it all to go horribly wrong.

The simple fact is that mistakes are made and injustices occur. People spent decades in jail for crimes they didn't commit, and in countries like the US, the innocent are executed. Sometimes, to our eternal shame, technical arguments are used to justify gross injustices- 'It's too late, the appeal time has past or we can't hear new evidence at this stage.'

There is a very established, sophisticated system of law in the US, and an abundance of some of the finest lawyers in the world. The commercial law courts have exceptional acumen, and many bright, inquisitive minds presiding.

However, around the edges, especially in the criminal law context, things are far from perfect.

Indeed, if the Russian State wants a good example of how not to do things, the administration of the death penalty in the US would be a good place to start.

Racism and discrimination still permeate many aspects of the US criminal law system, especially around the administration of the death penalty. I profess my deep-seated opposition to it. It degrades any system of law that applies it and brutalizes those who administer it.

An 'eye for an eye' is a doctrine that many Americans support. I deplore it. It is primitive and medieval and has no part in any civilized society. By its very existence, we declare ourselves to have evolved little since the days when political opponents were publicly hung, drawn and quartered.

There are numerous examples of prisoners wrongly accused, wrongly convicted and wrongly executed for crimes they did not commit. In addition, the reassuring notion that prisoners condemned to death in the US are 'put-down' in a humane fashion, like dogs or cats, is simply untrue: The record is strewn with examples of botched executions in which men and women literally choked to death or burst into flames, dying a slow, painful, degrading death.

I was always utterly aghast at the fact that US states used the gas chamber to execute the condemned. The last such execution occurred on March 3, 1999 in Arizona. After the Nazi death camps and the horrors of the concentration camps, the foremost democratic state in the world used Nazi methods to dispense justice, and dispose of the unwanted: An utterly grotesque concept.

In March 2010, at a Russian parliamentary discussion on 'Images of Russia: Stereotypes, Paradoxes and Reality,' reports indicate[192] that Nikolay Levichev, the head of the Just Russia faction in the Duma, acknowledged that Moscow's efforts in recent years to 'create a positive image of Russia' have not succeeded.

He believed that it had 'missed a chance at the Vancouver Olympics to improve its image.' observing that jokes were made about Russia's victory in the Para-Olympics, which became not a cause for pride, but rather a source of off-colour jokes on the Internet.

Levichev also noted that 'certain countries in general do not have any idea where Russia is located or what our country represents.' He thought that other countries 'associate the words 'Russian' and 'Russia' 'not with the cosmos, ballet or hockey but with disasters, the absence of democracy, and Moscow's failure to eliminate the death penalty.'

I thought I had heard it all, but I have never heard the latter charge against Russia.

In November 2009, Russia's Constitutional Court ruled that a ban on the death penalty would remain after a moratorium established in 1996 expired in January, 2010. It ruled that the use of the death penalty was now impossible because Russia had signed international treaties banning it. The 1996 moratorium was announced when it joined the Council of Europe, although Russia retains capital punishment in its criminal code.

Most Russians support capital punishment, but the Russian government has stated it is in favour of entirely eliminating it, in line with the European tradition. The last execution in Russia was on September 2, 1996. In this regard, Russia is a far more civilized place than the US, which uses the death penalty extensively.

As well as executing the innocent, the US has no issue executing the mentally ill, making a laughing stock of the paramount rule of law that mandates a guilty mind or guilty knowledge before conviction for a serious crime. A serious mental illness will frequently negate the possibility that an accused can posses such a guilty mind, or have a real consciousness of the magnitude of a crime committed.

US lawyers who represent death penalty defendants have indicated[193] that they are aware that Texas has executed at least six mentally retarded inmates. Up until 2002, mentally retarded persons were executed in the US. The US Supreme Court left it to the States to determine how to decide whether a person had mental disabilities. Prior to this decision, an estimated 44 mentally retarded people were executed between 1984 and 2002.

Before 2002, US governors Georg Bush and Rick Perry both opposed legislation in Texas that would have barred execution of individuals with mental issues. The standard to determine what constitutes mental illness remains capricious and arbitrary.

Several mentally challenged death row prisoners have been executed in Texas over the past decade. Kelsey Patterson, executed on May 18, 2004 suffered from paranoid schizophrenia, and believed that electronic devices implanted in his body were controlling him. Such convictions make a mockery of the concept of rule of law.

Texas defence lawyers have slept through capital murder trials, ignored exculpatory evidence, used drugs or alcohol while presenting poor defendants and even ingested cocaine on the way to trial. However, the Texas Court of Criminal Appeal has denied relief to death row inmates whose lawyers slept through their trials. In addition, non-whites in Texas are essentially excluded from jury service in capital cases, and the punishment of the death penalty is disproportionally applied to blacks.

There have been numerous instances in the US of foreign nationals denied access to their Consulate until they have incriminated themselves. Some have been subsequently executed in dubious circumstances.

Only the US and Somalia have refused to ratify the *UN Convention on the Rights of the Child,* which rules out life sentences with no chance of release for crimes committed before the age of 18. It was not until 2005 that the US Supreme Court abolished the death penalty for under-18s. In May 2010, it ruled that juveniles could not be subjected to life without parole for any crime other than homicide.

US Supreme Court Justices and higher courts bar death row inmates from appealing sentence of death even in cases where new evidence is strongly suggestive of innocence because of procedural errors in the process of bringing such matters to the attention of the courts.

There is an incomprehensible rigid adherence to applying 'rules' that merely serve to catch out indigent accused, punishing them for their reliance on incompetent and inexperienced lawyers, often court appointed for them. In adopting such a formulistic approach, any pretence at doing justice, except in the most primitive sense, is abandoned.

US politicians, on all sides of the political divide simply won't speak out about the scandalous inequities inherent in the application and administration of the death penalty in the US, most particularly the fact that innocent persons are executed for crimes they did not commit- for fear it will cost them votes.

I simply cannot take seriously US politicians hectoring the Russians about 'rule of law' in the face of such insults to the concept. Ironically, with blinding indifference to its own shortcomings, every year since 1976, the US Department of State has published a self-righteous report on the State of human rights in the world, often with emphasis on alleged abuses in China and Russia.

As previously stated, the Russians are now fighting back with a report of their own, examining the US and Europe's own shortcomings in the human rights arena. The US, however, as I will explain in a later chapter, is far better at spinning its case.

The many inequities that exist in our Western legal system, some of them very grave indeed, manifest on a routine basis, but they very rarely make the news. Local politicians are simply not interested in them, even though they occur under their very noses.

The fact is that our markedly imperfect system stumbles along, some days more elegantly, more justly than others. Some days, the outcome would make you plain weep. This is as good as it gets after decades, even centuries, trying to perfect it. Through its aggressive foreign policy, the US assumes that it has the moral high ground. Yet it most decidedly does not.

The US government simply cannot run around the world picking off its enemies, and at the same time lecture the rest of the world about rule of law. As previously observed, these lawless tactics set an appalling precedent. They are a blatant perversion of the law, sacrificed on the altar of political ideology and expediency- and an invitation to anarchy.

Osama Bin Laden was a bad man. There can be little doubt about that. However, it is unquestionably the case that he was summarily executed by US forces on the order of the President. I have read the various excruciating explanations from his legal team trying to justify (in law) this action. They are markedly unconvincing.

Both Bin Laden and Gaddafi met violent ends. Both were very bad men. The world is a better place without them. However, let's call a spade a spade. Can anyone seriously suggest that anything other than mob justice was meted out in either case? When I took my oath as a lawyer (three times, as it turns out), I didn't sign up for this.

According to a New Yorker article,[194]*Getting Bin Laden,'* there was 'never any question of detaining or capturing him – it wasn't a split-second decision. No-one wanted detainees.' The author of the article in the New Yorker was told this by a Special Operations Officer involved in the mission.

One may think he got his just desserts, as undoubtedly he did, but the rule of law did not prevail on that occasion. It was frontier justice. Principles of justice that are integral to a civilized society cannot be set aside capriciously if and when we encounter 'very bad people.'

Who determines how bad you must be before you are deprived of the basic tenets of rule of law? Politicians, bureaucrats, the media? I shudder at such a concept, and where it will lead us.

As seen in Chapter One, the concept of rule of law has also been dispensed with in the cyber- war arena. There have been recent statements by US state lawyers indicating that the rules of war do apply in cyberspace (if not in the real world). In this regard, however, talk is cheap. The facts belie the assertion.

Another problem with setting legal norms aside where terrorism is concerned is that there tends to be 'mission creep.' and officials and bureaucrats will use laws and policies supposed to be for very limited means to investigate far less serious crimes.

Indeed, under the guise of fighting terrorism, the UK and many Western democracies have done far more damage to rule of law than terrorists could ever hope to achieve. Legal protections that evolved over centuries, and were viewed as integral to the fair administration of justice and the rights of an accused person, have been quietly removed or rolled-back over the past decade, with more to come.

There are many reports from organisations such as Amnesty International about the extremely harsh pre-trial conditions that anybody accused of having anything remotely related to Al-Qaeda experience in the US. Torture of inmates by American soldiers is on video for all to see, and mass killings of Afghanese citizens by rogue American soldiers appear to have gone unpunished.

I am very disillusioned and saddened, as both a lawyer and citizen of the world, with the disingenuous, intellectually-barren arguments made to support rampant disregard for the rule of law in the West. When the end justifies the means, we can easily dispense with everything else in between (the rule of law being one obvious casualty).

The 'war on terrorism' in the West has been, and will remain, a hugely convenient hot-button justification for the militarists, extreme right wing politicians, jingoists, and plain mad men to run amok, with cowed, well-meaning politicians beating their drum.

Where it will all end, I have no idea, but pretending that nothing has changed is too rich for me. Quantanimo is the ultimate example of this 'pragmatic' Western approach to the rule of law.

All our cherished principles of fundamental justice have been thrown out the window, to our collective shame, in that notorious compound. American judges have been de facto declared incapable of trying terrorism suspects in a public court of law: This is nonsense, and does the US judiciary a grave injustice in the process, despite my misgivings with respect to death penalty cases.

Can we possibly expect that inmates that emerge (assuming they ever do) from such exposure to Western 'justice' will respect it? No, we seem like monumental hypocrites to them. They invariably come out bitter enemies of Western democratic principles, having been on the boot end of it.

A few brave souls in the US, primarily legal academics, dared call a spade a spade after the Bin Laden execution, but they faced heavy rebuke and censure for doing so-their patriotism was called into question. Free we may be, but it still takes guts to fight the majority view.

Similarly, the Western fixation with sanctions and boycotts has become another ploy to force our way of doing things on others - invariably under the guise of 'protecting human rights' in the countries in question.

Sanctions and the Western PR machine are also used to irreparably damage the reputation of the targeted countries, crippling local economies, impoverishing and intimidating the locals, and obliterating any hope of inbound investment or tourism. There is a significant bully boy element to many of these initiatives.

Even worse, we use the grandiose cover of rule of law to justify the whole sordid business.

The concept of rule of law is trotted out over and over to justify great inequities. In UN debates about the application of sanctions on Iraq, various pious pronouncements were made by Western governments to justify the measures. The UK government argued that sanctions would reinforce a 'world order based on respect for the law.' Similarly, in 1992, in UN debates about Libyan sanctions, the US argued that sanctions would 'preserve the rule of law.'[195]

Just recently, I heard Western commentators lauding the US for cancelling 'food aid' to North Korea after its failed 'missile' launch. Was that something to boast about-starving the North Koreans? What have we come to?

Putin has expressed the desire for a peaceful solution to the Syrian conflict and deplores, as do I, the 'race to sanctions' and the desire to 'punish' certain countries. He has expressed hope that North Korea will not be unnecessarily provoked- pointing out that such countries are on Russian borders and that Russia cannot 'choose their neighbours.'

Numerous hard cases present on a daily basis. There is little to celebrate in the frequently wildly disproportionate nature of these draconian measures. The spectre of double standards and overt political gerrymandering looms large; for instance, Western enthusiasm for sanctions on Arab countries guilty of flagrant human rights abuses is non-existent.

In addition, many financial institutions have opted to cease doing business with sanctioned countries and their nationals entirely, for fear of incurring the wrath of regulators keen to levy huge fines for even the most technical transgressions. For that reason, the impact of supposedly 'targeted' sanctions is way in excess of what was intended.

It is almost nigh impossible to get delisted once you are unfortunate enough to 'make' a sanctions list. There is little or no due process enabling one to do so, although the European Union is making long overdue improvements in the EU sanctions appeals process.

It is an extraordinary state of affairs that individual lives can be destroyed, their reputations left in tatters, with no recourse to the law available to them. The pretence that 'justice' prevails in any appreciable guise is so disingenuous as to verge on the delusional.

Reports indicate the individuals have been placed on sanctions lists on the basis of Google searches.

In his fine book on the topic[196], mentioned elsewhere in this Part, Australian legal academic Jeremy Matam Farrall is blunt in his assessment that the UN Security Councils' 'rhetorical commitment to promoting the rule of law does not yet extend to its sanctions practice.'

In addition to vociferous support for the sanctions regime, the US makes few friends abroad with various attempts to impose US law on an extra-territorial basis throughout the world.

For instance, the EU was upset over the fact that the US Patriot Act requires US corporations outside the US, such as Microsoft, with huge amounts of European personal data on EU citizens, to hand it over on demand to US authorities in breach of EU privacy laws. Numerous other heavy handed examples exist on the American side.

More recently, Western politicians have started applying self-created 'bans' on attending sporting competitions in countries with whom we have some 'beef,' such as the Ukraine, with EU politicians falling over themselves to proclaim they would not attend European Soccer Championship matches in that country as a sign of solidarity with the imprisoned 'Gas Princess.' ex-premier Yulia Tymoshenko.

This high-handed attitude involves a race to judgment with respect to the charges against her- demonstrably a domestic matter. It sets a very bad precedent.

More recently, there were equally wrong-headed and sanctimonious calls to boycott the Eurovision Song Contest in former Soviet republic of Azerbaijan, ostensibly by human rights activists.

The simple fact is that these high profile events are often the only ray of sunshine the local people get in many developing countries. Boycotting them only adds to their misery and sense of isolation. We need to butt out and put down the moral high ground cudgel we have not earned the right to wield.

If matters continue as they are, I fear we will begin boycotting countries because the local people have funny accents, or eat the wrong kind of breakfast cereal. Sanctions and bans only hurt the people behind the politicians, who are nearly always well insulated from their consequences.

We simply lack imagination in dealing with international crises. Even when people are clearly captive to despotic leaders, do Western sanctions, bans and geo-political posturing achieve a positive outcome for them? I am deeply sceptical that is the case. It is simply the established knee jerk reaction of Western politicians to complex problems.

Will countries like Saudi Arabia, sponsors of the Syrian rebel forces and suppliers of arms, promote democratic values in that country if the current Syrian regime is ousted?

As matters stand, however, it appears that if anyone looks sideways at us, we will sanction, ban or 'Magnitsky' them, in no particular order. It's all quite ingenious, as in doing so we manage to side-step the rule of law entirely, but do great offence to the concept in the process.

Despite our hypocrisy, there is, as we have seen in Part One, a notion in the West, much loved by the UK media in particular, that the Russian government can just 'hit a switch' and bingo, like Jack in the Box, out pops the elusive rule of law. This contention is fanciful.

Lon Fuller was a famous American legal philosopher, who wrote *The Morality of Law* in 1964. He was professor of Law at Harvard University for years. In *The Morality of Law*, he set out eight 'principles of legality' that he asserted were necessary in any legal system.

Law or rules must be: (1) sufficiently general; (2) publicly promulgated; (3) sufficiently prospective; (4) clear and intelligible; (5) free of contradiction; (6) sufficiently constant through time so that individuals can order their behaviour accordingly; (7) not impossible to comply with; and (8) administered in a way sufficiently congruent with their wording so that individuals can abide by them.

He debated certain core aspects of the rule of law with Briton, HLA Hart in the pages of the Harvard Law Review in 1958 – the famous exchange between the two mighty legal scholars became known as the Hart-Fuller debate. Every law student worth his or her salt should, in my estimation, know all about it.

Hart was an exponent of what is known as 'legal positivism,'and Fuller defended so-called 'natural law.' Hart worked for MI5 in counter-intelligence in the Second World War, worked as a barrister and subsequently became Professor of Jurisprudence at Oxford University.

He wrote 'The Concept of Law.' a standard text for Western law students studying legal jurisprudence (the philosophy of law). He was also a humane, intelligent man, with a deep aversion to the death penalty. His wife, Jenifer Hart, was a colourful woman, a senior UK civil servant, a communist in the 1930's, an Oxford don and a self professed 'entrenched atheist and socialist.'[197]She was accused in later life of having been a Soviet spy, a charge she denied.

A very simplistic explanation of legal positivism is that legal and moral rights are not related- the focus is on what the law says or means, not on what it ought to say or mean. The natural law view is that the law should be based on a kind of fundamental morality and that laws should be viewed in the context of their purpose, not on a literal meaning of the words used.

Fuller maintained that the law's authority derives from an inter-active, reciprocal relationship with those it seeks to govern. Citizens will obey laws if they believe them to be 'necessary, right, and good.' Fuller believed in the notion of man as a 'responsible agent.' The key to this reciprocal arrangement was, however, the necessity that the governing laws are predictable and easily understood- they must conform to his 'eight principles.'

I adhere to Fuller's view.

During my time as an undergraduate student of German, and subsequently, when I began my legal training, I studied the monumental decline of the German legal system under the Nazis, which putrefied from within- intact at first glance, but upon deeper inspection, fetid, rotten to the core.

This metamorphosis occurred with the widespread and indeed frequently enthusiastic collusion of the caretakers of the system, who subsequently relied on 'legal positivism' (in lay mans' terms, roughly the idea that they followed the (written) law- a gloss on, 'we were just following orders.') to justify behaviour, morally corrupt by any standards, that degraded in the most fundamental sense, the meaning of rule of law.

Indeed, Fuller and Hart debated the Nazi context at length, and I cannot do justice to the debate in this book. However, Fuller's view, roughly corresponds to my own, namely that notwithstanding the existence of a complex system of law in Nazi Germany, and jurists to administer and interpret it, failure to adhere to his 'eight principles' led to the inevitable conclusion that the German legal system had simply collapsed. It was morally bankrupt, although literally intact.

Fuller believed, as seems rather obvious today, that the question 'what is law?' is far more complex than just words on a page. As he wrote: the ' internal morality of law is not something added to, or imposed on, the power of law, but is an essential condition of that power itself.... Some minimum adherence to legal morality is essential for the practical efficacy of law.'

I see little reason to argue with such a simple, but ultimately profound statement.

In a truly extraordinary turn of events, the Nazi jurists, lawyers, members of the judiciary, academics and legislators who colluded in the collapse of the German legal system under the Nazis were allowed to retain their positions after the war- many remained in them well into the 1970s and even the 1980's.

The Allies initially were adamant about the need to 'clean house.' but quickly concluded that without the Nazi jurists, there would be a huge deficit in individuals to run the post-war German legal system. So the incumbents gradually retrieved their old status (many were subsequently promoted), clawed back pension benefits, and ousted anti-Nazi jurists, many of whom remained unemployed for decades.

It was as if nothing had changed. Nazi laws were tidied up- to remove any overt references to the period and its pernicious ethos, but much remained behind, of a more subtle nature.

In 1987, a rather brave German official in the Department of Justice in Bremen, Ingo Mueller, also a law professor, wrote a bestselling 'expose' about the period, called *Furchtbare Juristen:Die unbewaeltigte Vergangenheit unserer Justiz*[198]- roughly translated as 'Terrible (more like 'reprehensible') Lawyers: The Unresolved Past of Our Legal System.'

The book caused a scandal in Germany, keen to turn the page and put the Nazi era behind it. It was translated and re-published by the Harvard University Press in 1991. It is a splendid book, with a fine translation by Deborah Lucas Schneider, and ought to be required reading on every legal syllabus in the world. It would also bear reading by politicians and indeed citizens at large. It is a sobering, cautionary tale.

For lawyers who are disillusioned with the practice of law, and have lost sight of what it means to be a lawyer, and what our oath means, this book reminds us what it is not.

As Mueller describes it, it was a shameful period, a truly low watermark for the legal profession everywhere, made demonstrably worse by the fact that many German jurists, collectively, relied on 'legal positivism' to justify their actions.

There were highly moral lawyers who tried to fight back, such as Count Helmuth James von Moltke, a man of integrity who was ultimately tried for treason and executed by the Nazis at the age of 37. Sadly, he was in the minority. His poignant letters to his wife, Freya, are re-produced in a book of the same name.[199]

In my mind, the Nazi experience, and the subsequent brazenly disingenuous self-justification of great swathes of the legal profession in Germany is the ultimate counter-argument to the view that law and morality are separate.

I have been told by continental jurists, usually Germans (the Italian lawyers of my acquaintance, pragmatically, take no such view), that their legal system is incorruptible, near perfect in every respect (usually in the context of a discussion about rule of law in Russia). I remind them that this halcyon situation, assuming it exists, is a relatively recent phenomenon.

There is no escaping the fact, however (to some extent, Hart's argument) that even if the 'eight principles' are in force and operational, irrational or corrupt actors can subvert an entire 'on the face of it' morally defensible system of rule of law.

We must accept a certain degree of flexibility in the law, and grant powers of discretion to judges and other enforcers- and, as stated, if these people are 'tough on crime' or fixed in their views on certain topics, the application of laws will never be constant, predictable or just.

Human actors, integral to devising and applying the rule of law, however defined, will, inevitably, on occasion, run aground the best laid plans of mice and men. Such is our destiny.

However, that rather sobering conclusion is not an excuse for inaction, or acquiescence to the lowest common denominator, but it does mean that there are no easy solutions to very complex problems.

Indeed, if you speak to seasoned rule of law practitioners-yes, such people exist, usually lawyers and other professionals that work for international aid agencies and organizations like the World Bank, they will tell you that there have been many failed (and well-funded) attempts to establish rule of law, for instance, in post-conflict countries. A degree of soul searching is now going on, probably long overdue.

Depending on who you talk to, the reasons for failure vary, but there is a consensus of sorts, that there is no 'one size fits all' Western solution to recalcitrant problems in countries vastly different to our own. What worked in Minnesota or Oxford is unlikely to mesh with local customs and culture in a third world country.

Local needs and expectations were often ignored in the well-meaning desire to rapidly 'on budget, and on time' bring order to chaos, the logical, Western way. It does not take a legal genius to predict that such a patronising, top down approach is generally ill-fated.

Thankfully, at least amongst the people I have spoken with, there seems to be a realization that a mindset change is in order. Establishing rule of law is not just a job for lawyers, but rather must be an iterative, long term dialogue with many actors and stakeholders across various sectors of society, with a valid perspective on what will work and what will not, what is needed on the ground, urgently, and what would merely be nice to have.

Some more jaded rule of law practitioners, with whom I have considerable sympathy, have told me that many rule of law projects, usually funded by big Western aid agencies, are heavily biased, with an underlying political, economic and even social/moral agenda that may be anathema to local needs and culture. Both US President Bush's denial of US aid to family planning services that provided any abortion related services leaps to mind in this regard.

Many rule of law practitioners, however, bristle at this suggestion, but the facts tend to belie their assertions that no such bias exists. Bias need not be malicious. Indeed, it may stem from entirely laudable principles, but at its core, derive from a colonial, paternalistic mindset ('we know best') that is well wide of the mark.

Although it may seem like an esoteric topic at first glance, Fuller's views are highly relevant, in my view, to discussions about the establishment of the rule of law in post conflict countries, or in places that have traditionally known little of it, such as Russia.

At present, a complex power play is in motion in Egypt following recent elections, in which the courts are playing a pivotal role. The risk is that the court system will be exploited by powerful protagonists to give their machinations the patina of legality.

Fuller's views on the purpose and genesis of law, and whether law is, or ought to be, inherently 'moral' (and what that even means), and how law ought to be interpreted and applied in the real world are as valid today as when written. We can have all the law we like, but if immoral actors preside, as in Nazi Germany, justice will not prevail, or any semblance of it.

Rogue actors aside, on a more mundane level, it is prudent that lawmakers seek and obtain input from local communities, where feasible, before laws are introduced that are supposed to benefit such communities. If laws are not fit for purpose, they will be ignored or the subject of covert, passive resistance.

As outlined in Part One, the concept of 'rule of law'- although highly complex in actuality- has become a rather hackneyed expression, rolled out by every journalist with a check-list, and especially popular in the Russian context.

The Western media is enamoured with it, but lacks, in the main, the slightest understanding of what it means. They have little or no appreciation of the mammoth complexity of a subject that compounds legal practitioners, academics, politicians and aid agencies in equal measure.

In his book, '*United Nations Sanctions and The Rule of Law,*[200] previously referred to, Jeremy Matam Farrall referred to the fact that although the concept of rule of law is routinely trotted out by the UN and national governments to justify, inter alia, economic sanctions, there is no consensus as to what 'rule of law' actually means[201].

He notes that the term has been described as 'an unqualified human good.' as 'the most important political concept today,' ' a solution to the world's troubles,' and 'its promises ..trumpeted by presidents of countries with vastly different political, economic, religious and traditions, such as China, Indonesia, Iran, Mexico, Russia, the United States and Zimbabwe.'[202]

The term, he notes, is also 'used as a trump card in contentious discussions.' He noted that claim was laid to the term with equal fervour by both the Bush and Gore political camps in the bitter 2000 US political showdown in Florida. He describes the emotive term as possessing 'a power or force of its own- that is often considered 'so self-evidently good that it cannot be challenged and it need not be defined.'

However, Farrall observed, the term is 'a remarkably slippery concept' – a political ideal which has 'preoccupied political philosophers and legal theorists alike for 2,500 years.'[203] It has been criticized as 'opaque.' chameleon-like,''impossible,' 'a slogan without substance, 'mere ideology.' etc. The concept of rule of law, as Farrall notes, has 'attracted, inspired and perplexed countless scholars.'

The Western media and our politicians imbue it with a mystical quality, and wield it over the heads of the Russians like the French guillotine. But we don't really know what it means. It simply becomes whatever we want it to mean – and it can mean very different things depending on the political end game.

It has, however, reared its head in recent times closer to home, in Romania, as a dispute between the Prime Minister and President has resulted in draconian emergency power ordinances that purport to limit important checks and balance in the legal system.

It really doesn't matter who holds the reins of power in Russia- the facts remain the same. We extolled the Russian leadership after the collapse of communism to let the genie out of the bottle. Now, they must try to stuff him back in.

The Russian state will, assuredly, have to set an example, and not be seen to suck and blow at the same time, but the kind of grassroots change necessary to convince people that the concept of rule of law has meaning will be a slow process.

It will take time for the decades old practice of bribe seeking and taking to dissipate and for citizens to look with disapproval and approbation at those who participate. Peer pressure is hugely influential in setting and changing behaviour, as is popular culture and the media. They all act as cues as to what constitutes acceptable behaviour, as people tend to want to fit in.

In this regard, GRECOs comments about the need for the Russian state to include Russian civil society (a fancy term for community representatives) in corruption-fighting initiatives, for them to have any credibility, have considerable merit.

As more Russians travel abroad, especially to the West, and see how others live and understand their expectations of their legal system, things will change for the better at home. Education, from the ground up is also important to assist in the emergence of a true, civil society. Mindsets can also change.

It is not just public officials in Ireland who have a history of corrupt behaviour. 'Bilking the system' was tacitly condoned for generations by Irish people. Indeed, it was a badge of honour to get away with 'it' any way you could. The Irish people were quite prepared to bilk each other too, not just the state.

Politicians were routinely given money under the table by constituents who wanted something from them, especially in the planning and property domain, as the Mahon report highlights. One of the longest standing Prime Ministers in Irish History, Charlie Haughey, was notoriously corrupt-kitting himself out in grand, sartorial style off the back of the taxpayer. For the longest time, however, he was regarded as a 'loveable rogue.'

Yet, ingrained behaviour can change. Tolerance level for social welfare fraud and tax fraud generally used to be very high in Ireland. Not anymore. There has been a huge spike in reports to confidential government anti-fraud 'tip' lines. Many people report on transgressors anonymously by email. Jail sentences for tax evasion are now commonplace and lengthy.

Change is also possible in the social sphere. The Irish used to be incorrigible smokers. It was impossible to enter a pub or restaurant without emerging reeking of cigarette smoke. I never imagined I would live to see the day when it was otherwise. A smoking ban was introduced in 2004 to uproar from pub owners and dyed- in- the-wool smokers. Tempers frayed and lawsuits were filed; dire predictions were made that the hospitality sector would be decimated.

When the penny dropped that the government wouldn't budge, and that resistance was indeed futile, the unimaginable happened: Smoke free dining and a significant drop in smoking generally that has saved lives and reduced health care costs.

Official sources indicate that large price hikes contributed to a very significant extent in the success of the ban. Putin, a health conscious man, would like to get Russians off the weed too, and phased in bans on smoking in public places are on the agenda. Russians, like the Irish, can be expected to put up strong resistance, but I expect that it will eventually whittle away.

The West can help Russia defeat corruption and to instil rule of law, in a meaningful sense.

There are many outstanding lawyers and specialists in the world, with skills and relevant experience to offer. At the end of the day, however, these are Russian problems to be solved by Russians, in a way that works for them.

It should be recognized that there are many courageous lawyers in Russia, doing their best, sometimes in exigent circumstances, and a harsh climate, to take a stand for what they believe is right. However, the standard of legal training is inconsistent and national standards lacking, and they lack support. That can be fixed.

400

Sometimes, however, lawyers simply have to be brave, to set an example. No-one, not even the surly British press, can accuse the Russians of not being brave.

Examples abound: The courageous US civil rights lawyers who faced down, at great risk to themselves and their families, racists and the Klu Klux Klan thugs in the US South, for example; the Italian lawyers, judges and prosecutors who routinely take on the Italian mafia, perfectly capable, as has occurred in the past, of blowing them to smithereens, and police and lawyers in Ireland who target vicious drug gangs and seize the proceeds of their crimes.

I also have great admiration for the US legal aid lawyers, paid a pittance, who defend capital cases, with negligible resources.

Indeed, the American Bar Association[204] does fine work. Many thousands of lawyers give their time and energy in trying to make a difference, from big firm lawyers to sole practitioners.

One does not have to be a US lawyer to join, or to even be a lawyer to join. It is, to my mind, the most egalitarian law society in the world- the most inclusive- and all for a very fair annual membership fee. One can join countless sections and committees, focused on different areas of law, and network with US and international colleagues.

Without a doubt, the ABA is way ahead of the curve when it comes to identifying, researching and developing the most cutting edge areas of law. (By way of disclosure, I have been involved with the ABA for years and was honoured to be made a Fellow of the association).

For all its faults, and idiosyncrasies, the US has exceptional lawyers and many practitioners would be more than willing (and indeed are currently involved) in assisting

Russian lawyers any way they can, on completely apolitical grounds. Americans have a generous spirit.

We do not lack for global legal talent or experience to lend impartial assistance. We need, however, to provide such assistance, upon request, respectfully, in the full understanding that the Russians may ultimately choose to do things their own way, and not clone our experience. One size does not fit all.

Ultimately, the goal of any rational Russian government must be to gain the trust and confidence of the Russian population in the rule of law, and to convince Russian business people and foreign investors that Russian law is a viable choice of law in contracts (the law that governs the deal) rather than (as is currently the case), UK or US law.

There are still gaps in Russian law today- and a gap analysis would be prudent, but all laws, including civil and administrative law should conform to what Fuller described. They cannot be capricious or lead to unpredictability. There is an opportunity to create important checks and balances, and to learn from the colossal mistakes made in the West that led to the current meltdown in global financial markets.

The administrative laws also need reforming, including the environmental regulation system. Market participants have described existing environmental laws as 'confusing and inefficient' and the procedures for obtaining environmental permits 'extremely complicated.'

The cost of compliance with top heavy bureaucracy and red tape is substantial and prevents Russian businesses from spending more on modernisation and environmental protection, a very significant issue in a resource heavy economy.

The cost to business of compliance with regulations generally is very high in Russia. According to the World

Bank's Enterprise surveys, in 2009, Russian managers spent 20% of their time dealing with government regulations, more than twice as much as their peers in the ten EU emerging countries

In the environmental domain, Russian businessman, Oleg Deripaska, has estimated that every year Russian businesses 'spend up to RUR 175 billion to gain permits and approvals for emissions and waste discharges to allow them to exceed their allotted quotas as well as for bribes to officials.'

In addition, the cost of the huge bureaucracy is very high, and constitutes an additional burden on the State that yields a negative return on investment.

Reports of turf wars between Russian prosecutors and various investigative committees need to be rapidly sorted out. Such wrangling is counter-productive and sends out a bad signal to the public. The UK has recently had similar issues.

I worked for a period in Canada as a senior Federal crown counsel- focusing on multi accused drug trials- where there was a lot of money involved. My job was simple enough- put them in jail, find, seize and ultimately confiscate the money.

It was easier said than done. We used wiretap evidence to convict any we could, but at the time, the Canadian law was simply inadequate to enable us confiscate the drug money. So off they went to jail, for less time than you'd like (Canada is not as fond of long, draconian sentences as the US), in the happy knowledge that when they got out, they could live in the lap of luxury. The law was eventually changed and considerable progress has now been made.

In Ireland, a serious problem with vicious drug dealing gangs came to a head with the shooting to death in her car, in broad daylight, of a well-known, female investigative journalist (depicted by Cate Blanchett in the movie, *Veronica Guerin*).

The brutal slaying was a bridge too far for horrified Irish citizens and politicians alike, and almost overnight, extremely tough laws were passed enabling law enforcement to hit the criminals where it hurt them most- in their pocket books. The seizure of 'drug related assets' is now commonplace in Ireland, and has certainly muzzled the thugs, although by no means obliterated the problem.

Although these laws are arguably unconstitutional without a rather generous reading of the law, the people support the measures, and the judiciary has shown little appetite for rowing against the tide.

Defeating determined, sophisticated, well-resourced criminals isn't easy anywhere, and even in the West, supposedly the high watermark for such initiatives, we make a poor fist of it. Drug cartels, for instance, and organized crime generally do not suffer from budgetary constraints; they employ top flight talent to assist them in running their vertically integrated, global operations.

In other words, the battle against organised crime will never really be won – even in the West. However, widespread corruption and deficiencies in the administration of justice in Russia currently negatively impact the lives of regular folk in Russia. They deserve better.

In terms of getting to grips with the problem, Putin has written that 'together with the expert community, with the judges, with the entrepreneurs.' the State must 'publicly discuss' the issues and make concrete proposals by 'the end of this year' (2012)

I hope he is sincere. I believe he is. More to the point, the Russian people expect him to deliver. However, patience will be a virtue, assuming it does not run out.

Part Four: More like us than not

Chapter Fourteen

Labels

A National Institute on Aging (NIA) study,[205] *National Character Does Not Reflect Mean Personality Trait Levels in 49 Cultures,* which appeared in the October 7, 2005 issue of *Science,* examined the accuracy of national character stereotypes in 49 cultures worldwide. The National Institute on Aging is one of 27 Institutes and Centers that constitute the US National Institutes of Health.

According to the study, national character stereotypes are not generalizations based on observation of the personality traits of people in a country. Instead, they are social constructions, probably based on the socio-economic conditions, history, customs, myths, and values of a culture.

The study was conducted by Antonio Terracciano, Ph.D, and Robert R. McCrae, Ph.D, investigators in the NIA's Laboratory of Personality and Cognition. Joining them were 85 colleagues from around the world who participated in the Personality Profiles of Cultures Project, a basic research study on features of personality traits across cultures that is supported by the NIA.

'This study contributes to a basic understanding of stereotypes, which affect social interactions for many groups,' McCrae said. He also made an important observation, with which I wholeheartedly concur (discussed to some extent in Part Two of this book), namely that 'National stereotypes can provide some information about a culture, but they do not describe people. In fact, unfavorable stereotypes of national or ethnic groups are potentially very dangerous, forming the bases for prejudice, discrimination, persecution, or even genocide.'

Historical examples abound: The Holocaust, the Hiroshima/Nagasaki nuclear bombs, the slave trade, racial discrimination in the US, the Rwanda massacre, and apartheid: The list is long and depressing.

The Second World War, as fought in the Pacific, was particularly brutal and atrocities on all sides were commonplace. Historians have described how US troops collected 'trophies' from dead Japanese soldiers, including body parts, even skulls, and sent them home to loved ones as souvenirs.

Unless we have psychopathological tendencies, it is only by de-humanizing the enemy that we can commit barbarous acts against fellow human beings. It is only when we are convinced that 'they' are 'not like us,' but rather inferior, treacherous, monstrous in some way, that we accept the need for brutality.

This perception shift that shows us at our very worst has been routinely achieved throughout history with the connivance and support of the media, politicians, and popular culture.

Stereotypes also become 'cultural phenomena' and are perpetuated through media, hearsay, education, history, and jokes, according to the NIA study. How we perceive our own culture is also frequently skewed.

The NIA study found, for instance, that Americans believe 'the typical American is very assertive, and Canadians believe the typical Canadian is submissive, but in fact Americans and Canadians have almost identical scores on measures of assertiveness, a little above the world average.'

'People should understand that we are all prone to these kinds of preconceptions and likely to believe that they are justified by our experience, when in fact they are often unfounded stereotypes. We need to remind ourselves to see people as individuals, whether they are Americans or Lebanese, Gen Xers or senior citizens,' McCrae said.

Or Russians, I would add. However, the fact that many Westerners have never met a Russian, and must rely on the wildly biased, Russophobic Western media and similarly biased, stereotype-laden Western popular culture hardly aids mutual understanding.

The researchers in the NIA study observed (findings largely endorsed by subsequent studies[206]) that 'Most people hold beliefs about personality characteristics typical of members of their own and others' cultures. These perceptions of national character may be generalizations from personal experience, stereotypes with a 'kernel of truth,' or inaccurate stereotypes.' However, by and large, they concluded that most stereotypes are simply inaccurate.

A 2007 NIA study titled *Perceptions of Americans and the Iraq invasion: Implications for Understanding National Character Stereotypes*, also observed that 'National character stereotypes appear to be extremely durable phenomenon.' In other words, they are a tough nut to crack.

The researchers also concluded that they are not benign, even when positive: 'Stereotypes about reserved Englishmen or compliant Canadians might appear to be relatively harmless. However, the literature suggests that stereotypes can have a negative effect on academic performance (e.g. the ingrained, even institutionalized belief that girls are bad at mathematics may be a self-fulfilling prophecy) and health.

Studies quoted suggest that African Americans suffer from high blood pressure, possibly as a result of racist stereotyping towards them. It is hardly a major leap to suggest that the physical and mental health of generations of Russians has suffered as a result of the extraordinarily harsh conditions they have had to endure for centuries.

Outside the ambit of these extreme consequences, the impact of stereotyping can be subtle and insidious over time. We can only hypothesize about the impact of stereotyping on contemporary Russians. However, it is easy to envisage that it may over time result in feelings of isolationism, insecurity and paranoia.

Indeed, a recent Pew Study[207] suggested that slightly more than half of Russians surveyed (55%) believe their country is generally disliked by other countries – an increase of 8 percentage points since 2010. Fully 73% of respondents said that Russia deserves to be more respected around the world than it currently is, with only 16% believing that Russia is as respected internationally as it should be.

Only 31% thought that Russia is generally liked around the world, while 14% give no opinion. The sense that Russia deserves greater respect from other countries was' fairly constant across age, education and income groups.'

I have personally observed that a good proportion of Russians travelling in Ireland are reluctant to say where they come from, and are visibly surprised when I tell them they are welcome and express affection for their homeland.

Similarly in Ireland, Nigerian nationals are often loath to reveal their country of origin for fear of being associated with a certain criminal element that gets wide publicity. Many Canadians travel with conspicuous Maple Leaves on their bags to signal to the world that they are not Americans. People are not oblivious to stereotypes about them and they may alter their behaviour to counter such beliefs or hide their nationality completely.

Thankfully, despite some disheartening findings, the NIA researchers observed that all was not lost: 'Given a strong enough commitment, however, societies can modify such beliefs.' noting that 'Ethnic stereotypes and attitudes about African Americans have changed markedly in the United

States, but only as a result of sustained work by generations committed to social change.'

Indeed, as we well know, that particular battle was very hard fought, with lynchings, hate-crimes and immoral 'race' laws strewn across the battle-scarred landscape. I doubt the war has yet been decisively won, despite significant progress in the right direction.

The NIA researchers tried, and failed, to explain in any comprehensive fashion the origins of stereotyping, in no small part due to the fact that 'it' defies 'logical' analysis, but they made important observations along the way.

For instance, they noted that the 'impact of contact on stereotypes has been extensively researched and discussed.' They observed that research has concluded that contact alone (for instance through tourism) will not dispel stereotypes we hold about each other.

However, I believe personal contact must form part of the solution if we have any hope of getting to know one another. The fact that the Western media pounds us with negative imagery about Russia does not, however, burnish Russia's allure as a tourist destination.

Additionally, the NIA researchers observed that different cultural 'values' may hold the key (or, at least part of it) to explaining difference in stereotypes we hold about each other. For instance, although right on the US border, Canadians are loath to acknowledge any similarity between them and the caricature of the 'Ugly American.' They strive to be different.

There is considerable merit in these observations. Yet, I contend that politics, the mass media and popular culture all play a decisive role in perpetuating perceived differences between ostensibly similar cultures and people far more like each other than not.

As stated in Part One, my own studies in this field while doing my undergraduate degree in German led me to a strong belief that hundreds of years of stereotyping contributed in a very significant way to the subsequent Nazi genocide. Frequent images and stories about sub-human Jews de-sensitized people to propaganda and hateful stereotyping about them.

In the nineteenth century in Germany, popular pamphlets (distributed like newspapers today) and even fairy tales (the Brothers Grimm/Hans Christian Andersen) portrayed the Jews, both in word and image, in stridently anti-Semitic terms. Although some of the propaganda was unsophisticated and grotesque, even lewd, much of it had the patina of respectability.

Composer Richard Wagner, a virulent anti-Semite, wrote ostensibly rational, pseudo-scientific articles about the 'fact' that Jewish musicians and composers could not write truly creative music due to racial characteristics than prevented them doing so[208].

The NIA researchers also concluded that 'The media and interpersonal communication have a powerful role in shaping and maintaining these stereotypical beliefs.'.which are 'enshrined in literature and history disseminated through jokes, and perpetuated by travellers' tales.'

Eminent US psychologist and Harvard Professor, Gordon Allport, writing in 1954 in his seminal text, *The Nature of Prejudice*[209] observed that stereotypes can become 'cultural phenomena' and that 'the media and interpersonal communication have a powerful role in shaping and maintaining these stereotypical beliefs.'

The German mass market newspaper Bild recently criticized the possible choice of Mario Draghi (ex-governor of the Italian Central Bank) as the next President of the European Central Bank on the basis of a stereotype about

Italians: 'Mama mia, with Italians, inflation is a way of life, like tomato sauce with spaghetti.'[210] The suggestion was that only a fiscally prudent German should run the bank.

After what may have been political pressure, Bild changed its mind and endorsed Draghi, granting him the ultimate compliment by depicting him in a Pickelhaube- the traditional Prussian spiky helmet.

Allport also believed that stereotypes can be used to 'justify hostility,' and he noted that there was 'an additional, exceedingly important reason for their existence: They are socially supported, continually revived and hammered in, by our media of mass communication – by novels, short stories, newspaper items, movies, stage, radio and television.'

In the Iraq study, the NIA researchers made a conclusion that I consider to be an incontrovertible fact, namely that 'At a collective level, national stereotypes can contribute to international tension and conflict.'

Although there is no easy fix, they wisely noted that we all have a role to play in displacing stereotypes and diffusing the hostility that is often fuelled by them. Their observations in this respect give me renewed hope that my book is not an entirely useless endeavour:

'Psychologists cannot easily alter these entrenched ideas, but they can remind themselves, their students, and the public that national character stereotypes are a poor guide to understanding people in any country or culture. We cannot cure optical illusions but we can learn not to be deceived by them.'

Clearly we can't make stereotypes vanish in a puff of smoke- 'abracadabra.' Nothing is ever that simple, but it doesn't mean we shouldn't try. It's also conceivable that we will eventually find a new scapegoat to replace the Russians. I do not welcome that day, as clearly two wrongs do not make a right. In an ideal world, we would not feel the need to vilify or stereotype anyone, but that Valhalla is not on the horizon, human nature being what it is.

The basic premise of this book is that Russia and Russians are routinely stereotyped in the West, and the subject of biased and distorted media coverage that exacerbates the problem. Part One provides what I believe to be copious example of this latter phenomenon.

Most of us are subjected to stereotyping at some stage in our lives. It is also true that almost no nationality gets off scot-free; for instance, the Godfather movies and endless TV series like the Sopranos portray Italian-Americans as Mafiosi and closet psychopaths, always on the verge of bludgeoning someone to death while humming La Traviata.

Yet the Russian situation is unique, I believe, as for various complex reasons that I try to tease out in this book, Russians invariably get the short end of nearly every straw. Americans are not fed the daily Putin Ogre diet that is as common as fish and chips in the UK, but stereotyping Russians nevertheless infuses Hollywood movies, day to day media, print and TV coverage.

It follows many of us from dusk to dawn, each negative portrayal reinforcing the other, and there is no countervailing argument, no case for the defence. Judgment is frequently rendered as the first order of business, and then the 'facts' are marshalled to support the verdict.

I recently sat down to watch the first part of a four-part BBC 2 documentary about Putin. It turned out to be the mother of all hatchet jobs.

At the outset, the narrator described the series as, 'Telling the chilling story of Russia under Vladimir Putin.' An inauspicious start if one had any expectation that it would challenge the prevailing Western orthodoxy about Putin or

Russia, or present an even-handed, impartial view. Talk about laying your cards on the table.

The narrator advised that the show would explain how Putin dominates Russia and 'tries to dominate his neighbours;' how his behaviour has 'made the world uneasy about him' with his desire to 'restore Russia as a world power' after Russia's recent 'humiliation.'

The formula was in full flight.

The disjointed narrative jumped about through recent Russian history, interspersed with profoundly depressing interviews with American neo-conservatives and Cold War veterans such as Colin Power, who made reference to 'gentlemen' understanding how certain things work, implying that the Russians were not gentlemen. He also referred to the Russians as 'These fellows,' as if they did not belong in polite society- a theme that frequently occurs in UK media coverage.

The BBC presented interviews with Putin foes such as Khodorskovsky. He was portrayed as a softly-spoken, long-suffering martyr. Putin, by contrast, is the ogre from Jack in the Beanstalk. I half expected him to boom, 'Fee-fi-fo-fum, I smell the blood of an Englishman.' The documentary was so biased it lacked all credibility.

It also failed utterly to get the measure of the man. In my estimation, this complex, highly intelligent human being bears no resemblance to the stock cartoon-character portrayed. I have never met anyone who is that black and white; so clichéd in every respect.

Putin's dispute with Khodorkovsky was naively described as 'a war about democracy.' It was not. The BBC inaccurately described the affair as a 'political conflict' that 'divides Russians to this day.' As I described in Part One, most Russians have no love for Khodorkovsky whatsoever. They view him as a robber baron who stole state assets to feather his nest and then cried foul when his toys were taken from him.

The BBC made light work of how he acquired his vast wealth, and rather than painting any kind of unflattering picture, simply indicated that his wealth was obtained at a time 'when Russian business law was in its infancy,' a neat phrase that got him off the hook, and that failed utterly to capture his well-documented rise from obscurity.

In the context of a completely one-sided 'analysis' of the Russian-Georgian war, I was stupefied to hear a quote from Condoleezza Rice, the former US Secretary of State, an avowed right-wing hawk, ' To see the Russians beat up on a small country was really unpalatable to us.'

At first I thought I must be dreaming. 'Beating up on small countries'? She had to be pulling our leg. But no, the BBC was serious. The truly monumental irony of that statement seemed to go right over Rice's head.

Rice was gung ho about the Iraq war. She was a member of the inner sanctum of US Republican politicians who persuaded Tony Blair to send thousands of young British soldiers to their death to fight a war in Iraq about weapons of mass destruction that didn't exist. To hear her lecture Russia was a monumental exercise in hypocrisy that I found hard to stomach.

After the first episode, I called a few friends and colleagues, all educated people interested in Russia, not Russia-haters, who had watched the show, and asked their opinion. Every last one said, and I paraphrase, 'Putin seems like a monster. Russia seems very dangerous, and the poor people really suffering.' I asked them if they would visit Russia after watching the BBC show. They uniformly replied they would not: It just seemed 'too violent.'

There it was: A one hour, prime time segment by a major UK news organisation had convinced educated, sympathetic people that Russia is a basket case run by a Russian Idi Amin.

It is trite and disingenuous to argue that the media has no influence as both anecdotal evidence (such as the conversations with my colleagues) and more academic studies strongly suggest otherwise. Indeed, the BBCs own research shows a shift in negative sentiment towards Russia in the UK.

The 2011 BBC World Service County Rating poll, an annual survey conducted across 27 countries by GlobeScan, an international polling firm, and the Program on International Policy Attitudes (PIPA) at the US University of Maryland, found that views towards Russia have 'cooled very significantly: negative views jumped to 55 percent (up 22 points), and opinion shifted from being divided to strongly negative in 2011 (29% vs 55%).

How could it possibly be otherwise?

The fact the BBC's contributes with its own programming to the attitudinal shift is deeply saddening. I note that when the 2009 BBC poll results were announced, a press release from 6 February, 2009, quoted the GlobeScan Chairman Doug Miller as saying, 'As for Russia, the more it acts like the old Soviet Union, the less people outside its borders seem to like it.'

Quite astonishing: That was the (impartial) view of the pollsters!

The subject of stereotyping may seem esoteric, but in the current economic climate with huge numbers of people unemployed, stressed and fearful, and seeking answers and solutions to their plight that politicians cannot supply, there is serious potential we will resort to stereotyping and scapegoating as a means to vent our anger.

By way of recent example, there has been an outbreak of hostility between the Greeks and the Germans, with whom the Greeks have a fractious history: Greece was devastated by the Nazis in the Second World War; the Nazis met with fierce resistance from the locals. The Greeks perceive themselves beholden to the Germans in their current battle for economic survival, under crippling levels of debt- and deeply resent this fact.

Greek newspapers have responded with ferocious attacks on the Germans. Greek politicians have accused the Greek government trying to negotiate with the European Union and IMF (collectively depicted as Nazis) of being traitors and collaborators.

Greeks have voiced the opinion that whatever they own the Germans should be set-off against unpaid war reparations (Germany paid Greece $67m in war reparations in the 1960s). Horst Reichenbach, the German who heads the European Commission Task Force for Greece is frequently depicted in Greek newspapers in German military uniform.

This outbreak of vitriol and stereotyping intensified after reports that the Germans want complete control over Greek finances- to ensure they tackle the vast debt load as a priority before the average Greek gets a morsel from Greek state coffers.

As matters unfold, tempers may fray and it could get even uglier, degenerating, at best, into name-calling and increasingly nasty stereotyping. If we could count on Western politicians and the media to keep a cool head, we might avoid serious tensions, but I would not bet on it.

What is doubly concerning is that there is bountiful historical precedent for this phenomenon (seeking someone to blame in a crisis) and it rarely ends well if allowed get out of hand. The spotlight frequently falls on immigrants and vulnerable ethnic minorities who are easy targets, as well as people more generally who are perceived as 'not like us'-people like the Russians who have only quite recently emerged from behind their Iron Curtain.

It is sad to acknowledge, but undeniable, that we dearly love to hate, and who we choose to hate is a moveable feast. If we can find a convenient scapegoat to blame for whatever mess we have got ourselves into, so much the better, especially if they come from a big scary place like China or Russia that our ancestors didn't come from.

It may be fair to say, however, that certain stereotypes and prejudices, such as anti-semitism, may be particularly durable, for various complex reasons way beyond the scope of this book.

In his book, *War Without Mercy*[211], referred to in Part Two, John Dower wrote about the relationship between the Allies and the Japanese after their defeat in the Second World War, and the fact that the vicious racist stereotyping of the latter seemed, miraculously, to vanish over-night.

Yet, what was apparent was how malleable the stereotypes really were; the 'herd' imagery applied to the Japanese people en masse during the war morphed into positive imagery. They were suddenly depicted as pro-American and anti-Communist. The motif of parent and child, teacher and pupil also emerged, as the Japanese were portrayed in paternalistic terms as good students, wiling to learn, sitting at the feet of the Western Teacher.

According to Dower, the war-time stereotypes of the Japanese were 'free-floating and easily transferred from one target to another, depending on the exigencies and apprehensions of the moment. The war hates and race hates of World War Two, that is, proved very adaptable to the Cold War.'

He observed that traits which the Americans and English had associated with the Japanese, 'with great empirical sobriety, were suddenly perceived to be really more relevant to the Communists (deviousness and cunning, bestial and atrocious behaviour, homogeneity and monolithic control, fanaticism divorced from any legitimate goals or realistic perception of the world, megalomania bent on world conquest).'

At the height of the Cold War, it was, Dower noted, occasionally pointed out that the Russians were really an Asiatic, or Oriental people. 'They were, as Churchill liked to say even before the war ended, the real menace from the East.'[212]

What was extraordinary was how 'Enemies changed, with wretched suddenness, but the concept of 'the enemy' remained impressively impervious to drastic alteration, and in its peculiar way provided psychological continuity and stability from the world war to the Cold War.'[213]

This transferral of 'hate' sentiments was, as Dower noted, 'even more vivid when China joined the Communist camp and Japan and China changed places in the eyes of the Americans and the British.'

'Heralded during the war for their individualism and love of democracy,' the Chinese, virtually in the blink of an eye became 'the unthinking horde; the fanatics, the 500 (or 600 or 700) million blue ants of Asia; the newest incarnation of the Yellow Peril- doubly ominous now that it had become inseparable from the Red Peril.'[214]

In 1950, a US diplomat, and supposed expert on China, O. Edmund Chubb, explained how the 'The Chinese, like the Russians, 'do not think like other men.' Rather, they 'acted out of 'a madness born of xenophobia.'[215]

Ever ready to lend a helping hand, the media and the cartoonists set about depicting the Communists with 'horns on their heads, as befitted the new demons. And the Japanese leadership set about the task of replacing the task of replacing China as a 'free world' ally in American eyes.'[216]

What is saddening, and deeply concerning, is how Dowers observations still apply today, as the Russians remain 'the enemy' in the eyes of great swathes of the media and Cold War fixated Western politicians.

Historical revisionism also occasionally rears its ugly head as we conveniently forget the truly monumental sacrifice made by rank and file Russians fighting the Nazis in bloody battles on Russian soil and in Russian cities.

Initially, when the Wall fell, and communism ended, there was euphoria in the West at the concept that the Russians might join the ranks of the Japanese and be docile in 'defeat' (as the botched transition from communism to wild-West democracy was perceived in many quarters- and still is today). The stereotypes were temporarily put on hold while it all played out.

However, when Putin came to power, very much his own man, all bets were off. They still are. Putin could do cartwheels to accommodate us, but his fiercely independent streak, and that of his people, is threatening to the West- which must always be the biggest gorilla in the room. This is particularly true in the US, but it is a sentiment easily understood by the British establishment, the once-mighty colonist, which still mourns the loss of Empire.

As Dower cogently observed, 'it is natural for the language of war to be applied to the battlefields of commerce.' He wrote about how 'Japan bashing' reared its ugly head in the US once more 'when the balance of trade began to get out of hand'- the pupils had learnt a little too fast and too well, and were kicking American butt in the economic arena.

As the level of competition from the Japanese, especially in the automobile sector became intense, and American hegemony was no longer assured, 'the old pejorative stereotypes were resurrected.'[217]

In 1983, at a Democratic Party gathering, the head of a US congressional trade delegation to Japan referred to 'the little yellow men, you know, Honda'- a comment that became well known in Japan.'[218]A US senator described a Japanese decision to export more cars to the United States as 'an economic Pearl Harbor.'[219]The cycle repeats itself over and over.

Popular movies and American best-selling authors like Michael Crichton (*Rising Sun*) and Tom Clancy (*Debt of Honor*) all painted a picture of rapacious, ruthless and unethical Japanese business men, and corrupt practices. However, in the 1990's when the economic situation in the US improved, 'Jap bashing' was less prevalent.

As Dower noted, as is profoundly concerning to me in the current economic climate, 'It is predictable that harsher racist attitudes reminiscent of the war years will again arise at times of heightened competition or disagreement.'

It's not simply the case that we stereotype people in other countries, we often do so to our own. I have observed that some Russians, often affluent, educated people living abroad, appear to look down, even scapegoat, poorer members of Russian society. Unfortunately, it is often these same people who are interviewed by the Western media to provide (mainly hostile) views of Russia.

I have heard it said by Westerners and Russians alike, and read it in news reports and articles, that ordinary Russians have a 'serf' mentality and are thus unfit to lead or to comprehend the lofty aspirations of free men. Some Russian dissidents and well-educated, wealthy members of the Russian diaspora appear fond of this elitist hypothesis.

They use it to explain to Westerners why Russians who remain home don't revolt against the current ruling political elite- namely because they are intellectually challenged, less worthy than those who leave. I find this sentiment revolting.

The historical context, I have been told, explains it. Centuries of rule by the Russian nobility, intellectuals, aristocrats of all stripes, has condemned the unwashed, untitled, uneducated masses to perpetual ignorance and sloth.

I am also markedly unsympathetic to the notion held by some factions of the governing Russian political elite, the Russian diaspora, and the Western media alike, that the Russian people are remorselessly corrupt. This is a sentiment I have also heard from Russian human rights and anti-corruption activists.

Indeed, I take issue with ex-President Medvedev's comments about the prevalence of 'legal nihilism' in Russia, or rather the implication that Russians are somehow naturally inclined towards iniquity in that respect.

The same charges were laid against the Irish population in times gone by, and we have succeeded by or own hands in bringing order to chaos, although as the Mahon report makes clear, there is much room for improvement.

It's not that long ago, however, that the Irish were viewed by their colonial British masters as peasant savages, unfit to govern themselves-unfit to live amongst 'civilized' people. However, over the past few decades, the peasant Irish have come into their own and shown they are well capable of holding their own with the nations of the world.

The peasant savages have made good and have shown tenacity and resilience in facing current economic problems. My uncles went to London in the 50's to work on the construction sites and they still talk about racism and rampant hostility towards the immigrant Irish, including signs outside pubs that read ' No blacks and no Irish.' We've come a long way since then.

In my view, we are all equally capable of good and evil, of living by rules and ethics and codes of behaviour (or not), of living dignified 'moral' lives, of respecting the right of our fellow man and woman to exist, but it does not happen overnight, nor does it happen in a vacuum.

As previously noted, rules and regulations are necessary, but by no means sufficient, to establish a fair and equitable society. The state must also set an example, that much is obvious, but everyone has a role to play in realizing the concept of a 'Just Society.'

We are supposed to know right from wrong. We have had decades, even centuries to let it seep in, to comprehend what is expected of us in a civilized, 'just' society. We do not have the excuse of seven decades of communist rule to justify our 'incorrigible' willingness to flout the rules. Yet, we fall short over and over again.

Some older members of the Russian diaspora left Russia during Soviet time, and understandably do not have many fond memories to impart. However, making due allowance for this fact, many influential members of the Russian diaspora appear steadfast in their determination to run down Russia any chance they get, despite its strong economic fundamentals, and other positive indicators.

By contrast, in Ireland, the government and media have it ingrained in the locals that we are essentially Brand Ambassadors for Ireland in our contact with tourists, and more generally. This attitude arguably took a bit of a beating during the selfish Celtic Tiger years, but locals are now very much aware how important Ireland's reputation and tourism revenue is to the country, and the traditional Irish welcome is more visible again.

We are all very conscious that for decades television images of burnt out neighbourhoods and the carnage caused by bombing campaigns and open-warfare in the north of Ireland did little to burnish Ireland's reputation as both a stable democracy and a place a rational tourist might want to visit. This fraught legacy makes the transition from a rural, backward island economy to a modern, peaceful, innovative, technology savvy territory all the more remarkable.

The Celtic Tiger is currently on life-support, but despite the current predicament that Ireland finds itself in, few people truly relish the prospect of Ireland on its knees. Simply more people wish Ireland well than those who do not. The Irish have many friends around the world-not least the Americans, and when the dust settles and the panicking subsides, as it inevitably will, goodwill towards the country and its engaging people will be fertile soil from which new beginnings can grow.

Our diaspora, particularly in the US, has been described by the Irish government as our 'single greatest asset.' By contrast, Putin cannot depend on much support from the Russian diaspora, or at least from its more 'elite' contingent.

Irish America has unquestionably helped our development and remains an extremely valuable resource. Although Ireland is a tiny country-with a mere 4,581,269 inhabitants (the highest it has been in 150 years), nearly 36 million Americans claim Irish ancestry, making them one of the most significant ethnic groups in the country (not including those reporting Scots-Irish ancestry: another 5 million Americans).

The link has proven to be hugely valuable: US corporations account for about 74% of all inbound investment into Ireland. The considerable goodwill that exists towards Ireland and the Irish around the world, in turn, has helped the Irish government garner largely positive media coverage throughout the current financial crisis for its efforts to keep us plunging deeper into the abyss.

In marked contrast to the treatment meted out to the Russians, the international media (including the FT) has given our efforts in this regard a generally positive spin, with sympathetic headlines such as '*Proud Ireland Struggles to Keep Lid on the Begging Bowl.*'[220]

Sadly, Russia cannot depend on goodwill towards it and goodwill is an extremely valuable commodity.

Goodwill towards a people, a company or even a country often impacts reputation, and reputation matters a very great deal. At the national level, it helps Irish politicians attract in-bound investment and talented people, who are willing to move to Ireland to work, bringing much needed skills and expertise with them.

Studies suggest that we sometimes stereotype ourselves unjustly. In effect, we come to believe our own bad press. It may be easier to adopt a defeatist, resigned stance and accept the stereotype or 'bad seed' notion ('we're simply made that way') than to get to the root of the problem. In the Russian context, the Western media has much to answer for.

Based on personal observation and media reports (an unreliable source, by times), I believe that there is a significant element of defeatism in Russian society today, as reflected in the results of the Pew Research study already referred to, which suggests that Russians feel they are disliked in the world.

Certainly, many Russians living abroad express disillusionment with their homeland and lack of confidence in the future, if not outright hostility towards it. This is odd in light of the fact that compared to the dire situation in the West, Russia is in good economic shape, and its young people have every reason to be optimistic about the future.

In their studies, the NIA researchers have hypothesized, however, that national character stereotypes may be formed in part as a result of how others see us, e.g. 'Americans may perceive themselves as arrogant because they have so often been described that way by others.'

Indeed, it must be dispiriting for Russians to always be on the receiving end of clichéd Western stereotypes, bias and misconceptions about them. Russian friends tell me how depressing it is to go to Western movies to watch Russian gangsters, psychopathic, demented scientists, terrorists and blond half-naked 'slappers.' They tell me they are resigned to it; they don't see what they can do about it.

As I will discuss, there are small, hopeful signs that the tide may yet turn in their favour. However, the fact that Russians are treated in such a boorish manner by the West must take its toll on them. At some basic level, we all want to be liked, and to be treated fairly and with respect. It doesn't seem like too much to ask.

I like to travel. I often ask people about their impressions of Russia as I go walkabout. I hear many strange things.

Westerners do not believe that there are bears on Russian streets, as Russians curiously think they do, but many assume it is 'very far away.' I asked people in Dublin, 'How far away is Russia.' and most of them thought Moscow was 'about a ten hour flight.' They equated it to flying to California.

When I told them it is just over three hours flight from London, they were astonished. Many EU tourists fly to Greece and other sun locations that require a longer flight and think nothing of it.

Stereotyping, especially if uniformly bad, may create a perception of 'distance' between us that is both geographical and inter-personal in nature, i.e. they are 'not like us.' and they are 'very far away.'

Sarah Palin, the dim but attractive ex-governor of Alaska, and one-time US Presidential hopeful was infamous for her lack of knowledge about geography and foreign affairs. Her tour de force was when she told US media in an interview that 'You can actually see Russia from land here in Alaska.'[221]

This faux pas resulted in a wonderful front page cartoon in the *New Yorker* magazine showing her at her home looking at Russia on the horizon through a set of binoculars. Palin was also lampooned in a hilarious skit on Saturday Night Live (a famous US/New York City comedy show) by genius comedienne Tina Fey (with a pretend Hillary Clinton), who bore an uncanny resemblance to Palin.

However, Palin is not alone in being challenged when it comes to her knowledge of geography.

The *2006 National Geographic-Roper Survey of Geographic Literacy* surveyed the geographic knowledge of 18-to 24-year-olds across the United States.[222]

According to the findings, 'Americans are far from alone in the world, but from the perspective of many young Americans, we might as well be. Most young adults between the ages of 18 and 24 demonstrate a limited understanding of the world, and they place insufficient importance on the basic geographic skills that might enhance their knowledge.'

The findings suggested that:

Only 37% of young Americans can find Iraq on a map — though US troops have been there since 2003.

- 6 in 10 young Americans don't speak a foreign language fluently.

- 20% of young Americans think Sudan is in Asia. (It's the largest country in Africa.)

- 48% of young Americans believe the majority population in India is Muslim. (It's Hindu—by a landslide.)

- Half of young Americans can't find New York on a map.

The researchers wrote that 'These results suggest that young people in the United States—the most recent graduates of our educational system—are unprepared for an increasingly global future. Far too many lack even the most basic skills for navigating the international economy or understanding the relationships among people and places that provide critical context for world events.'

By contrast, in July 2011, a team of 16-year-olds from Russia won gold for the first time in the nearly 20-year history of the National Geographic World Championship, beating out finalists from China and Canada. The United States' team finished in fourth place and failed to qualify for the finals. The final was held at Google headquarters in Mountain View, Calif. Google have sponsored it for the past several years. More than 4 million students compete annually in the bee.

The head of the competition said she hopes the students' success will help bring more publicity to geography, a subject largely ignored in US high schools. I hope she is right.

Many Westerners have told me they would love to visit Russia, but they do not view it as a country ordinary people can visit. They think Russia is freezing and dangerous. They think of Russians as dour and unsmiling (a common Western misconception about the Russian character) - and either 'very poor' or 'very rich.' I have been asked if Russians still have 'gold teeth.'

It is largely true, however, that Russians don't sport great big grins on their faces as they go about their business, or upon meeting a stranger for the first time.

An interesting article in the Moscow Times in April 2011 by Michael Bohm suggested that the Russian reluctance to smile comes in part from Soviet propaganda that portrayed the American smile as 'an 'imperialist wolf revealing its ferocious teeth..'The seemingly friendly American smile, Soviets were told, is really a trick used to entice trusting Soviet politicians to let their guard down, allowing Americans to deceive them both in business deals and in foreign policy.'

That seems plausible to me, but another explanation simply may be that there wasn't much to smile about for a very long time. Additionally, it is not that long ago that communist society encouraged, even mandated, that people, even family members, betray each other to Soviet authorities.

Russians value sincerity. Trust is considered a very valuable commodity not to be dispensed lightly: It has to be earned. Such a dynamic does not beget the easy, meaningless smile.

On my first trip to Russia, I was warned by Irish people familiar with Russia to 'lose the smile,' or I'd be considered an imbecile. Irish people smile a lot, so this edict was a tall order. The first few days were absolute agony as I went about with a grimace on my face, trying desperately to curb the nearly irresistible urge to beam at whoever crossed my path.

Eventually, it was all too much, and I gave up the ghost. I realized that Russians have a very dry, laconic sense of humour- and that even in a business setting, provided you don't actually sound like an imbecile, the odd smile isn't fatal. What a relief that was.

However, it may also be the case that the Russians and the Irish have a natural affinity. In a recent edition of the Lonely Planet travel guide to Ireland, our national character is described as 'fatalistic and pessimistic to the core' and skilled at 'the peculiar art of self-deprecation.' In this regard we can appreciate Russian fatalism, despite the fact we are incorrigibly 'smiley.'

Another observable fact is that Russians are not phony. They tend to be very frank, even brutally so, at least by Western standards. For that reason, fake camaraderie is something you rarely encounter. It's not that people won't suck up to you if they want something from you, but Russians are poor fakers. They have considerable charm, but you can positively hear them cringe if forced to lay it on in circumstances where they feel it is unwarranted.

My own people, by contrast, can turn the Celtic charm tap on at will. It is rarely a cynical ploy, however. From travelling extensively abroad, I can say, quite sincerely that the Irish are genuinely interested in other people; within short order they will extract your life story from you. They are also inveterate travellers. It is practically impossible to go anywhere that an Irish person wasn't before you.

In Soviet times, it was official government policy to lay out the red carpet for foreign dignitaries to make a good impression, with smiles a-plenty. However, if the current Russian government attempted to mandate universal smiling at tourists, I fear the result would be catastrophic. Russians are not so easily manipulated.

By contrast, James Kynge, in his excellent book, *China Shakes the World*,[223] referred to it Part Two, writes about official Chinese government policy to 'create feelings' in foreigners, with elaborate and simulated ploys to gain their confidence, such as racing after hotel guests to return the most insignificant item left behind in a hotel room. They call it 'waishi' or 'foreign affairs.[224]'

Westerners who have obtained copies of secret 'waishi' training manuals reveal that 'foreign affairs workers' are told that making friends with foreigners 'is the effective way to strive for international sympathy and support. It is an important task of foreign affairs work.'

However, it is reiterated that foreigners and Chinese 'are different.' Indeed, Kynge describes the stereotyping of foreigners as endemic in China (getting their own back?); we are often compared to monkeys, and it is generally believed that we have big noses.[225] He also describes hostility towards the Japanese as deep-seated and ugly. This antipathy is bred from childhood and the historical context: Chinese children memorize text at school describing the Japanese as 'devils' and 'evil.'

However, important Western guests to China have received huge, staged Elvis style welcomes. Craig Barrett, the US Intel CEO was dazzled by a rock-star welcome he received in China and duly approved a significant investment in the county.[226]

It's not that the Irish don't suck up to Intel as well- the government most certainly does, but the notion that Enda Kenny, our Prime Minister could get out a huge crowd to chant 'Intel, Intel' as the CEO drove by (as apparently happened in China) sounds a bit far-fetched. However, in the current economic climate, with jobs very scarce, anything is possible.

Special handbooks were published in China for the 2008 Olympics in Beijing- 'to teach people how to make a good impression on foreigners.' The order of the day was, Kynge writes, 'Scrupulous politeness, high standards of personal hygiene (no spitting) and the creation of 'warmth' towards visitors.'

He notes that Chinese school children are still taught about the treachery of the Western powers in humiliating China. Although much of what they are taught is true, it is not presented in the spirit of rapprochement. Rather, as Kynge describes it, the authorities nurture radical nationalism, and make no effort to teach current realities, such as the fact the Japanese have provided extensive aid and investment to China over the years, or simply that times have changed.

Rather, by Kynge's account, the Chinese government feeds the masses with the opium of resentment and the gratifying notion that China's traditional enemies will get their comeuppance. This notion is familiar to the Irish. In the fight for independence from England, the Gaelic phrase was often used in the Republican cause: 'Tiocfaidh ar La'- meaning 'Our day will come.'

We, too, were victims of colonial aggression, so the Chinese stance, racism aside, is not inexplicable. However, in a global economy, where everyone and everything is at some level inter-connected, we all need to let bygones be bygones. Right now, the Chinese can console themselves with the fact that the Big Nose post-colonialists are up to their eyeballs in debt that they own.

However, as much as Russia needs to try to improve its image and reputation abroad, in part by putting on a welcoming face to foreigners, I recommend the sincere approach. No faking it.

I had read Kynge's book before my first trip to China, so I was wise to 'waishi,' which I did encounter- and hated. I found myself wistful for a frigid day in Moscow with women in Fendi fur and beggars alike scowling at me, and then the odd, furtive hesitant smile: The real deal- and all the more precious for it.

Russians are well capable of acting as ambassadors without gushing all over us. However, sometimes they don't help themselves. There is a disconcerting tendency in Russia to put a raft of tough looking men with hard edges in front of the camera, or on official websites.

Even US multinationals, including those in traditionally hard-men industries usually realize that it is imprudent to pack the board of directors or management team with men who look like they could go ten rounds with Muhammad Ali in his heyday, or, even worse, a bunch of white guys with obvious entitlement complexes.

These gender imbalances are a significant issue in the West, but Russia has a huge wealth of attractive, brilliant women: It should put them up front, with Russians of both sexes from multi-ethnic minority groups and help soften the country's image.

Creating a modern, diversified economy requires a modern sensibility and a diversified workforce. It won't happen by simply putting a new plaque on the wall. This is an issue in most Western countries as much as in Russia. However, the men and women chosen to represent Russia should help neutralize existing stereotypes, rather than accentuating them.

Another commonly held view of Russia in the West is that flying internally is dangerous.

An appalling recent aircraft crash record has Russia at the bottom of the international safety league tables at the time of writing. A total of 121 people have been killed in seven crashes this year, which clearly is 121 too many. The 2018 World Cup soccer matches will be held at venues all over Russia, so this situation will have to be drastically improved by the time the soccer fans arrive en masse.

Medvedev ordered a review and many aircraft have been grounded, and must be replaced-an expensive proposition. There will be a major shakeup in the sector. However, one challenge is that only really tough airplanes (Russian planes are hardy and extremely well built) can service the vast and inhospitable terrain- and a great many Russians depend on tiny regional airlines to get around. So if they are all shut down, people and businesses are cut off.

The problem is rarely with the planes themselves, but rather with a lack of integrated, consistent standards and regulatory oversight, compounded by poor training, maintenance and abysmal salaries for pilots and airline staff. In some instances where planes have crashed, investigations revealed that pilots had flown drunk or ignored instructions from air traffic control.

However, the news is not all bad. Although air disasters are more common than they should be, it is still a very safe way to travel. In addition, the view that Westerners have about air travel in Russia is well wide of the mark. They imagine huge, dilapidated, ancient Aeroflot planes with steel seats, chickens out back and surly hostesses.

When I told friends I flew from Moscow to Sochi on Russian airline S7, I was treated like Amelia Earhart, a veritable pioneer. I explained that the plane was brand new, beautifully fitted out, the food free and excellent, and the stewardesses attractive and kind. No-one believed me, but my reputation as an intrepid world traveller was secure.

Irish air travellers are used to rough treatment at the hands of local budget airline Ryanair and CEO, Michael O'Leary (of taxi plate fame), who relishes his image as a Neanderthal, intent on inflicting every indignity imaginable on passengers to save money. He has suggested that toilets on board be fitted with coin slots. He hates it when we get anything for free.

As the Irish are big soccer fans, many of us will visit Russia for the World Cup. Assuming we get to our destination alive, we will have low expectations when it comes to air travel in Russia. We will be easy to impress. Give us a free coffee or drink, a reasonable baggage allowance, a few crumbs to eat and a nice magazine, and we will think we are on Pan Am in the 60's.

The Sochi Winter Olympics in 2014 and the 2018 World Cup are clearly a phenomenal opportunity for the Russian government to showcase the country. With many thousands of people expected to visit Russia for both events, there is no time to waste to start the vital work to showcase Russia-and Russians.

Hearts and minds need to be won. And it's not just about building stadiums and roads, and setting up hot dog and drinks stands, it's a golden opportunity to break down stereotypes. However, it's not a one-way street: We must visit Russia with an open mind and a generous spirit. I have every confidence the Russians will put on a great show.

It's worth noting that not all the stereotypes about Russians are overtly negative. Some verge on the positive, such as the view that Russians are mysterious, even sexy, in a cloak and dagger kind of way. It's partly the accent, and too many James Bond movies.

The first time I landed in Moscow, I felt a tremendous excitement at breaching the 'Evil Empire.' I was intensely curious about Russians and Russianness-I wanted to suck it all in. It was all quite intoxicating, in a way that going to Paris is not.

Another Western stereotype about Russia is that Russian women are 'hot'- as in sexy. Western men often imbue Russian women with enchantress qualities and great physical beauty. It is rare that a Western man will say anything negative about Russian woman, although there is little focus on their intellectual prowess. There is a mild assumption that most Russian woman wish to marry Western men, to escape the drunken savages at home.

I think it is fair to say that the Russian people are blurry figures to many people in the West. They have little substance in our imagination, except for the cliché-ridden caricatures we see in the movies and read in the mass media.

What is extraordinary, but inevitably the case when propaganda does its job well, is how far removed from reality the Western view of Russia really is. My personal impressions are shared by many people I have met and spoken with over the years, but that is all they are.

In my experience, rather than being stern and dour, Russians are extremely passionate, intense people. They love a good argument and debate, nice food and wine (on occasion, like the Irish, to excess). In Soviet times, one of the few commodities readily available for purchase was cheap vodka.

However, the Western notion, quite obnoxiously repeated ad nauseum by reputable UK newspapers, that all Russian males are legless in the middle of the day is nonsense. I have seen far more drunken louts in both Dublin and London, where binge-drinking is an epidemic.

Russians love dancing and singing and they have a black humour and ready wit. They are superstitious, pessimistic, and their daily lives, despite adversity, are often full of drama. They are erratic, temperamental, enigmatic and fiercely proud. Many Russians still believe in old-fashioned concepts of 'duty and honour,' long extinct in the West.

They either love you or they hate you, or they are utterly dismissive of you-and possibly all in the same day: They have fire in them.

Indeed, those I have met are brimful of contradictions. These extremes of personality have long attracted Westerners who like to 'live large.' Russia is not a place for people who like everything under control. Russia tends to attract people who crave and relish the complex kaleidoscope of colour and experiences that this unique country has to offer.

For this reason, and the fact that many of them seem to loath the place, several Western Moscow-based media correspondents really need to find another posting. Russia can be messy, so if you like to canter around the paddock on a nice, well behaved horse, move to Toronto. For better or worse, Russia is one hell of a ride and has much to commend it.

The US author and Pulitzer Prize winner, Michael Cunningham (his book *The Hours* was made into a Hollywood movie) was interviewed by the Moscow Times in December, 2011.[227]He provided an eloquent perspective on the Russians he met in Moscow on his first Russian book tour.

He said that 'Russians ask questions unlike questions I have encountered anywhere else. One man asked me, 'What is the meaning of life?' No one has ever asked me that question before...Russians want to pose the big questions.'

He observed that his books, much-loved in Russia, are 'more emotional, more earnest, more psychological than a lot of what is fashionable in America right now.' He said that he 'may be a Russian writer born accidentally in America.'

He said that 'The current American idea about Moscow is that it is some hybrid of Tokyo and the Wild West, that it is incredibly prosperous and has as many Pradas as we have delicatessens in New York City, and that gangsters are driving their Mercedes on the sidewalks, shooting at random pedestrians.'

However, he noted 'That the vitality of the city is palpable even from a moving cab. That it is inspired and chaotic and full of energy. It's full of greed and life and fear and all the qualities that animate the great cities: New York, Tokyo, maybe Berlin, London. There is a fabulous combination of hope and discouragement and incredible materialism. Food, beautiful clothes, beautiful stuff. Will it end tomorrow? Maybe, so we better grab it while we can.'

Many Russians appear to have a 'live for today' mentality that likely originated from pragmatism born of decades of deprivation. Russians of my acquaintance rarely save. I once asked a Russian friend why she didn't save for a rainy day, and she said 'every day is a rainy day, so why bother.' I filed it under 'justification' for my next splurge. It rains a lot in Ireland.

Russians are great spenders, unlike the Chinese, who save like crazy. They spend multiples more at airport duty free shops than other nationals. They have high disposable income-due to the 13% flat income tax rate. Russians also have subsidized energy, and many live in low-cost housing.

In the 2011 Xmas season, the UK department store, Selfridges, did well in no small part due to an influx of Russian tourists. An estimated 24 million Russians now travel abroad each year, and they are big spenders. The fact the middle class is growing and has high discretionary spending power makes Russians very enthusiastic consumers.

They have supported the UK's high end housing market, high end restaurants, and boutiques for a decade or more. They deserve a little respect for their troubles. However, they may have to work a little harder to get it.

I have heard several high-end boutique staff in London complain that Russian 'high-rollers' treat store staff like dogs-'Give me this, that. No hello, please, thanks, goodbye.'

I have, unfortunately, observed this phenomenon for myself, and I cannot condone it. I can't explain it either. I can only attribute it to 'New-Moneyism'- an unwarranted arrogance born of recent access to more money than is good for you. London store keepers are happy for Russian custom, but consider Russians rough around the edges.

The bizarre concept of perceiving oneself as 'elite' may also have something to do with this bad behaviour. The Irish tend to be egalitarian- very much in the US 'Republican' tradition (in the best sense of the word) - so I struggle to understand such an attitude.

A suitable punishment, in the UK context at least, might be enforced viewing, back-to-back, of every episode of hit TV series *Downton Abbey* to learn how proper English people treat the 'staff.'

Russian tourists took a record 60 million trips abroad in the first half of 2011. The most popular travel destinations were Turkey, China, Egypt, Thailand and Finland. They are increasingly choosing independent travel over package holidays, a sign the market is maturing.

Although Russian tourists abroad could conceivably act as brand ambassadors for Russia, some of them may do more harm than good, in terms of debunking Westerns stereotypes, if Western surveys are to be believed.

The US travel site Expedia.com surveyed 15,000 hoteliers around the world, and revealed that Russians are considered to be among the most unpleasant tourists, only losing out in terms of 'unbearability' to Chinese, French and Indian nationals.

Many Russians despair at the behaviour of their own abroad, for acting like lewd boors, drinking and smoking to excess, talking loudly and wearing garish jewellery and clothing, or no clothes at all. They are also criticized for not speaking other languages. Americans rarely do either, but they will use guide books to try to say a few words.

During communist times, Russians tended to horde food for bad times, and they sometimes behaved in an equally parsimonious manner when they travelled abroad, to the bemusement of Westerners. I have heard charges about bad Russian behaviour in restaurants, especially at buffets. However, in my experience, buffets bring out the worst in people, Westerners included.

Only recently, at a luxury hotel in Rome, I watched a well-heeled American woman surreptitiously pack her handbag full with food from the breakfast buffet, much to the horror of the keen eyed waiters. I wondered why one might visit Italy, renowned for its food, only to behave as if food shortages were widespread.

The behavior of some Russian tourists may not be exemplary, but one only has to visit Ibiza and observe British and German tourists in their full glory to realize that Russians have strong competition for the title 'world greatest travel boor.'

The Irish also frequently lose the run of themselves on vacation, much to my dismay. However, incidents where they cause havoc on airplanes by drinking the plane dry, fighting and acting like idiots are less frequent. Nonetheless, crimes against civilized behaviour are still observable.

Americans too, when travelling abroad have a poor reputation for loud, boorish behaviour and unsophisticated attire. The American tourist's obsession with wearing white running shoes and large shorts (also an epidemic amongst Canadians) positively everywhere, including fine dining establishments, has intrigued me for years.

Are there no comfortable shoes and long pants available for purchase in the US? Is it attributable to the fact that Americans drive everywhere so that the prospect of walking in a foreign city is so intimidating it mandates professional feet wear?

Regardless of the reason, the 'shorts and runners' uniform raises eyebrows and even hackles in places where it is considered that 'clothes maketh the man.' Casual dress may be viewed as a mark of disrespect.

If many Westerners think Russians dour, with criminal tendencies, what do Russians think of us?

Stereotypes of Westerners also exist on the Russian side. It is not a one way street.

Yevgeny Bazhanov, the Vice Chancellor of Research and International Relations at the Russian Foreign Ministry's Diplomatic Academy was quoted in the Moscow Times[228] as saying that he had noticed a ' disturbing new trend among my students: In the past 10 years, the number of them who sincerely believe ridiculous conspiracy theories about US aggression and global domination is increasing.'

Such conspiracy theories include a belief that US President George W. Bush was behind the Sept. 11, 2001 attacks to give him a pretext to invade Iraq. According to Bazhanov, some 'highly influential public figures' espouse these conspiracy theories on Russian television and in the print media. He indicated that a 'seasoned military analyst' had tried to convince him that the US States was behind the recent Moscow subway bombings.

On a more benign note, an article in the Moscow Times[229] discussed what Russian students in an American history class at the Russian State University for the Humanities thought of when they think about America. For a 19-year-old Kazan native with an American stepfather, it was Elvis, Washington, democracy. For his friend, it was baseball and hot dogs.'

However, the Moscow Times article quoted a Soviet dissident who moved to the United States in 1976, and returned to Russia over a decade later, as saying that Russians and Americans 'don't know what's really going on' in each other's countries, and that some Russians think America 'is still full of cowboys and Marines.'

It is fortunately by no means the case that all bias, prejudice, or stereotyping is intentionally malicious. In all likelihood, most of it is not. When we invoke stereotypes, we rarely intend to cause offence or do harm to anyone. We just don't think. Indeed, many of us, if challenged, will readily acknowledge that our perspective is ill-informed, outdated, or plain silly.

I believe it is important to attack stereotypes and ignorance with facts, but also with humour.

An illustrator called Yanko Tsvekov created *Mapping Stereotypes,*[230]European country maps labelled with stereotypes as viewed by individual countries- e.g. the US map of Europe has Russia in red as 'Commies.' Germany has Russia as 'Gas Vault.' the Vatican has labelled Russia 'Arch-Nemesis.' Britain has dubbed it 'Big Spenders.' and so on.

I know someone who is head of anti-money laundering at a huge US bank in London and he has the US map on his wall, but he hides it when his American bosses come to town. He told me they 'wouldn't get it.'

How we perceive others (and the stereotypes we give credence to about them) can impact how we do our jobs, and even how companies, including banks, rank countries in terms of risk exposure.

Occasionally we add fuel to the flames by 'playing to' a stereotype for our own ends.

In 2008, Russian billionaire, Mikhail Prokhorov, piled a fortune into an upscale Russian magazine venture called 'Snob'- aimed at educated, sophisticated Russians living abroad. It is in Russian only at present, but sells in major international cities such as New York and London. The name was intended to be ironic, but it goes down like a lead balloon in the West where the word has few positive connotations.

Prokhorov stood against Putin in the March 2012 Presidential election. The UK media seemed to like the idea. But why? Prokhorov, no dummy, despite his international playboy image, was one of the winners in the fire sale of Russian state assets in the wild 90's. He is not, however, the Russian peoples' champion and he has little popular support.

He can be droll. A while back, he was asked why he'd never married: He is considered one of the most eligible bachelors in Russia. He responded that he didn't 'do' small business, and that marriage is the ultimate small business: Ergo, it wasn't for him. It was funny, after a fashion, but telling.

In a subsequent US PR campaign to increase his profile as owner of the New York Jets basketball team, when asked the same question by a US journalist, he gave a more PC answer- he hadn't met a woman yet who could cook well enough.

Russia needs a profusion of small businesses- perhaps even run by beautiful women who can cook. All big businesses start small, unless you were given your empire off the back of a truck during the boot sale of the century. A President with a derisory attitude towards small business is the last thing Russia needs.

Snob magazine is beautifully produced with gorgeous art work, but the pre-launch publicity made it clear it is aimed at 'elite' intellectual Russians at home and abroad, rather than the nameless rank and file Russians who toil in office towers in the West.

It is unlikely to register much with a Western audience. However, the name, the extravagant caviar and champagne launch parties, and a few rather pompous interviews given by writers associated with it, does not help debunk existing stereotypes about Russians.

I read an article which quoted a writer for the magazine in which he referred to Russians who work in regular jobs in the US as not the kind of people that Snob wants to target. I took from what he said that these people were not 'elite' enough to be of interest to the magazine.

However, these ordinary, unassuming Russians are far better ambassadors for Russia than their more supercilious (and rather boring) 'elite' countrymen and women.

The US and UK coverage of the Snob venture that I have read was vaguely positive, but sardonic, covering the rather flash launch parties the magazine held. Russian critics have, however, described the magazine as typical of the Russian intelligentsia, living in an Ivory Tower that has little to do with ordinary Russians.

As part of his US charm campaign to promote his purchase of New York Jets, Prokhorov gave interviews to US TV stations, such as CNBC. As well as expressing his desire for a wife who can cook, Prokhorov camped it up for the US networks, speaking in animated, but quixotic English, about his vast wealth, love of beautiful women, ownership of fine yachts, and his high-octane hobbies.

I recall him saying he didn't know where his yacht was parked- people look after these paltry details for him. The male interviewer lapped it up and was plainly wildly jealous.

It may all seem like harmless fun, especially when there's nothing shameful about having lots of money in the US, and flaunting it. Indeed, not having it is far more suspect. However, such publicity likely inspires creative endeavours such as the stereotype-ridden advertising campaign, 'Gregor-The Russian Billionaire'- made for US cable TV provider DirectTV by New York ad agency Grey.[231]

Needless to say, wealthy men behaving badly, or simply kicking up some dust, is hardly a phenomenon exclusive to

Russia: Such antics are commonplace in the West, and tolerated as vaguely endearing: Men will be men. It's not even a barrier to a career in politics. Berlusconi, Strauss-Kahn, and Bill Clinton are examples on point.

However, as Russians are arguably a special case, it's risky to add fuel to the fire. In the case of Gregor, one might argue that Prokhorov brought it on himself - and did Russians no favours in the process.

Every possible stereotype about 'new Russians' is rolled out for the Gregor advertising campaign. I didn't know whether to laugh or to cry. It is hilarious, or deeply worrisome, depending on your perspective, but it's feeding Russian stereotypes in a major way.

There were two Gregor ads that I know of; the first was aired in August 2010 and called 'Opulence.' The second was 'Epic-Win.' They seem to be still up on YouTube.

Both feature the ultimate caricature of the Russian Billionaire, Gregor. Gregor is tall, lean, semi-bald, with a trendy one day shadow. He sports many gold rings and a large 'opulent' watch. His belt looks like Versace. He has an appalling Russian accent. No one I have ever met in Russia sounds like this- maybe after 12 shots of vodka, but even then it's a stretch.

Gregor meanders through a gold festooned room, in which dogs sit playing poker, and beef-cake security goons stand guard. Along the route, he chooses one gold statue over another (both indistinguishable) from two suited women, presumably art dealers, as they have on more clothes than the other women in the room, dressed in short, sparkly evening dresses.

Gregor walks in a leisurely fashion-a man clearly at peace with his world- and along the way snacks on gold covered sweets (candy) from a crystal container.

His opening line is, 'Opulence- I has it.' But he also likes saving 'za money,' hence his interest in DirectTV's premium (TV) package. He gives a demented laugh (one is thus left wondering how this imbecile made his billions) and kisses a mini–giraffe sitting on a cushion beside him. Two gorgeous women sit alongside. His TV channel changers are shaped like gold bars, and are served up to him stacked on a tray.

In the Epic-Win ad, grunting and groaning men lift weights that appear to be solid gold. Gregor, however, is working out with the assistance of leads on his arms that enable him exercise with 'no pain'- indeed no movement whatsoever. Exercise without exertion.

Clearly, this bleeding-edge technology should be front and centre at the new Moscow Skolkovo Technology Centre.

He is seated in a chair, with mini Faberge eggs beside him (a sly reference to the fact Russian billionaires having bought rare Faberge eggs at auction for repatriation back to Russia) on an opulent side-table, attended to by women in skin-tight spandex.

The best thing about both ads- and mercifully the public agreed- was the cute and extremely life-like mini-giraffe. In Epic-Win, the mini giraffe is jogging on a mini treadmill.

With the success of the mini giraffes, the New York ad agency, Grey, responsible for the ads, showcased a fictional, but very real looking 'live' video feed (previously at http://www.petitelapgiraffe.com) where you could watch the animals at their breeding farm in Russia, at Sokoblovsky Farms, '80 kilometers outside Krasnodar.'The site's text is in faux broken English.

One comment on the YouTube site under the Epic Win video link was apt:'Who the fuck is Gregor.' Who indeed? Although friends in LA told me that 'everyone' assumed Gregor was Prokhorov.

At one point when I checked, nearly 800,000 people had clicked to buy Gregor's mini–giraffe, a subsequent twist to the ad campaign. More recently, I viewed the Opulence ad on YouTube-it had 935,158 views (hits). Nearly a million people watched the Gregor ad- on YouTube alone!

Now, it's just fun, you say, keep your hair on- and I'd agree, if it was not for the fact that popular images of Russians in the movies, on TV, in print, in newspapers, and in popular literature, all re-hash the same jaded stereotypes of Russians, and not always with as much panache as the DirectTV ads. Sadly, most representations of Russians are not funny at all.

Chapter Fifteen

Movies

It is a sad fact, but many kids today are mesmerized by reality TV and low-brow celebrity culture. They are hugely influenced by what they see on TV, on social networking sites and in movies they download for free. It's not just kids though. Popular culture is undeniably a force to be reckoned with: We ignore it at our peril.

The international Jewish community is often involved in initiatives promoting tolerance. This is good news, because the US creative community has a highly influential cadre of Jewish writers, directors, producers, comedians, and actors. I believe that if they were approached in the right manner, they would be willing to work to eliminate or at least lessen stereotypes that target Russians in the movies, on network TV, etc.

They should know better in portraying Russians as cartoon characters, treacherous, remorseless villains, Mafiosi and hookers. Superstar producers such as Steven Spielberg, who has directed movies about the Holocaust, and worked hard to preserve the testimony of survivors, ought to be fully aware of the dangers of stereotyping and its potentially very adverse consequences.

In Spielberg's 2008 *Indiana Jones and the Kingdom of the Crystal Skull* movie, Russians replace the Nazi villains in the previous Indiana movies. I read that at one point, Nazis were to be the villains, but Spielberg had just directed Schindler's List and felt disinclined to treat the Nazis 'lightly.' In addition, supposedly Harrison Ford believed they had 'plumb worn the Nazis out.'

George Lucas may ultimately have to take the blame, reportedly thinking that if the movie was to be set in the 1950s, it would have to feature the Cold War, and the matter was resolved when he read that Stalin was interested in crystal skulls. With the flip of a coin, the Russians, who died in millions to stop Hitler in his tracks, replaced the Nazis.

It's not good enough.

Over the last few years, alongside clipping mountains of negative print media, I started to notice that Hollywood movies are absolutely over-run with Russian villains. Pay more attention, and you will notice it too. A major studio movie that doesn't feature a Russian villain is a scarce commodity. TV shows, especially in the spy, crime or 'gangster' genre are little better.

As noted in Part One, the writers on UK hit series 'Spooks' seemed hard pressed to make an episode without a Russian caricature. I found it monotonous, lacking imagination as to what might constitute a future terrorist threat against Britain.

Hollywood wields great power in the public consciousness, and is, unquestionably a powerful source of soft-power for the US government and US industry. The industry contributes more than $175 billion annually to the US economy.[232] In terms of reach, over two-thirds (68%) of Americans went to the movies at least once in 2011. PG-13 movies constituted 12 out of the top 25 movies in release in 2010.

Movie theatres in the US/Canada attract more people than all theme parks and US sports combined.[233] The Motion Pictures Association of America's (MPAA) 2010 theatrical market statistics (box office numbers)[234] show that international box office numbers are up significantly over five years ago-with big growth in China and Asia in general, making up for lacklustre domestic numbers.

Hispanics are more likely to go to the movies: In 2011, 43 million Hispanics bought 351 million movie tickets in the US – they also go to the movies more often than anyone else (on average 7 times a year, compared to an average of about 4 a year for other people).

One might expect, therefore, that Hollywood will hesitate before making movies like *Man on Fire*, (with Denzel Washington running riot through Mexico, portrayed as a deadly hell-hole) that portray Hispanic countries as crime-ridden backwaters.

In 1999, the US Cartoon Network pulled Speedy Gonzales from the US airwaves in part because Speedy was not political correct. However, Speedy was popular south of the border and thousands of Hispanic people signed petitions to bring him back. He subsequently made a short comeback.

In 2007, Ivan Katchanovski (I have already mentioned his paper on bias on US network TV) wrote a paper about political incorrectness in Hollywood movies that portray Russia, the Ukraine and Kazakhstan. He analysed more than one hundred movies and films for his paper.[235]His findings mimic my own.

He concluded that most of the movies he viewed 'incorrectly' present these countries as 'economically and technologically backward, extremely anti-American and anti-Semitic countries, which have pervasive 'Russian mafia' and widespread female prostitution.'

A lack of knowledge about geography is prevalent; smash hits such as *Independence Day* (1996) depicted a map supposed to be of Russia that in fact shows the borders of the old Soviet Union. In addition, a Russian TV news broadcast portrayed in the movie is described as the 'Soviet Central News.' In *Borat*, Katchanovski notes that 'the fictional Kazakh journalist played by UK comedian Sasha Cohen does not object when American students in the movie refer to Kazakhstan as 'Russia.'

Indeed, it pained me to watch Cohen in the thoroughly vile *Borat* movie (full title:*'Borat: Cultural Learnings of America for Make Benefit Glorious Nation of Kazakhstan*) ridiculing an entire country that most people had never heard of- a blank slate on which to paint any image his imagination could conjure up. I nearly threw up watching it.

The film was released in 2006 by 20th Century Fox. Kazakhstan's President Nursultan Nazarbayev and his country took offense at the work. Fox, expecting the worst, set up One America as a separate entity to produce the film: Prudent litigation management.

According to the Hollywood Reporter, Cohen and Fox Studios were sued, but commented that 'most of the 'Borat' cases were essentially filed (but defeated) by a bunch of people who felt duped into signing release forms (or who Cohen failed to get signatures from).'[236]

A bizarre fall-out from the movie was that Britain's Prince Andrew was asked to help rehabilitate the business reputation of Kazakhstan, which government ministers believed had been damaged by stereotypes included in *Borat*. At the time, Prince Andrew was a UK trade ambassador until he fell out of favour.

The Kazakhstani government ran full page ads in *The New York Times, US News and World Report* and commercials on CNN and the local ABC affiliate in Washington, D.C as part of a PR campaign ahead of President Nazabayev's trip to the United States, to try to neutralize the harm done to the country's reputation by *Borat*. Subsequently, Kazakhstan, which borders Russia, tried to play it down, but Russia banned *Borat* citing concerns it might offend its neighbour and 'some viewers' religious or national sensibilities.'

Banning movies is rarely the answer.

At one stage in 2008- 2009, the Russian government proposed taking the *South Park* cartoon series off air- as posing a threat to young minds. *South Park* is indeed as subversive and rude as it gets, but it has brilliant moments. In one episode, Kenny is killed waiting for the bus when the Mir Space Station crashes and flattens him. The Russian government has also threatened to ban video games with an anti-Russian slant, apparently a common theme.

Cohen won a Golden Globe for his performance in Borat. However, notoriety aside, his contribution to Western society is such that the only thing most Westerners will ever know about Kazakhstan is what Cohen said about it: It'll stick. It is cheap, unsophisticated humour posturing disingenuously as a worthy endeavour to expose the irrationality of stereotypes.

I confess I heartily dislike Cohen's crude, vulgar humour in general, which seems to primarily revolve around giving him the tiniest excuse to remove all his clothes and flash his bits: Put it away Sasha.

I heard his 'in-character' justification for the movie. Sometimes, you just can't make a silk purse out of a sow's ear. There are too many people out there happy to mock and jeer others in the Sasha Baron Cohen tradition. They don't learn from the experience. We kid ourselves if we think they do. A tiny minority may view Cohen as a modern day Jonathan Swift and see deep meaning in his antics. I, for one, do not. Of course, he is box office gold.

By contrast, US comedian Larry David's humour (David is not slow to tackle stereotyping head on, in his rather inimitable fashion) is of the hummingbird variety compared to Cohen's blunderbuss approach. I would love to meet him, but fear we would spiral into mutual loathing of the universe in short order.

Hugely popular American comedians command the crowd at the Coliseum. Popular entertainers have huge clout. Men like Adam Sandler, Eddie Murphy, Jerry Seinfeld and Larry

David function as modern day philosophers, albeit under the guise of Court Jester.

In my favourite Woody Allen movie, *Hannah and Her Sisters* (1986), Frederick, the cynical artist played beautifully by Max van Sydow, made the following marvellously trenchant observation (with which I have much sympathy) to his lover, played by Mia Farrow:

'You missed a very dull TV show on Auschwitz. More gruesome film clips, and more puzzled intellectuals declaring their mystification over the systematic murder of millions. The reason they can never answer the question 'How could it possibly happen?' is that it's the wrong question. Given what people are, the question is 'Why doesn't it happen more often?'

Real humour, that has a tender heart, can make us think twice and question our baser instincts and poorly conceived assumptions about others. If we only laughed at ourselves more often, we might be less likely to kill each other over meaningless differences.

Films released in Spain can now get a new rating called 'specially recommended for the equality of sexes.' The focus is on gender bias, and the initiative is backed by the Spanish Secretary of State for Equality. However, it is an interesting development that may leave room for heightened awareness of other types of stereotyping. No doubt, Hollywood lobbyists will keep a watchful eye. Certainly, the Russians have legitimate cause to complain.

National character stereotyping is (and always has been) rife in Hollywood; the drunken, but charming Irish idiot was a stable for years. However, a distinction can be made with respect to the portrayal of Russia and Russians is that there is generally nothing affectionate about the manner in which they are presented. By contrast, even Italians mobsters love their mothers, opera and good food. An underlying affection for them comes through.

In the 1996 Arnold Schwarzenegger movie, 'Eraser'- a typical Arnold tour de force in which he blows everything up- the Russian mafia is in league with terrorists. Arnold forms an alliance with the Italian mobsters who run the US ports that the terrorists are using to store and move the deadly weapons.

The Italian mob helps Arnold foil the terrorist operation. In one scene, the mobsters express contempt for their Russian brethren, calling them 'Commie bastards.' Another Italian hood corrects him, 'They are not Commies any more, they have a Federation.' 'Don't make me hurt you, Mikey' is the dry response.

In Hollywood, even Italian mobsters are portrayed as American patriots prepared to team up with law enforcement to fight Russian terrorists intent on nuclear Armageddon.

In his movie study, Katchanovski noted that 43% of all the movies he reviewed focused on "Russian mafia, assassins, or other criminals'- and in 'most of these films, 'Russian Mafiosi' kill or threaten to kill Americans, predominantly on US soil: a frequent theme is the threat of nuclear Armageddon.'

He notes that in hit TV series 24- a former Soviet General employs terrorists to detonate portable nuclear devices in major US urban centres 'to avenge the Soviet Unions' defeat in the Cold War.' In another episode in 2006, a billionaire leader of a Russian separatist group attempts to use nerve gas and nuclear missiles against US citizens.

He also notes- and I find this conclusion particularly alarming- that 'Several major Hollywood movies undertake historical revisionism concerning World War II in the Soviet

Union.' By way of example in *Hell Boy (2004)* the Russian mystic (Rasputin) is portrayed as a Nazi ally.

Similarly, in the Hannibal Lector Prequel, *Hannibal Rising (2007)*, the explanation given for Lector's metamorphosis into a terrifying cannibal is that he watched as his baby sister was eaten by starving Russian soldiers in Lithuania near the end of World War Two. The Russian soldiers in this movie, I recall, are portrayed as sub-human. Hannibal was released in the CIS countries, making nearly 5 million USD at the box office.

I can only imagine Russian faces watching their soldiers, Western allies in the Second World War, devouring the tender young girl. The movie is, of course, loosely based on the blockbuster novel by Tom Harris.

I recall that in *Defiance* (2008) starring Bond Daniel Craig as a Polish- Jewish resistance leader, the Russian allies are portrayed as anti-Semitic, boorish drunks. It would not appear to have been released in the CIS region. According to Katchanovski, many Western World War II movies depict soldiers in the Soviet army not as allies, but as rapists and monsters. In addition, the vast numbers of Russian and Ukrainians killed during the war are ignored.

Katchanovski noted, most depressingly, that a 2004 Gallup Poll suggested that more than half of High School graduates in the US did not know that the Soviet Union was a US ally during the Second World War. Only 11% thought that the Soviet Union contributed most to the defeat of Nazi Germany- 65% believing instead that the US did so.

In fact, 80% of German casualties were inflicted on the Eastern Front. Indeed, it is indisputable that without the appalling sacrifice and heroism of the people of the Soviet Union, the allies would not have defeated the Nazis.

One million Russians died in the siege of Stalingrad alone, more than all combat deaths suffered by the allied forces combined. At the end of the war, over 8.6 million Soviet soldiers had died, and at least 17 million Russian civilians had been killed; twenty five million people were also left homeless. Drought, famine, and disease followed in the wars' wake. [237]

When Hollywood movies change these facts, or Western school books or curricula fail to impart them to our young people, we denigrate the enormous sacrifice made by the Russian people to keep us safe from Nazism.

Katchanovski also cites another depressing 2003 Gallup Poll that suggested that 15% of Americans thought that the Soviet Union was involved in the assassination of President Kennedy.

Katchanovski believes that because Russians, Ukrainians and the other CIS nationals are not perceived as protected minorities in the US, it is open season as to how they are portrayed by Hollywood and in network television in the US. The concept of 'political correctness' does not extend to them.

He notes, however, that other minorities, such as Muslims, have vociferously protested movies and TV shows that portray them in a negative light, with success. For instance, he states that episodes of TV show '24' that had Arab villains, and similarly, the movie *True Lies* (1994) drew loud protests from organisations such as the Council on American-Islamic Relations)- resulting in anti-racist disclaimers being shown with them to appease critics.

He also gives the example of the Tom Clancy book, *Sum of All Fears*- the plot was changed for the movie (2002) to replace Palestinian terrorists with European neo- Nazis, with Russian and Ukrainian villains in tow. He explains that even the Japanese get some accommodation as the movie *Pearl Harbor* (2001) was toned down to remove overtly anti-Japanese sentiment to appeal to (large and lucrative) Japanese audiences.

The result of protests by Muslim communities in particular (and also, in my view, Western fear of violent retaliation by extremist Muslim groups) has been that US film makers have tended to shy away from any negative representations of Muslims and Arabs, even after 9/11. Negative portrayals of Russians, however, continue unabated.

As Katchanovski notes, the Russians and other CIS communities lack political representation and clout in the US. Furthermore, he notes that countries not perceived as significant US allies get a particularly rough ride. He observes that economic factors also inevitably play a role, as 'US film-makers largely ignore reception of their films in these post-Soviet countries.'

Not any more, as I will explain.

Katchanovski notes that there is little information available to American High School students about post-Soviet countries; in the period 1997-2005, no more than 0.2 percent of the US population visited Russia- and far fewer visited Ukraine and Kazakhstan. Therefore, any views that they have about Russia and the CIS countries likely come from popular culture, including movies.

In 2010, I note that 20 million Americans visited Mexico[238] (top destination) – followed by Canada (11.7 million) and the UK (2.4 million) A paltry 257,000 US visitors went to Russia, down slightly from 2009- a mere 2.6% of the total Western European numbers.

Katchanovski noted that a 2001 Parrillo/Donoghue survey of 2,916 students in 22 US colleges and universities revealed that Russians were viewed as more 'distant' to Americans (defined as 'willingness to marry, befriend, accept as neighbours and co-workers, or allow into the United States') than virtually any other ethnic group. In addition,

American women viewed Russian males (compared to 30 other ethnic and religious groups) as more alien to them than other men. US males placed them closer to the middle.

I haven't the faintest idea why American women would shun Russian men (often gallant and very charming) except for a concern about their propensity (gleaned from Hollywood movies) to make bio-weapons and plot terrorist conflagrations. If you watched enough Hollywood movies, you would certainly think twice before dating a Russian physicist- pronounced 'phys-ee-ceest' as they seem to have especially diabolic predilections.

I agree with Katchanovski's concern that it is entirely conceivable that the predominantly negative images of persons from post-Soviet countries in movies 'negatively affect Americans' perceptions of social distance from Russians.' The fact, according to National Geographic surveys, that many Americans struggle to find New York City on a map (let alone Russia) is also inauspicious.

Katchanovski concludes that 'analysis of polls, media coverage, and web hits shows that such films have real impact in promoting stereotypes of and prejudices' against people from these regions. In his view, they are not merely harmless fun.

In *The Nature of Prejudice,* Gordon W. Allport[239] referred to a study done in 1944 by the Writer's War Board in the US, with Columbia University, that 'made an extensive study of the 'stock characters' portrayed in the mass media.' 'Popular light fiction was found to be perhaps the most striking offender': Anglo Saxons constituted over ninety percent of the 'reputable' characters in 185 short stories.

'Menials' or bad guys like thieves or gamblers were 'seldom Anglo-Saxon.' The study found that in general, 'the behaviour of these fictional characters could easily be used to 'prove' that Negroes are lazy, the Jews wily, the Irish superstitious, and the Italians criminal.'

The 1944 study also analysed 100 motion pictures involving 'Negro characters.' and found that in seventy five cases, the portrayal was 'disparaging and stereotyped.' In only 12 cases, 'was the Negro presented in a favourable light as an individual human being.'

Allport quoted 'hard-headed businessmen' explaining their preference for Anglo-Saxons in advertising in economic terms: 'You'd lose your audience if a colored man appeared in the ad.'

We can take some solace from the fact that such utterly abhorrent sentiments are no longer acceptable in our society, but it is not that long ago that these views were mainstream in the US. Homosexual men and women were also the subject of witch-hunts and discriminatory legislation.

Allport pointed out that over the years, minority groups who had previously been silent filed complaints about how they were portrayed by the studios, with the result, at the other extreme, that Hollywood directors were afraid to cast anyone in the role of villain.

For instance, in 1949, there was a controversy over the British version of *Oliver Twist*, the movie. The controversy was over the portrayal of Fagin as the archetypical Jew. The movie was withdrawn from showing in certain parts of the US due to protests.

In addition, Allport referred to concerns about the study of Shakespeare's *The Merchant of Venice* in schools, because of the fear that the character Shylock might 'lead to stereotyped impressions on young people.' Pinocchio was also considered harmful because 'it features Italians and 'assassins' in close association.'[240]

Allport was sanguine about our ability to eliminate all stereotypes, and instead suggested we strengthen our ability to differentiate among them, and 'handle their impact with critical power.'

Children clearly lack such critical power, in short supply amongst adults. In this respect, Allport noted that textbooks used in schools have come in for close scrutiny and criticism.' He noted that a very thorough report concluded that 'the treatment given minority groups in over three hundred textbooks reveals that many of them perpetuate negative stereotypes.'

However, he concluded that 'the fault seems to lie not in any malicious intent, but in the culture-bound traditions which the authors of the textbooks unwittingly adopted.'

In the past, there have been controversial suggestions that textbooks used in the Palestinian territories contained obnoxious stereotypes of Jewish people. Subsequent studies have concluded that the matter has been over-stated, and that there is fault on both sides, with additional studies noting that Israeli textbooks contained stereotypes about Arabs and perpetuated anti-Arab sentiments and views of historical events. Efforts are being made to try to advance the peace process on both sides by removing inflammatory textbook references.

In recent times, Hong Kong residents have expressed similar concerns about efforts by the Chinese to change school books to reflect Chinese communist values. School children are especially susceptible to the power of suggestion and, if unchallenged, they may, quite conceivably, take whatever stereotypes and mischaracterisations are fed to them as children into adulthood, with negative effect.

I grew up in Southern Ireland when the 'Troubles' in the north of Ireland were at their bloodiest and most violent. As kids, we started our school day singing patriotic songs and learning by heart the poetry of dead martyrs to the Irish cause against the British oppressors. It would be naive to assume that this routine did not leave an impression that took years to shake off.

Despite the fact that Russian stereotypes are pervasive in Western society today, the answer, hinted at by Allport, is not radical political correctness or banning movies. I lived in Canada for many years, and in my view, there is a case to be made that political correctness in that country has gone too far; it has reached a point where one is frequently struck dumb trying to think of anything to say that would not conceivably offend someone or something.

Free speech is an extremely important freedom in a democratic society and should not be dispensed with lightly. I detest Sasha Cohen's comedy, but I would not purport to stop him making it. A disclaimer saying- 'Truly nasty comedy'- as the credits go up, would likely make him all the more popular.

What is needed, instead, as Allport intimated, is more education about the impact of stereotyping on people, to try to encourage us to have more empathy and tolerance for our fellow human beings, whatever their race, colour, creed, or sexual orientation. If we achieve that lofty goal at some distant point in our evolution, we may have a more nuanced and sophisticated view of what forms of entertainment deserve our hard-earned money.

That does not mean we become hyper-sensitive to every perceived slight. Such a person will not prosper in the real world, where a hard head is a useful commodity. However, that is not to condone egregious examples of stereotyping in movies.

I recently watched 'Gone with the Wind' again, and cringed the whole way through it. The African-American slaves in it

460

are portrayed as fawning, simpering, duplicitous imbeciles: Horrible stuff. I am also really uncomfortable watching the Ferengi in the *Star Trek* TV series as they bear a startling resemblance to the most repellent Nazi caricatures of Jews. The Ferengi are an ugly, lascivious, money-grubbing alien race. I am not alone in my discomfort. Critics have pointed out similar concerns.

The dreadful character, Jar Jar Binks in the *Star Wars* movie series was a hybrid of many stereotypes, resembling a near-racist caricature of a Rastafarian Jamaican on acid. I was not alone in my reaction to Jar Jar, quite possibly the most irritating character in a modern movie, although there are many contenders for that title.

Putin was supposedly upset (and threatened litigation) over a purported resemblance[241] between him and the annoying Dobby character in the *Harry Potter* movies. Although there is a passing resemblance (a BBC children's website poll found that 54 per cent of respondents saw the resemblance), after a long night, or too much alcohol, I too (having somewhat protruding eyes) could do a fair Dobby impersonation.

Based on my analysis, Putin has much to be aggrieved about as far as the West is concerned. I would not, however, put Dobby top of the list.

A tongue in cheek Guardian newspaper report stated that US President George Bush was upset about a resemblance between him and the thoroughly nasty Gollum creature in the *Lord of The Rings-Two Towers* movie hit. I had another look: Maybe.

In Ireland, when I was in College, the government, in league with the Catholic Church, banned the hilarious Monty Python movie, *The Life of Brian* (and later *The Meaning of Life*). The engineering society smuggled the reel into a lecture theatre and we all gave secret handshakes, and probably a few quid, to gain admission to what was the highlight of the term.

The movie, *Lara Croft Tom Raider- Cradle of Life* was banned in China. Censors said the film portrayed China as a country in chaos. 'After watching the movie, I feel that the Westerners have made their presentation of China with malicious intention,' an unidentified official said in reports. The Chinese also complained the film had made the country appear to have no government and run by secret societies. 'The movie does not understand Chinese culture. It does not understand China's security situation. In China there cannot be secret societies,' the official said.

I take issue with Hollywood screenwriters in a few respects, but banning an entertaining movie is daft.

A few years back, one of my favourite UK childhood puppet characters, *Basil Brush* (a hard talking, loud laughing fox puppet) got in trouble for allegedly disparaging gypsies in a skit. According to the BBC, an official complaint was made to Northamptonshire Police, 'by a gipsy living on a travellers' site in Northamptonshire.' The gentleman in question, unidentified, was stated to be upset as he'd watched the episode in question with his daughter and found it insulting.

The police referred the matter to the Hate Crimes Unit and 'after speaking to police officers, the BBC reviewed the tapes and offered not to show the episode again.' The episode was made six years prior to this airing. The offending skit showed 'a gipsy woman trying to sell the puppet fox wooden pegs and heather.'

I pondered the fact that a single gypsy in Northampton was more effective seeking redress against a Western media outlet for stereotyping his people than the entire Russian nation taking on Hollywood and the Western media. I am not sure what the lesson is in that sobering observation, but it must mean that there is hope.

I recall British comedians *Morecombe and Wise* in one of their popular Christmas shows mocking famous Russian dancer Rudolph Nureyev, by calling him Rudolph 'Near-Enough.' It was very funny. Nureyev was a good sport, and many other celebrities similarly played along. As matters currently stand, Russians are very good sports, but enough is enough.

Clearly, no-one today in Hollywood today, of sound mind, will portray African Americans as they did in 1944. In addition, they are extremely careful with Islamic figures, as discussed.

As Gordon Allport pointed out, a finding also noted by Katchanovski in his analysis, stereotypes and prejudice often follow the political context. Allport also noted that when the Soviet government and the United States were wartime allies, the Russians were portrayed as 'rugged, brave and patriotic.' However, after the War when hostilities resumed, the Russians were portrayed as 'fierce, aggressive and fanatic.'

One of the rare positive portrayals of Russians in Hollywood movies and on TV is in the *Star Trek* TV series that was also made into a successful movie series.

Russians were not, until recently, familiar with this phenomenon, a personal favourite. I wish there was even the tiniest prospect that our future might resemble the world depicted in it- except for the Ferengi. The series remains enormously successful and influential because it shows us what he might become if we put our differences aside to realize our potential.

Obama is believed to be a *Star Trek* fan. He is reported[242] to have given 'the Vulcan peace sign' (Vulcans are a cerebral, highly logical alien species in Star Trek) to Leonard Nimoy, the actor who played the Vulcan character Spock for many years in the original Star Trek series when he met him at a convention.

If Obama is indeed a Star Trek fan- a 'Trekkie'-there may be hope that the 'United Federation of Planets' depicted in the series might someday include Russia, although I wouldn't hold my breath.

I was absolutely glued to Star Trek as a child and teenager. The original series was first aired in the US in the 1960s. The crew of the space vessel integral to the series, the Star Trek Enterprise, included a Russian man, Pavel Andreievich Chekov, and a black woman, Lieutenant Uhura.

These were gutsy casting choices in the 60's in the US, with the Cold War in full flight and racism and race riots part of the US landscape. The creator of the series, Gene Roddenberry, considered himself a secular humanist. He is lucky he is not alive today, as atheists and secular humanists are more despised in the US than pretty well any minority group. Soon the only safe place for an atheist to live will be in France.

Reports suggest that the actress who played Uhura, Michelle Nichols, intended to leave the series in 1967 after the first season, but was persuaded by Martin Luther King to stay on as she was considered a role model for the black community, as one of the first African American characters in a US TV series, and certainly one of the first to be portrayed in such a positive light.

I have no idea if this story is true, but it would certainly add credence to the suggestion that popular culture matters in promoting tolerance. Star Trek featured the first multi-racial kiss on television, when Captain Kirk kissed Uhura.

At NASA's invitation, Nichols acted as a spokesperson to encourage African-Americans to join the space programme.

464

Indeed, many US astronauts have credited Star Trek with inspiring them to go into space.

Chekhov assumed his first posting on the Star Trek Enterprise bridge as a lowly 'ensign' and acting navigator, but he rose through the ranks, according to some accounts making the grade Commander in Chief of all Star Fleet. The young Chekov was portrayed as proud and hot-heated, with many romantic attachments.

There are many urban legends surrounding the Star Trek phenomenon, and it is hard to separate fact from fiction, but there is a story that Roddenberry devised the Chekhov character in response to a letter from the Soviet Pravda newspaper on behalf of the Kremlin to the US TV network NBC that aired the show, decrying the lack of a Soviet character on board the space craft. As they were the first into space with Sputnik in 1957, the Russians were purportedly aggrieved that there was no Russian cosmonaut on board.

As far as I can gather, Pravda did not write such a letter, but there appears to be evidence that Roddenberry did write to Mikhail Zinyanin, editor of Pravda in October 1967 telling him that about the introduction of the Chekhov character, and an NBC press release around the same time mentioned a Pravda article as an impetus for creating the character. No doubt, PR and spin have long over-whelmed the facts, but it is a great story nonetheless.

A big budget 2009 *Star Trek* movie remake was directed by Hollywood whizz-kid and Spielberg protégé, JJ Abrams, with talented Russian actor, Anton Yelchin playing Chekhov. His accent is mocked in a few reasonably funny scenes. Early on, the computer fails to recognize his voice commands because of his difficulty pronouncing the letter V- 'Victor, Victor' sounding like 'Wicktor, Wicktor.'

Russians do, indeed, find it difficult as there is no V in Russian. This is an old gag, however, taken from the original series: In one scene, Chekhov has trouble saying, 'nuclear vessels'- it sounded instead like nuclear 'wessels.'

Mercifully, Chekhov ends up the hero in the Abrams movie. His computing gaming skills save a young James Kirk and his colleague Zulu after their parachutes fail to open and they hurtle towards the ground in free fall. He manages to beam them on board.

The movie was a huge international hit, grossing nearly 500 million dollars globally- with just over half that made in the US. It had a production budget of circa USD 150 million. It was released in Russia- grossing in excess of USD 4 million, and made over USD 8 million in China. The 2009 movie introduced *Star Trek* to a whole new generation, too young to have seen the original series- and to the Russians and Chinese, who'd never seen it at all.

Anton Yelchin was interviewed about his role as Chekov. He was asked[243] about the fact that 'back in the '60s, in the midst of the Cold War, the series was groundbreaking for its inclusion of a positive Russian character' and whether it was important to him that the new movie retain some of Gene Roddenberry's (the Star Trek creator) sense of unity'?

Yelchin replied, 'Yes, absolutely. Chekov is, honestly, one of the few positive Russian characters is American film and TV history. Roddenberry's vision of unity - that he saw us coming together in the future rather than falling apart - is a beautiful thing, especially in a world like ours where, more often than not, it seems as if we are coming apart. And that message pervades our film too.'

J.J. Abrams, the director, has talked about how important it was to him that Star Trek be optimistic. Yelchin said that 'the micro message of the new film is about a diverse crew coming together but the larger message is about everyone in the world coming together...'

In many instances, based on my analysis, the movie studios would not break even on US box office numbers alone- the foreign box office is, thus, highly important to overall profitability. Russians like going to the movies, and the Russian/CIS box office take for many movies looks increasingly attractive, especially with US numbers flattening out.

Iron Man 2 (2010) grossed over USD $14 million in the CIS region- with over USD $7 million in Russia alone, a quite remarkable take considering the fact the dastardly villain is Ivan Vanko aka 'Whiplash.' a brilliant but demented Russian 'phys-ee-ceest' played to the hilt by Mickey Rourke.

One entertaining account I read stated that the Vanko role was created by Rourke, in collaboration with director Jon Favreau and screenwriter Justin Theroux. 'I wanted to redeem him as much as we possibly could without shaking up the Marvel people,' Rourke said in a phone interview.

'I didn't want to do a one-dimensional bad guy like you'd see in a comic book,' Rourke said. 'Get some schmuck to do that. Hollywood always does that, especially when it's a Russian bad guy. I wanted to add layers to it, represent where he's coming from, and have a sense of humor.'

Rourke spent a few hours in lockup in Moscow's notorious Butyrka Prison, as part of his preparation, and appears to have learned a great deal about Russian prisoners' tattoos by talking to them. Rourke is a fine actor and his efforts, seemingly well-intentioned, to add nuance to a cartoon character Russian villain does him credit.

Unfortunately, even Russian-Western movie co-productions serve up stereotypes while trying to present Russians in a positive light.

In the (2009) movie, *2012*, a co-production with the Russians, John Cusack plays a small time writer who discovers that the world is going to come to an end. The inveterate Chinese have, however, built huge arcs that will survive the incoming tidal wave that will engulf the planet. The arcs will house dignitaries, and the lucky few who can afford to pay one billion euro each for a place onboard.

One of the main characters in the movie is a Russian 'oligarch' who is fat, sleazy, an ex-boxer, and a billionaire. Cusack acts as chauffeur for his two bratty, portly kids, both boys. The oligarch's mistress is blond, kind-hearted, and silly with prominent breast implants. By contrast, Cusack's ex-wife, married to a plastic surgeon, is flat-cheated, and nauseatingly wholesome. The oligarch's mistress, the blond 'fluff.' is surreptitiously, but quite understandably, having an affair with the oligarch's blond, buffed, dashing pilot.

Although stereotypes abound in the movie, there are a few sops to the Russians.

The oligarch ultimately dies bravely, saving his children before he falls to his death. The Russian pilot saves everyone, having heroically landed a huge Soviet plane in snow and ice. The air-headed Russian mistress dies trying to save her mini-poodle. The blonde Russian President (not unlike a taller Putin) is the first Head of State to agree to open the doors to save the people who have been locked out of the arcs, showing a level of humanity not exhibited by the hard-nosed, immoral American Head of State.

It was interesting to note how little faith the screen-writers had in American technology. In the movie, only the Chinese have the technical ability to build the super arcs in time to save a small section of humanity from extinction.

Having survived the tides, the survivors see Africa on the horizon above the water level, presumably their new home.

Screenwriters are not without wit or irony. I recall that at the conclusion of one disaster movie, the US President must ask the Mexican authorities for safe harbour in return for the cancellation of debt.

2012 grossed far more abroad (78.4% of the overall take) than in the US where it performed poorly (circa USD 166 million only). It cost 200 million to make. It made a whopping USD 603 million outside the US, with big numbers in France, Germany, Japan, Brazil and Mexico too. It was a hit in Russia/CIS- grossing circa USD $36 million and a half. It made just over USD $31 million in the UK.

In the recent alien flick *'The Darkest Day'*- another co-production (filmed in Moscow), the Russians and Americans (and a dastardly, cowardly Swede) fight side by side to best an invisible but deadly alien menace. The Russians are tough and brave, but when their leaders are killed, trite stereotypes take centre stage: They are portrayed as helpless, unable to assume control of their own destiny, forced to look to the 'take-charge' (hugely irritating) American kid-hero for direction as to what to do. There are also a number of jabs at the Russian legal system.

I went to see Madonna's latest movie, 'W.E' about the life of Wallis Simpson with low expectations, beyond seeing some pretty clothes and elegant interiors. There is a sub-plot about a young American woman in an abusive marriage and her obsession with Simpson. She is fascinated with an auction of Simpson's possessions to be held at Sotheby's in New York City.

She forms a bond, and ultimately an intimate relationship with a handsome Sothebys's security guard, a Russian émigré called Evgeny, described by her friend, dismissively, as a 'dime a dozen' Russian intellectual 'slumming as a security guard.' The young woman is given sanctuary by him in his tasteful loft apartment (one must bury any incredulity that a security guard could afford such a flat in Manhattan) after he finds her battered and bruised from a beating by her psychiatrist husband.

There is a piano in his place, which he plays for her with aplomb. She tells him that he 'plays beautifully.' He responds, 'You see, we are not all gangsters.'

That got my attention.

Madonna's theme, as I saw it, was a motif close to her heart- that of the outsider- and so she presents Simpson, hated by the British Press and the establishment.

According to Madonna, the Evgeny character was inspired by Ukrainian gypsy punk Eugene Hutz (real name Evgeny Nikolaev), actor and lead singer of the New York Gypsy punk bank, Gogol Bordello. Madonna is a fan.

Hutz has been quoted as saying that Russian song lyrics are far more sophisticated than Western lyrics, but beyond that fact, I am not sure I see the connection between Evgeny's character and Huiz, the wild-man, Ukrainian gypsy. However, positive Russians characters in Western movies are so rare, that it is best not to be too fastidious.

Evgeny is an elegant, sensitive man- mercifully not a brute intent on nuclear Armageddon. Although one might quibble and argue that his character is also a stereotype- the romantic idealized view of Russians, beloved of my childhood, it's better than the alternative.

It is interesting to me that celebrities like Madonna and Tom Ford, the designer who directed the wonderful film, *The Silent Man,* show hidden depths in their movies, a willingness to look beneath the surface of things and to challenge the prevailing orthodoxy. The Western creative community may be an important ally in beating back the stereotypes about Russians, despite the hullabaloo about the Pussy Riot storm in a teacup.

It doesn't look promising at present, but, the Hollywood studios may decide that they should stop vilifying the Russians if they expect them to show up in record numbers to watch their movies.

The Chinese understand full well the power that the Hollywood studios wield in terms of global 'soft power.' Although India has Bollywood and the Russians do have a vibrant local movie scene, there is still nothing in the world to compete with Hollywood.

The Chinese are shopping to buy a major Hollywood movie studio and doing deals left, right and centre. They are also paying to embed Chinese brands into Hollywood movies. For instance, in the *Transformers 3* movie, Chinese household brand names are depicted. The Chinese want to familiarise Western audiences with their brand names. In some cases, the movie characters refer to Chinese brands by name.

These product 'placements' were negotiated by Hollywood agents with the Chinese. According to reports, the producers were initially sceptical about why they would put a Chinese product that is not known in the West in their movies. However, after a charm campaign was launched by the Chinese, which brought the producers to China (undoubtedly a large cheque also changed hands), the Chinese got what they wanted.

This is a shrewd move. As well as acclimatising Western audiences to Chinese brands that have ambitions on the global stage, product placements arguably help diffuse prejudices or stereotypes that the Chinese believe exist in the media[244].

The Russian market is also increasingly important to several US movie studios, including Disney. Disney recently bought a stake in local Russian TV station, Seven TV. The last *Pirates of the Caribbean* movie grossed $64m at the Russian box office, a 50% increase in box office take from the previous movie in the series. Reports indicate that Putin met the Russian Disney CEO in Moscow.

I do not recall any Russian villains on board *The Black Pearl*. Nor do I don't expect Disney to be so dumb as to add one now. If I pay my ten dollars, or ruble equivalent, for admission, I don't expect to be insulted with it.

Old school Hollywood tough guys like Bruce Willis are still hugely popular in Russia and doing product endorsements: You see their faces on billboards. They are more than happy to exploit their continued popularity in Russia.

The French do an excellent job of promoting the French film industry abroad. The French state has a hugely successful organisation, *UniFrance.org*, created in 1949 to support and promote French film worldwide. *UniFrance*[245] is, as its website attests 'present at every stage in the life of a French film abroad.' The Russians may try to emulate its success.

Modern day Russian movie-makers produce stunning films, often huge hits at international movie festivals. The Russian State could do a great deal more to promote them, their genre- and Russia at large. There are hopeful signs. Russia joined *Eurimages*[246] in March 2011. Under the umbrella of the Council of Europe, it aims to promote the European film industry by encouraging the production and distribution of films and fostering co-operation between professionals.

While he was President, Medvedev signed a decree on the creation of Public Television channel in Russia which is scheduled to go on-air on January 1, 2013. The new digital channel will be broadcast throughout Russia for free. The reaction was mixed, with many Russians in the creative community mocking the initiative. I would give it a chance.

In an interesting article in the US Baltimore Sun from 1991,[247] Alexei Vinogradsky writes about Russians, at their peril, watching US movies on black market DVDs in the 70's and 80's. He wrote that after watching the movie *Hair* in 1979, Moscovites began wearing fetching hippy outfits (and presumably sporting large hair) around Moscow. He commented that he expected to see hordes of hippies in the US when he went there, and was disappointed to see none.

He also wrote that during communism Russians watched Hollywood movies on black market videos a few months after their US release. He noted that sometimes hit US movies flopped because Russian audiences did not understand the references- e.g. *Batman*. 'Who is Batman? Unfortunately, in Russia nobody knows who he is.'

However, other action heroes fared better. Russians loved Sylvester Stallone and Arnold Schwarzenegger- and pumped iron to look like both. Alexei used to worry that hostilities might break out between the US and the USSR over the treatment meted out to Russian boxer, Ivan Drago ('the Siberian Bull') in Rocky IV, until he realized that Russians loved Rambo too. Drago was portrayed as a decorated Soviet war hero.

Some critics suggested that 'Drago was meant to symbolize America's perception of Russia: Immense, powerful, and emotionless.' [248] At the end, when Rocky prevails in a Moscow ring, he gives a rousing 'reset' speech to the once hostile Russian audience.

Alexi wrote that he was a US movie buff and liked 'thrillers, horrors and love dramas.' So much so, that when he went to the US, he 'expected to see a life like in '9 1/2 Weeks' or in Dirty Harry movies.' He had been warned by Russians and Americans alike about US crime levels. He expected to be told to 'stick im up' at every intersection, and was amazed when 'nobody touched me during two days in New York. Not criminals, not police.'

He also noticed that there were far fewer police in the streets than in the movies- 'So I lost another of my stereotypes.' In a fine example of how travel does broaden the mind, he wrote rather poignantly:

'But I lost in USA. not all my stereotypes about this country, which I got after watching the videos. I keep the main one: Americans are beautiful people, and America is nice country. Most people in Russia had never hated Americans. They always thought about Americans if not with love then with constant interest and respect. I think it shouldn't be obstacle for normal relationships between our countries if all American men don't look like Indiana Jones and all women like Kim Bassinger. It doesn't matter, does it?'

As well as creating them, movies can clearly also break down stereotypes between people and help spark an interest in each other's culture. However, their influence can also be a little more pernicious.

In November, 2011, Russian Viktor Bout was found guilty by a US jury of various offences including arms dealing. Despite the conviction, in my estimation, the proceedings against him do not easily pass a smell test. This is not to suggest that Bout is a choir boy. However, I have considerable doubts that the rule of law emerged untainted from the affair.

The Americans were out to 'get their man'- and get him they did. He was already convicted by Hollywood and the mass media (labelled the *Merchant of Death* before trial)- before he set foot on US soil in handcuffs and leg irons. Bout appears to possess information from his activities that would embarrass both governments-Russian and American. The fact the Americans were so desperate to get him first speaks volumes.

The whole affair was political theatre, and I doubt the truth will ever be known. However, the US's strong arm, extra-territorial efforts to locate and arrest him in Thailand where he spent years in custody, without charge or conviction, leaves much to be desired from the perspective of the rule of law purist.

The Thai government resisted US efforts to extradite him for years, and then, in interesting circumstances, released him to US authorities. There have been suggestions-supported in part by WikiLeaks cables- that the Thai government handed him over as a quid pro quo for the US muting its criticism of its violent suppression of riots in May 2010: The Thai army killed 89 people, in what was de facto civil war. Once Bout was handed over, however, the once vociferous calls by the US for sanctions against Thailand for human rights violations mysteriously ceased.

After the guilty verdict, Bout's defence appealed. A juror gave an interview to the New York Times after the trial, in which she said she had seen 'that terrible Nicolas Cage movie,' referring to the movie *Lord of War* based rather obviously on Bout's life. The juror denied knowing it was meant to portray Bout. She was believed by the court, and the appeal (essentially alleging jury bias) failed.

A cursory review of the Internet would have revealed that the movie was indeed largely based on Bouts' alleged activities before trial. When I saw the Cage movie, I immediately made the connection to Bout. In *Mission Impossible- Ghost Protocol*, there is a character with a Russian accent who plays an arms dealer and bears a stunning resemblance to Bout.

The internet raises many issues for jury trials, as jurors substitute or augment real evidence presented at trial with untested, likely erroneous information gleaned from social networking sites, movies, TV and the internet more generally, despite warnings from trial Judges not to do so.

The Chief Justice of England and Wales has warned that the integrity of jury trials may be in jeopardy as a result of such activity. Repercussions can be severe: in some cases convictions have been quashed and retrials ordered (resulting in significant delays and expense). Early in 2011, a Manchester woman was the first juror to be jailed for contacting a defendant via Facebook.

A 2010 report by the UK Ministry of Justice on the fairness of UK jury trials[249] noted that at least 12% of jurors admitted to seeing (rather than 'looking') at the internet in standard cases, with a much bigger proportion doing so in high profile cases. It is unclear whether in fact they went looking for information on matters or persons before the court, but it is entirely conceivable that they did.

What do these concerns and the Bout case have to do with the subject at hand?

A great deal, I suggest. Such incidents suggest that people are indeed influenced by what they see on the big screen and what they read in the mass media and on social networking sites. They may be unable to distinguish fantasy, the power of suggestion or pure conjecture from reality.

In addition, to compound matters, the current obsession with reality TV and social networking sites has, arguably, created a social dynamic where everyone is an 'expert.' Conducting internet 'research' on subjects well beyond one's competency level is now ubiquitous, as doctors will attest, as people purport to diagnose their complaints with online medical 'research.'

History has taught us- through studies on the impact of propaganda more generally- that a great number of people draw potentially damning conclusions from movies, TV shows, rumour-mongering, salacious gossip, poorly crafted and researched newspaper articles, or simply media reports that are biased and riddled with stereotypes.

Some of it is harmless, but some of it inevitably sticks.

At the end of the day, however, having watched countless movies and TV shows featuring remorseless Russian villains, I asked myself, why are movie makers so obsessed with Russians? Can it be attributed to simple lack of imagination, or do Russians just make better villains?

Maybe it is the sexy accent and the Godless, haters of the Free World vibe that makes them such compulsive viewing. Perhaps we simply yearn for an enemy with a recognizable 'face'- a welcome foil to today's shape-shifting terrorists.

During the Cold War, Americans were bombarded with US propaganda that portrayed Russians as rapacious, cold-hearted ideologues, who wanted to snatch capitalism and its joys from the American population. On the other side of the equation, the Russians were told not to trust the smiling face of the American capitalist, which disguised a wolf in sheep's clothing.

During the Hoover era in the US, the notorious Committee Against Un-American activities, persecuted Hollywood actors and writers who were exposed as 'having Communist sympathies.' To be called a Communist was like being called a Nazi. Many lives were ruined by Hoover's hatred and paranoiac endeavours to root Communism out of America.

Such a legacy is unquestionably hard to shake off, but the time to break free has surely long passed us by.

The stereotyping of Russia and Russians does not just occur in Hollywood movies and in TV shows in the West, it also extends to mainstream literature. I note that bestselling author John Le Carre's new novel is called *Our Kind of Traitor* and features an urbane English hero and several Russian Mafiosi and money launderers. The Russian gangsters are called the 'Armani kids.' Le Carre made his name with his spy thrillers set in the Cold War. He has returned to the genre he knows best and that just keeps on selling.

In another example, a novel called *Snow Drops*, written by A.D. Miller, formerly the Moscow correspondent for *The Economist*, the Russians are given a rough ride. A review by Benjamin Evans in The Sunday Telegraph magazine stated that it was .'.A bravura setting for a study in morality, although Russians may balk at being portrayed as beady – eyed chancers with hearts as cold as the frozen Moskva river.'

I think, unfortunately, that Russians are so accustomed to being portrayed in the West as 'beady-eyed chancers'- that another novel portraying them in this light is unlikely to register over much.

Despite the overwhelmingly negative portrayal of Russia and Russians in the movies and popular culture, I do not believe- or rather I don't want to believe- that this dynamic is malicious or representative of some deep-seated hostility towards Russians.

The current crop of film makers simply want to entertain, and Russians undoubtedly make great, sexy villains. They are less scary than Muslim terrorists, and less of a cliché, maybe, than the well-worn Nazis. However, let's dig deep and find other fish to fry.

If a plea for tolerance and empathy isn't enough, the perpetrators might reflect on simple economics- Russians buy movie tickets, and there's plenty of room for growth in Russia as revenues stagnate at home. That fact alone may buy them some respect.

Chapter Sixteen

Fighting Back

The Russian state has tried to fight back against the endemic stereotyping, but its efforts to do so are usually thrown back in its face. Indeed, in some instances, these efforts are seized upon by the Western media and used to lampoon Russia, and to set in motion a whole new round of stereotyping and negative press.

A particularly vitriolic article in *The New Republic* in 2009,[250] written by neo-conservative pundit James Kirchick described various attempts by the Russian state to fight back, including efforts to set the record straight on the Georgian conflict. He described these initiatives as 'only deserving laughter on the part of those who read them.'

He described them as cynical efforts to convince an American audience of Russia's good intentions. 'Russia must sell a rotten apple by pretending its foie gras. It would be a worrying effort, if only the Russians did it better.'

Kirchick wrote that Russia hired the US PR agency Ketchum Inc. and paid them $845,000 US dollars for a two month contract. This paltry sum pales into insignificance compared to what the Bush/Cheney regime spent on the failed Brand America campaign to rehabilitate its own flagging brand image abroad after the disastrous foray into Iraq.

In his article, Kirchick wrote about the Time Magazine publication in November 2007 in which Putin won 'Person of the Year.' Kirchirck credits Ketchum with this result. However, rather than being gracious and giving Putin credit for his achievement in moving Russia from chaos to an investment grade country in short order, he dredges out a quote from the equally uncivil managing editor of Time Magazine in which readers were reminded that the 'Person of the Year' title was 'not and never has been an honour.'

Kirchick clearly derived satisfaction from his statement that 'international press coverage of the conflict (the Georgian conflict) was almost uniformly critical of Russia' – and his observation that 'no matter how hard Russia tries, or how much money it spends, its flacks don't have much to write home to Moscow about.'

Based on my own research, I can certainly attest that is a fact. However, unlike Kirchick, I do not believe the situation is anything to boast about.

This article was a classic example of Russophobia. It was mean-spirited, condescending and plain un-impressive in every respect. For many hard men in the West, there can be no reset with the old enemy.

Shortly after September 11 2001, America launched a TV advertising campaign for Brand America, broadcast to predominantly Muslim countries.[251]In 2004, the Bush administration spent $685m (about £380m) on these PR initiatives to rehabilitate its image abroad after the Iraq war. The expensive campaign is widely considered to have been a failure- and may even have done more harm than good.

Brand USA is the new name for America's tourism body encompassing all 50 states, part of a new national image campaign. Congress approved a public-private partnership to revitalize America's brand image with a global campaign, promoting the US as a tourist destination. At least they could agree on that much.

It has a $200 million budget and a new website for tourists, DiscoverAmerica.com. The tagline is 'Fresh, welcoming and inclusive,' as a reminder that 'the United States of awesome possibilities welcomes everyone.' This strikes me as incredibly corny. It sounds like clothes detergent. The web site embraces social media with the usual Facebook and Twitter interfaces, and bloggers onside.

The US has so much to commend it as a tourist destination that it doesn't need such banal hype to promote it.

By contrast, Russia is to spend up to a mere $60 million on a six-year advertising campaign to bolster its image as a tourist destination-a smaller budget than countries like Spain and Italy, with much of the budget to be spent on attracting Chinese tourists.

Although it is not clear from academic studies, at least, that tourism and personal contact alone can dispel stereotypes about a country or people, I remain convinced that getting to know one another has to be part of the solution. As well as tourism, student exchanges at all levels, through to university students are desirable to help break down barriers.

It is critical we reach tomorrow's leaders. I have cousins who visited Russia on school tours as children during the communist era, and still talk fondly of Russia as a result.

As emerging and developing countries seek to move out into the wider world, there will be an increased desire on their part to manage their brands and neutralize bad publicity about corruption, internal strife, war, violence, etc. The international PR and advertising agencies are lining up to help them. It is highly debatable whether any of these efforts are worth spending huge money on.

As matters now stand, in my estimation, no matter how hard they try, the Russians are likely to remain on the back foot. The Western media, tacitly egged on by certain Western politicians, wealthy Russians and sundry foreigners with an axe to grind with the Russian state, make sure that is the outcome.

Some of the efforts to fight back, mainly led by the Russian state, have been well-intentioned, but poorly construed and executed. However, there is no doubt in my mind that their efforts are nearly redundant in the face of relentlessly negative Western media coverage. They are damned if they do, and damned if they don't.

Even (rare) good news stories are parodied and turned upside down by the Western media and bloggers. As already mentioned, Russia's victory in the 2010 Vancouver Paralympics (it won the most medals) was ridiculed on the Internet, which was shockingly bad form.

Russians also lack the home-crowd advantage in trying to fight back. They lack Western experience and acumen in PR and marketing. Americans and Britons are savvy at 'managing the message.'

Business and politics in both places-although the US has the edge-are dominated by branding. US politicians strut their stuff like movie stars, although the dismal slate of the US Republican Presidential nominees made for a very tough sell, outside the US at least.

In addition, reality TV has infused many Westerners from all walks of life with an impassioned, usually delusional belief that they have 'Star' quality. Bookstore shelves are groaning under the weight of tomes that promote 'Brand You.'

Russia does not lack celebrities skilled in the art of self promotion, but' Brand Me' is not, I surmise, as ingrained a concept as in the West. Although Russians are decidedly not stern-faced automatons, Stalin, communism and centuries of communal living and collectivism have arguably left a mark.

Even today, some Russians, especially the generations that grew up under communism, see a virtue in laying low and keeping their mouth shut. It is not that long ago that such reticence to stand out was integral to survival.

Like chalk and cheese, surveys shown that Americans, by contrast, bask in the public domain. They are adamant they can 'make their own luck.' with no help from Government or the state. Everyone seems to want to become a reality star, rather than a doctor, engineer or lawyer. Fame, however fleeting, and however acquired, is the new Holy Grail.

In 2011, the US Pew Research Center conducted a survey examining American-Western European Values, as part of its Global Attitudes Project. It concluded that Americans are 'more individualistic' than Western Europeans- with 62% of Americans disagreeing with the survey statement that 'Success in life is determined by forces outside our control.'[252]

Britons were pretty gung-ho as well, 55% agreed with the statement, but only 43% did so in France, and a mere 27% of Germans. Americans have traditionally also expressed strong belief in their cultural superiority, and the 2011 survey suggests that confidence levels remain high at 49%, although down significantly from 60% in previous surveys.

Other surveys support the view that Russians, like the Germans, have no illusions about their ability to pull themselves up by their bootstraps: They don't buy it.

The art of self-promotion and confidently blowing one's trumpet is bred into Americans, but it is, in my experience, considered gauche in Europe, reality TV notwithstanding.

Pontificating about one's genius and general merit was traditionally frowned upon in the UK: There was no quicker way to get yourself parodied in satirical magazines like Private Eye, with its 'Pseuds' and 'Luvvies' columns. However, Britons tend to be rather good at self-promotion, albeit in a rather more self-effacing, sardonic manner than would fly in the US, e.g. the affable Hugh Grant persona.

The Irish are also fine self-promoters, more in the US tradition, although at home we are expected to keep a lid on it, or face similarly scathing put-downs as to be expected in the UK.

Russians, by contrast, in my experience, are uncomfortable talking themselves up. Different communication styles also make it challenging for them to do so effectively with a Western audience. In this regard, they may be further disadvantaged when taking on the slick and hostile Western media machine.

Reputation is an important commodity that impacts brand value. Although the concept of brand is usually associated with physical products, like Coca Cola or the Apple iPhone, countries have brands too. Countries with solid brands and a positive reputation have a distinct advantage over those that do not.

As indicated, my country, Ireland, enjoys many positive county brand associations- e.g. the image of smiling, welcoming, funny people has served us well throughout the current financial crisis, as more people wish us well than those who do not.

Alas, Westerners are not nearly as accommodating towards Russia and Russians, and my perception is that they are given very little quarter. Sadly, Russian lows are celebrated and highs ignored or denigrated.

The Western media use their biased portrayal of Russia as a 'gangster state.' with 'gangster leaders.' as justification for emptying the verbal piss pot on Russia's head. It is a vicious circle, because as long as they continue to do so, Russia's attempts to salvage its international reputation will be an uphill battle, akin to rowing against the tide in Niagara Falls.

Although assessing country brand stature, as a relative concept, is a daunting task, it does not mean that someone won't try. The Anholt Nation Brands Index is an analytical ranking of the world's nations as brands developed by author Simon Anholt, the editor of 'Place Branding,' a quarterly British journal devoted to the topic.

It recently polled 25,903 online consumers from 35 countries in North America, Europe, Asia and Latin America. Israel finished in the survey, behind Estonia, Indonesia and Turkey. Russians rated Britons 9th out of 50 countries- evidence of the continued Russian love affair with that market, but sadly Britons rated Russians a mere 35th. The UK media's tug of war with the 'gangster state' undoubtedly has an impact.

Other companies and surveys that attempt to rank countries by brand or reputation image include the East-West Global Index, and the Future-Brands Index.

East-West Communications is a US based company. It publishes the *East West Nation Brand Perception Index*, based on 'analysizing millions of mentions of countries in hundreds of thousands of news articles, every quarter.' In 2010, it ranked Singapore first and Canada second in 2010, Kuwait was in third place and Qatar was Fourth. Russia was ranked 171, the Ukraine was 23,rd and Georgia 132rd. Ireland was ranked 20, down from 16 in 2009. The UK was ranked 18, down 9 places, and the US was ranked 55, down 19.

The *2010 FutureBrand Country Brand Index*, in partnership with BBC World News, rates 110 countries. Canada is rated first, up from second place in 2009- attributed to the success of the Winter Olympics- the US is in 4th place, down from first, UK is 9th, down from eight, Ireland s 17th, down from 12. Russia is ranked 81.

After reading these surveys, I asked myself: Is Russia 170 times less interesting than tiny Singapore, or 153 times less worthy than the UK?

The methodology of the Country Brand 'Index' is worth examining. It sounds vague, grand and frightfully scientific.

It is described as 'based on FutureBrands proprietary research methodology. The sixth edition of CBI incorporates a global quantitative research study with 3,400 international business and leisure travellers from 13 countries on all five continents, qualified by in-depth expert focus groups that took place in 14 major metropolitan areas around the world...'

Besides the fact that much of the description of the underlying research methodology reads like sheer gobbledegook, I was much struck by the clear implication that Russia's 'value system' is perceived more kindly by 3400 international leisure and business travellers than that of Saudi Arabia (ranked 69). How can that be?

A summary of the Index findings states with a flourish, that 'This year's leading country brands share some common features. They are all democratic, progressive, relatively politically and economically stable, and doing business in English.'

It is noteworthy that amongst the top 25 county brands (i.e. economically stable places) are countries such as the US, the UK, Greece, Ireland and Spain, that are either bankrupt in all but name, or mired in colossal levels of debt that threaten economic prosperity for decades to come. Russia, by contrast, has effectively no debt and has significantly potential for economic growth that these countries lack.

Reading and cutting out hateful media about Russia over the past few years has been a dispiriting exercise. I used to wonder if Russia has any friends in the West who aren't investment bankers out to make a quick buck. I concluded it has, although they are definitely in the minority. There are a number of well-informed, even-handed journalists, film makers and writers who do not seek to make a career out of Russia-bashing.

In addition, I believe there are many 'ordinary people' in the West who feel as I do. We just don't make front page news, but we are out there, and with the advent of the internet and social networking, our influence is growing.

According to Guy Kawasaki, former Chief Evangelist for Apple, in his book, *Enchantment: The Art of Changing Hearts, Minds and Actions* (Portfolio/Penguin 2011), 'If a change is a big deal, then it's a big deal to make it happen.' but he suggests a novel way to bring change about.

Instead of chasing the known 'influencers,' Kawasaki states that social media has changed the dynamic. He suggests that we must 'embrace the nobodies' - folk who are passionate about a cause and will spread the word. Rather than playing to the converted or seeking out the Big Names, Kawasaki believes that 'nobodies' are 'the new somebodies.'

In my view, Russia needs to tap into the considerable swell of goodwill-often from relative 'nobodies' that exists towards it around the world. This goodwill currently finds little expression as it is drowned out by the Russophobes. I believe that we can make a difference if we challenge the status quo and encourage our media to 'up their game' and abandon the formula.

Conclusion

Times have changed, even if the old stereotypes have not. However, they remain weapons in our arsenal to deploy against 'the enemy' whether the battlefield is on the fields of war, or the battlefields of commerce.

Although these weapons are old, they have proven their mettle over centuries, as they will again, in large part because of our gullibility and incorrigible tendency to want to blame someone in a crisis. We are loath to accept responsibility for our own fate, or to face up to chronic errors in judgment.

As John Dower pointed out in 1986, however, 'What is new is the perception that the West is no longer materially and technologically preeminent.' If that was apparent in 1986, how very apt it is today. Like a man with a crystal ball, Dower wrote, ' it follows that the paternalistic pose which the United States and European powers have hitherto adopted toward non-white and less developed peoples has had the ground cut out from under it.'

Although writing primarily about Japan, in his final paragraph, Dower noted that returning to the Second World War and particularly the vicious war fought in the Pacific is 'thus inevitable and essential-and fraught with peril. It can teach us many things, but can also fan the fires of contemporary anger and self-righteousness. In whatever way, the World War Two in Asia has become central to our understanding not only of the past, but of the present as well.'

I commend Dower's book in its entirety to you. All politicians should be required to read it, as well as compelled to take classes in tolerance, and cross-cultural studies.

In 1950, in his seminal work on *The Rise and Fall of the Third Reich*, William L. Shirer wrote, 'In our new age of terrifying, lethal gadgets, which supplanted so quickly the old one, the first great aggressive war, if it should come, will be launched by suicidal madmen pressing an electronic button. Such a war will not last long and none will ever follow it. There will be no conquerors and no conquests, but only the charred bones of the dead on an uninhabited planet.'

As we have seen in Part Two, it is the Chinese Red-Yellow Peril that engages us in the West at present. Media reports and statements from US politicians, in particular, show how they are desperate to make money in this vast, beguiling market, in increasingly tough economic times, positively tripping over themselves to meet the Chinese (Communist) leadership, cap in hand.

On the other hand, however, playing to the home crowd, cognizant of the fact they are plain out of ideas about how to fix things at home, they wheel out the old belligerent, self-serving stereotypes about the threat posed by the Yellow Peril (not framed in quite these racist terms, but the implication remains the same) to the US heartland, threatening protectionist trade measures and generally sabre-rattling.

The old weapon is being used again, to serve one purpose, and one purpose only, to take the heat off them at home, and to get re-elected, whatever the cost.

Russia is an unusual case, no longer a Red Peril, but, as I have tried to outline in this book, still bizarrely viewed with hostility and suspicion by Western politicians, a warped viewpoint echoed by nearly every channel of communication that we've got at our disposal.

The biased and stereotypical imagery of Russians and their elected leaders, whatever we might think of them - they compare rather well with our own sorry lot at present- are rife, ugly and relentless. They do a grave disservice to a brave, resilient, even brilliant people.

The entire boorish affair isn't pretty. We aren't pretty. As a species, we pretty well suck: This is my less than erudite conclusion after years of disheartening research.

But I do retain a smidgeon of hope-hope that fair-minded, rational people will conclude that we ought not, like the lemmings of history, fall into the age-old trap of demeaning and denigrating millions of people about whom we know far too little, but who are far more like us than not.

Russians have suffered indeterminable injustices and hardships over decades, even centuries, and endured it all with grace, dignity and indomitable courage. For God's sake (or whatever it is you believe in), give them a break, and call to account those who refuse to do so.

490

Bibliography

I read a great deal to write this book. Here is a smattering of books that may be of interest, in no particular order.

Leon Poliakov, *The History of Anti-Semitism*, Volume 1-4, University of Pennsylvania Press, 1977

John W. Dower, *War Without Mercy: Race & Power In The Pacific War*, Pantheon Books, New York, 1986

James Kynge, *China Shakes The World-The Rise of a Hungry Nation*, Phoenix, 2006

David E. Hoffman, *The Oligarchs: Wealth and Power in the New Russia*, Public Affairs, New York, 2002

Mark Hollingsworth and Stewart Lansley, *London Grad-From Russia With Cash: The Inside Story Of The Oligarchs*, Fourth Estate, London, 2009

James Bamford, *The Puzzle Palace: Inside the National Security Agency, America's Most Secret Intelligence Organization*, Penguin, 1983

Kevin Poulsen, *Kingpin: How One Hacker Took Over the Billion-Dollar Cybercrime Underground*, Crown, 2011

Gregory L. Freeze (Editor), *Russia: A History*, Third Edition, 2009, Oxford University Press

Orlando Figes, *Crimea: The Last Crusade*, Penguin, 2010

Joseph E. Stiglitz, *Freefall: America, Free Markets, and the Sinking of the World Economy*, W.W. Norton & Co., January 2010

Alexander Stille, *Excellent Cadavers*, Vintage Books, New York, 1995

Jeremy Matam Farrall, *United Nations Sanctions and the Rule of Law*, Cambridge Studies in International and Comparative Law, 2007

Robert Moore, *A Time To Die: The Untold Story of the Kursk Tragedy*, Crown, New York, 2002

John Keegan, *Intelligence In War*, Vintage Canada, 2004

William Cohen, *House of Cards: How Wall Streets' Gamblers Broke Capitalism*, Allen Lane, 2009

Edward Chancellor, *Devil Take The Hindmost- A History of Financial Speculation*, A Plume Book, 2000

Michael Lewis, *The Big Short: Inside the Doomsday Machine*, Allan Lane, 2010

Carl F. Fey, Stanislav Shekshnia, Faculty and Research Working Paper, *The Key Commandments for Doing Business on Russia*, Insead, January 2008

Gordon W. Allport, *The Nature of Prejudice*, Addison-Wesley Publishing Company, 1954

Ingo Mueller, translated by Deborah Lucas Schneider, *Hitler's Justice: The Courts of the Third Reich*, Harvard University Press, 1991 (originally published in German by Kindler Verlag, Munich, 1987)

Edited and translated by Beate von Oppen, *Letters to Freya*, 1939-1945, Knopf, New York, 1990

Richard Wagner, *Das Judenthum in der Musik* (Judaism in Music), Leipzig, 1869

Text in German: http://mydocs.strands.de/MyDocs/05845/05845.pdf

Translation: http://mydocs.strands.de/MyDocs/05845/05845.pdf

William L.Shirer, *A History of Nazi Germany-The Rise And Fall of The Third Reich*, Fawcett Crest, New York, 1950

Robert Jay Lifton, *The Nazi Doctors: Medical Killing and The Psychology of Genocide*, Basic Books, 1986

David R. Dow, *Killing Time: One Man's Race To Stop An Execution*, William Heinemann, New York, 2010

Steven Luckert and Susan Bachrach, *State of Deception-The Power of Nazi Propaganda*, published in conjunction with the exhibition, *State of Deception-The Power of Nazi Propaganda*, held at the United States Holocaust Memorial Museum from January 2009-October 2011, Washington, D.C.

Daniel Treisman, *The Return- Russia's Journey from Gorbachev to Medvedev*, Free Press, 2011

Andrei Makine, *The Life of an Unknown Man*, Sceptre, 2009

Sheila Fitzpatrick, *Everyday Stalinism- Ordinary Life In Extraordinary Times: Soviet Russia In The 1930s*, Oxford University Press, 1999

Frances Stonor Saunders, *Who Paid the Piper? The CIA and the Cultural Cold War*, Granta Books, London, 1999

Joseph T. Hallinan, *Going Up The River- Travels in a Prison Nation*, Random House, New York, 2001

Dennis Lloyd, *The Idea of Law*, Penguin Books, 1964

Lon L. Fuller, *The Morality of Law*, Yale University Press, 1964

H.L.A Hart, *The Concept of Law*, Oxford University Press, 1961

H.L.A Hart, *Positivism and the Separation of Law and Morals*, Harvard Law Review 71 (4): 593–629, 1958

Lon L. Fuller, *Positivism and Fidelity to Law- A Reply to Professor Hart*, Harvard Law Review 71 (4): 630–672, 1958

Cheshire, North & Fawcett, *Private International Law*, Fourteenth Edition, Oxford University Press, 2008

Guy Kawasaki, Enchantment, *The Art of Changing Hearts, Minds and Actions*, Penguin, 2011

Notes

Part One

[1] Leon Poliakov, *The History of Anti-Semitism*, Volume 1-4, University of Pennsylvania Press, 1977

James Kirkup, *Obituary*, The Independent, 11 December, 1997

[2]*Lifting the veil?* Irish Times Editorial, 26 September 2011

[3] *Putin's speech* at the St Petersburg International Economic Forum, June 21, 2012

[4] The Economist, World Debt Comparison, *The global debt clock*

[5] RESOLUTION 1003 (1993)⁻ *On the ethics of journalism*, Assembly debate on 1 July 1993 (42nd Sitting) (see Doc.6854, report of the Committee on Culture and Education, Rapporteur: Mr Núñez Encabo). Text adopted by the Assembly on 1 July 1993 (42nd Sitting)

[6] Catherine Belton, *FT Investigation*, Financial Times, December 1, 2011

[7] Washington Post Editorial, *Trade and Consequences*, June 20, 2011

[8] FT editorial – July 16, 2012- *The Sergei Magnitsky bill*

[9] Michael Foley, *'Journalism is about giving people something important, not making them feel good,'* The Irish Times, 4th November 2011

[10] Andrew Sullivan, *Tough luck, Mitt, Brits fight dirty*, The Sunday Times, July 29, 2012

[11] Lionel Barber's Hugh Cudlipp Lecture: *The Business of Journalism: a View from the Frontline*, Speech by the Financial Times editor at London College of Communication, 31 January, 2012

[12] Catherine Belton, *A battle too far for Vekselberg*, Financial Times, March 17, 2012

[13] Supra, note 11

[14] David S. and Ann M. Barlow Professor of Political Economy and Strategy, Emeritus, Stanford University

[15] Baron, David P, *Persistent Media Bias*, Stanford University, August 2004

[16] American Association of Newspaper Editors, 1999, *Examining our Credibility: Examining Credibility, Explaining Ourselves*, Reston, Va. (www.asne.org)

[17] Zaller, John, *A Theory of Media Politics*, Manuscript, UCLA, October 24, 1999

[18] Goldberg, Bernard, *Bias: A CBS Insider Exposes How the News Media Distort the News*, Regnery Publishing, Washington, DC, 2002

[19] Patterson, Thomas E. and Wolfgang Donsbach, *News Decisions: Journalists as Partisan Actors*, Political Communication, 13:453-68, 1996

[20] Supra, note 16

[21] Press release:

http://www.people-press.org/1995/10/31/a-content-analysis-international-news-coverage-fits-publics-ameri-centric-mood/

The report:

http://www.people-press.org/files/legacy-pdf/19951031.pdf

[22] Gideon Rachman, *American journalism still a model*, Financial Times, July 15, 2008

Gideon Rachman has written a book entitled 'Zero Sum' in which he describes Russia as an authoritarian regime that is part of an axis of authoritarianism that includes China and Iran.

[23] Julia Hobsbawn and John Lloyd, Joint Editorial Intelligence and Reuters Institute report, *Power of the Commentariat*, May 6, 2008

[24] Gideon Rachman, *Respect for the law is in Russia's interest*, Financial Times, June 10, 2008

[25] Supra, note 11

[26] Phillip Stephens, The *Vulnerabilities that lie behind Mr. Putin's Belligerence*, Financial Times, August 15, 2008

[27] Heidi Tagliavini (Swiss diplomat), *Independent International Fact- Finding Mission On the Conflict in Georgia* Report, Council of the European Union, September 2009

[28] Chrystina Freeland, *As crazy as it sounds, the Oligarchs could save Russia*, the Financial Times, August 22, 2008

[29] Paul Betts, *The Humbling of Russia's Masters of the Universe*, Financial Times, November 27, 2008

[30] *What's Next* – In Focus Section, The Sunday Times, 31st August 2008

[31]

http://www.aclu.org/files/images/asset_upload_file945_218 57.pdf

[32] FT editorial, August 18, 2012

[33] Gil Plummer and Borzou Daragahi, *UK groups poised for Libya work*, Financial Times, May 14, 2012

http://www. ukti. Gov.uk

[34] Sam Fleming, *The Brics' growth story starts to lose its way*, Sunday Telegraph, January 2, 2012

[35] David Morgan, *One in four Americans without health coverage: study*, Reuters, April 19, 2012

[36] The Central Intelligence Agency (CIA), World Factbook, COUNTRY COMPARISON :: DISTRIBUTION OF FAMILY INCOME - GINI INDEX

https://www.cia.gov/library/publications/the-world-factbook/rankorder/2172rank.html

[37] http://www.unicef-irc.org/publications/pdf/rc9_eng.pdf

[38] http://www.un.org/esa/population/publications/worldageing19502050/pdf/173russi.pdf

[39] James Kynge, *China Shakes The World-The Rise of a Hungry Nation*, Phoenix, 2006

[40] Alexander Domrin, Candidate of Law (Russia), Doctor of Juridical Science (S.J.D., University of Pennsylvania Law School) Head of Department for International Programs, Pepeliaev Group, *Corruption in the Name of 'Democracy': Sad Lessons of the 1990s*, May 2011

[41]   http://www.gpo.gov/fdsys/pkg/CREC-2002-09-20/pdf/CREC-2002-pt1-PgS8998.pdf

Russia Democracy Act of 2002

[42] David E. Hoffman, *The Oligarchs: Wealth and Power in the New Russia*, Public Affairs, New York, 2002

[43] Mark Hollingsworth and Stewart Lansley, *London Grad-From Russia With Cash: The Inside Story Of The Oligarchs*, Fourth Estate, London, 2009, p243

[44] Supra, note 44, quoting Berezovsky speaking to the Frontline Club, June 6, 2007, p70

[45] Supra, note 44, p253-254

[46] *Berezovsky v Abramovich* (Summary) [2012] EWHC B15 (Ch) (August 31, 2012)

http://www.bailii.org/ew/cases/EWHC/Ch/2012/B15.html

Full judgment (498 pages): http://www.bailii.org/cgi-bin/markup.cgi?doc=/ew/cases/EWHC/Comm/2012/2463.html&query=abramovich&method=boolean

[47] Supra, note 43, p100-126; Berezovsky is covered in pages 127-149

[48] Supra, note 44, p223

[49] Supra, note 44, p229

[50] Supra, note 44, p228-229

[51] Supra, note 44, p230

[52] Supra, note 44, p245

[53] Supra, note 44, p243

[54] Supra, note 44, p231

[55] Supra, note 44, p293

[56] Supra, note 44, p293

[57] Supra, note 44, p276

[58] Daniel Mitchell, Ph.D, *Russia's Flat Tax Miracle*, The Heritage Foundation, March 24, 2003

http://www.heritage.org/research/commentary/2003/03/russias-flat-tax-miracle

[59] KPMG, *Corporate tax rates table*

http://www.kpmg.com/global/en/whatwedo/tax/tax-tools-and-resources/pages/corporate-tax-rates-table.aspx

[60] Supra, note 59

[61] GAO, *Tax Administration, Comparison of the Reported Tax Liabilities of Foreign- and US-Controlled Corporation 1998-2005*, July 2008

http://www.gao.gov/new.items/d08957.pdf

[62] David Kocieniewski, *US Business Has High Tax Rates but Pays Less*, The New York Times, May 2, 2011

http://www.nytimes.com/2011/05/03/business/economy/03rates.html

[63] Gideon Rachman, FT, September 27, 2011

[64] Joshua Green, *Playing Dirty*, The Atlantic Monthly, June 2004

[65] Nick Collins and Duncan Gardham, *Russian 'spy rock' was genuine, former chief of staff admits*, The Telegraph, 19, January, 2012

http://www.telegraph.co.uk/news/worldnews/europe/russi a/9022827/Russian-spy-rock-was-genuine-former-chief-of-staff-admits.html

[66] A hit US TV series, with dim, attractive housewives amusing themselves by sleeping with younger men, each others husbands, etc.

[67] June Blitz , *Secrecy Essential to Protect Nation, says MI6 Chief*, The Financial Times, October 29, 2010

[68] Office of the National Counterintelligence Executive, *Foreign Spies Stealing US Economic Secrets in Cyberspace*, Report to Congress on Foreign Economic Collection and Industrial Espionage, 2009-2011, October 2011

http://www.ncix.gov/publications/reports/fecie_all/Foreign _Economic_Collection_2011.pdf

[69] Duncan Campbell, *Inside Echelon, 25 July 2000*

http://www.heise.de/tp/artikel/6/6929/1.html

[70] Duncan Campbell, *I spy an ally- All is fair in the world of espionage, even eavesdropping on your friends*, 15 March 2000

http://www.guardian.co.uk/comment/story/0,3604,181794,0 0.html

[71] European Parliament, Final Report, A5-0264/2001, PAR1,11 July 2001

http://www.fas.org/irp/program/process/rapport_echelon_e n.pdf

[72] R. James Woolsey, *Why We Spy on Our Allies*, The Wall Street Journal, March 17, 2000

http://cryptome.org/echelon-cia2.htm

[73] Martin Asser, *Echelon: Big brother without a cause?* BBC News, 6 July, 2000

http://news.bbc.co.uk/2/hi/europe/820758.stm

[74] UK Home Office page on the *Regulation of Investigatory Powers Act (RIPA)*

http://www.homeoffice.gov.uk/counter-terrorism/regulation-investigatory-powers/

[75] James Bamford, *The Puzzle Palace: Inside the National Security Agency, America's Most Secret Intelligence Organization,* Penguin, 1983

[76] James Bamford, *The NSA Is Building the Country's Biggest Spy Center (Watch What You Say),* Wired, March 15, 2012

http://www.wired.com/threatlevel/2012/03/ff_nsadatacenter/all/1

[77] Kevin Poulsen, *Kingpin: How One Hacker Took Over the Billion-Dollar Cybercrime Underground,* Crown, 2011

[78] Supra, note 75

[79] http://www.symantec.com/threatreport/

[80] John Leyden, *Cyberspy attacks targeting Russians traced back to UK and US,* The Register, September 22, 2011

http://www.theregister.co.uk/2011/09/22/russia_cyberespionage_attack/

[81] http://www.whitehouse.gov/blog/2011/07/12/us-and-russia-expanding-reset-cyberspaceJoint press release:
http://www.whitehouse.gov/sites/default/files/uploads/2011_klimashin_schmidt_cyber_joint_statement.pdf

[82] David E. Sanger, *Obama Order Sped Up Wave of Cyberattacks Against Iran,* The New York Times, June 1, 2012

[83] Edward Lucas, *The Spies Next Door,* Irish Daily Mail, March 19, 2012

[84] *Latin America leads the world in business optimism* says Grant Thornton survey, January 2011

http://www.gtrus.com/main.php?year=2011&chapter=press&page=pr/2011/pr_1102

[85]

http://themoscownews.com/sports/20101203/188252004.html

[86] Courtney Weaver, *All to play for*, Financial Times, December 11/12, 2010

[87] Rod Liddle, *Notes on a Scandal*, The Sunday Times, December 5, 2010

[88] Liam Halligan, *Why the World Cup Decisions are Beneficial for the Global Economy*, The Sunday Telegraph, December 5, 2010.

[89] The Competitiveness Roadmap: 2011-2050

http://www.imd.org/research/publications/wcy/upload/roadmapPrint_A4.pdf

[90] *Police hunt cruel Russian donkey owner who attached it to parachute for sick advertising stunt*, The Daily Mail, July 21, 2010

[91] *Russia's flying donkey dies of heart attack*, The New York Post, Feb 5, 2011

[92] Roger Boyes, *Finger of Suspicion points to Kremlin as Khodorkovsky Film is Stolen from Studio*, The Times, February 8, 2011

[93] Will Stewart, *Poland's Presidential Plane Crash: Accident or Assassination*, The Sunday Telegraph Magazine, March 6, 2011

[94] *Trade and Consequences* – Editorial – The Washington Post, June 20, 2011

[95] *Obama Says Economics Key to Relations*, The Moscow Times, August 3, 2011

[96] By Adam Entous, Alan Cullison And Richard Boudreaux, *Mr. Putin's Return Complicates US Policy- in Washington and in Moscow*, The Wall Street Journal, September 26, 2011

[97]

http://www.kyivpost.com/news/russia/detail/113542/#ixzz1 Z3RRhSm0

[98] Mike Emanuel, *Boehner Rips Russia's Soviet-Style Behavior*, FoxNews.com, October 25, 2011

[99] Richard McGregor, *A Cold-Blooded Tale of Two Conflicts*, Book Review, Financial Times, September 5, 2011

[100] Khristina Narizhnaya, *Stereotypes Fuel Jackson-Vanik*, The Moscow Times, June 29, 2011

[101] PRESS RELEASE -Entry into force of the Agreement between the Russian Federation and the United States on visa formalities

http://www.mid.ru/brp_4.nsf/newsline/FF947816BE3701604 4257A59005462B3

[102] Ivan Katchanovski, Ph.D , *US TV Coverage of Post-Communist Countries: Politics and Virtual Reality*, paper prepared for presentation at the Annual Conference of the Canadian Political Science Association, Carlton University, Ottawa, Canada, May 27 – 29, 2009

[103] Lieven, Anatol (2000a), *Through a Distorted Lens: Chechnya and the Western Media, Current History*, 99 (639): 321-328 and Lieven, Anatol (2000b). *Against Russophobia*, World Policy Journal, 17 (4), 25-32

[104] *Letters to the Editor*, Financial Times, August 15 2008

[105] Owen Slot, Russian *Spooked by Lack of Trust from the West dating back to Iron Curtain*, The Times, October 20, 2010

[106]Mark Franchetti, *In a Third World War, Russia Would Survive*, The Sunday Times Magazine, August 14, 2011

[107] David McWilliams, *Russian Still has Unfinished Business with its Neighbours*, Irish Times, August 17, 2008.

[108] Sir Ivor Roberts, *Pay-Back Time as Kosovo Chickens Come Home to Roost*, The Irish Times

[109] Tom McGurk, *EU Caught in Caucasian Crossfire*, The Sunday Business Post, August 17, 2008

Part Two

[110]Pew Research Center, Global Attitudes Project, *The Pulse of Europe 2009: 20 Years After the Fall of the Berlin Wall: End of Communism Cheered but Now with More Reservations*, November 2, 2009

http://www.pewglobal.org/2009/11/02/end-of-communism-cheered-but-now-with-more-reservations/3/

[111] Supra, note 1

[112] David E. Hoffman, *The Oligarchs: Wealth and Power in the New Russia*, Public Affairs, New York, 2002

[113] Supra, note 4

[114] Gregory L. Freeze (Editor), *Russia: A History*, Third Edition, 2009, Oxford University Press

[115] Supra, note 5, p481

[116] Supra, note 5, p495

[117] Supra, note 111

[118] Supra, note 115

[119] Orlando Figes, *Crimea: The Last Crusade*, Penguin, 2010

[120] John W. Dower, *War Without Mercy: Race & Power In The Pacific War*, Pantheon Books, New York, 1986, p172, 347 and 364

[121] Supra, note 121

[122] Supra, note 121, p154

[123] Supra note 121, p150, 154

[124] Supra, note 121, p151

[125] Supra, note 121, p163

[126] Supra, note 121, p162

[127] Supra, note 121, p170, 171

[128] Supra, note 121, p171

[129] Supra, note 121, p156

[130] Supra, note 121, p5, 6, 7

[131] Supra, note 121, p78, 79, 80

[132] Supra, note 121, p80

[133] Supra, note 121, p81

[134] Supra, note 121, p7

[135] James J. Weingartner, Trophies of War: US Troops and the Mutilation of Japanese War Dead, 1941–1945, *Pacific Historical Review* 61 (1): 53–67, JSTOR 3640788, February 1992

[136] Supra, note 111,

[137] Supra, note 115, p505-506

[138] Supra, note 115

[139] The White House, Office of the Press Secretary

http://www.whitehouse.gov/the_press_office/Remarks-by-the-President-on-Strengthening-Missile-Defense-in-Europe/

Peter Baker, *White House Scraps Bush's Approach to Missile Shield*, The New York Times, September 17, 2009

[140] Liam Halligan, *The World Will Have Failed if we put a European in Charge at the IMF again*, The Sunday Telegraph, May 22, 2011

141 Joseph E. Stiglitz, *Freefall: America, Free Markets, and the Sinking of the World Economy*, W.W. Norton & Co., January 2010

142 Ross P. Buckley, *The Bankruptcy of Nations; An Idea Whose Time Has Come*, The American Bar Association/Section of International Law, The International Lawyer, Volume 43, Number 3, Fall 2009

143 Bretton Woods Project, *IMF's latest prescription: Cure the crisis with austerity*, June 17, 2010

http://www.brettonwoodsproject.org/art-566364

144 Roland Oliphant, *Q&A: Boeing Chief Rejects Cold War Mentality*, Moscow Times, December 16, 2011

145 *OECD Reviews of Labour Market and Social Policies: Russian Federation*, December 12, 2011

http://www.oecd.org/els/socialpoliciesanddata/oecdreviews oflabourmarketandsocialpoliciesrussianfederation.htm

146 Alan Beattle, *IMF Failed to Spot Crisis Risk – Watchdog Says*, Financial Times, February 10, 2011

147 Frank Newport, *China Tops List of Countries Vitally Important to US*, February 9, 2011

http://www.gallup.com/poll/146039/China-Tops-List-Countries-Vitally-Important-Egypt-9th.aspx

148 James Kynge, *China Shakes the World: The Rise of a Hungry Nation*, Phoenix, UK, 2006

149 Hal Weitzman, *Debt Fears Lead US Youth to Question Value of University*, FT, July 15, 2011

150 Supra, note 40

151 Supra, note 40, p156

152 John W. Miller, *Bread Basket: In the Ukraine Mavericks Gamble on Scarce Land*, Wall Street Journal, May 12, 2008

153 CHRISTOPHER GRIFFIN AND JOSEPH E. LIN, *China's space ambitions*, Armed Forces Journal

http://www.armedforcesjournal.com/2008/04/3406827/

Part Three

154 *The Queen on the Application of Corner House Research and Campaign against Arms Trade and The Director of the Serious Fraud Office and BAE Systems PLC*, in the High Court of Justice, Queens' Bench Division, Administrative Court, April 10, 2008, (2008), EWHC, 714 (Admin)

http://www.thecornerhouse.org.uk/sites/thecornerhouse.org.uk/files/JR-Judgment.pdf

155 Supra, note 155, para. 101

156 House of Lords, On appeal from: [2008] EWHC 246 (Admin), SESSION 2007-08, July 30, 2008

http://www.bailii.org/uk/cases/UKHL/2008/60.html

157 Mark Tran, *BAE finally pays out £29.5m for educational projects in Tanzania*, the Guardian, March 15, 2012

http://www.guardian.co.uk/global-development/2012/mar/15/bae-pays-for-tanzania-education-projects

158 *Anti-Bribery Act 2010*, in force July 11, 2011

http://www.legislation.gov.uk/ukpga/2010/23/contents

http://www.fco.gov.uk/en/global-issues/conflict-minerals/legally-binding-process/uk-bribery-act

159 *Joint First and Second Evaluation Rounds -Evaluation Report on the Russian Federation*, GRECO, December 5 2008

http://www.coe.int/t/dghl/monitoring/greco/evaluations/round2/GrecoEval1-2(2008)2_RussianFederation_EN.pdf

160 *Compliance Report on the Russian Federation*, GRECO, December 3 2010

http://www.coe.int/t/dghl/monitoring/greco/evaluations/ro
und2/GrecoRC1&2(2010)2_RussianFederation_EN.pdf.

[161] Second Mutual Evaluation Report - Anti-Money
Laundering And Combating The Financing Of Terrorism
Russian Federation, Fatf, 20 June 2008

http://www.fatf-gafi.org/countries/n-
r/russianfederation/documents/mutualevaluationoftherussi
anfederation.html

[162] *Mutual Evaluation of the Russian Federation, FATF,* April
2012

http://www.fatf-
gafi.org/topics/mutualevaluations/documents/merrussia.ht
ml

[163] *How to Profit in the new Russia Without Sidelining Ethics:
An Insiders' Guide to Successful Dealmaking,* Sponsored by
Russia/Eurasia Committee, Chair and Moderator: Mary P.
Kirwan, Barrister & Solicitor, Dublin; Speakers: David
Cranfield, CMS Legal, Moscow, John Goodwin, Linklaters
LLP, Moscow, Mike Hogan, Enterprise Ireland, Ilya
Nikiforov, Egorov, Puginsky, Afanasiev & Partners, St
Petersburg, American Bar Association, Section of
International Law, 2011 Fall Meeting, Dublin, Ireland

[164] Transparency International, *Corruption Perceptions Index,*
2011

http://cpi.transparency.org/cpi2011/

[165] Forbes, *2010 Despotism Survey*

[166] John Hooper , *Move over, Cosa Nostra,* Guardian, June 8,
2006

[167] *US saw mafia-ridden Italian region as 'failed state'-*
(WikiLeaks cable), The Canadian Press, January 13, 2011

[168] Supra, note 43, p261-262

[169] Supra note 43, p262

[170] Alexander Stille, *Excellent Cadavers*, Vintage Books, New York, 1995

[171] Mahon Tribunal Final Report

http://www.planningtribunal.ie/images/finalReport.pdf

Paul Cullen, *Give me a crash course in . . . the Mahon tribunal report*, Irish Times, March 24, 2012

http://www.irishtimes.com/newspaper/weekend/2012/0324/1224313801698.html

[172] Paul Krugman, *How crony capitalism is warping criminal justice*, Irish Times, March 27, 2012

[173] *On Progress in Romania under the Cooperation and Verification Mechanism Report from the Commission to the European Parliament and the Council*, Brussels, 18.7.2012 COM (2012) 410 Final.

[174] *Serious and Organised Crime Threat Assessment 2010-2011*, Centre for the study of Democracy, Sofia, April 2012

[175] *On Progress in Bulgaria under the Cooperation and Verification Mechanism Report from the Commission to the European Parliament and the Council*, Brussels, 18.7.2012 COM (2012) 411 Final

[176] Supra, note 21

[177] Supra, note 21

[178] Supra, note 19 and 21

[179] Alan Rappeport, *Mafia Still Holding US Ports to Ransom*, FT, January 24, 2011

[180] Antoaneta Bezlova, *China's mobile death fleet*, Asia Times, June 21, 2006
http://www.atimes.com/atimes/China/HG21Ad01.html

[181] *Death Row FAQs*, State of Delaware

http://doc.delaware.gov/information/deathrow_history.shtml

[182] Adam Thomson *Mexico Mourns Fifty Two Killed when Casino set alight by Armed Gang*, Financial Times, August 27, 2011

[183] Supra note 43

[184] *The Pulse of Europe 2009: 20 Years After the Fall of the Berlin Wall*

End of Communism Cheered but Now with More Reservations, Pew Global Attitudes Project, Pew Research Center, Released November 2, 2009

http://www.pewglobal.org/2009/11/02/end-of-communism-cheered-but-now-with-more-reservations/

[185] Committee to Protect Journalists (CPJ)

http://www.cpj.org/2012/02/attacks-on-the-press-in-2011-in-russia-pr-is-bette.php

[186] *Russia-Press Country Profile*, European Court Of Human Rights

http://www.echr.coe.int/NR/rdonlyres/7CF42EB0-0481-4ACD-9B49-1B92D396D126/0/PCP_RUSSIA_EN.pdf?

[187] *Statistical information (1959-2011)*, European Court Of Human   Rights
http://www.echr.coe.int/ECHR/EN/Header/Reports+and+Statistics/Statistics/Statistical+data/

[188] Vanessa Wozniak, *Ken Clarke: law and lawyers among the UK's 'greatest exports,'* The Lawyer, September 14, 2011

http://www.thelawyer.com/ken-clarke-law-and-lawyers-among-the-uks-greatest-exports/1009193.article

[189] Neil Buckley, *A shady business*, FT, October 8/9 2011

[190] Thomas Firestone, *Criminal Corporate Raiding in Russia*, The International Lawyer, ABA/Section of International Law, Winter 2008, Volume 42, Number 4

[191] Andrei Postelnicu, *'Dynastic will' is rare in Russia*, Camden Research, 19 September, 2012

http://www.campdenfb.com/article/dynastic-will-rare-russia-campden-research-finds

[192] http://www.novopol.ru/-imidju-rossii-postavili-dvoyku--text82775.html

In Russian only

[193] Excellent resources available at The American Bar Association's *Death Penalty Representation Project*

http://www.americanbar.org/advocacy/other_aba_initiatives/death_penalty_representation.html

[194] Lara Marlowe, *No-One Wanted Detainees' in Raid on Bin Laden House*, Irish Times, August 3, 2011

[195] Jeremy Matam Farrall, *United Nations Sanctions and the Rule of Law*, Cambridge Studies in International and Comparative Law, 2007, p23

[196] Supra note 196, p24

[197] *Obituary- Jenifer Hart*, The Telegraph, April 9, 2005

http://www.telegraph.co.uk/news/obituaries/1487412/Jenifer-Hart.html

[198] Ingo Mueller, translated by Deborah Lucas Schneider, *Hitler's Justice: The Courts of the Third Reich*, Harvard University Press, 1991 (originally published in German by Kindler Verlag, Munich, 1987)

[199] Edited and translated by Beate von Oppen, *Letters to Freya*, 1939-1945, Knopf, New York, 1990

[200] Jeremy Matam Farrall, *United Nations Sanctions and The Rule of Law*, Cambridge Studies in International and Comparative law, Cambridge University Press, 2007

[201] Supra, note 196, p24

[202] Supra, note 196, p25

[203] Supra, note 196, p25

[204] The American Bar Association

www.americanbar.org

Part Four

[205]Press release October 6, 2005

http://www.nia.nih.gov/newsroom/2005/10/national-stereotypes-common-mistaken-study-reports

Terraciano, R.R.McCrae (and others), *National Character Does Not Reflect Mean Personality Trait Levels in 49 Cultures*:: 7 October 2005, VOL 310- SCIENCE: www.science.org

[206] Terracciano and Robert McCrae, *Perceptions of Americans and the Iraq Invasion: Implications for Understanding National Character Stereotypes,'* Journal of Cross- Cultural Psychology 2007

Robert McCrae, Antonio Terracciano (and others), *Climatic Warmth and National Wealth: Some Culture-level Determinants of National Character Stereotypes*, European Journal of Personality, *Eur.J. Pers.*21:953-976 (2007)

[207] *Russians Back Protests, Political Freedoms-And Putin*, Pew Research Center, Pew Global Attitudes Project, May 23, 2012

http://www.pewglobal.org/2012/05/23/russians-back-protests-political-freedoms-and-putin-too/

[208] Richard Wagner, *Das Judenthum in der Musik* (Judaism in Music), Leipzig, 1869

German Text:

http://mydocs.strands.de/MyDocs/05845/05845.pdf

Translation:
http://mydocs.strands.de/MyDocs/05845/05845.pdf

[209] Gordon W. Allport, *The Nature of Prejudice*, Addison-Wesley Publishing Company, 1954

[210] Quentin Peel, *Draghi wins over German broadsheet*, FT, April 30/May 1 2011

[211] Supra, 121, p308, 309

[212] Supra, note 121, p308, 309

[213] Supra, note 121, p309

[214] Supra, note 121, p309, 310

[215] Supra, note 121, p309, 310

[216] Supra, note 121, p310

[217] Supra, note 121, p312, 313

[218] Supra, note 121, p313

[219] Supra, note 121, p314

[220] Sam Coates, Rory Watson, Laura Dixon, *Proud Ireland Struggles to Keep Lid on the Begging Bowl*, The Times, November 18, 2010

[221] http://www.youtube.com/watch?v=JXL86v8NoGk

[222] *2006 National Geographic-Roper Survey of Geographic Literacy*

http://www.nationalgeographic.com/roper2006/findings.html

[223] Supra, note 40

[224] Supra, note 40, p206

[225] Supra, note 40, p204

[226] Supra, note 40, p207

[227] Michele A. Berdy, *A 'Russian' Writer Born in the US*, December 12, 2011

228 Yevgeny Bazhanov, *The Future Faces of Russia*, Moscow Times, May 27, 2010

20 Andrew Squire, *Hot Dogs, Baseball Meet Borscht, Hockey*, Moscow Times, July 15, 2011

230 http://alphadesigner.com/about.html

231   http://www.adweek.com/adfreak/directvs-opulence-czar-flexes-his-epic-win-126935

http://www.adweek.com/adfreak/directvs-opulence-ad-rich-subtleties-12404

232 The Motion Pictures Association of America

http://www.mpaa.org/policy

233   http://www.mpaa.org/Resources/93bbeb16-0e4d-4b7e-b085-3f41c459f9ac.pdf

234 Supra, note 233

26 Ivan Katchanovski, Ph.D, *Politically Correct Incorrectness: Kazakhstan, Russia, and Ukraine in Hollywood Films*, paper prepared for presentation at the Annual Meeting of the American Political Science Association in Chicago, August 30-September, 2, 2007

236 Matt Belloni, The Hollywood Reporter, December 21, 2010

237 Supra, note 115, p382, 392

238 *2010 US Resident Travel to Europe*, US Department of Commerce, International Trade Administration, Office of Travel and Tourism Industries
http://www.tinet.ita.doc.gov/outreachpages/download_data_table/2010_US_to_Europe.pdf

239 Supra, note 210

240 Supra, note 210, p201-202

241 *Lawyers say Dobby is based on Putin*, Guardian, January 30, 2003

http://www.guardian.co.uk/film/2003/jan/30/harrypotter.news

242 *The First Vulcan in the Oval Office?*, The Times, May 13, 2009

243 May Durlong, *From TREK to TERMINATOR - Actor Anton Yelchin's Big Month*, Newsarama, 5 May, 2009
http://www.newsarama.com/film/090505-anton-yelchin.html

244 Kathrin Hille, *Chinese Brands Starring Hollywood Movie*, FT, July 20, 2011

245 uniFrance Films

www.unifrance.org

246 Eurimages, European Cinema Support Fund, Council of Europe
http://www.coe.int/t/dg4/eurimages/default_en.asp

247 Alexei Vinogradsky, *The Soviet Union's growing taste for American movies*, The Evening Sun

January 4, 1991

248 http://en.wikipedia.org/wiki/Ivan_Drago

249 Cheryl Thomas, *Are juries fair?* UK Ministry of Justice, February, 2010
http://www.justice.gov.uk/publications/docs/are-juries-fair-research.pdf

250 James Kirchick, *Pravda On the Potomac*, The New Republic, February 18, 2009

251 James Harkin, *The PR Campaign for Brand America*, The Guardian, September 17, 2005

252 Pew Research Center: Pew Global Attitudes Project, *The American- Western European Values Gap*, November 17, 2011

http://www.pewglobal.org/2011/11/17/the-american-western-european-values-gap/

5940601R00305

Printed in Great Britain
by Amazon.co.uk, Ltd.,
Marston Gate.